The Essentials of Modern
Software Engineering

The Essentials of Modern Software Engineering

Edited by Cheryl Jollymore

CLANRYE INTERNATIONAL
www.clanryeinternational.com

Clanrye International,
750 Third Avenue, 9th Floor,
New York, NY 10017, USA

ISBN: 978-1-64726-590-8

Cataloging-in-publication Data

The essentials of modern software engineering / edited by Cheryl Jollymore.
p. cm.
Includes bibliographical references and index.
ISBN 978-1-64726-590-8
1. Software engineering. 2. Computer programming. 3. Computer networks. 4. Computer science.
5. Information science. 6. Automatic programming (Computer science). I. Jollymore, Cheryl.
QA76.758 .S64 2023
005.1--dc23

For information on all Clanrye International publications
visit our website at www.clanryeinternational.com

Contents

Preface..VII

Chapter 1   **A Generalized Formal Semantic Framework for Smart Contracts**..................................... 1
Jiao Jiao, Shang-Wei Lin and Jun Sun

Chapter 2   **Global Reproducibility through Local Control for Distributed Active Objects**... 23
Lars Tveito, Einar Broch Johnsen and Rudolf Schlatte

Chapter 3   **TracerX: Dynamic Symbolic Execution with Interpolation (Competition Contribution)**... 44
Joxan Jaffar, Rasool Maghareh, Sangharatna Godboley and Xuan-Linh Ha

Chapter 4   **Integrating Topological Proofs with Model Checking to Instrument Iterative Design**... 49
Claudio Menghi, Alessandro Maria Rizzi and Anna Bernasconi

Chapter 5   **Computing Program Reliability using Forward-Backward Precondition Analysis and Model Counting**.. 71
Aleksandar S. Dimovski and Axel Legay

Chapter 6   **An Empirical Study on the Use and Misuse of Java 8 Streams**....................................... 91
Raffi Khatchadourian, Yiming Tang, Mehdi Bagherzadeh and Baishakhi Ray

Chapter 7   **Improving Symbolic Automata Learning with Concolic Execution**........................113
Donato Clun, Phillip van Heerden, Antonio Filieri and Willem Visser

Chapter 8   **LLVM-based Hybrid Fuzzing with LibKluzzer (Competition Contribution)**... 137
Hoang M. Le

Chapter 9   **Extracting Semantics from Question-Answering Services for Snippet Reuse**...142
Themistoklis Diamantopoulos, Nikolaos Oikonomou and Andreas Symeonidis

Chapter 10   **Family-Based SPL Model Checking Using Parity Games with Variability**.. 163
Maurice H. ter Beek, Sjef van Loo, Erik P. de Vink and Tim A.C. Willemse

Chapter 11   **Skill-Based Verification of Cyber-Physical Systems**...**184**
Alexander Knüppel, Inga Jatzkowski, Marcus Nolte, Thomas Thüm,
Tobias Runge and Ina Schaefer

Chapter 12   **Combining Partial Specifications using Alternating Interface**
Automata...**204**
Ramon Janssen

Permissions

List of Contributors

Index

Preface

Software engineering is the application of engineering principles for maintaining, designing and developing of software. There are two parts of software engineering, which include software and engineering. Software is basically a collection of triggers, codes and documents, which perform a certain task and meet a specific need. Engineering is the process of creating products by applying best methods, practices and principles. Some of the major subdivisions of software engineering are software design, software construction, and requirements engineering. Software design involves defining the components, architecture, interfaces, and other properties of a system or component. Software construction involves integration testing, programming, unit testing and debugging. This book attempts to understand the discipline of modern software engineering and the practical applications of its concepts. Its aim is to present researches that have transformed this discipline and aided in its advancement. The book is a resource guide for experts as well as students.

This book is the end result of constructive efforts and intensive research done by experts in this field. The aim of this book is to enlighten the readers with recent information in this area of research. The information provided in this profound book would serve as a valuable reference to students and researchers in this field.

At the end, I would like to thank all the authors for devoting their precious time and providing their valuable contribution to this book. I would also like to express my gratitude to my fellow colleagues who encouraged me throughout the process.

Editor

A Generalized Formal Semantic Framework for Smart Contracts

Jiao Jiao[1]($\boxtimes$)(ID), Shang-Wei Lin[1](ID), and Jun Sun[2](ID)

[1] Nanyang Technological University, Singapore
{jiao0023,shang-wei.lin}@ntu.edu.sg
[2] Singapore Management University, Singapore
{junsun}@smu.edu.sg

Abstract. Smart contracts can be regarded as one of the most popular blockchain-based applications. The decentralized nature of the blockchain introduces vulnerabilities absent in other programs. Furthermore, it is very difficult, if not impossible, to patch a smart contract after it has been deployed. Therefore, smart contracts must be formally verified before they are deployed on the blockchain to avoid attacks exploiting these vulnerabilities. There is a recent surge of interest in analyzing and verifying smart contracts. While most of the existing works either focus on EVM bytecode or translate Solidity contracts into programs in intermediate languages for analysis and verification, we believe that a direct executable formal semantics of the high-level programming language of smart contracts is necessary to guarantee the validity of the verification. In this work, we propose a generalized formal semantic framework based on a general semantic model of smart contracts. Furthermore, this framework can directly handle smart contracts written in different high-level programming languages through semantic extensions and facilitates the formal verification of security properties with the generated semantics.

Keywords: Blockchain · Smart contracts · Generalized semantics

1 Introduction

Blockchain [17] technologies have been studied extensively recently. Smart contracts [16] can be regarded as one of the most popular blockchain-based applications. Due to the very nature of the blockchain, credible and traceable transactions are allowed through smart contracts without relying on an external trusted authority to achieve consensus. However, the unique features of the blockchain introduce vulnerabilities [10] absent in other programs.

Smart contracts must be verified for multiple reasons. Firstly, due to the decentralized nature of the blockchain, smart contracts are different from programs written in other programming languages (e.g., C/Java). For instance, the storage of each contract instance is at a permanent address on the blockchain. In this way, each instance is a particular execution context and context switches are possible through external calls. Particularly, in Solidity, `delegatecall` executes programs in the context of the caller rather than the recipient, making it possible to modify the state of the caller. Programmers must be aware of the execution context of each statement to guarantee the programming correctness. Therefore, programming smart contracts is error-prone without a proper understanding of the underlying semantic model. Secondly, a smart contract can be deployed on the blockchain by any user in the network. Vulnerabilities in deployed contracts can be exploited to launch attacks that lead to huge financial loss. Verifying smart contracts against such vulnerabilities is crucial for protecting digital assets. One famous attack on smart contracts is the DAO attack [41] in which the attacker exploited the reentrancy vulnerability and managed to take 60 million dollars under his control. Thirdly, it is very difficult, if not impossible, to patch a smart contract once it is deployed due to the very nature of the blockchain.

Related Works. There is a surge of interest in analyzing and verifying smart contracts [32,12,24,28,26,9,25,31,21,44,20,22,38,36,4,34,43,19,30,35,29,23,46,14]. Some of the existing works focus on EVM [2,47] (Ethereum Virtual Machine). For instance, a symbolic execution engine called Oyente is proposed in [32] to analyze Solidity smart contracts by translating them into EVM bytecode. In addition, a complete formal executable semantics of EVM [24] is developed in the K-framework to facilitate the formal verification of smart contracts at bytecode level. A set of test oracles is defined in [26,45] to detect security vulnerabilities on EVM bytecode. In [21], a semantic framework is proposed to analyze smart contracts at EVM level. Securify [44] translates EVM bytecode into a stackless representation in static-single assignment form for analyzing smart contracts. In other works, Solidity smart contracts are translated into programs in intermediate languages for analysis and verification. Specifically speaking, Solidity programs are formalized with an abstract language and then translated into LLVM bitcode in Zeus [28]. Similarly, Boogie is used to verify smart contracts as an intermediate language in the proposed verifiers in [31,23]. In addition, the formalization in F* [12] is an intermediate-level language for the equivalence checking of Solidity programs and EVM bytecode. In [22], a simple imperative object-based programming language, called SMAC, is used to facilitate the online detection of Effectively Callback Free (ECF) objects in smart contracts. To conclude, most of the existing approaches either focus on EVM bytecode, or translate Solidity smart contracts into programs in intermediate languages that are suitable for verifying smart contracts or detecting potential issues in associated verifiers or checkers. Furthermore, none of the existing works can directly handle smart contracts written in different high-level programming languages without translating them into EVM bytecode or intermediate languages.

Motivations. A direct executable formal semantics of the high-level smart contract programming language is a must for both understanding and verifying smart contracts. Firstly, programmers write and reason about smart contracts at the level of source code without the semantics of which they are required to understand how Solidity programs are compiled into EVM bytecode in order to understand these contracts, which is far from trivial. In addition, there may be semantic gaps between high-level smart contract programming languages and low-level bytecode. Therefore, both high-level [27,48,49,15,11] and low-level [24,21] semantics definitions are necessary to conduct equivalence checking to guarantee that security properties are preserved at both levels and reason about compiler bugs. Secondly, even though smart contracts can be transformed into programs in intermediate languages to be analyzed and verified in existing model checkers and verifiers, the equivalence checking of the high-level smart contract programming language and the intermediate language considered is crucial to the validity of the verification. For instance, most of the false positives reported in Zeus [28] are caused by the semantic inconsistency of the abstract language and Solidity.

As domain-specific languages, high-level smart contract programming languages, such as Solidity, Vyper, Bamboo, etc, intend to implement the correct or desired semantics of smart contracts although they may not actually achieve this. This means that these languages are semantically similar in order to interpret the same high-level semantics of smart contracts. For instance, Vyper is quite similar to Solidity in spite of syntax differences and the semantics interpreted by Bamboo is consistent with that of Solidity (cf. Section 2.1 for details). Considering this fact, we propose a generalized formal semantic framework based on a general semantic model of smart contracts. Different from previous works which either analyze and verify smart contracts on EVM semantics or interpret Solidity semantics with the semantics of intermediate languages, the proposed framework aims to generate a direct executable formal semantics of a particular high-level smart contract programming language to facilitate the high-level verification of contracts and reason about compiler bugs. Furthermore, this framework provides a uniform formal specification of smart contracts, making it possible to apply verification techniques to contracts written in different languages.

Challenges. The challenges of developing a generalized formal semantic framework mainly lie in the construction of a general semantic model of smart contracts. Firstly, different high-level smart contract programming languages differ in syntax which limits state transitions. Compared with Solidity, Vyper [8] and Bamboo [1] have more syntax limits to exclude some vulnerabilities reported in Solidity. For instance, Vyper eliminates `gasless send` by blocking recursive calls and infinite loops, and `reentrancy attacks` by excluding the possibility of state changes after external calls [40]. In addition, there are no state variables in Bamboo and each contract represents a particular execution state, making it possible to limit operations to certain states to prevent attacks. Therefore, we need to take into account the syntax differences when constructing a general semantic model for smart contracts. Secondly, semantics developed with the general semantic model must be direct to guarantee the validity of the verification. For instance, as discussed above, even though intermediate languages may be a good solution to construct a general semantic model, they introduce semantic-level equivalence checking issues due to pure syntax translations.

Contributions. In this work, we develop a generalized formal semantic framework for smart contracts. The contributions of this work lie in three aspects. Firstly, our work is the first approach, to our knowledge, to a generalized formal semantic framework for smart contracts which can directly handle contracts written in different high-level programming languages. Secondly, a general semantic model of smart contracts is constructed with rewriting logic in the K-framework. With the general semantic model, a direct executable formal semantics of a particular high-level smart contract programming language can be constructed as long as its core features fall into the ones defined in this model. The general semantic model is validated with its interpretation in Solidity using the Solidity compiler test set [6] and evaluation results show that it is complete and correct. Lastly, the generated semantics facilitates the formal verification of smart contracts written in a particular high-level programming language as a formal specification of the corresponding language. Together with low-level specifications [24,21], it allows us to conduct equivalence checking on high-level programs and low-level bytecode to reason about compiler bugs and guarantee that security properties are preserved at both levels.

Outline. The remaining part of this paper is organized as follows. In Section 2, we introduce smart contracts and the K-framework. The general semantic model of smart contracts is introduced in Section 3. In Section 4, we take Solidity as an example to illustrate how to generate a direct executable formal semantics of a particular high-level smart contract programming language based on the general semantic model. Section 5 shows the evaluation results of the proposed framework. Section 6 concludes this work.

2 Preliminaries

In this section, we briefly introduce smart contracts and the K-framework.

2.1 Smart Contracts

Solidity Smart Contracts. Ethereum [2,47], proposed in late 2013 by Vitalik Buterin, is a blockchain-based distributed computing platform supporting the functionality of smart contracts. It provides a decentralized international network where each participant node equipped with EVM can execute smart contracts. It also provides a cryptocurrency called "ether" (ETH) which can be transferred between different accounts and used to compensate participant nodes for their computations on smart contracts.

Solidity is one of the high-level programming languages to implement smart contracts on Ethereum. A smart contract written in Solidity can be compiled into EVM bytecode and executed by any participant node equipped with EVM. A Solidity smart contract is a collection of code (its functions) and data (its state) that resides at a specific address on the Ethereum blockchain [7]. Fig. 1 shows an example of Solidity smart contracts, named `Coin`, implementing a very simple cryptocurrency. In line 2, the public state variable `minter` of type `address` is declared to store the address of the minter of the cryptocurrency, i.e., the owner of the smart contract. The constructor, denoted by `constructor()`, is defined in lines 5–7. Once the smart contract is created and deployed[3], its

---

[3] How to create and deploy a smart contract is out of scope and can be found in: https://solidity.readthedocs.io

```
1    contract Coin {
2       address public minter;
3       mapping (address => uint) public balances;
4
5       constructor() public {
6          minter = msg.sender;
7       }
8
9       function mint(address receiver, uint amount) public {
10         if (msg.sender != minter) return;
11         balances[receiver] += amount;
12      }
13
14      function send(address receiver, uint amount) public {
15         if (balances[msg.sender] < amount) return;
16         balances[msg.sender] -= amount;
17         balances[receiver] += amount;
18      }
19   }
```

Fig. 1. Solidity Smart Contract Example

constructor is invoked automatically, and `minter` is set to be the address of its creator (owner), represented by the built-in keyword `msg.sender`. In line 3, the public state variable `balances` is declared to store the balances of users. It is of type `mapping`, which can be considered as a hash-table mapping from keys to values. In this example, `balances` maps from a user (represented as an address) to his/her balance (represented as an unsigned integer value). The `mint` function, defined in lines 9–12, is supposed to be invoked only by its owner to mint coins, the number of which is specified by `amount`, for the user located at the `receiver` address. If `mint` is called by anyone except the owner of the contract, nothing will happen because of the guarding `if` statement in line 10. The `send` function, defined in lines 14–18, can be invoked by any user to transfer coins, the number of which is specified by `amount`, to another user located at the `receiver` address. If the balance is not sufficient, nothing will happen because of the guarding `if` statement in line 15; otherwise, the balances of both sides will be updated accordingly.

A blockchain is actually a globally-shared transactional database or ledger. If one wants to make any state change on the blockchain, he or she has to create a so-called *transaction* which has to be accepted and validated by all other participant nodes. Furthermore, once a transaction is applied to the blockchain, no other transactions can alter it. For example, deploying the `Coin` smart contract generates a transaction because the state of the blockchain is going to be changed, i.e., one more smart contract instance will be included. Similarly, any invocation of the function `mint` or `send` also generates a transaction because the state of the contract instance, which is a part of the whole blockchain, is going to be changed. Transactions have to be selected and added into blocks to be appended to the blockchain. This procedure is the so-called *mining*, and the participant nodes are called *miners*.

Vyper Smart Contracts. Vyper is a high-level programming language for smart contracts running on EVM. As an alternative to Solidity, Vyper is con-

```
1   minter: public(address)
2   balances: map(address, wei_value)
3
4   @public
5   def __init__():
6       self.minter = msg.sender
7
8   @public
9   def mint(receiver: address, amount: wei_value):
10      if (msg.sender != self.minter): return
11      self.balances[receiver] += amount
12
13  @public
14  def send(receiver: address, amount: wei_value):
15      if (self.balances[msg.sender] < amount): return
16      self.balances[msg.sender] -= amount
17      self.balances[receiver] += amount
```

Fig. 2. Vyper Smart Contract Example

sidered to be more secure by blocking recursive calls and infinite loops to avoid `gasless send`, and excluding the possibility of state changes after external calls to prevent `reentrancy attacks` [40]. Thus, it is more difficult to write vulnerable code in Vyper. In addition, it supports bounds and overflow checking, and strong typing. Particularly, timing features such as block timestamps are supported as types, making it possible to detect the vulnerability of `timestamp dependence` [32] on Vyper semantics. This is not possible on Solidity semantics since Solidity does not support timing features. Apart from security, simplicity is another goal of Vyper. It aims to provide a more human-readable language, and a simpler compiler implementation. An example Vyper smart contract corresponding to the Solidity smart contract illustrated in Fig. 1 is shown in Fig. 2.

Bamboo Smart Contracts. Bamboo is another high-level programming language for Ethereum smart contracts. In Bamboo, state variables are eliminated and each contract represents a particular execution state, making state transitions explicit to avoid reentrancy attacks by default. This is because operations in functions are limited to certain states. An example Bamboo smart contract which is equivalent to the Solidity smart contract illustrated in Fig. 1 is shown in Fig. 3. In this example, explicit state transitions are applied to strictly limit operations in the constructor to a certain state. To be specific, the default part in the contract `PreCoin` which is equivalent to the constructor in Fig. 1 can only be invoked once, after which the state is always `Coin`. This is consistent with the fact that the constructor of a Solidity smart contract is only invoked once when a new contract instance is created.

Comparison. As introduced above, Vyper smart contracts are similar to Solidity smart contracts regardless of the differences in syntax formats. Compared with Solidity, Vyper simply excludes the vulnerabilities reported in Solidity at syntax level. Apart from the syntax differences, explicit state transitions are applied in Bamboo to prevent potential attacks. Despite the limits in syntax and state transitions, high-level smart contract programming languages have a lot in common in semantics due to the fact that they have to be functionally the same.

```
1   contract PreCoin(address => uint balances){
2       default{
3           return then become Coin(sender(msg), balances);
4       }
5   }
6
7   contract Coin(address minter, address => uint balances){
8       case(void mint(address receiver, uint amount)){
9           if (sender(msg) != minter)
10              return then become Coin(minter, balances);
11          balances[receiver] = balances[receiver] + amount;
12          return then become Coin(minter, balances);
13      }
14      case(void send(address receiver, uint amount)){
15          if (balances[sender(msg)] < amount)
16              return then become Coin(minter, balances);
17          balances[sender(msg)] = balances[sender(msg)] - amount;
18          balances[receiver] = balances[receiver] + amount;
19          return then become Coin(minter, balances);
20      }
21  }
```

Fig. 3. Bamboo Smart Contract Example

2.2 The K-framework

The K-framework ($\mathbb{K}$) [39] is a rewriting logic [33] based formal *executable* semantics definition framework. The semantics definitions of various programming languages have been developed using $\mathbb{K}$, such as Java [13], C [18], etc. Particularly, an executable semantics of EVM [24], the bytecode language of smart contracts, has been constructed in the K-framework. $\mathbb{K}$ backends, like the Isabelle theory generator, the model checker, and the deductive verifier, can be utilized to prove properties on the semantics and construct verification tools [42].

A language semantics definition in the K-framework consists of three main parts, namely the language syntax, the configuration specified by the developer and a set of rules constructed based on the syntax and the configuration. Given a semantics definition and some source programs, the K-framework executes the source programs based on the semantics definition. In addition, specified properties can be verified by the formal analysis tools in $\mathbb{K}$ backends. We take IMP [37], a simple imperative language, as an example to show how to define a language semantics in the K-framework.

The configuration of the IMP language is shown in Fig. 4. There are only two cells, namely k and state, in the whole configuration cell T. The cells in the configuration are used to store some information related to the program execution. For instance, the cell k stores the program for execution Pgm, and in the cell state a map is used to store the variable state.

$$\left\langle \left\langle \text{\$PGM:Pgm} \right\rangle_k \quad \left\langle \text{.Map} \right\rangle_{state} \right\rangle_T$$

Fig. 4. IMP Configuration

Here, we introduce some basic rules in the K-IMP semantics. These rules are allocate, read and write. The syntax of IMP is also given in Fig. 5.

```
Pgm  ::= "int" Ids ";" Stmt   Ids ::= List{Id, ","}
AExp ::= Int | Id | "-" Int | AExp "/" AExp  > AExp "+" AExp | "(" AExp ")"
BExp ::= Bool | AExp "<=" AExp | "!" BExp  > BExp "&&" BExp | "(" BExp ")"
Block ::= "{" "}" | "{" Stmt "}"
Stmt ::= Block | Id "=" AExp ";" | "if" "(" BExp ")" Block "else" Block |
  "while" "(" BExp ")" Block > Stmt Stmt
```

Fig. 5. Syntax of IMP

RULE ALLOCATE
$$\left\langle \frac{\text{int X,Xs;S}}{\text{int Xs;S}} \cdots \right\rangle_k \quad \left\langle \frac{\text{Rho:Map}}{\text{Rho (X |-> 0)}} \right\rangle_{state}$$
requires notBool (X in keys(Rho))

RULE FINISH-ALLOCATE
$$\left\langle \frac{\text{int .Ids;S}}{\text{S}} \cdots \right\rangle_k$$

RULE READ
$$\left\langle \frac{\text{X:Id}}{\text{I}} \cdots \right\rangle_k \quad \left\langle \ldots \text{ X |-> I } \ldots \right\rangle_{state}$$

RULE WRITE
$$\left\langle \frac{\text{X = I:Int;}}{.} \cdots \right\rangle_k \quad \left\langle \ldots \frac{\text{X |-> \_}}{\text{X |-> I}} \cdots \right\rangle_{state}$$

Let us start with the rule of memory allocations in IMP shown in ALLOCATE. When Pgm, interpreted as int X,Xs;S, is encountered, we need to store a list of variables (X,Xs) starting from X in the cell state with a list of mappings. Here state can be regarded as a physical memory or storage, and Xs is also a list of variables which can be empty. X is popped out of the cell k and a new mapping from X to 0 is created in the cell state, which means that a memory slot has been allocated for X to store its initial value 0. No duplicate names are allowed in state, which is guaranteed by the require condition. Then we go like this until Xs becomes empty, which means that all the variables have already been stored in state. At this point, the execution of the first part of Pgm has been finished and we proceed to the execution of the statement S. This can be summarized in FINISH-ALLOCATE where .Ids is an empty list of identifiers, which means that the variable list is empty. Please note that . means an empty set in the K-framework. If a rule ends with ., it means that nothing will be executed.

Then we come to the rules of read and write for variables. As shown in READ, if we want to look up the value of the variable X, we need to search it in the cell state by mapping the variable name X to its value I. So the evaluation of this expression X is its value I. If we cannot find a mapping for X, the program execution will stop at this point. Particularly, ... means there can be something in the corresponding position. For instance, the mapping of X can be in any position in the cell state. However, for rules in the cell k, ... can only be at the end since the program which is stored in k is executed sequentially. As illustrated in WRITE, if we want to assign the integer I to the variable X, similarly we need to search it in state by mapping the variable name. We also need to rewrite the value of X, denoted by "_" which is a placeholder, to I.

Rewriting logic facilitates the construction of a general semantic model for smart contracts. This is because a rewriting logic style semantics consists of a set of rewriting steps from the language syntax to its evaluations. In spite of syntax differences, different smart contract languages have a lot in common in logical

RULE ALLOCATE-GENERAL
$$\left\langle \frac{\texttt{\#allocate(X, I)}}{\texttt{.}} \cdots \right\rangle_k \quad \left\langle \frac{\texttt{Rho:Map}}{\texttt{Rho (X |-> I)}} \right\rangle_{state}$$
requires notBool (X in keys(Rho))

RULE READ-GENERAL
$$\left\langle \frac{\texttt{\#read(X)}}{\texttt{I}} \cdots \right\rangle_k$$
$$\langle \ldots \texttt{X |-> I} \ldots \rangle_{state}$$

RULE WRITE-GENERAL
$$\left\langle \frac{\texttt{\#write(X, I)}}{\texttt{.}} \cdots \right\rangle_k \quad \left\langle \cdots \frac{\texttt{X |-> \_}}{\texttt{X |=> I}} \cdots \right\rangle_{state}$$

RULE ALLOCATE-IMP
$$\left\langle \frac{\texttt{int X,Xs;S}}{\substack{\texttt{\#allocate(X, 0)} \ldots \\ \curvearrowright \texttt{int Xs;S}}} \cdots \right\rangle_k$$

RULE READ-IMP
$$\left\langle \frac{\texttt{X:Id}}{\texttt{\#read(X)}} \cdots \right\rangle_k$$

RULE WRITE-IMP
$$\left\langle \frac{\texttt{X = I:Int;}}{\texttt{\#write(X, I)}} \cdots \right\rangle_k$$

```
MemoryOperations ::= #read(Id) | #write(Id, Int) | #allocate(Id, Int)
```

Fig. 6. Syntax of General Memory Operations

aspects to achieve the equivalent functionality. Rewriting logic makes it possible to separate the language syntax from the common logical aspects based on which the general semantic model is constructed. The semantics rules introduced above can be general and not specific to IMP. We show the general rules for read, write and allocate in READ-GENERAL, WRITE-GENERAL and ALLOCATE-GENERAL, respectively. In these rules, #read, #write and #allocate represent the functions to read, write and allocate memory slots for variables with specified parameters and their syntax is shown in Fig. 6. The semantics rules for memory operations in IMP can be obtained by rewriting the corresponding IMP syntax to the general memory operations defined above, namely #read, #write and #allocate, which form a general semantic model. The semantics rules for read, write and allocate in IMP based on the general semantic model are shown in READ-IMP, WRITE-IMP and ALLOCATE-IMP, respectively. Particularly, the symbol $\curvearrowright$ means "followed by". The semantics rules interpreted with the internal semantics of the general memory operations defined in Fig. 6 are equivalent to those developed from scratch, namely READ, WRITE and ALLOCATE. Rather than pure syntax translations to intermediate languages, a general semantic model enables semantic-level mappings to commonly shared high-level features.

3 A General Semantic Model

Different high-level smart contract programming languages vary in syntax but have a lot in common semantically to achieve the equivalent functionality. Considering this fact, we construct a general semantic model for smart contracts based on the commonly shared high-level semantic features that are independent of any specific language or platform. The semantics of a high-level smart contract programming language can be summarized into three aspects in terms of its functionality, namely memory operations, new contract instance creations and function calls. Particularly, new contract instance creations and function calls are the two kinds of transactions on the blockchain. In this section, we present an overview of the desired semantics of these three core features.

3.1 Syntax

The syntax of the general semantic model is defined in the K-framework and shown in Fig. 7. Due to limit of space, we only present the syntax of rewriting steps related to memory operations, new contract instance creations and function calls with MemOp, NewInstanceCreation and InstanceStateUpdate, respectively. Particularly, ExpressionList is a list of Expressions. TypeName consists of ElementaryTypeName which takes one memory slot, ComplexTypeName which is composed of a set of ElementaryTypeNames, and ReferenceTypeName which refers to a pre-defined instance. For Solidity, ElementaryTypeName consists of all the elementary types defined in the official documentation [7] except Byte. ComplexTypeName refers to mappings, arrays and Byte. ReferenceTypeName involves user-defined types and function types. Id stands for identifiers. Int and Bool represent integers and Boolean values, respectively. Values, a subset of ExpressionList, is a list of Value types which can be integers (Int) or Boolean types (Bool). Msg is the type of transaction information. VarInfo stores variable information. MemberAccess deals with expressions in member access formats.

```
RewritingSteps  ::= MemOp | NewInstanceCreation | InstanceStateUpdate

MemOp  ::= read(Expression) | readAddress(Int, Id) | write(Expression, Value)
         | writeAddress(Int, Id, Value) | allocate(Int, VarInfo)
         | allocateAddress(Int, Int, Id, Value)

NewInstanceCreation  ::= createNewInstance(Id, ExpressionList)
         | updateState(Id) | allocateStorage(Id)
         | initInstance(Id, ExpressionList)

InstanceStateUpdate  ::= functionCall(Expression; Expression; Id;
         ExpressionList; Msg) | functionCall(Id; ExpressionList)
         | switchContext(Int, Int, Id, Msg) | returnContext(Int)
         | exception() | updateExceptionState() | revertState()

Expression  ::= Id | Value | Msg | VarInfo | MemberAccess
ExpressionList  ::= List{Expression, ","} | Values
Value  ::= Int | Bool  Values ::= List{Value, ","}
Msg  ::= #msgInfo(Int, Int, Int, Int)
VarInfo  ::= #varInfo(Id, TypeName, Id, Value)
MemberAccess  ::= #memberAccess(Expression, Id)
TypeName  ::= ElementaryTypeName | ComplexTypeName | ReferenceTypeName
```

Fig. 7. Syntax of the General Semantic Model

3.2 Configuration

The runtime configuration indicates program states at each execution step, making detailed runtime features available. The runtime configuration of the general semantic model is illustrated in Fig. 8. Due to limit of space, only a part of the cells is presented here. In this configuration, there are six main cells in the whole configuration cell T and they are k, controlStacks, contracts, functions, contractInstances and transactions. The value of each cell is initialized in the configuration with its type specified. A dot followed by any type represents an empty set of this type. For instance, .List is an empty list. Particularly, K is the most general type which can be any specific type defined in the K-framework.

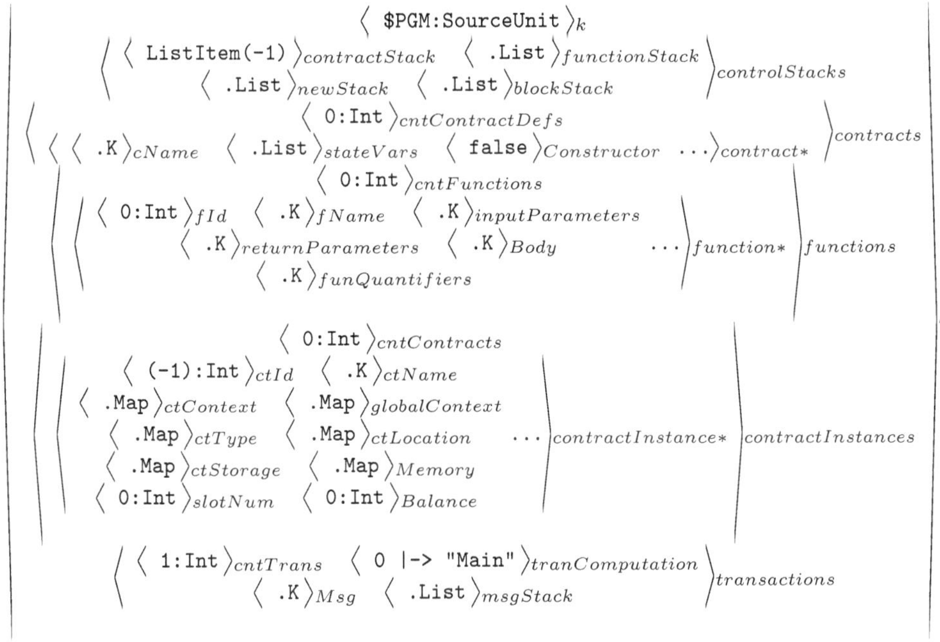

Fig. 8. Runtime Configuration of the General Semantic Model

In k, source programs, called SourceUnit, are stored for execution. If the programs stored in k terminate in a proper way, there will be a dot in this cell, indicating that this cell is empty and there are no more programs to execute.

controlStacks consists of contractStack, functionStack, newStack and blockStack. To be specific, contractStack keeps track of the current contract instance. functionStack stores a list of function calls. newStack records a list of new contract instance creations. blockStack stores a list of variable contexts to look up and assign values to variables in different scopes.

In contracts, a set of contract definitions is stored. Each cell contract represents a contract definition. The number of distinct contracts is counted in cntContractDefs. In contract, the contract name is stored in cName. State variable information is stored in stateVars. In addition, Constructor indicates whether the contract has a constructor or not and its initial value is false.

Similarly, functions stores a set of function definitions. Each cell function represents a function definition. The total number of function definitions is stored in cntFunctions. For each function definition, the function Id and the function name are stored in fId and fName, respectively. In addtion, function parameters, including input parameters and return parameters, are recorded in the corresponding cells. We also store the function body in the cell `Body` and the function quantifiers which can be modifiers or specifiers in the cell `funQuantifiers`.

In `contractInstances`, there is a set of contract instances. Each cell `contract-Instance` represents a contract instance. The number of contract instances is counted in `cntContracts`. We store the contract instance Id and the name of its associated contract in the cells `ctId` and `ctName`, respectively. Four different mappings are applied to keep track of more information of a variable. Specifically speaking, `ctContext`, `ctType`, `ctLocation` and `ctStorage`/`Memory` record the mappings from a variable name to its logical address in the storage or memory, a variable name to its type, a variable name to its location information, namely "global" or "local", and the logical address of a variable in the storage or memory to its value, respectively. `globalContext` keeps track of the state variable context. The number of memory slots taken by variables is calculated in `slotNum`. The cell `Balance` records the balance of each contract instance.

In the cell `transactions`, we keep track of the number of transactions in `cntTrans`, every transaction in `tranComputation` and also "msg" information in `Msg` and `msgStack`. "msg" is a keyword in smart contracts to represent transaction information. For instance, "msg.sender" is the caller of the function and "msg.value" specifies the amount of ether to be transferred in Solidity. The cell `msgStack` stores a list of transaction information tuples while `Msg` records the current one. We simulate transactions of smart contracts with a "Main" contract which is similar to the main function in C. In the "Main" contract, new contract instances can be created and external function calls to these instances are available. The Id of the "Main" contract is "-1", since other contract instances start from 0. Therefore, the initialized content in `contractStack` is `ListItem(-1)`, and `cntTrans` is counted from 1, which means that the creation of the "Main" contract is the first transaction recorded in `tranComputation`.

3.3   Semantics of the Core Features

We introduce the semantics rules for the core features in smart contracts. Due to limit of space, the implementation details (cf. [3]) of the sub-steps are omitted.

Memory Operations. We present an overview of the semantics rules for memory operations on elementary types, such as `int`, `uint` and `address` in Solidity, each of which takes only one memory slot. Complex types, such as arrays, mappings, etc, are compositions of elementary types. A memory operation on a complex type can be regarded as a set of recursive memory operations on elementary types. For instance, the memory allocation for a one-dimensional fixed-size array is equivalent to allocating an elementary type for each index of this array. Reading and writing a particular index involve recursive steps to retrieve the logical address of this index from the base address of the array. Mappings are similar to dynamic arrays. For a mapping from `address` to `uint`, the memory allocation for this mapping is equivalent to allocating an unsigned integer type at each address involved. Reference types which refer to pre-defined instances can be simply implemented as mappings in the K-framework.

RULE READ
$$\left\langle \frac{\texttt{read(X:Id)}}{\texttt{readAddress(Addr, L)}} \dots \right\rangle_k \quad \langle \texttt{ ListItem(N:Int) } \dots\rangle_{contractStack}$$
$$\left\langle \begin{array}{l} \langle\texttt{ N }\rangle_{ctId} \quad \langle\texttt{... X |-> Addr ...}\rangle_{ctContext} \\ \qquad \langle\texttt{... X |-> L ...}\rangle_{ctLocation} \\ \langle\texttt{... X |-> T:ElementaryTypeName ...}\rangle_{ctType} \end{array} \quad \dots \right|_{contractInstance}$$

RULE WRITE
$$\left\langle \frac{\texttt{write(X:Id, V:Value)}}{\texttt{writeAddress(Addr, L, V)}} \dots \right\rangle_k \quad \langle \texttt{ ListItem(N:Int) } \dots\rangle_{contractStack}$$
$$\left\langle \begin{array}{l} \langle\texttt{ N }\rangle_{ctId} \quad \langle\texttt{... X |-> Addr ...}\rangle_{ctContext} \\ \qquad \langle\texttt{... X |-> L ...}\rangle_{ctLocation} \\ \langle\texttt{... X |-> T:ElementaryTypeName ...}\rangle_{ctType} \end{array} \quad \dots \right|_{contractInstance}$$

RULE ALLOCATE
$$\left\langle \frac{\texttt{allocate(N:Int, \#varInfo(X:Id, T:ElementaryTypeName, L:Id, V:Value))}}{\texttt{allocateAddress(N, Addr, L, V)}} \dots \right\rangle_k$$
$$\left\langle \begin{array}{l} \langle\texttt{ N }\rangle_{ctId} \quad \left\langle\dfrac{\texttt{Addr}}{\texttt{Addr +Int 1}}\right\rangle_{slotNum} \quad \left\langle\dfrac{\texttt{TYPE:Map}}{\texttt{TYPE (X |-> T)}}\right\rangle_{ctType} \\ \left\langle\dfrac{\texttt{CON:Map}}{\texttt{CON (X |-> Addr)}}\right\rangle_{ctContext} \quad \left\langle\dfrac{\texttt{LOC:Map}}{\texttt{LOC (X |-> L)}}\right\rangle_{ctLocation} \end{array} \quad \dots \right|_{contractInstance}$$

RULE NEW-CONTRACT-INSTANCE-CREATION
$$\left\langle \frac{\texttt{createNewInstance(X:Id, E:ExpressionList)}}{\texttt{updateState(X)} \curvearrowright \texttt{allocateStorage(X)} \curvearrowright \texttt{initInstance(X, E)}} \dots \right\rangle_k$$

RULE FUNCTION-CALL
$$\left\langle \frac{\texttt{functionCall(C:Int; R:Int; F:Id; Es:Values; M:Msg)}}{\texttt{switchContext(C, R, F, M)} \curvearrowright \texttt{functionCall(F; Es)} \curvearrowright \texttt{returnContext(R)}} \dots \right\rangle_k$$

Let us start with the **read** operation on elementary types shown in READ. Here, we consider the object X as a variable which is an Id type. The first thing to do is to get the current execution context. This is achieved by retrieving the current contract instance Id N in **contractStack** and mapping the corresponding contract instance with N in the cell **ctId**. After that, we retrieve the logical address of X, denoted by Addr, in **ctContext** and the location information of X, denoted by L, in **ctLocation**. With these two parameters, we can obtain the evaluation of X through **readAddress** which retrieves the value located at Addr in the associated cell specified by L. To be specific, if L specifies this variable as a global one, the search space is **ctStorage**. Otherwise, the value is retrieved in Memory. **write** is similar to **read**. After retrieving the logical address of X, denoted by Addr, and the location information of X, denoted by L, we rewrite the value at Addr to the value V in the cell specified by L through **writeAddress**.

Then we come to the allocation for elementary types shown in ALLOCATE. The first input parameter N indicates the object contract instance Id. The variable information including the name X, the type T, the location information L and the initial value V, is stored in **#varInfo**. First, we retrieve the corresponding instance by mapping the Id N in **ctId**. Then the number of memory slots is increased by 1 in **slotNum**. After that, the variable information is recorded in the associated cells. To be specific, we record the logical address Addr, the type T, and the location information L in `ctContext`, `ctType` and `ctLocation`, respectively. Finally, a memory slot is allocated for this variable through `allocateAddress`.

New Contract Instance Creations. As illustrated in NEW-CONTRACT-INSTANCE-CREATION, the contract name X and the arguments in the constructor E are taken as input parameters to create a new instance of X. There are altogether three sub-steps for this transaction and they are `updateState`, `allocateStorage` and `initInstance`. To be specific, `updateState` updates the blockchain states, including the states of contract instances and transactions, and the stack information to indicate the new contract instance creation. In addition, `allocateStorage` allocates state variables and `initInstance` deals with initialization issues, such as calling the constructor, in the new instance.

Function Calls. In order to make the semantics of function calls general for all kinds of calls and extensible for different smart contract languages, a uniform format is applied to generalize the semantics. The uniform format is `functionCall(Id_of_Caller; Id_of_Recipient; Function_Name; Arguments; Msg_Info)`. Particularly, `Msg_Info` represents the transaction information, including the Ids of the caller and the recipient instances, the value of digital assets to be transferred and the transaction fees to be consumed. The semantics rule for function calls based on this format is shown in FUNCTION-CALL.

In the rule FUNCTION-CALL, the caller of this function is C and the recipient is R. F is the function name and Es specifies the function call arguments. M is the "msg" information to keep track of transactions. In particular, the types of these parameters have been specified. The semantics of function calls is designed from a general point of view. Each external function call is regarded as an extension of an internal function call. Whenever there is an external function call, we first switch to the recipient instance and then call the function in this instance as an internal call. Finally, we switch back to the caller instance. In this way, external function calls can be achieved through internal function calls and switches of contract instances. This mechanism also applies to internal function calls where the caller is the same as the recipient. There are three sub-steps in FUNCTION-CALL. The first one is to switch to the recipient instance from the caller through `switchContext`. The second is an internal function call `functionCall`. The last one is to return to the caller instance through `returnContext`.

Particularly, the semantics of function calls is equipped with exception handling features. If an exception is encountered, it will be propagated to the transactional function call to revert the whole transaction. The propagation of exceptions is a sub-step in `returnContext`. The exception handling mechanism is also general, making it possible to deal with all kinds of exception handling features in smart contracts, such as **revert** and **assert** in Solidity, in a similar way.

RULE EXCEPTION-PROPAGATION

$$\left\langle \frac{\text{exception()}}{\text{updateExceptionState()}} \cdots \right\rangle_k$$
$$\left\langle \text{ListItem(R)ListItem(C)} \cdots \right\rangle_{contractStack}$$
requires C >=Int 0

RULE TRANSACTION-REVERSION

$$\left\langle \frac{\text{exception()}}{\text{updateExceptionState() ...}} \right\rangle_k$$
$$\curvearrowright \text{revertState()}$$
$$\left\langle \text{ListItem(R)ListItem(-1)} \right\rangle_{contractStack}$$

There are two stages in handling exceptions. The first one is the propagation of exceptions to the transactional function call as shown in EXCEPTION-PROPAGATION, and the second is the reversion of the transaction as shown in TRANSACTION-REVERSION. The first stage is present in nested calls to propagate exceptions to the transactional function call, while the second stage is only present in the transactional function call stemming from the "Main" contract. In the stage of propagating exceptions, the exception state is updated through updateExceptionState() to indicate that an exception has been encountered. Particularly, the Id of the caller instance should be larger than or equal to 0 since the caller cannot be the "Main" contract. And in the stage of reverting transactions, the caller is the "Main" contract whose Id is "-1". In addition to updating the exception state, the whole transaction is reverted through revertState().

4 Direct Semantics Generation

A direct semantics of a high-level smart contract programming language can be developed based on the general semantic model introduced above. From the perspective of rewriting logic, a language semantics is a set of rewriting steps from the language syntax to its evaluations. Each of these rewriting steps implements a function to move the syntax a step further to its final evaluations. The general semantic model which consists of a set of internal rewriting steps and defines the desired semantics of smart contracts can be regarded as a logical intermediate language. A direct semantics of a high-level smart contract programming language can be constructed by rewriting its syntax to the features in the general semantic model with several functional steps. This also indicates the process of smart contract language design. We take Solidity as an example to illustrate how to generate the semantics based on the general semantic model. The semantics rules presented below are based on the Solidity syntax defined in [7].

Let us start with the look-up operation in Solidity. As shown in LOOK-UP, the object is considered to be a variable X. X is evaluated with read in the general semantic model. We simply rewrite the corresponding Solidity syntax to read. assignment is similar to look-up. As shown in ASSIGNMENT, we simply rewrite the assignment syntax in Solidity to write in the general semantic model.

RULE LOOK-UP   RULE ASSIGNMENT   RULE NEW-INSTANCE-SOLIDITY

$$\left\langle \frac{\texttt{X:Id}}{\texttt{read(X)}} \cdots \right\rangle_k \quad \left\langle \frac{\texttt{X:Id = V:Value}}{\texttt{write(X, V)}} \cdots \right\rangle_k \quad \left\langle \frac{\texttt{new X:Id (E:ExpressionList)}}{\texttt{createNewInstance(X, E)}} \cdots \right\rangle_k$$

Both state and local variable allocations are achieved through allocate in the general semantic model. State variables are allocated when new contract instances are created, while local variables are allocated right after declarations.

In NEW-INSTANCE-SOLIDITY, the syntax of new contract instance creations in Solidity is rewritten to createNewInstance in the general semantic model.

Function calls in Solidity are written in a format similar to member access. For instance, target.deposit.value(2)() is a typical function call in Solidity. To be specific, target specifies the recipient instance and deposit is the function

RULE FUNCTION-CALL-SOLIDITY

$$\left\langle \frac{\texttt{\#memberAccess(R:Int, F:Id)} \curvearrowright \texttt{Es:Values} \curvearrowright \texttt{MsgValue:Int} \curvearrowright \texttt{MsgGas:Int}}{\texttt{functionCall(C; R; F; Es; \#msgInfo(C, R, MsgValue, MsgGas))}} \cdots \right\rangle_k$$
$$\left\langle \texttt{ListItem(C:Int)} \cdots \right\rangle_{contractStack}$$

RULE REVERT

$$\left\langle \frac{\texttt{revert(.ExpressionList);}}{\texttt{exception()}} \cdots \right\rangle_k$$

RULE ASSERT

$$\left\langle \frac{\texttt{assert(true);}}{.} \cdots \right\rangle_k \quad \left\langle \frac{\texttt{assert(false);}}{\texttt{exception()}} \cdots \right\rangle_k$$

RULE REQUIRE

$$\left\langle \frac{\texttt{require(true);}}{.} \cdots \right\rangle_k \quad \left\langle \frac{\texttt{require(false);}}{\texttt{exception()}} \cdots \right\rangle_k$$

to be called in that instance. `value` specifies `msg.value` as 2. In addition, we can specify other parameters, such as `msg.gas`, function arguments, etc. When it comes to the semantics of function calls in Solidity, the first thing to do is to decompose the member access like format and transform it into the one in the general semantic model. As shown in FUNCTION-CALL-SOLIDITY, each decomposed part in Solidity calls is reorganized in `functionCall`. Specifically speaking, `#memberAccess(R:Int, F:Id)` specifies the recipient instance R and the function to be called in this instance F. `Es` specifies the function arguments. `MsgValue` and `MsgGas` represent `msg.value` and `msg.gas`, respectively.

The semantics rules for function calls apply to all kinds of function calls in Solidity, including high-level and low-level calls, constructors and fallback functions. For instance, if there is no function name specified in a function call or the specified function name does not match any existing function in the recipient instance, the first decomposed part in FUNCTION-CALL-SOLIDITY will be `#memberAccess(R:Int, String2Id("fallback"))` where R is the Id of the recipient instance and "fallback" refers to the fallback function in that instance. In this case, the fallback function in R will be invoked. In addition, in the case of `delegatecall`, the recipient instance R is the same as the caller instance C since the execution takes place in the caller's context.

Exception handling features in Solidity can be interpreted with the semantics of `exception()` in the general semantic model. The semantics rules for `revert`, `assert` and `require` are shown in REVERT, ASSERT and REQUIRE, respectively.

5 Evaluation

We evaluate the proposed generalized formal semantic framework for smart contracts by showing that the generated semantics, an interpretation of the general semantic model with a particular language, is consistent with the semantics interpreted by the corresponding official compiler on benchmarks. The testing language makes no difference to the evaluation since it aims to validate the semantics of the commonly shared high-level features defined in the general semantic model. We take Solidity as an object for the evaluation since there are sufficient Solidity smart contracts available for testing the generated Solidity

Table 1. Coverage of the Generated Solidity Semantics

Features	Coverage	Features	Coverage
Types(Core)		**Statements(Core)**	
Elementary Types		If Statement	FC
address	FC	While Statement	FC
bool	FC	For Statement	FC
string	FC	Block	FC
Int	FC	Inline Assembly	N
Uint	FC	Statement	
Byte	FC	Do While Statement	FC
Fixed	N	Place Holder Statement	FC
Ufixed	N	Continue	FC
User-defined Types	FC	Break	FC
Mappings	FC	Return	FC
Array Types	FC	Throw,Revert,Assert,Require	FC
Function Types	FC	Simple Statement	FC
address payable	FC	Emit Statement	FC
Functions(Core)		**Expressions(Core)**	
Function Definitions		Bitwise Operations	FC
Constructors	FC	Arithmetic Operations	FC
Normal Functions	FC	Logical Operations	FC
Fallback Functions	FC	Comparison Operations	FC
Modifiers	FC	Assignment	FC
Function Calls		Look Up	FC
Internal Function Calls	FC	New Expression	FC
External Function Calls	FC	Other Expressions	FC
Using For	FC	**Inheritance**	FC
Event	FC		

FC: Fully Covered and Consistent with Solidity IDE   N: Not Covered

semantics. The Solidity semantics developed with the proposed framework is publicly available at https://github.com/kframework/solidity-semantics.

The generated Solidity semantics is evaluated from two perspectives: the first one is its coverage (i.e., completeness), and the second is its correctness (i.e., consistency with Solidity compilers). Evaluation results show that the Solidity semantics developed with the proposed framework completely covers the supported high-level core language features specified by the official Solidity documentation [7] and is consistent with the official Solidity compiler Remix [5].

We evaluate and test the Solidity semantics developed with the proposed framework with the Solidity compiler test set [6]. This test set is regarded as a standard test set or benchmarks for evaluating Solidity semantics since the test programs are written in a standard or correct way defined by the language developers and cover all the features in Solidity. There are altogether 482 tests in the Solidity compiler test set. The evaluation is done by manually comparing the execution behaviours of the generated Solidity semantics with the ones of the Remix compiler on the test programs. We consider the generated Solidity semantics is correct if the execution behaviours indicated in the configuration are consistent with the ones of the Remix compiler. A feature is considered to be fully covered if all the compiler tests involving this feature are passed. We list the coverage of the generated Solidity semantics in Table 1 from the perspective of each feature specified by the official documentation.

From Table 1, we can observe that the generated Solidity semantics completely covers the supported high-level core features of Solidity. As for types, the generated Solidity semantics covers the following elementary types: `address`, `bool`, `string`, `Int`, `Uint` and `Byte`. `Fixed` and `Ufixed` are not covered because they are not fully supported by Solidity yet [7]. User-defined types, including `struct`, contract types and `enum`, are covered. Mappings, arrays, function types and `address payable` are also covered. In addition, the semantics associated with functions, such as function definitions and function calls, is fully covered. The semantics of statements is completely covered except that of `inline assembly statements` which are considered to be low-level features accessing EVM (i.e., this part of semantics can be integrated with KEVM [24]). All kinds of expressions in Solidity are covered. Lastly, the semantics of `event` is also covered and the parts of semantics for `using for` and `inheritance` are covered with rewriting. For all the parts of covered semantics, they are considered to be correct since the execution behaviours involved are consistent with the ones of Remix. Therefore, the generated Solidity semantics can be considered to be complete and correct in terms of the supported high-level core features of Solidity, indicating the completeness and correctness of the general semantic model.

Threats to Validity. We validate the general semantic model with its interpretation in Solidity. The validity of the proposed framework holds for any particular high-level smart contract programming language as long as its core features fall into or can be properly rewritten to the ones defined in the general semantic model. The proposed framework may not work if the core features cannot be interpreted with the ones defined in the general semantic model. However, this is unlikely due to the nature of smart contract executions. For instance, transactions in existing instances are implemented with or can be transformed into function calls regardless of the platforms of smart contract programs.

6   Conclusion

In this paper, we propose a generalized formal semantic framework for smart contracts. This framework can directly handle smart contracts written in different high-level programming languages, such as Solidity, Vyper, Bamboo, etc, without translating them into EVM bytecode or intermediate languages. In this framework, a direct executable formal semantics of a particular high-level smart contract programming language is constructed based on a general semantic model with rewriting logic. The general semantic model is validated with its interpretation in Solidity and evaluation results show that it is complete and correct. Furthermore, the proposed framework provides a formal specification of smart contracts written in different languages.

Acknowledgements. This work is supported by the Ministry of Education, Singapore under its Tier-2 Project (Award Number: MOE2018-T2-1-068) and partially supported by the National Research Foundation, Singapore under its NSoE Programme (Award Number: NSOE-TSS2019-03).

References

1. Bamboo (2018), https://github.com/pirapira/bamboo
2. Ethereum (2020), https://www.ethereum.org
3. Implementation Details (2020), https://github.com/SmartContractSemantics/SemanticFrameworkforSmartContracts
4. Mythril (2020), https://github.com/ConsenSys/mythril
5. Remix - Solidity IDE (2020), https://remix.ethereum.org
6. Solidity Compiler Test Set (2020), https://github.com/ethereum/solidity
7. Solidity Documentation (2020), https://solidity.readthedocs.io/en/latest
8. Vyper Documentation (2020), https://vyper.readthedocs.io/en/latest
9. Amani, S., Bégel, M., Bortin, M., Staples, M.: Towards Verifying Ethereum Smart Contract Bytecode in Isabelle/HOL. In: Proceedings of the 7th ACM SIGPLAN International Conference on Certified Programs and Proofs. pp. 66–77. CPP 2018, ACM, New York, NY, USA (2018)
10. Atzei, N., Bartoletti, M., Cimoli, T.: A Survey of Attacks on Ethereum Smart Contracts (SoK). In: Maffei, M., Ryan, M. (eds.) Principles of Security and Trust - 6th International Conference, POST 2017, Held as Part of the European Joint Conferences on Theory and Practice of Software, ETAPS 2017, Uppsala, Sweden, April 22-29, 2017, Proceedings. Lecture Notes in Computer Science, vol. 10204, pp. 164–186. Springer (2017). https://doi.org/10.1007/978-3-662-54455-6_8
11. Bartoletti, M., Galletta, L., Murgia, M.: A Minimal Core Calculus for Solidity Contracts. In: DPM/CBT@ESORICS (2019)
12. Bhargavan, K., Delignat-Lavaud, A., Fournet, C., Gollamudi, A., Gonthier, G., Kobeissi, N., Kulatova, N., Rastogi, A., Sibut-Pinote, T., Swamy, N., Béguelin, S.Z.: Formal Verification of Smart Contracts: Short Paper. In: Murray, T.C., Stefan, D. (eds.) Proceedings of the 2016 ACM Workshop on Programming Languages and Analysis for Security, PLAS@CCS 2016, Vienna, Austria, October 24, 2016. pp. 91–96. ACM (2016)
13. Bogdanas, D., Rosu, G.: K-Java: A Complete Semantics of Java. In: Rajamani, S.K., Walker, D. (eds.) Proceedings of the 42nd Annual ACM SIGPLAN-SIGACT Symposium on Principles of Programming Languages, POPL 2015, Mumbai, India, January 15-17, 2015. pp. 445–456. ACM (2015)
14. Chen, T., Zhang, Y., Li, Z., Luo, X., Wang, T., Cao, R., Xiao, X., Zhang, X.: TokenScope: Automatically Detecting Inconsistent Behaviors of Cryptocurrency Tokens in Ethereum. In: Cavallaro, L., Kinder, J., Wang, X., Katz, J. (eds.) Proceedings of the 2019 ACM SIGSAC Conference on Computer and Communications Security, CCS 2019, London, UK, November 11-15, 2019. pp. 1503–1520. ACM (2019)
15. Crafa, S., Pirro, M., Zucca, E.: Is Solidity Solid Enough? In: Financial Cryptography Workshops (2019)
10. Delmolino, K., Arnett, M., Kosba, A.E., Miller, A., Shi, E.: Step by Step Towards Creating a Safe Smart Contract: Lessons and Insights from a Cryptocurrency Lab. In: Clark, J., Meiklejohn, S., Ryan, P.Y.A., Wallach, D.S., Brenner, M., Rohloff, K. (eds.) Financial Cryptography and Data Security - FC 2016 International Workshops, BITCOIN, VOTING, and WAHC, Christ Church, Barbados, February 26, 2016, Revised Selected Papers. Lecture Notes in Computer Science, vol. 9604, pp. 79–94. Springer (2016). https://doi.org/10.1007/978-3-662-53357-4_6
17. Drescher, D.: Blockchain Basics (2017)
18. Ellison, C., Rosu, G.: An Executable Formal Semantics of C with Applications. In: Field, J., Hicks, M. (eds.) Proceedings of the 39th ACM SIGPLAN-SIGACT

Symposium on Principles of Programming Languages, POPL 2012, Philadelphia, Pennsylvania, USA, January 22-28, 2012. pp. 533–544. ACM (2012)

19. Feist, J., Grieco, G., Groce, A.: Slither: A Static Analysis Framework for Smart Contracts. In: Proceedings of the 2nd International Workshop on Emerging Trends in Software Engineering for Blockchain, WETSEB@ICSE 2019, Montreal, QC, Canada, May 27, 2019. pp. 8–15. IEEE / ACM (2019)

20. Grech, N., Kong, M., Jurisevic, A., Brent, L., Scholz, B., Smaragdakis, Y.: Mad-Max: Surviving Out-of-gas Conditions in Ethereum Smart Contracts. PACMPL **2**(OOPSLA), 116:1–116:27 (2018)

21. Grishchenko, I., Maffei, M., Schneidewind, C.: A Semantic Framework for the Security Analysis of Ethereum Smart Contracts. In: Bauer, L., Küsters, R. (eds.) Principles of Security and Trust - 7th International Conference, POST 2018, Held as Part of the European Joint Conferences on Theory and Practice of Software, ETAPS 2018, Thessaloniki, Greece, April 14-20, 2018, Proceedings. Lecture Notes in Computer Science, vol. 10804, pp. 243–269. Springer (2018). https://doi.org/10.1007/978-3-319-89722-6_10

22. Grossman, S., Abraham, I., Golan-Gueta, G., Michalevsky, Y., Rinetzky, N., Sagiv, M., Zohar, Y.: Online Detection of Effectively Callback Free Objects with Applications to Smart Contracts. PACMPL **2**(POPL), 48:1–48:28 (2018)

23. Hajdu, Á., Jovanovic, D.: solc-verify: A Modular Verifier for Solidity Smart Contracts. arXiv preprint **abs/1907.04262** (2019)

24. Hildenbrandt, E., Saxena, M., Rodrigues, N., Zhu, X., Daian, P., Guth, D., Moore, B.M., Park, D., Zhang, Y., Stefanescu, A., Roşu, G.: KEVM: A Complete Formal Semantics of the Ethereum Virtual Machine. In: 31st IEEE Computer Security Foundations Symposium, CSF 2018, Oxford, United Kingdom, July 9-12, 2018. pp. 204–217. IEEE Computer Society (2018)

25. Hirai, Y.: Defining the Ethereum Virtual Machine for Interactive Theorem Provers. In: Brenner, M., Rohloff, K., Bonneau, J., Miller, A., Ryan, P.Y.A., Teague, V., Bracciali, A., Sala, M., Pintore, F., Jakobsson, M. (eds.) Financial Cryptography and Data Security - FC 2017 International Workshops, WAHC, BITCOIN, VOTING, WTSC, and TA, Sliema, Malta, April 7, 2017, Revised Selected Papers. Lecture Notes in Computer Science, vol. 10323, pp. 520–535. Springer (2017). https://doi.org/10.1007/978-3-319-70278-0_33

26. Jiang, B., Liu, Y., Chan, W.K.: ContractFuzzer: Fuzzing Smart Contracts for Vulnerability Detection. In: Huchard, M., Kästner, C., Fraser, G. (eds.) Proceedings of the 33rd ACM/IEEE International Conference on Automated Software Engineering, ASE 2018, Montpellier, France, September 3-7, 2018. pp. 259–269. ACM (2018)

27. Jiao, J., Kan, S., Lin, S., Sanán, D., Liu, Y., Sun, J.: Executable Operational Semantics of Solidity. arXiv preprint **abs/1804.01295** (2018)

28. Kalra, S., Goel, S., Dhawan, M., Sharma, S.: ZEUS: Analyzing Safety of Smart Contracts. In: 25th Annual Network and Distributed System Security Symposium, NDSS 2018, San Diego, California, USA, February 18-21, 2018. The Internet Society (2018)

29. Kolluri, A., Nikolic, I., Sergey, I., Hobor, A., Saxena, P.: Exploiting the Laws of Order in Smart Contracts. In: Zhang, D., Møller, A. (eds.) Proceedings of the 28th ACM SIGSOFT International Symposium on Software Testing and Analysis, ISSTA 2019, Beijing, China, July 15-19, 2019. pp. 363–373. ACM (2019)

30. Krupp, J., Rossow, C.: teEther: Gnawing at Ethereum to Automatically Exploit Smart Contracts. In: Enck, W., Felt, A.P. (eds.) 27th USENIX Security Sym-

posium, USENIX Security 2018, Baltimore, MD, USA, August 15-17, 2018. pp. 1317–1333. USENIX Association (2018)

31. Lahiri, S.K., Chen, S., Wang, Y., Dillig, I.: Formal Specification and Verification of Smart Contracts for Azure Blockchain. arXiv preprint **abs/1812.08829** (2018)

32. Luu, L., Chu, D., Olickel, H., Saxena, P., Hobor, A.: Making Smart Contracts Smarter. In: Weippl, E.R., Katzenbeisser, S., Kruegel, C., Myers, A.C., Halevi, S. (eds.) Proceedings of the 2016 ACM SIGSAC Conference on Computer and Communications Security, Vienna, Austria, October 24-28, 2016. pp. 254–269. ACM (2016)

33. Martí-Oliet, N., Meseguer, J.: Rewriting Logic: Roadmap and Bibliography. Theor. Comput. Sci. **285**, 121–154 (2002)

34. Mossberg, M., Manzano, F., Hennenfent, E., Groce, A., Grieco, G., Feist, J., Brunson, T., Dinaburg, A.: Manticore: A User-Friendly Symbolic Execution Framework for Binaries and Smart Contracts. In: 34th IEEE/ACM International Conference on Automated Software Engineering, ASE 2019, San Diego, CA, USA, November 11-15, 2019. pp. 1186–1189. IEEE (2019)

35. Nehai, Z., Bobot, F.: Deductive Proof of Ethereum Smart Contracts Using Why3. arXiv preprint **abs/1904.11281** (2019)

36. Nikolic, I., Kolluri, A., Sergey, I., Saxena, P., Hobor, A.: Finding the Greedy, Prodigal, and Suicidal Contracts at Scale. In: Proceedings of the 34th Annual Computer Security Applications Conference, ACSAC 2018, San Juan, PR, USA, December 03-07, 2018. pp. 653–663. ACM (2018)

37. Nipkow, T., Klein, G.: IMP: A Simple Imperative Language. Concrete Semantics. Springer, Cham (2014)

38. Rodler, M., Li, W., Karame, G.O., Davi, L.: Sereum: Protecting Existing Smart Contracts Against Re-Entrancy Attacks. In: 26th Annual Network and Distributed System Security Symposium, NDSS 2019, San Diego, California, USA, February 24-27, 2019. The Internet Society (2019)

39. Roşu, G., Şerbănuţă, T.F.: An Overview of the K Semantic Framework. Journal of Logic and Algebraic Programming **79**(6), 397–434 (2010)

40. Sergey, I., Kumar, A., Hobor, A.: Scilla: A Smart Contract Intermediate-level Language. arXiv preprint **abs/1801.00687** (2018)

41. Siegel, D.: Understanding the DAO Attack (2016), https://www.coindesk.com/understanding-dao-hack-journalists

42. Stefanescu, A., Park, D., Yuwen, S., Li, Y., Roşu, G.: Semantics-based Program Verifiers for All Languages. In: Visser, E., Smaragdakis, Y. (eds.) Proceedings of the 2016 ACM SIGPLAN International Conference on Object-Oriented Programming, Systems, Languages, and Applications, OOPSLA 2016, part of SPLASH 2016, Amsterdam, The Netherlands, October 30 - November 4, 2016. pp. 74–91. ACM (2016)

43. Tikhomirov, S., Voskresenskaya, E., Ivanitskiy, I., Takhaviev, R., Marchenko, E., Alexandrov, Y.: SmartCheck: Static Analysis of Ethereum Smart Contracts. In: 1st IEEE/ACM International Workshop on Emerging Trends in Software Engineering for Blockchain, WETSEB@ICSE 2018, Gothenburg, Sweden, May 27 - June 3, 2018. pp. 9–16. ACM (2018)

44. Tsankov, P., Dan, A.M., Drachsler-Cohen, D., Gervais, A., Bünzli, F., Vechev, M.T.: Securify: Practical Security Analysis of Smart Contracts. In: Lie, D., Mannan, M., Backes, M., Wang, X. (eds.) Proceedings of the 2018 ACM SIGSAC Conference on Computer and Communications Security, CCS 2018, Toronto, ON, Canada, October 15-19, 2018. pp. 67–82. ACM (2018)

45. Wang, H., Li, Y., Lin, S., Ma, L., Liu, Y.: VULTRON: Catching Vulnerable Smart Contracts Once and for All. In: Sarma, A., Murta, L. (eds.) Proceedings of the 41st International Conference on Software Engineering: New Ideas and Emerging Results, ICSE (NIER) 2019, Montreal, QC, Canada, May 29-31, 2019. pp. 1–4. IEEE / ACM (2019)
46. Wang, S., Zhang, C., Su, Z.: Detecting Nondeterministic Payment Bugs in Ethereum Smart Contracts. PACMPL **3**(OOPSLA), 189:1–189:29 (2019)
47. Wood, G.: Ethereum: A Secure Decentralised Generalised Transaction Ledger. Ethereum project yellow paper **151**, 1–32 (2014)
48. Yang, Z., Lei, H.: Lolisa: Formal Syntax and Semantics for a Subset of the Solidity Programming Language. arXiv preprint **abs/1803.09885** (2018)
49. Zakrzewski, J.: Towards Verification of Ethereum Smart Contracts: A Formalization of Core of Solidity. In: Piskac, R., Rümmer, P. (eds.) Verified Software. Theories, Tools, and Experiments - 10th International Conference, VSTTE 2018, Oxford, UK, July 18-19, 2018, Revised Selected Papers. Lecture Notes in Computer Science, vol. 11294, pp. 229–247. Springer (2018). https://doi.org/10.1007/978-3-030-03592-1_13

2

Global Reproducibility through Local Control for Distributed Active Objects

Lars Tveito, Einar Broch Johnsen, and Rudolf Schlatte

Department of Informatics, University of Oslo, Oslo, Norway
{larstvei,einarj,rudi}@ifi.uio.no

Abstract. Non-determinism in a concurrent or distributed setting may lead to many different runs or executions of a program. This paper presents a method to reproduce a specific run for non-deterministic actor or active object systems. The method is based on recording traces of events reflecting local transitions at so-called stable states during execution; i.e., states in which local execution depends on interaction with the environment. The paper formalizes trace recording and replay for a basic active object language, to show that such local traces suffice to obtain global reproducibility of runs; during replay different objects may operate fairly independently of each other and in parallel, yet a program under replay has guaranteed deterministic outcome. We then show that the method extends to the other forms of non-determinism as found in richer active object languages. Following the proposed method, we have implemented a tool to record and replay runs, and to visualize the communication and scheduling decisions of a recorded run, for Real-Time ABS, a formally defined, rich active object language for modeling timed, resource-aware behavior in distributed systems.

1   Introduction

Non-determinism in a concurrent or distributed setting leads to many different possible runs or executions of a given program. The ability to reproduce and visualize a particular run can be very useful for the developer of such programs. For example, reproducing a specific run representing negative (or unexpected) behavior can be beneficial to eliminate bugs which occur only in a few out of many possible runs (so-called Heisenbugs). Conversely, reproducing a run representing positive (and expected) behavior can be useful for regression testing for new versions of a system.

Deterministic replay is an emerging technique to provide deterministic executions of programs in the presence of different non-deterministic factors [1]. In a first phase, the technique consists of *recording* sufficient information in a trace during a run to reproduce the same run during a *replay* in a second phase. Approaches to reproduce runs of non-deterministic systems can be classified as either *content-based* or *ordering-based* replay. Content-based replay records the results of all non-deterministic operations whereas ordering-based replay records the ordering of non-deterministic events.

This paper considers deterministic replay for non-deterministic runs of Active Object languages [2], which combine the asynchronous message passing of Actors with object-oriented abstractions. Compared to standard OO languages, these languages decouple communication and synchronization by communicating through asynchronous method calls without transfer of control and by synchronizing via futures. We develop a method to reproduce the runs of active objects. The method is ordering-based, as we represent the parallel execution of active objects as traces of events. We show that locally recording events at so-called *stable states* suffice to obtain deterministic replay. In these states, local execution needs to interact with the environment, e.g., to make a scheduling decision or to send or receive a message. We formalize execution with record and replay for a basic active object language, and show that its executions enjoy confluence properties which can be described using such traces. These confluence properties justify the recording and replay of local traces to reproduce global behavior.

Active object languages may also contain more advanced features [2], such as *cooperative scheduling* [3,4], *concurrent object groups* [3,5] and *timed, resource-aware behavior* [6]. With cooperative scheduling, an object may suspend its current task while waiting for the result of a method call and instead schedule a different task. With concurrent object groups, several objects share an actor's lock abstraction. With timed, resource-aware behavior, local execution requires resources from resource-centers (e.g., virtual machines) to progress. These features introduce additional non-determinism in the active object systems, in addition to the non-determinism caused by asynchronous calls. We show that the proposed method extends to handle these additional sources of non-determinism.

The proposed method to deterministically replay runs has been realized for Real-Time ABS [6], a modeling language with these advanced features, which has been used to analyze, e.g., industrial scale cloud-deployed software [7], railway networks [8], and complex low-level multicore systems [9,10]. Whereas the language supports various formal analysis techniques, most validation of complex models (at least in an early stage of model development) is based on simulation. The tracing capabilities have a small enough performance impact to be enabled by default in the simulator. The simulator itself is implemented as a distributed system in Erlang [11]. The low performance overhead comes from only recording local events in each actor, which does not impose any additional communication or synchronization, which are typically bottlenecks in a distributed system.

Contributions. Our main contributions can be summarized as follows:

- we propose a method to reproduce runs for active object systems based on recording events reflecting local transitions from stable object states;
- we provide a formal justification for the method in terms of confluence and progress properties for ordering-based record & replay for a basic actor language with asynchronous communication and synchronization via futures;
- we show that the method extends to address additional sources of non-determinism as found in richer active object languages; and
- we provide an implementation of the proposed method to record, replay and visualize runs for the active object modeling language Real-Time ABS.

```
class C {
  Int n = 1;
  Unit m1() { n = n - 1; }
  Unit m2() { n = n * 3; }
}

// Main block
{
  C o = new C();
  o!m1();
  o!m2();
}
```

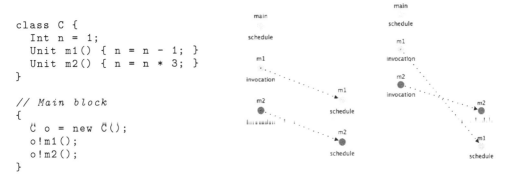

Fig. 1: A simple program, with two possible results

Fig. 2: The executions leading to the two different results for the simple program.

Paper overview Section 2 provides a motivating example, Section 3 considers the problem of reproducibility for a formalization of a basic active object language and Section 4 formalizes record and replay over the operational semantics of the basic language. Section 5 considers reproducibility for extensions to the basic language. Section 6 presents our implementation of the method for Real-Time ABS. Section 7 discusses related work and Section 8 concludes the paper.

2 Motivating Example

Consider the program in Fig. 1. It consists of a class C, with a single integer field, initialized to 1 and two methods m1 and m2. The main block of the program creates an active object *o* as an instance of the class, and performs two asynchronous calls on *o*, o!m1() and o!m2() respectively. Since the calls are asynchronous, the caller can proceed to make the second call immediately, without waiting for the first call to complete. The two calls are placed in the queue of *o* and scheduled in some order for execution by *o*. (We here assume method execution is atomic, but this assumption will be relaxed in Section 5.)

Thus, even the execution of this very simple program can lead to two different results, depending on whether o!m1() is scheduled before o!m2(), and conversely, o!m2() is scheduled before o!m1(). In the first case, the field n (which is initially 1) will first be decremented by 1 and then be multiplied with 3, resulting in a final state in which the field n has the value 0. In the second case, the field n is first multiplied by 3, then decremented by 1, resulting in a final state in which the field n has the value 2. Fig. 2 depicts the two cases (using the visualization support in our tool, described in Section 6.3). Note that this problem still occurs for languages with ordered message passing between two actors (e.g., Erlang [11]) when the two calls are made by different callers.

The selection of run to execute is decided by the runtime system and is thus non-deterministic for the given source program. In general, there can be much more than two possible runs for a parallel active object system. If only a few of the possible runs exhibit a particular behavior (e.g., a bug), it can be very interesting to be able to reproduce a particular run of the given program. We propose a method to instrument active objects systems which allows global reproducibility of runs through local control for each active object.

3   A Formal Model of Reproducibility

To formalize the problem of global reproducibility through local control for active object systems, we consider a basic active object language in which non-determinism stems from the order in which method calls are selected from the queue of the active objects.

3.1   A Basic Active Object Language

Consider a basic active object language with asynchronous method calls and synchronization via futures. The language has a Java-like syntax, given in Fig. 3. Let T, C and m range over type, class and method names, respectively, and let e range over side-effect free expressions. Overlined terms denote possibly empty lists over the corresponding syntactic categories (e.g., $\bar{e}$ and $\bar{x}$).

$$
\begin{aligned}
P &::= \overline{CL}\ \{\overline{T\ x};\ s\} \\
CL &::= \texttt{class}\,C\,\{\overline{T\ x};\ \overline{M}\} \\
M &::= T\ m\ (\overline{T\ x})\,\{\overline{T\ x};\ s\} \\
s &::= s;s \mid \texttt{skip} \mid x = rhs \\
&\quad \mid \texttt{if}\ e\ \{s\}\,\texttt{else}\,\{s\} \\
&\quad \mid \texttt{while}\ e\,\{s\} \mid \texttt{return}\ e \\
rhs &::= e \mid \texttt{new}\ C\,(\bar{e}) \mid e!m(\bar{e}) \mid x.\texttt{get}
\end{aligned}
$$

Fig. 3: BNF for the basic active object language.

A program P consists of a list $\overline{CL}$ of class declarations and a main block $\{\overline{T\ x}; s\}$, with variables x of type T and a statement s. A class C declares fields (both with types T) and contains a list $\overline{M}$ of methods. A method m has a return type, a list of typed formal parameters and a method body which contains local variable declarations and a statement s. Statements are standard; assignments $x = rhs$ allow expressions with side-effects on the right-hand side rhs.

Asynchronous method calls decouple invocation from synchronization. The execution of a call $f = o!m(\texttt{args})$ corresponds to sending a message $m(\texttt{args})$ asynchronously to the callee object o and initializes a future, referenced by f, where the return value will be stored. The statement $x = f.\texttt{get}$ retrieves the value stored in the future f. This operation synchronizes with the method return; i.e., the execution of this statement *blocks* the active object until the future f has received a value. Messages are *not* assumed to arrive in the same order as they are sent. The selection of messages in an object gives rise to non-determinism in the execution. An example of a program in this language was given in Section 2.

3.2   An Operational Semantics for the Basic Language

We present the semantics of the basic active object language as a transition relation between configurations cn. In the runtime syntax (Fig. 4), a configuration cn can be empty (ϵ), or a set of objects, futures, and invocation messages. We let o and f be dynamically created names from a set of object and future

$$
\begin{aligned}
cn &::= \epsilon \mid object \mid future \mid invoc \mid cn\ cn \\
future &::= fut(f, val) \\
object &::= ob(o, a, p, q) \\
process &::= \{a \mid s\} \\
invoc &::= inv(o, f, m, \overline{v})
\end{aligned}
\qquad
\begin{aligned}
q &::= \epsilon \mid process \mid q\ q \\
val &::= v \mid \perp \\
a &::= x \mapsto v \mid a, a \\
p &::= process \mid \mathtt{idle} \\
v &::= o \mid f \mid \mathtt{true} \mid \mathtt{false} \mid t
\end{aligned}
$$

Fig. 4: Runtime syntax; here, o and f are object and future identifiers.

identifiers, denoted *Identifiers*. An active object $ob(o, a, p, q)$ has an identifier o, attributes a, an active process p (that may be $\mathtt{idle}$) and an unordered process pool q. A future $fut(f, val)$ has an identifier f and a value val (which is $\perp$ if the future is not resolved). An invocation $inv(o, f, m, \overline{v})$ is a message to object o to activate method m with actual parameters $\overline{v}$ and send the return value to the future f. Attributes bind program variables x to values v. A process $\{a \mid s\}$ has local variables a and a statement list s to execute. Values are object identifiers o, future identifiers f, Boolean values $\mathtt{true}$ and $\mathtt{false}$, and other literal values t (e.g., natural numbers). The initial state of a program consists of a single active objects $ob(o_{\mathtt{main}}, a, p, \varnothing)$, where the active process p corresponds to the main block of the program. Let $names(cn)$ denote the set of object and future identifiers occurring in a configuration cn.

Figure 5 presents the main rules of the transition relation $cn \to cn'$. A *run* is a finite sequence of configurations $cn_0, cn_1, \ldots, cn_n$ such that $cn_i \to cn_{i+1}$ for $0 \leqslant i < n$. We assume configurations to be associative and commutative (so we can reorder configurations to match rules), where $\overset{*}{\to}$ denotes the reflexive and transitive closure of $\to$. Let $bind(m, \overline{v}, f, C)$ denote method lookup in the class table, returning the process corresponding to method m in class C with actual parameters $\overline{v}$ and with future f as the return address of the call. Thus, every process has a local variable *destiny* which denotes the return address of the process (i.e., the future that the process will resolve upon completion), similar to the self-reference *this* for objects. We omit explanations for the standard rules for assignment to fields and local variables, conditionals, while and skip.

Rule ACTIVATE formalizes the scheduling of a process p from the unordered queue q when an active object is idle. In ASYNC-CALL, an asynchronous method call creates a message to a target object o' and an unresolved future with a fresh name f. Object creation in NEW-ACTOR creates a new active object with a fresh identifier o', and initializes its attributes with initAttributes(C, o'), including reference to itself ($\mathtt{this}$). These are the only rules that introduce new names for identifiers; let a predicate fresh(o) denote that o is a fresh name in the global configuration (abstracting from how this is implemented). Rule LOAD puts the process corresponding to an invocation message in called object's queue. Rule RETURN resolves the future associated with a process with return value v, and READ-FUT fetches the value v of a future f into a variable. With rule CONTEXT, parallel execution in different active objects has an interleaving semantics.

Definition 1 (Stable configurations). *A configuration cn is stable if, for all objects in cn, the execution is blocked or the object needs to make a scheduling*

$$\text{(Activate)}\quad \frac{p \in q}{\begin{array}{l} ob(o, a, \mathtt{idle}, q) \\ \to ob(o, a, p, q \backslash \{p\}) \end{array}}$$

$$\text{(Assign1)}\quad \frac{v = [\![e]\!]_{(a \circ l)} \quad x \in \mathrm{dom}(l)}{\begin{array}{l} ob(o, a, \{l \mid x = e; s\}, q) \\ \to ob(o, a, \{l[x \mapsto v] \mid s\}, q) \end{array}}$$

$$\text{(Assign2)}\quad \frac{v = [\![e]\!]_{(a \circ l)} \quad x \notin \mathrm{dom}(l)}{\begin{array}{l} ob(o, a, \{l \mid x = e; s\}, q) \\ \to ob(o, a[x \mapsto v], \{l \mid s\}, q) \end{array}}$$

$$\text{(Cond1)}\quad \frac{\mathtt{true} = [\![e]\!]_{(a \circ l)}}{\begin{array}{l} ob(o, a, \{l \mid \mathtt{if}\ e\ \{s_1\}\ \mathtt{else}\ \{s_2\}; s\}, q) \\ \to ob(o, a, \{l \mid s_1; s\}, q) \end{array}}$$

$$\text{(Cond2)}\quad \frac{\mathtt{false} = [\![e]\!]_{(a \circ l)}}{\begin{array}{l} ob(o, a, \{l \mid \mathtt{if}\ e\ \{s_1\}\ \mathtt{else}\ \{s_2\}; s\}, q) \\ \to ob(o, a, \{l \mid s_2; s\}, q) \end{array}}$$

$$\text{(While)}\quad \frac{s_1' = s_1; \mathtt{while}\ e\ \{s_1\}}{\begin{array}{l} ob(o, a, \{l \mid \mathtt{while}\ e\ \{s_1\}; s_2\}, q) \\ \to ob(o, a, \{l \mid \mathtt{if}\ e\ \{s_1'\}\ \mathtt{else}\ \{\mathtt{skip}\}; s_2\}, q) \end{array}}$$

$$\text{(Skip1)}\quad \begin{array}{l} ob(o, a, \{l \mid \mathtt{skip}; s\}, q) \\ \to ob(o, a, \{l \mid s\}, q) \end{array}$$

$$\text{(Skip2)}\quad \begin{array}{l} ob(o, a, \{l \mid \mathtt{skip}\}, q) \\ \to ob(o, a, \mathtt{idle}, q) \end{array}$$

$$\text{(New-Actor)}\quad \frac{a' = \mathrm{initAttributes}(C, o') \quad \mathrm{fresh}(o')}{\begin{array}{l} ob(o, a, \{l \mid x = \mathtt{new}\ C(); s\}, q) \\ \to ob(o, a, \{l \mid x = o'; s\}, q)\ ob(o', a', \mathtt{idle}, \varnothing) \end{array}}$$

$$\text{(Context)}\quad \frac{cn_1 \to cn_1'}{cn_1\ cn_2 \to cn_1'\ cn_2}$$

$$\text{(Async-Call)}\quad \frac{o' = [\![e]\!]_{(a \circ l)} \quad \overline{v} = [\![\overline{e}]\!]_{(a \circ l)} \quad \mathrm{fresh}(f)}{\begin{array}{l} ob(o, a, \{l \mid x = e!m(\overline{e}); s\}, q) \\ \to ob(o, a, \{l \mid x = f; s\}, q)\ inv(o', f, m, \overline{v})\ fut(f, \bot) \end{array}}$$

$$\text{(Load)}\quad \frac{p' = \mathrm{bind}(m, \overline{v}, f, \mathrm{classOf}(o))}{\begin{array}{l} inv(o, f, m, \overline{v})\ ob(o, a, p, q) \\ \to ob(o, a, p, q \cup \{p'\}) \end{array}}$$

$$\text{(Return)}\quad \frac{v = [\![e]\!]_{(a \circ l)} \quad l(\mathrm{destiny}) = f}{\begin{array}{l} ob(o, a, \{l \mid \mathtt{return}\ e\}, q)\ fut(f, \bot) \\ \to ob(o, a, \mathtt{idle}, q)\ fut(f, v) \end{array}}$$

$$\text{(Read-Fut)}\quad \frac{v \neq \bot \quad f = [\![e]\!]_{(a \circ l)}}{\begin{array}{l} ob(o, a, \{l \mid x = e.\mathtt{get}; s\}, q)\ fut(f, v) \\ \to ob(o, a, \{l \mid x = v; s\}, q)\ fut(f, v) \end{array}}$$

Fig. 5: Semantics of the basic active object language.

decision. An object is blocked if it needs to execute a get-statement. An object needs to make a scheduling decision if its active process is idle.

Let G denote a stable configuration. We say that two stable configurations G_1 and G_2 are *consecutive* in a run $G_1 \xrightarrow{*} G_2$ if, for all cn such that $G_1 \xrightarrow{*} cn$ and $cn \xrightarrow{*} G_2$, if $cn \neq G_1$ and $cn \neq G_2$ then cn is not a stable configuration.

Lemma 1 (Reordering of atomic sections). *Let G_1 and G_2 be stable configurations. If $G_1 \xrightarrow{*} G_2$, then there exists a run between G_1 and G_2 in which only a single object executes between any two consecutive stable configurations.*

Proof (sketch). Observe that the notion of stability captures any state of an object in which it needs input from its environment. The proof then follows from the fact that the state spaces of different objects are disjoint and that message passing is unordered. This allows consecutive independent execution steps from different objects to be reordered. ☐

$$\frac{\text{(LOCAL-ASSIGN1)}}{v = \llbracket e \rrbracket_{(a \circ l)} \quad x \in \text{dom}(l)}{a, \{l \mid x = e; s\} \rightsquigarrow a, \{l[x \mapsto v] \mid s\}} \qquad \frac{\text{(LOCAL-ASSIGN2)}}{v = \llbracket e \rrbracket_{(a \circ l)} \quad x \notin \text{dom}(l)}{a, \{l \mid x = e; s\} \rightsquigarrow a[x \mapsto v], \{l \mid s\}}$$

$$\frac{\text{(LOCAL-WHILE)}}{s_1' = s_1; \texttt{while } e \ \{s_1\}}{a, \{l \mid \texttt{while } e \ \{s_1\}; s_2\} \rightsquigarrow a, \{l \mid \texttt{if } e \ \{s_1'\} \texttt{ else } \{\texttt{skip}\}; s_2\}} \qquad \frac{\text{(LOCAL-SKIP1)}}{a, \{l \mid \texttt{skip}; s\} \rightsquigarrow a, \{l \mid s\}}$$

$$\frac{\text{(LOCAL-COND1)}}{\texttt{true} = \llbracket e \rrbracket_{(a \circ l)}}{a, \{l \mid \texttt{if } e \ \{s_1\} \texttt{ else } \{s_2\}; s\} \rightsquigarrow a, \{l \mid s_1; s\}} \qquad \frac{\text{(LOCAL-COND2)}}{\texttt{false} = \llbracket e \rrbracket_{(a \circ l)}}{a, \{l \mid \texttt{if } e \ \{s_1\} \texttt{ else } \{s_2\}; s\} \rightsquigarrow a, \{l \mid s_2; s\}} \qquad \frac{\text{(LOCAL-SKIP2)}}{a, \{l \mid \texttt{skip}\} \rightsquigarrow a, \texttt{idle}}$$

$$\frac{\text{(GLOBAL-ACTIVATE)}}{p \in q \quad a, p \overset{!}{\rightsquigarrow} a', p' \quad p = \{l \mid s\}}{l(\text{destiny}) = f \quad q' = q \backslash \{p\}}{\overset{sched\langle o,f \rangle}{ob(o, a, \texttt{idle}, q)} \xrightarrow{\quad} ob(o, a', p', q')}$$

$$\frac{\text{(GLOBAL-RETURN)}}{v = \llbracket e \rrbracket_{(a \circ l)} \quad l(\text{destiny}) = f}{ob(o, a, \{l \mid \texttt{return } e\}, q) \ fut(f, \perp)}{\xrightarrow{futWr\langle o,f \rangle} ob(o, a, \texttt{idle}, q) \ fut(f, v)}$$

$$\frac{\text{(GLOBAL-CONTEXT)}}{cn_1 \xrightarrow{ev?} cn_1'}{\frac{cn_1 \ cn_2}{\xrightarrow{ev?} cn_1' \ cn_2}}$$

$$\frac{\text{(GLOBAL-NEW-ACTOR)}}{a'' = \text{initAttributes}(C, o')}{\text{fresh}(o') \quad a, \{l \mid x = o'; s\} \rightsquigarrow a', p'}{ob(o, a, \{l \mid x = \texttt{new } C(); s\}, q)}{\xrightarrow{new\langle o,o' \rangle} ob(o, a', p', q) \ ob(o', a'', \texttt{idle}, \varnothing)}$$

$$\frac{\text{(GLOBAL-READ-FUT)}}{v \neq \perp \quad f = \llbracket e \rrbracket_{(a \circ l)}}{a, \{l \mid x = v; s\} \overset{!}{\rightsquigarrow} a', p}{ob(o, a, \{l \mid x = e.\texttt{get}; s\}, q) \ fut(f, v)}{\xrightarrow{futRe\langle o,f \rangle} ob(o, a', p, q) \ fut(f, v)}$$

$$\frac{\text{(GLOBAL-ASYNC-CALL)}}{o' = \llbracket e \rrbracket_{(a \circ l)} \quad \overline{v} = \llbracket \overline{e} \rrbracket_{(a \circ l)}}{\text{fresh}(f) \quad a, \{l \mid x = f; s\} \overset{!}{\rightsquigarrow} a', p}{ob(o, a, \{l \mid x = e!m(\overline{e}); s\}, q)}{\xrightarrow{inv\langle o,f \rangle} ob(o, a', p, q) \ inv(o', f, m, \overline{v}) \ fut(f, \perp)}$$

$$\frac{\text{(GLOBAL-LOAD)}}{p' = \text{bind}(m, \overline{v}, f, \text{classOf}(o))}{inv(o, f, m, \overline{v}) \ ob(o, a, p, q)}{\rightarrow ob(o, a, p, q \cup \{p'\})}$$

Fig. 6: Coarse-grained, labelled semantics of the basic active object language.

3.3 A Labelled Operational Semantics for the Basic Language

Based on Lemma 1, we can define a semantics of the basic active object language with a more coarse-grained model of interleaving which is equivalent to the semantics presented in Fig. 5. We let this coarse-grained semantics be labeled by events to record the interaction between an active object and its environment. The events are defined as follows:

Definition 2 (Events). *Let $o, f \in \text{Identifiers}$. The set $\mathcal{E}$ of events ev is given by*

$$ev ::= new\langle o, o \rangle \mid inv\langle o, f \rangle \mid sched\langle o, f \rangle \mid futWr\langle o, f \rangle \mid futRe\langle o, f \rangle.$$

In the coarse-grained semantics, a transition relation $a, p \rightsquigarrow a', p'$ captures *local execution* in an active object with attributes a. These rules are given in

Fig. 6 (top) and correspond to the rules ASSIGN1, ASSIGN2, WHILE, COND1, COND2, SKIP1 and SKIP2 of Fig. 5. These rules are deterministic as there is at most one possible reduction for any given pair a, p. Let $\overset{*}{\leadsto}$ denote the reflexive, transitive closure of $\leadsto$, let the unary relation $\not\leadsto$ denote that there is no transition from a given pair a, p, and let the relation $\overset{!}{\leadsto}$ denote the reduction to normal form according to $\leadsto$; i.e.,

$$a, p \overset{!}{\leadsto} a', p' \iff a, p \overset{*}{\leadsto} a', p' \wedge a', p' \not\leadsto$$

In the remaining rules, given in Fig. 6 (bottom), a labelled transition relation $cn \overset{ev}{\longrightarrow} cn'$ captures transitions in which the local execution of an active object interacts with its environment through scheduling, object creation, method invocation, or interaction with futures. These rules also correspond to the similar rules in Fig. 5, with two differences:

1. The rules are labelled with an event reflecting the particular action taken in the transition, and
2. the rules perform a local deterministic reduction to normal form according to the $\leadsto$ relation in each step.

Remark that rule GLOBAL-LOAD is identical to LOAD of Fig. 5; although we do not need to add an explicit label the rule is kept at the global level since it involves both an object and a message. Rule GLOBAL-CONTEXT is labeled by $ev?$ to capture that the label is optional (i.e., the rule also combines with GLOBAL-LOAD). We henceforth consider runs for the basic active object language based on this labelled semantics.

3.4   Execution Traces and their Reordering

This section looks at traces reflecting the runs of programs in the basic active object language according to the semantics of Section 3.3, and their reordering. We consider traces over events in $\mathcal{E}$. Let ϵ denote the empty trace, and $\tau_1 \cdot \tau_2$ the concatenation of traces τ_1 and τ_2. For an event ev and a trace τ, we denote by $ev \in \tau$ that ev occurs somewhere in τ and by τ **ew** ev that τ ends with ev (i.e., $\exists \tau'. \tau = \tau' \cdot ev$). Define τ/o and τ/f as the projection of a trace τ to the alphabet of an object o and a future f, by their first or second argument respectively (where an alphabet is the set of events involving that name). Finally, let $names(\tau)$ denote the inductively defined function returning the set of identifiers that occur in a trace τ (e.g., $names(inv\langle o, f \rangle) = \{o, f\}$). We assume that every initial configuration has a main object and process, and let $names(\epsilon) = \{o_{\mathrm{main}}, f_{\mathrm{main}}\}$.

Given a run $cn_0 \overset{ev_0}{\longrightarrow} \cdots \overset{ev_n}{\longrightarrow} cn_{n+1}$, we denote $cn_0 \overset{\tau}{\Rightarrow} cn_{n+1}$ that a trace τ is the trace of the run if $\tau = ev_0 \cdots ev_n$ (where τ ignores the unlabeled transition steps of the run). Well-formed traces can be defined as follows, based on [12]:

Definition 3 (Well-formed Traces). *Given $o, o', f \in$ Identifiers. Let $wf(\tau)$ denote that τ is* well-formed, *defined inductively:*

$$wf(\epsilon) \iff True$$
$$wf(\tau \cdot new\langle o, o'\rangle) \iff wf(\tau) \land o \in names(\tau) \land o' \notin names(\tau)$$
$$wf(\tau \cdot inv\langle o, f\rangle) \iff wf(\tau) \land o \in names(\tau) \land f \notin names(\tau)$$
$$wf(\tau \cdot sched\langle o, f\rangle) \iff wf(\tau) \land o \in names(\tau) \land \tau/f = inv\langle o', f\rangle$$
$$wf(\tau \cdot futWr\langle o, f\rangle) \iff wf(\tau) \land \tau/f \text{ ew } sched\langle o, f\rangle$$
$$wf(\tau \cdot futRe\langle o, f\rangle) \iff wf(\tau) \land futWr\langle o', f\rangle \in \tau$$

Wellformedness thus captures a happens-before relation over events while ensuring that certain identifiers are new at given points in the trace. Din and Owe have shown that the trace of any run of the semantics of an active object language similar to ours is well-formed [12]. For example, no process can be scheduled unless it has been invoked (which again requires the GLOBAL-LOAD rule to apply in between GLOBAL-ASYNC-CALL and GLOBAL-ACTIVATE). Given a trace τ, we can now define the equivalence class $[\tau]$ of traces which preserve the local ordering and the wellformedness of τ, as follows:

Definition 4 (Global trace set). *Let τ be a trace and define*

$$[\tau] = \{\tau' \mid \tau'/o = \tau/o \text{ for all object identifiers } o \in names(\tau) \land wf(\tau')\}.$$

Remark that this construction is closely related to equivalence classes in Mazurkiewics trace theory [13], with wellformedness as the dependency relation of the equivalence classes.

Example 1. The program from Fig. 1 (Section 2) has the following traces:

$$\tau_1 = new\langle o_{\mathrm{main}}, o\rangle \cdot inv\langle o_{\mathrm{main}}, f_{\mathrm{m1}}\rangle \cdot inv\langle o_{\mathrm{main}}, f_{\mathrm{m2}}\rangle \cdot sched\langle o, f_{\mathrm{m1}}\rangle \cdot sched\langle o, f_{\mathrm{m2}}\rangle$$
$$\tau_2 = new\langle o_{\mathrm{main}}, o\rangle \cdot inv\langle o_{\mathrm{main}}, f_{\mathrm{m1}}\rangle \cdot sched\langle o, f_{\mathrm{m1}}\rangle \cdot inv\langle o_{\mathrm{main}}, f_{\mathrm{m2}}\rangle \cdot sched\langle o, f_{\mathrm{m2}}\rangle$$
$$\tau_3 = new\langle o_{\mathrm{main}}, o\rangle \cdot inv\langle o_{\mathrm{main}}, f_{\mathrm{m1}}\rangle \cdot inv\langle o_{\mathrm{main}}, f_{\mathrm{m2}}\rangle \cdot sched\langle o, f_{\mathrm{m2}}\rangle \cdot sched\langle o, f_{\mathrm{m1}}\rangle$$

Observe that traces τ_1 and τ_2 belong to the same global trace set (i.e. $[\tau_1] = [\tau_2]$), and will produce the same final state.

Let $G \xrightarrow{o:f} G'$ denote a run between consecutive stable configurations which executes the process identified by f on object o in the stable configuration G until the next stable configuration G'. If $sched\langle o, f\rangle \cdot \tau$ is the trace of $G \xrightarrow{o:f} G'$, then τ is a trace over the event set $\{inv\langle o, f'\rangle, new\langle o, o'\rangle, futWr\langle o, f\rangle \mid o', f' \in$ Identifiers$\}$. This observation provides an intuition for the following lemma:

Lemma 2 (Local confluence). *Let G_1, G_2, G_3 be stable configurations, o, o' object and f, f' future identifiers, with $o \neq o'$, $f \neq f'$. If $G_1 \xrightarrow{o:f} G_2$ and $G_1 \xrightarrow{o':f'} G_3$, then there is a stable configuration G_4 such that $G_2 \xrightarrow{o':f'} G_4$ and $G_3 \xrightarrow{o:f} G_4$.*

Proof (sketch). The proof follows from the fact that execution in an object does not inhibit a process to run in another object.   □

The following theorem shows that local confluence implies global confluence for executions in the *same global trace set* (which means that the two executions agree on the local trace projections).

Theorem 1 (Global confluence). *Let G_1, G_2, G_3 be stable configurations and τ_1, τ_2 traces such that $G_1 \stackrel{\tau_1}{\Rightarrow} G_2$ and $G_1 \stackrel{\tau_2}{\Rightarrow} G_3$. If $\tau_2 \in [\tau_1]$ then $G_2 = G_3$.*

Proof (sketch). Observe that runs with traces in the same global trace set must agree on the naming of objects and futures. The result then follows by induction over the length of $G_1 \stackrel{\tau_1}{\Rightarrow} G_2$ from local confluence (Lemma 2).   □

4   Global Reproducibility with Local Traces

The global confluence of executions with traces in the same global trace set provides a formal justification for a method to obtain global reproducibility for distributed active object systems which exhibit non-deterministic behavior. The method is based on enforcing the local trace projection from the global trace set on each active object. For the basic active object language, the method is based on recording the events from the set $\mathcal{E}$ during an execution. This set of events, which includes events capturing the scheduling decisions of the runtime system as well as the choice of dynamically created names during a particular execution, is sufficient to establish the wellformedness of the recorded trace and identify the global trace set of the recorded run. Furthermore, if we record local traces for each active object, these will correspond to the local trace projections of the global trace set. In fact, any composition of local traces recorded during a run will result in the same global trace set. Similarly, any composition of local trace projections enforced during a replay will result in a trace in the same global trace set. Thus, Theorem 1 guarantees that local recording and replay of different traces from the same global trace set will result in the same final state. It remains to show that for any such trace in the global trace set corresponding to a recorded run, the execution during replay will not get stuck. For this purpose, we now formalize record and replay as extensions to the semantics of the basic active object language.

We extend the operational semantics of Fig. 6 to record and replay traces. Let $\tau \triangleright cn$ denote an extended runtime configuration, where τ is a witness for cn, playing dual roles for recording and replaying. A *recorded run* starts from an initial configuration $\epsilon \triangleright cn$, where cn is the initial configuration of the run to be recorded. The reduction system for recording a trace is given as a relation $\stackrel{\bullet}{\longrightarrow}$ by the rules in Fig. 7; the two rules correspond to the unlabeled (just GLOBAL-LOAD) and labeled transitions of the semantics, respectively. A replay starts from an initial configuration $\tau \triangleright cn$, where τ is a trace and cn the initial configuration of the run to be replayed. The reduction system for replaying a trace is given as a relation $\stackrel{\bullet}{\longrightarrow}$ by the rules in Fig. 8, the two rules are symmetric to those for recording a run. The rules in Fig. 7 and Fig. 8 formalize the obvious relation between the recording and replaying of a trace and a run in the semantics of the

(UNLABELED-RECORD)
$$\frac{cn \to cn'}{\tau \rhd cn \overset{\bullet}{\longrightarrow} \tau \rhd cn'}$$

(UNLABELED-REPLAY)
$$\frac{cn \to cn'}{\tau \rhd cn \overset{\blacktriangleright}{\longrightarrow} \tau \rhd cn'}$$

(LABELED-RECORD)
$$\frac{cn \overset{ev}{\longrightarrow} cn'}{\tau \rhd cn \overset{\bullet}{\longrightarrow} \tau \cdot ev \rhd cn'}$$

(LABELED-REPLAY)
$$\frac{cn \overset{ev}{\longrightarrow} cn'}{ev \cdot \tau \rhd cn \overset{\blacktriangleright}{\longrightarrow} \tau \rhd cn'}$$

Fig. 7: Semantics of Record   Fig. 8: Semantics of Replay

basic active object language. Let $\overset{\bullet}{\Longrightarrow}$ and $\overset{\blacktriangleright}{\Longrightarrow}$ denote the reflexive, transitive closures of $\overset{\bullet}{\longrightarrow}$ and $\overset{\blacktriangleright}{\longrightarrow}$, respectively.

Lemma 3 (Freshness of names). *For any recording $\epsilon \rhd cn \overset{\bullet}{\Longrightarrow} \tau \rhd cn'$ or replay $\tau \cdot \tau' \rhd cn \overset{\blacktriangleright}{\Longrightarrow} \tau' \rhd cn'$, we have that $names(\tau) = names(cn')$.*

Proof (sketch). Follows by induction over the length of $\epsilon \rhd cn \overset{\bullet}{\Longrightarrow} \tau \rhd cn'$ and $\tau \cdot \tau' \rhd cn \overset{\blacktriangleright}{\Longrightarrow} \tau' \rhd cn'$, respectively.   □

It follows from Lemma 3 that given an identifier $x \in Identifiers$ and a run $\epsilon \rhd cn \overset{\bullet}{\Longrightarrow} \tau \rhd cn'$, if $x \notin names(\tau)$, then $x \notin names(cn')$ and consequently, the predicate $fresh(x)$ will hold as a premise for any rule in the semantics that one may want to apply to cn'. Consequently, fresh-predicates in the premises of the transition rules of the basic active language will accept the identifier names chosen from the recorded trace when replaying a run.

Lemma 4 (Progress for replay by global trace). *Let G, G' be stable configurations. If $\epsilon \rhd G \overset{\bullet}{\Longrightarrow} \tau \rhd G'$ then $\tau \rhd G \overset{\blacktriangleright}{\Longrightarrow} \epsilon \rhd G'$.*

Proof. The proof is by induction over the length of the run $\epsilon \rhd G \overset{\bullet}{\Longrightarrow} \tau \rhd G'$. The base case is obvious. We assume (IH) that if $\epsilon \rhd G \overset{\bullet}{\Longrightarrow} \tau \rhd cn$ then $\tau \rhd G \overset{\blacktriangleright}{\Longrightarrow} \epsilon \rhd cn$ and show that if $\epsilon \rhd G \overset{\bullet}{\longrightarrow} \tau \cdot ev \rhd cn'$ then $\tau \cdot ev \rhd G \overset{\blacktriangleright}{\longrightarrow} \tau \rhd cn'$. By the IH, this amounts to showing that if $\epsilon \rhd cn \overset{\bullet}{\longrightarrow} \epsilon \cdot ev \rhd cn'$ then $ev \cdot \epsilon \rhd cn \overset{\blacktriangleright}{\longrightarrow} \epsilon \rhd cn'$. The proof proceeds by cases over the transition rules of the basic active object language (cf. Fig. 5). The interesting cases are the rules which need new names. Lemma 3 ensures that the predicate $fresh(o)$ will hold for a new name o in ev (and similarly for f), and the corresponding rules can be applied.   □

It follows from Theorem 1 that if we can replay a run which is equivalent to a recorded run τ, the final state of the replayed run will be the same as for the recorded run. It remains to show that any run in the equivalence class $[\tau]$ can in fact be replayed.

Theorem 2 (Progress for replay by local control). *Let G, G' be stable configurations, τ, τ' traces. If $\epsilon \rhd G \overset{\bullet}{\Longrightarrow} \tau \rhd G'$ and $\tau' \in [\tau]$, then $\tau' \rhd G \overset{\blacktriangleright}{\Longrightarrow} \epsilon \rhd G'$.*

Proof (sketch). We show by induction over the length of trace τ that if $\epsilon \rhd G \overset{\bullet}{\Longrightarrow} \tau \rhd cn$ and $\tau' \in [\tau]$, then $\tau' \rhd G \overset{\blacktriangleright}{\Longrightarrow} \epsilon \rhd cn'$. It then follows from Theorem 1 that $cn = cn'$.   □

5   Extensions for Richer Active Object Languages

The method for global reproducibility of executions for a basic active object language based on record & replay of local traces, may be extended to include features introducing other sources of non-determinism in richer active object languages [2]. We here briefly review some such features and how the method may be extended to cover them.

Cooperative scheduling. In cooperatively scheduled languages (e.g., [3–5, 14]), methods may explicitly *release control*, allowing other pending method invocations be scheduled. The criteria for being rescheduled may be that some boolean condition is met, or a future being resolved. Note that methods still execute until it cooperatively releases control; i.e., a method will not be interrupted because the condition of another method is satisfied. With cooperative scheduling, the same task may be scheduled several times, which means that the same scheduling event may occur multiple times in a trace. In the method for reproducibility, this extension can be covered by an additional suspension-event reflecting the processor release and an adjustment of the wellformedness condition to reflect that a scheduling event either comes after a invocation event (as for the basic language) or after a suspension event on the same future.

Concurrent object groups. In language with concurrent object groups (e.g., [3,5]), a group of concurrent objects (or cog) share a common scheduler, which becomes the unit of distribution; this gives an interleaved semantics between objects within the same cog, while separate cogs are truly concurrent. For record & replay, the events of a trace need to capture the cog, rather than the object, in which an event originated. Recording the names of cogs is sufficient for reproducibility without controlling the naming of objects. For the reproducibility method, the proofs in Section 4 would use an equivalence relation between configurations that only differ in the choice of object names inside the cogs and the global trace set (Def. 4) would project on cogs rather than objects.

Resource-aware behavior. Active objects may reside in a resource center with limited resources, e.g. CPU or memory restrictions, with regards to time (e.g., [6, 15]). Statements may have some associated cost which requires available resources in order to execute. If there are insufficient resources, then execution is blocked in that object until time advances. Here, object compete for resources, in the same sense that tasks compete for processing time. Following our method for deterministic replay, the traces can be extended with events for resource request in a similar manner as method invocations in the basic active objects language, and resource provision with events similar to the task scheduling events.

External non-determinism and random numbers. Active object languages may also feature external factors that may influence an execution, such as input from a user, fetching data from a database or receiving input from a socket, or random number generation. Here, a purely *ordering-based* method is insufficient. Our replay method needs to be extended with events which include the data received from the external source and the replay would need to fetch data from the trace rather than from the external source, similar to the reuse of object and future identifiers from the trace in the previous section. Random number generation can be seen as a special case of external non-determinism; for pseudo-random number generators it would be sufficient to only record the initial seed for reuse during replay.

6   Implementing Record & Replay for Real-Time ABS

We report on our implementation[1] of *record & replay*, based on the formalization in Section 4. The implementation was done for Real-Time ABS [6, 16], an active object modeling language which includes the following features discussed in Section 5: cooperative scheduling, concurrent object groups, and timed, resource-aware behavior, all of which are handled by our implementation. The simulator for Real-Time ABS models, written in Erlang, supports interaction with a model during execution via the Model API [17] in order to, e.g. fetch the current state of an object, advance the simulated clock or visualize the resource consumption of a running model. In addition, we have implemented a *visualizer* for recorded traces. In this section, we discuss the following aspects of the implementation: the recording of traces in a distributed setting, the handling of names, the visualization of traces, and performance characteristics for the implementation of record & replay.

6.1   Recording Traces in a Distributed Setting

For simulation, ABS models are transpiled to Erlang code by representing most entities as Erlang actors, e.g., concurrent object groups (or cogs), resource centers, futures and ABS-level processes. Thus, execution is concurrent and may be distributed over multiple machines. This leads to two important differences from the formalization in Section 4:

- *True concurrency:* The formalization is based on an interleaved concurrency model, which yields a total order of events. In the simulator, cogs are implemented as Erlang actors and may operate in true parallel, where two events may happen *simultaneously*, which corresponds to a partial order of events.
- *Distributed state:* Because the state of the model is distributed over many independent actors, we cannot easily synchronize over the state of different actors. In the implementation, such synchronization in the formalization must be realized by asynchronous message passing protocols.

---

[1] The Real-Time ABS simulator is available at
https://github.com/abstools/abstools
The accompanying visualization tool is available at
https://github.com/larstvei/ABS-traces

These differences pose challenges for recording and replaying global traces in the implementation. When recording a run, it is not trivial to obtain a global trace. If all cogs and resource centers were to report their recorded events to a single actor maintaining the global trace, races could occur between different asynchronous messages. For example, if an object o invokes a method on another object o', then the corresponding invocation and scheduling events could arrive in any order. Such races could be resolved by, e.g., introducing additional synchronization or using Lamport timestamps [18, 19]. Similarly, precisely replaying a global trace would require some synchronization protocol with the actor holding the global trace, severely increasing the level of synchronization during execution.

We address these challenges by only considering the local projections of the global trace for each cog and resource center. The information needed to construct local traces does not require any additional synchronization. During replay, only the local execution of an actor is controlled, which is sufficient to obtain a run with a trace in the same global trace set.

6.2   Names in the Erlang Simulator

The formalization allows recorded names to be reused when replaying a run. In contrast, in the Erlang system cogs, resource centers and futures are implemented as actors (i.e. Erlang actors) and identified by a process identifier (pid) determined by Erlang. To ensure that names in the events of the recorded trace are easily identifiable in a replay without modifying the naming scheme of Erlang, we construct additional names that are associated with the given pid. The constructed names follow a deterministic naming scheme, which guarantees that names are globally unique without depending on knowledge of names generated in other actors (in contrast to the fresh-predicate in the semantics).

Cogs, resource centers and futures can be named locally following a naming scheme based on existing actors already having such unique, associated names. The name $\langle A_{id}, i + 1 \rangle$ of a new actor can be determined by the actor A_{id} in which it is created, together with a local counter denoting the number i of actors previously created in A_{id}. Thus, the name of the actor corresponds to its place in the topology and is guaranteed to be fresh.

6.3   Visualization of Recorded Traces

The trace recorded during a simulation can give the user insight into that execution of a model, since it captures the model's communication structure. The recorded trace may be extracted from a running simulation via the Model API or written to file on termination. However, the terse format of the traces makes it hard for users to quickly get an intuitive idea of what is happening in the model. Complementing the replay facility, we have developed a tool to visualize recorded traces, which conveys information from traces in a more intuitive format. To facilitate visualization, the events in our implementation are slightly richer than those in Definition 2; e.g., they include the name of the method corresponding to the future in the event.

The visualization reconstructs a global trace τ from its local projections. Since the local ordering of events is already preserved by the recorded traces, we only need to compose local traces in a way that preserves wellformedness. We derive a happens-before relation $<$ from wellformedness (Definition 3), and denote its transitive closure by $\ll$.

The happens-before relation $\ll$ gives a partial order of events. In the visualization of the trace τ, all events are depicted by a colored dot. For any two events e_1, e_2, e_1 is drawn above e_2 if $e_1 \ll e_2$; the events are drawn in the same column only if they reside in the same cog or resource center. An arrow is drawn between any two events e_1, e_2 if $e_1 < e_2$. Events that are independent (i.e., neither $e_1 \ll e_2$ nor $e_2 \ll e_1$) may be drawn in the same row. Events with the same future as argument are drawn with the same color. The tool additionally supports simple navigation in the trace, gives visual indicators of simulated time steps, and supports time advancement in a running model through the model API, making it easy to step forward in time. Fig. 2 illustrates the visualization for two runs of the motivating example.

6.4 Example

Consider a Real-Time ABS model of an image rendering service which can process either still photos or video. The service is modeled as a class `Service` with two methods `photo_request` and `video_request`. The model captures *resource-sensitive behavior* in terms of cost annotations associated with the execution of `skip`-statements inside the two methods and in terms of deadlines provided to each method call. The processing cost for rendering an image is constant (here, the cost is given by the field `image_cost`), but the processing cost of rendering a video depends on the number of frames (captured by a parameter n to the method `video_request`). The success of each method call depends on whether it succeeded in processing its job, as specified by the cost annotation, before its deadline passes; this is captured by the expression in the return statement `return (Duration(0) < deadline())`. Remark that `deadline()` is a predefined read-only variable in Real-Time ABS processes. Its value is given by the caller.

In the main block, a server is created on which the service can run. This server is a resource-center with limited processing capacity (called a deployment component in Real-Time ABS [6]), restricting the amount of computation that can happen on the server per time interval in the execution of the model. The service is then deployed on the server (by an annotation [DC: server] to new-statement. We let a class `Client` (omitted here) model a given number of processing requests to the image rendering service in terms of asynchronously calling the two methods a given number of times (e.g., the call to `video_request` takes the form `[Deadline: Duration(10)] f = s!video_request(n)`, pushing the associated futures `f` to a list, and then counting the number of successful requests when the corresponding futures have been resolved. It is easy to see that the success of calls to the `video_request` method which requires more resources, may depend on whether it is scheduled before or after calls to `photo_request`,

```
class Service {
 Int image_cost = 1;

 Bool photo_request() {
  [Cost: image_cost] skip;
  return (Duration(0)
        < deadline());
 }

 Bool video_request(Int n) {
  [Cost: n*image_cost] skip;
  return (Duration(0)
        < deadline());
 }
}

// Main block
{
  DC server
  = new DC("Server", 2);
  [DC: server] Service s1
  = new Service();
  new Client(s1, 1, 100);
}
```

Fig. 9: Real-Time ABS code for the photo rendering service.

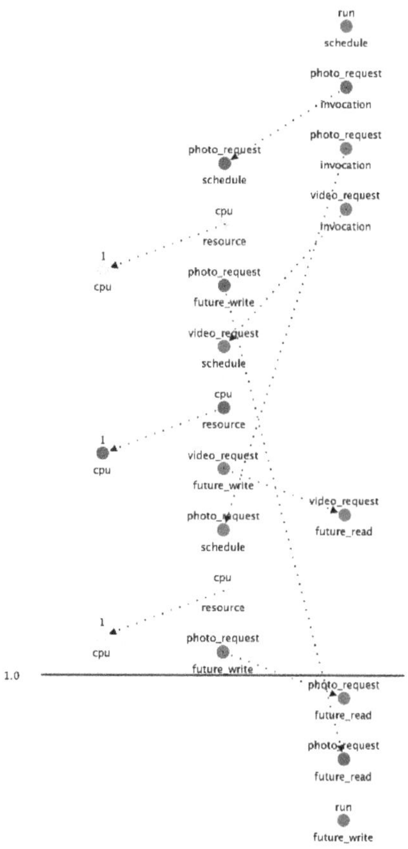

Fig. 10: Visualization of a run of the photo rendering service.

depending on the provided deadlines. Thus, the model exhibits both scheduling non-determinism for asynchronous calls and resource-aware behavior. The image in Fig. 10 depicts a trace from a simulation of the model, showing interactions between a deployment component (left), the service (middle) and the client (right).

6.5   Performance Characteristics of the Implementation

We give a brief evaluation of the performance characteristics of record & replay for Real Time ABS. The size of the traces is proportional to the number of objects, method invocations and resource provisions. Because we do not impose additional synchronization, we are able to achieve a constant-time overhead. To investigate how record & replay scales, we created a micro-benchmark performing method invocations on an active object, and recorded execution times for

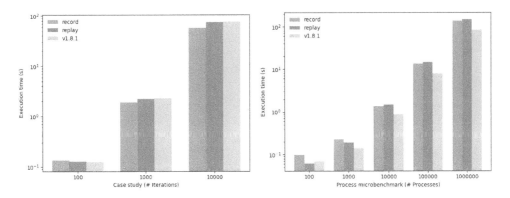

Fig. 11: Record and replay: example (left) and process microbenchmark (right)

$10^2, 10^3, \ldots, 10^6$ method calls. We also ran the example of Section 6.4, recording execution times for $10^2, 10^3$ and 10^4 Client iterations. These are worst-case scenarios for record & replay, as the invoked methods do not perform any computation that does not result in creating an event.

Fig. 11 shows the results of the two programs with replay enabled, with record enabled and the last release of Real-Time ABS which does not feature record & replay. Note that we only measure simulation time and do not include the time reading and writing trace files. We can see that the results of Fig. 11 (left) are slightly improved and the overhead observed in Fig. 11 (right) is about a factor of 1.8. We note that supporting record & replay in Real-Time ABS required extensive modifications to the Real-Time ABS simulators implementation.

7 Related Work

This work complements other analysis techniques for Real-Time ABS models, such as simulation [17], deductive verification [9], and parallel cost analysis [20] and testing [21]. We here discuss related work on deterministic replay. Deterministic replay is an emerging technique to reproduce executions of computer programs in the presence of different non-deterministic factors [1]. It enables cyclic debugging [22] in non-deterministic execution environments. Our focus is on software-level reproducibility in the context of actor-systems. Approaches to reproduce specific runs of non-deterministic systems can be either *content-based* or *ordering based* [23].

Content-based methods trace the values read from a shared memory location. These are particularly suitable when there is a lot of external non-determinism (typically I/O operations, like user input). Content-based replay for actor systems typically record messages, including the sender, receiver and message content, (see, e.g., [24–26]). This technique is typically used for rich debuggers like Actoverse [24] for Scala's Akka library, which provides visualization support similar to ours. However, content-based approaches do not scale well [27], because the traces can become very large for message-intensive applications.

Ordering-based (or control-based) methods trace a system's *control-flow*. Our work fits within this category. Without external non-determinism, replaying the control-flow will reproduce the data of the recorded run. Ordering-based methods exist for asynchronous message passing using the message passing interface (MPI) [19,28]. MPI assumes that messages from the same source are received in order, this does not generally hold for actor systems. Aumayr *et al.* in [27] study ordering-based replay for actor systems with a memory-efficient representation of the generated traces. Netzer *et al.* [29] propose an interesting method to only trace events directly related to races, rather than all events (removing up to 99% of the events). This line of work is complementary to our focus on formal correctness and low runtime-overhead during record and replay. We believe we could benefit from their work to obtain more efficient trace representations. Lanese *et al.* recently proposed a notion of causal-consistent replay based on reversible debugging [30], which enables replay to a state by only replaying its causal dependencies. Similar to our work, they also formalize record & replay for an actor language. In contrast to our work, their approach is based on a centralized actor for tracing, and can only be used in combination with a debugger [31].

8   Conclusion and Future Work

This paper has introduced a method for global reproducibility for runs of distributed Active Object systems, based on local control. The proposed method is order-based and decentralized in that local traces are recorded and replayed without incurring any additional synchronization at the global level. The method is formalized as an operational semantics for a basic active object language, with trace recording and replay. This system exhibits non-determinism through the scheduling of asynchronous method calls and synchronization using first-class futures. Based on this formalization, we justify in terms of properties of trace equivalence classes that local control suffices to reproduce runs with a final state which is equivalent to the final state of a recorded run. We then discuss how other features of active object languages which introduce additional non-determinism can be supported by our method, including cooperative concurrency, concurrent object groups and resource-aware behavior.

The proposed method has been implemented for Real-Time ABS, an Active Object modeling language which includes most of the above-mentioned features and which has a simulator written in Erlang. The implementation only records local ordering information, which allows the overhead of both the record and replay phases to be kept low compared to deterministic replay systems which reproduce an exact global run.

In future work, we plan to build on the proposed record & replay tool for systematic model exploration, by modifying traces between the record and replay phase to explore different runs. This can be done by means of DPOR-algorithms for actor-based systems [32–34]. Combining DPOR with our proposed tool for record & replay would result in a stateless model checker [35] for Active Object systems.

References

1. Chen, Y., Zhang, S., Guo, Q., Li, L., Wu, R., Chen, T.: Deterministic replay: A survey. ACM Comput. Surv. **48**(2) (September 2015) 17:1–17:47
2. de Boer, F., Serbanescu, V., Hähnle, R., Henrio, L., Rochas, J., Din, C.C., Johnsen, E.B., Sirjani, M., Khamespanah, E., Fernandez-Reyes, K., Yang, A.M.: A survey of active object languages. ACM Comput. Surv. **50**(5) (October 2017) 76:1–76:39
3. Johnsen, E.B., Hähnle, R., Schäfer, J., Schlatte, R., Steffen, M.: ABS: A core language for abstract behavioral specification. In Aichernig, B., de Boer, F.S., Bonsangue, M.M., eds.: Proc. 9th Intl. Symp. on Formal Methods for Components and Objects (FMCO 2010). Volume 6957 of Lecture Notes in Computer Science., Springer (2011) 142–164
4. Brandauer, S., Castegren, E., Clarke, D., Fernandez-Reyes, K., Johnsen, E.B., Pun, K.I., Tapia Tarifa, S.L., Wrigstad, T., Yang, A.M.: Parallel objects for multicores: A glimpse at the parallel language encore. In: Formal Methods for Multicore Programming (SFM 2015). Volume 9104 of Lecture Notes in Computer Science., Springer (2015) 1–56
5. Schäfer, J., Poetzsch-Heffter, A.: JCoBox: Generalizing active objects to concurrent components. In D'Hondt, T., ed.: Proc. 24th European Conference on Object-Oriented Programming (ECOOP 2010). Volume 6183 of Lecture Notes in Computer Science., Springer (2010) 275–299
6. Johnsen, E.B., Schlatte, R., Tapia Tarifa, S.L.: Integrating deployment architectures and resource consumption in timed object-oriented models. J. Log. Algebr. Meth. Program. **84**(1) (2015) 67–91
7. Albert, E., de Boer, F.S., Hähnle, R., Johnsen, E.B., Schlatte, R., Tapia Tarifa, S.L., Wong, P.Y.H.: Formal modeling and analysis of resource management for cloud architectures: an industrial case study using real-time ABS. Service Oriented Computing and Applications **8**(4) (2014) 323–339
8. Kamburjan, E., Hähnle, R., Schön, S.: Formal modeling and analysis of railway operations with active objects. Sci. Comput. Program. **166** (2018) 167–193
9. Din, C.C., Tapia Tarifa, S.L., Hähnle, R., Johnsen, E.B.: History-based specification and verification of scalable concurrent and distributed systems. In: Proc. 17th Intl. Conf. on Formal Engineering Methods (ICFEM 2015). Volume 9407 of Lecture Notes in Computer Science., Springer (2015) 217–233
10. Bezirgiannis, N., de Boer, F.S., Johnsen, E.B., Pun, K.I., Tapia Tarifa, S.L.: Implementing SOS with active objects: A case study of a multicore memory system. In: Proc. 22nd Intl. Conf. on Fundamental Approaches to Software Engineering (FASE 2019). Volume 11424 of Lecture Notes in Computer Science., Springer (2019) 332–350
11. Armstrong, J.: Programming Erlang: Software for a Concurrent World. Pragmatic Bookshelf Series. Pragmatic Bookshelf (2007)
12. Din, C.C., Owe, O.: A sound and complete reasoning system for asynchronous communication with shared futures. J. Log. Algebr. Meth. Program. **83**(5-6) (2014) 360–383
13. Mazurkiewicz, A.W.: Trace theory. In Brauer, W., Reisig, W., Rozenberg, G., eds.: Advances in Petri Nets 1986. Volume 255 of Lecture Notes in Computer Science., Springer (1987) 279–324
14. Johnsen, E.B., Owe, O.: An asynchronous communication model for distributed concurrent objects. Software and Systems Modeling **6**(1) (2007) 39–58

15. Albert, E., Genaim, S., Gómez-Zamalloa, M., Johnsen, E.B., Schlatte, R., Tapia Tarifa, S.L.: Simulating concurrent behaviors with worst-case cost bounds. In Butler, M.J., Schulte, W., eds.: Proc. 17th International Symposium on Formal Methods (FM 2011). Volume 6664 of Lecture Notes in Computer Science., Springer (2011) 353–368

16. Bjørk, J., de Boer, F.S., Johnsen, E.B., Schlatte, R., Tapia Tarifa, S.L.: User-defined schedulers for real-time concurrent objects. Innovations in Systems and Software Engineering **9**(1) (2013) 29–43

17. Schlatte, R., Johnsen, E.B., Mauro, J., Tapia Tarifa, S.L., Yu, I.C.: Release the beasts: When formal methods meet real world data. In: It's All About Coordination - Essays to Celebrate the Lifelong Scientific Achievements of Farhad Arbab. Volume 10865 of Lecture Notes in Computer Science., Springer (2018) 107–121

18. Lamport, L.: Time, clocks, and the ordering of events in a distributed system. Commun. ACM **21**(7) (1978) 558–565

19. Ronsse, M., Kranzlmüller, D.: Rolt^{mp}-replay of Lamport timestamps for message passing systems. In: Proc. 6th Euromicro Workshop on Parallel and Distributed Processing (PDP'98), IEEE (1998) 87–93

20. Albert, E., Correas, J., Johnsen, E.B., Pun, V.K.I., Román-Díez, G.: Parallel cost analysis. ACM Trans. Comput. Log. **19**(4) (2018) 31:1–31:37

21. Albert, E., Gómez-Zamalloa, M., Isabel, M.: SYCO: a systematic testing tool for concurrent objects. In Zaks, A., Hermenegildo, M.V., eds.: Proc. 25th Intl. Conf. on Compiler Construction (CC 2016), ACM (2016) 269–270

22. LeBlanc, T.J., Mellor-Crummey, J.M.: Debugging parallel programs with instant replay. IEEE Trans. Computers **36**(4) (1987) 471–482

23. Ronsse, M., Bosschere, K.D., de Kergommeaux, J.C.: Execution replay and debugging. In: AADEBUG. (2000)

24. Shibanai, K., Watanabe, T.: Actoverse: a reversible debugger for actors. In Koster, J.D., Bergenti, F., eds.: Proc. 7th Intl. Workshop on Programming Based on Actors, Agents, and Decentralized Control (AGERE 2017), ACM (2017) 50–57

25. Barr, E.T., Marron, M., Maurer, E., Moseley, D., Seth, G.: Time-travel debugging for javascript/node.js. In Zimmermann, T., Cleland-Huang, J., Su, Z., eds.: Proc. 24th Intl. Symp. on Foundations of Software Engineering (FSE 2016), ACM (2016) 1003–1007

26. Burg, B., Bailey, R., Ko, A.J., Ernst, M.D.: Interactive record/replay for web application debugging. In Izadi, S., Quigley, A.J., Poupyrev, I., Igarashi, T., eds.: Proc. 26th Symp. on User Interface Software and Technology (UIST'13), ACM (2013) 473–484

27. Aumayr, D., Marr, S., Béra, C., Boix, E.G., Mössenböck, H.: Efficient and deterministic record & replay for actor languages. In Tilevich, E., Mössenböck, H., eds.: Proc. 15th Intl. Conf. on Managed Languages & Runtimes (ManLang'18), ACM (2018) 15:1–15:14

28. de Kergommeaux, J.C., Ronsse, M., Bosschere, K.D.: MPL*: Efficient record/play of nondeterministic features of message passing libraries. In Dongarra, J.J., Luque, E., Margalef, T., eds.: Recent Advances in Parallel Virtual Machine and Message Passing Interface, proc. 6th European PVM/MPI Users' Group Meeting. Volume 1697 of Lecture Notes in Computer Science., Springer (1999) 141–148

29. Netzer, R.H.B., Miller, B.P.: Optimal tracing and replay for debugging message-passing parallel programs. The Journal of Supercomputing **8**(4) (1995) 371–388

30. Lanese, I., Palacios, A., Vidal, G.: Causal-consistent replay debugging for message passing programs. In Pérez, J.A., Yoshida, N., eds.: Proc. 39th Intl. Conf. on

Formal Techniques for Distributed Objects, Components, and Systems (FORTE 2019). Volume 11535 of Lecture Notes in Computer Science., Springer (2019) 167–184

31. Lanese, I., Nishida, N., Palacios, A., Vidal, G.: Cauder: A causal-consistent reversible debugger for erlang. In Gallagher, J.P., Sulzmann, M., eds.: Proc. 14th Intl. Symp. on Functional and Logic Programming (FLOPS 2018). Volume 10818 of Lecture Notes in Computer Science., Springer (2018) 247–263

32. Flanagan, C., Godefroid, P.: Dynamic partial-order reduction for model checking software. In Palsberg, J., Abadi, M., eds.: Proc. 32nd Symp. on Principles of Programming Languages (POPL 2005), ACM (2005) 110–121

33. Abdulla, P.A., Aronis, S., Jonsson, B., Sagonas, K.: Optimal dynamic partial order reduction. In Jagannathan, S., Sewell, P., eds.: Proc. 41st Symposium on Principles of Programming Languages (POPL'14), ACM (2014) 373–384

34. Albert, E., Arenas, P., de la Banda, M.G., Gómez-Zamalloa, M., Stuckey, P.J.: Context-sensitive dynamic partial order reduction. In Majumdar, R., Kuncak, V., eds.: Proc. 29th Intl. Conf. on Computer Aided Verification (CAV 2017). Volume 10426 of Lecture Notes in Computer Science., Springer (2017) 526–543

35. Godefroid, P.: Model checking for programming languages using Verisoft. In Lee, P., Henglein, F., Jones, N.D., eds.: Proc. 24th Symp. on Principles of Programming Languages (POPL 1997), ACM (1997) 174–186

3

TracerX: Dynamic Symbolic Execution with Interpolation (Competition Contribution)

Joxan Jaffar ⓘ, Rasool Maghareh ⓘ, Sangharatna Godboley ⓘ, and
Xuan-Linh Ha ⓘ

National University of Singapore, Singapore, Singapore
{joxan,rasool,sanghara,haxl}@comp.nus.edu.sg

Abstract. Dynamic Symbolic Execution (DSE) is an important method for testing of programs. An important system on DSE is KLEE [1] which inputs a C/C++ program annotated with symbolic variables, compiles it into LLVM, and then emulates the execution paths of LLVM using a specified backtracking strategy. The major challenge in symbolic execution is *path explosion*. The method of *abstraction learning* [7] has been used to address this. The key step here is the computation of an *interpolant* to represent the learned abstraction.

TracerX, our tool, is built on top of KLEE and it implements and utilizes *abstraction learning*. The core feature in abstraction learning is *subsumption* of paths whose traversals are deemed to no longer be necessary due to similarity with already-traversed paths. Despite the overhead of computing interpolants, the *pruning* of the symbolic execution tree that interpolants provide often brings significant overall benefits. In particular, TracerX can *fully* explore many programs that would be impossible for any non-pruning system like KLEE to do so.

Keywords: Dynamic Symbolic Execution, Interpolation, Testing, Code Coverage

1 Overview and Software Architecture

Symbolic execution has emerged as an important method to reason about programs, in both verification and testing. By reasoning about inputs as symbolic entities, its fundamental advantage over traditional black-box testing, which uses concrete inputs, is simply that it has better *coverage* of *program paths*. In particular, *dynamic symbolic execution* (DSE), where the execution space is explored *path-by-path*, has been shown effective in systems such as DART [4] and KLEE [1]. A key advantage of DSE is that by examining a single path, the analysis can be both precise, and efficient. However, the key disadvantage of DSE is that the number of program paths is in general *exponential* in the program size, and most available implementations of DSE do not employ a general technique to prune away some paths.

In TracerX, our primary objective is to address the path explosion problem in DSE. More specifically, we wish to perform path-by-path exploration of DSE to enjoy its benefits, but we include a *pruning mechanism* so that a generated path can be eliminated if it is guaranteed not to violate the stated safety conditions. Toward this goal, we employ the method of *abstraction learning* [7], which is more popularly known as *lazy annotations* [8,9].

The software architecture of TracerX is presented in Fig. 1. The core feature of TracerX is the use of *interpolation*, which serves to generalize the context of a node in the symbolic execution

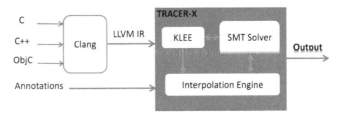

Fig. 1. TracerX Framework

tree (SET) with an approximation of the weakest precondition of the node. This method was implemented in the TRACER system [6], which was the first system to demonstrate DSE with pruning. TRACER was primarily used to evaluate new algorithms in verification, analysis and testing, e.g., [2,3,5]. While TRACER was able to perform bounded verification and testing on many examples, it could not accommodate industrial programs which often dynamically manipulate the heap memory. TracerX combines the state-of-the-art DSE technology used in KLEE with the pruning technology in TRACER to address this issue.

Now we explain *interpolation* in more detail. While exploring the SET, an *interpolant* of a state is an *abstraction* of it which ensures the safety of the subtree rooted at that state. In other words, if we continue the execution with the interpolant instead of the state we will *not* reach any error. Thus, upon

```
x = 0;
if ( b1 ) x += 12;
if ( b2 ) x += 15;
assert (x != 28);
```

Fig. 2. A Sample Program

encountering another state of the same program point, if the context of the state *implies* the interpolant formula, then continuing the execution from the new state will not lead to any error. Consequently, we can prune the subtree rooted at the new state.

Example 1. Consider the program in Fig. 2 and its SET explored by SE with interpolation in Fig. 3. The variables b1, b2 are symbolic and all combinations of the boolean conditions are satisfiable. The final statement assert($x \neq 28$) is the target. The path condition for every path is shown in the set in black color.

We traverse the SET in a left-right depth-first manner. In the end of the first path $x = 27$ which does not violate the assertion. Consider-

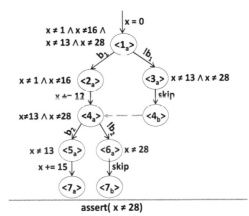

Fig. 3. SET with Interpolation of Program in Fig. 2

ing the target and the update on variable x between $\langle 5_a \rangle$ and $\langle 7_a \rangle$, we generate an interpolant which store the weakest precondition at $\langle 5_a \rangle$: $x \neq 13$ (Shown in purple color). Similarly, an interpolant is also computed at $\langle 6_a \rangle$: $x \neq 28$.

Now, combining these two interpolants, we generate an interpolant for the node $\langle 4_a \rangle$. Note that the weakest precondition here is $b_2 \longrightarrow (x \neq 13) \wedge !b_2 \longrightarrow (x \neq 28)$. We approximate this formula with the conjunction $(x \neq 13) \wedge (x \neq 28)$. Next, moving to $\langle 2_a \rangle$, the interpolant at $\langle 4_a \rangle$ is received and considering the update on variable x between $\langle 2_a \rangle$ and $\langle 4_a \rangle$, an interpolant is generated at $\langle 2_a \rangle$: $x \neq 1 \wedge x \neq 16$. Now moving to $\langle 4_b \rangle$, we check if the path condition at $\langle 4_b \rangle$ ($x = 0 \wedge !b_1 \wedge skip$) implies the interpolant that was generated at $\langle 4_a \rangle$ ($x \neq 13 \wedge x \neq 28$). Since the implication holds, node $\langle 4_b \rangle$ is subsumed with node $\langle 4_a \rangle$ (indicated by orange arrow) and the subtree below $\langle 4_b \rangle$ is pruned. The SET traversal continues by computing the interpolant at $\langle 3_a \rangle$ which is computed from $x \neq 13 \wedge x \neq 28$ subsuming $\langle 4_b \rangle$ and the updates between $\langle 3_a \rangle$ and $\langle 4_b \rangle$ (which is skip). The interpolants at $\langle 2_a \rangle$ and $\langle 3_a \rangle$ are then combined to generate an interpolant at $\langle 1_a \rangle$: $x \neq 1 \wedge x \neq 16 \wedge x \neq 13 \wedge x \neq 28$. Note that KLEE would explore the 4 paths in the SET while TracerX explores only two paths to the end.   □

2   Discussion on Strengths and Weaknesses

In Test-Comp 2020, TracerX stood at 6th rank in overall. Inspecting the results, TracerX was one of the teams having the highest score in: `cover-branches.BitVectors` and `cover-error.ControlFlow`. Moreover, TracerX was one of the top 3 scorers in: `cover-branches.DeviceDriversLinux64`, `cover-branches.ControlFlow`, and `cover-error.BitVectors`.

TracerX also accomplished more tasks by a meaningful margin compared to KLEE in: `cover-branches.BusyBox` and `cover-branches.MainHeap`. On the other hand, TracerX performed poorly in 3 sub-categories: `cover-error.ReachSafety-ECA`, `ReachSafety-Sequentialized` (both branches) and `cover-error.Floats`[1].

We should emphasize that TracerX in general requires symbolic execution trees to be bounded. Otherwise, interpolants cannot be computed. Moreover, TracerX is a heavy-weight approach and the overhead pays off as the problems gets harder. As a result it is expected for other light-weight approaches to have better results compared to TracerX in short timeout and memory limits.

Moreover, it appears that the configuration we used to explore unbounded programs (max-depth=1000) and also in the *benchexec tool-info* (wrongly running TracerX with the default memory (2GB) instead of 15GB RAM) might have had a profound effect in reaching timeout on the test programs.

---

[1] TracerX does not support symbolic expressions over floating point arithmetic.

3 Tool Setup and Configuration

The TracerX version used in TEST-COMP 2020 is available at https://gitlab. com/sosy-lab/test-comp/archives-2020/blob/testcomp20/2020/tracerx.zip[2]. The configuration/setting and running of TracerX is similar to KLEE. TracerX has some extra command line arguments. Firstly, the argument "solver-backend=z3" should be provided to run TracerX with interpolation. Without this option TracerX will run similar to **KLEE**. TracerX can do exploration in both the Random and DFS modes. However, the DFS exploration mode (using "-search=dfs") is preferred since it naturally increases the chance of generating interpolants. Furthermore, the option "-subsumed-test" should be used to generate a test-case from the subsumed nodes. This option is required for the coverage competition. The following is a sample full command line after compiling and running `tracerx.py`:

"`../tracerx-svcomp/bin/../tracerx_build/Release+Asserts/bin/klee -max-memory=14305 -output-dir=../tracerx-svcomp/bin/../test-suite -search=dfs -solver-backend=z3 -write-xml-tests -tc-orig=s3_clnt_3.BV.c.cil-2a.c -tc-hash=acd2272114f13977ea7bdc712c7567ec2e43dc8e07ef033eb67487bab7f66d59 --dump-states-on-halt=false -exit-on-error-type=Assert -max-depth=1000 -max-time=900 /tmp/tmpvwkb459r/s3_clnt_3.BV.c.cil-2a.c.bc`"

The two command line options, "-max-memory" and "-max-time" are used to set the maximum memory and time budget. The options "-write-xml-tests", "-tc-orig", and "-tc-hash" are to record the test input information. Once the halt instruction is invoked, "-dump-states-on-halt" creates a test case from all active states[3]. The option "-exit-on-error-type=Assert" terminates the search as soon as a bug is found (used only for coverage categories). The command line option "-max-depth=1000" is used to bound the maximum number of branches explored in unbounded paths.

4 Software Project and Contributors

The information about TracerX with self-contained binary is publicly available at https://www.comp.nus.edu.sg/~tracerx/. Also, the source code can be accessed at https://github.com/tracer-x/klee repository. Authors of this paper and other colleagues have contributed and developed TracerX at National University of Singapore, Singapore. The authors of this paper acknowledge the direct and indirect support of their students, former researchers, and colleagues.

---

[2] The *benchexec* tool-info file is https://github.com/sosy-lab/benchexec/blob/master/benchexec/tools/tracerx.py and the benchmark description file is https://gitlab.com/sosy-lab/test-comp/bench-defs/blob/master/benchmark-defs/tracerx.xml.

[3] This was disabled to save execution time. However, it would have been better to enable this option for maximum coverage.

References

1. Cadar, C., Dunbar, D., Engler, D.R., et al.: KLEE: unassisted and automatic generation of high-coverage tests for complex systems programs. In: Proceedings of the 8th OSDI. pp. 209–224 (2008)
2. Chu, D.H., Jaffar, J.: A complete method for symmetry reduction in safety verification. In: 24th International Conference on Computer Aided Verification (CAV). pp. 616–633, USA. Springer (2012)
3. Chu, D.H., Jaffar, J., Maghareh, R.: Precise cache timing analysis via symbolic execution. In: 22nd IEEE Real-Time and Embedded Technology and Applications Symposium (RTAS). pp. 1–12 (2016)
4. Godefroid, P., Klarlund, N., Sen, K.: DART: Directed automated random testing. In: Proceedings of the 2005 ACM SIGPLAN conference on Programming language design and implementation (PLDI). pp. 213–223 (2005)
5. Jaffar, J., Murali, V., Navas, J.A.: Boosting concolic testing via interpolation. In: Proceedings of the 9th Conference on Foundations of Software Engineering (FSE). pp. 48–58 (2013)
6. Jaffar, J., Murali, V., Navas, J.A., Santosa, A.E.: TRACER: a symbolic execution tool for verification. In: 24th International Conference on Computer Aided Verification (CAV). pp. 758–766. Springer (2012)
7. Jaffar, J., Santosa, A.E., Voicu, R.: An interpolation method for CLP traversal. In: 15th International Conference on Principles and Practice of Constraint Programming (CP). pp. 454–469. Springer (2009)
8. McMillan, K.L.: Lazy annotation for program testing and verification. In: 22nd International Conference on Computer Aided Verification (CAV). pp. 104–118 (2010)
9. Mcmillan, K.L.: Lazy annotation revisited. In: 26th International Conference on Computer Aided Verification (CAV). pp. 243–259 (2014)

4

Integrating Topological Proofs with Model Checking to Instrument Iterative Design

Claudio Menghi[1], Alessandro Maria Rizzi[2], and Anna Bernasconi[2]

[1] University of Luxembourg, Luxembourg, Luxembourg
claudio.menghi@uni.lu
[2] Politecnico di Milano, Milano, Italy
{alessandromaria.rizzi,anna.bernasconi}@polimi.it

Abstract. System development is not a linear, one-shot process. It proceeds through refinements and revisions. To support assurance that the system satisfies its requirements, it is desirable that continuous verification can be performed after each refinement or revision step. To achieve practical adoption, formal verification must accommodate continuous verification efficiently and effectively. Model checking provides developers with information useful to improve their models only when a property is not satisfied, i.e., when a counterexample is returned. However, it is desirable to have some useful information also when a property is instead satisfied. To address this problem we propose TOrPEDO, an approach that supports verification in two complementary forms: model checking and proofs. While model checking is typically used to pinpoint model behaviors that violate requirements, proofs can instead explain why requirements are satisfied. In our work, we introduce a specific notion of proof, called Topological Proof. A topological proof produces a slice of the original model that justifies the property satisfaction. Because models can be incomplete, TOrPEDO supports reasoning on requirements satisfaction, violation, and possible satisfaction (in the case where satisfaction depends on unknown parts of the model). Evaluation is performed by checking how topological proofs support software development on 12 modeling scenarios and 15 different properties obtained from 3 examples from literature. Results show that: (i) topological proofs are ≈60% smaller than the original models; (ii) after a revision, in ≈78% of cases, the property can be re-verified by relying on a simple syntactic check.

Keywords: Topological Proofs · Iterative Design · Model Checking · Theorem Proving · Unsatisfiable Core.

1 Introduction

One of the goals of software engineering and formal methods is to provide automated verification tools that support designers in producing models of an envisioned system which follows a set of properties of interest. Designers benefit from automated support to understand why their system does not behave as expected (e.g., counterexamples), but they might find it also useful to retrieve information when the system already follows the specified requirements. While model checkers provide the former, theorem provers sustain the latter. Theorem provers usually rely on some form of deductive mechanism that, given a set of axioms, iteratively applies a set of rules until a theorem is proved. The proof consists of the specific sequence of deductive rules applied to prove the theorem. In the literature, many approaches have dealt with an integration of model checking and theorem proving at various levels (e.g., [48,60,53,36]). These approaches are oriented to produce *certified model checking* procedures rather than tools that actually help the design process. Even when the idea is to provide a practically useful framework [49,50], the output consists of deductive proofs that are usually difficult to understand and hardly connectable with the designer's modeling choices. Moreover, verification techniques only take into account completely specified designs. This is a remarkable limitation in practical contexts, where the designer may start by providing an initial, high-level version of the model, which is iteratively narrowed down as design progresses and uncertainties are removed [13,42,8,19,65,43]. A recent work [4,5] considered cases in which a partial knowledge of the system model is available. However, the presented approach was mainly theoretical and lacked a practical implementation.

We formulate our problem on models that contain uncertain parts. We choose Partial Kripke Structures (PKSs) as a formalism to represent general models for the following reasons: (i) PKSs have been used in requirement elicitation to reason about system behavior from different points of view [19,8], and are a common theoretical reference language used in the formal method community for the specification of uncertain models (e.g, [26,9,27,10]); (ii) other modeling formalisms commonly used in software development [23,64], such as Modal Transition Systems [37] (MTSs), can be converted into PKSs through a simple transformation [26] making our solution easily applicable to those models.

Kripke Structures (KSs) are particular instances of PKSs that represent complete models. Requirements on the model are expressed in Linear-time Temporal Logic (LTL). As such, the approach presented in the following is generic: it can be applied on models that contain uncertain parts (PKSs) or not (KSs), and can be easily adapted to support MTSs.

Verification techniques that consider PKSs return three alternative values: *true* if the property holds in the partial model, *false* if it does not hold, and *maybe* if the property possibly holds, i.e., its satisfaction depends on the parts of the model that still need to be refined. As models are revised, i.e., they are modified during design iterations, designers need support to understand *why* properties are satisfied, or possibly satisfied.

A comprehensive and integrated design framework able to support software designers in understanding such motivation is still missing. We tackle this problem by presenting TOrPEDO (TOpological Proof drivEn Development frame-wOrk), a novel automated verification framework, that:

(i) supports a modeling formalism which allows a partial specification of the system design;

(ii) allows performing analysis and verification in the context of systems in which "incompleteness" represents a conceptual uncertainty;

(iii) provides guidance in producing model revisions through complementary outputs: counterexamples and proofs;

(iv) when the system is completely specified, allows understanding which changes impact or not the satisfaction of certain properties.

TOrPEDO is based on the novel notion of *topological proof* (TP), which tries to overcome the complexity of deductive proofs and is designed to make proofs understandable on the original system design. A TP is a *slice* of the original model that specifies which part of it impacts the property satisfaction. If the slice defined by the TP is not preserved during a revision, there is no assurance that the property holds (possibly holds) in the revised model. This paper proposes an algorithm to compute topological proofs—which relies on the notion of *unsatisfiable cores* (UCs) [56]—and proves its correctness on PKSs. It also proposes an algorithm that checks whether a TP is preserved in a model revision. This simple syntactic check avoids (in many cases) the execution of the model checking procedure. While architectural decomposition and composition of components can be considered during the system development [42], in this work we present our solution by assuming that the system is modeled as a single PKS. However, our framework can be extended to consider the composition of components, such as the parallel composition of PKSs or MTSs. This can be done by extracting the portions of the TP that refer to the different components.

TOrPEDO has been implemented on top of NuSMV [14] and PLTL-MUP [58]. The implementation has been exploited to evaluate TOrPEDO by considering a set of examples coming from literature including both completely specified and partially specified models. We considered 3 different example models and 4 variations for each model that was presented in the literature [12,20]. We considered 15 properties, i.e., 5 for each example, leading to a total of 60 ($3\times4\times5$) scenarios that require the evaluation of a property on a model. We evaluated how our framework supports model design by comparing the size of the generated topological proofs against the size of the original models. Results show that topological proofs are ≈60% smaller than the original models. Moreover, after a revision, in ≈78% of cases, our syntactic check avoids the re-execution of the model checker.

Organization. Section 2 describes TOrPEDO. Section 3 discusses the background. Sections 4 and 5 present the theoretical results and the algorithms that support TOrPEDO. Section 6 evaluates the achieved results. Section 7 discusses related work. Section 8 concludes.

2 TOrPEDO

TOrPEDO is a proof based development framework which allows verifying PKSs and evaluating their revisions. To illustrate TOrPEDO, we use a simple model describing the states of a vacuum-cleaner robot that has to satisfy the requirements in Fig. 2, specified through LTL formulae and English natural language.

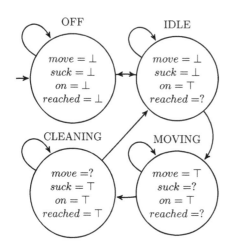

Fig. 1: PKS of a vacuum-cleaner robot.

LTL formulae

$\phi_1 = \mathcal{G}(suck \rightarrow reached)$
$\phi_2 = \mathcal{G}((\neg move)\, \mathcal{W}\, on)$
$\phi_3 = \mathcal{G}(((\neg move) \wedge on) \rightarrow suck)$
$\phi_4 = ((\neg suck)\, \mathcal{W}(move \wedge (\neg suck)))$

Textual requirements

ϕ_1: the robot is drawing dust (*suck*) only if it has *reached* the cleaning site.
ϕ_2: the robot must be turned *on* before it can *move*.
ϕ_3: if the robot is *on* and stationary ($\neg move$), it must be drawing dust (*suck*).
ϕ_4: the robot must *move* before it is allowed to draw dust (*suck*).

Fig. 2: Natural language and LTL formulation of the requirements of the vacuum-cleaner robot.
$\mathcal{G}$ and $\mathcal{W}$ are the "globally" and "weak until" LTL operators.

The TOrPEDO framework is illustrated in Fig. 3 and carries out verification in four phases: INITIAL DESIGN, ANALYSIS, REVISION, and RE-CHECK.

INITIAL DESIGN (❶). The model of the system is expressed using a PKS M (❶), which can be generated from other languages, along with the property of interest ϕ, in LTL (❷).

Running example. The PKS presented in Fig. 1 is defined over two atomic propositions representing actions that a robot can perform: *move*, i.e., the agent travels to the cleaning site; *suck*, i.e., the agent is drawing the dust, and two atomic propositions representing conditions that can trigger actions: *on*, true when the robot is turned on; *reached*, true when the robot has reached the cleaning site. The state *OFF* represents the robot being shut down, *IDLE* the robot being tuned on w.r.t. a cleaning call, *MOVING* the robot reaching the cleaning site, and *CLEANING* the robot performing its duty. Each state is labeled with the actions *move* and *suck* and the conditions *on* and *reached*. Given an action or condition α and a state s, we use the notation: $\alpha = \top$ to indicate that α occurs when the robot is in state s; $\alpha = \bot$ to indicate that α does not occur when the robot is in state s; $\alpha = ?$ to indicate that there is uncertainty on whether α occurs when the robot is in state s.

ANALYSIS (❷). TOrPEDO provides automated analysis support, which includes the following elements:

(i) Information about *what is wrong* in the current design. This information includes a definitive-counterexample, which indicates a behavior that depends on already performed design choices and violates the properties of interest. The definitive-counterexample (❸ $\bot$-CE) can be used to produce a revised version M' of M that satisfies or possibly satisfies the property of interest.

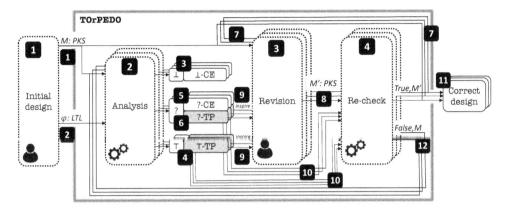

Fig. 3: TOrPEDO structure. Continuous arrows represent inputs and outputs to phases. Numbers are used to reference the image in the text.

(ii) Information about *what is correct* in the current design. This information includes definitive-topological proofs (**4** ⊤-TP) that indicate a portion of the design that ensures satisfaction of the property.

(iii) Information about *what could be wrong/correct* in the current design, depending on how uncertainty is removed. This information includes: a possible-counterexample (**5** ?-CE), indicating a behavior (which depends on uncertain actions and conditions) that violates the properties of interest, and a possible-topological proof (**6** ?-TP), indicating a portion of the design that ensures the possible satisfaction of the property of interest.

In the following we will use the notation x-topological proofs or x-TP to indicate arbitrarily definitive-topological or possible-topological proofs. The results returned by TORPEDO for the different properties in our motivating example are presented in Table 1. Property ϕ_2 is satisfied, ϕ_3 is not. In those cases TORPEDO returns respectively a definitive-proof and a definitive-counterexample. Since ϕ_1 and ϕ_4 are possibly satisfied, in both cases a possible-counterexample and a possible-topological proof are returned.

Running example. For ϕ_1 the possible-counterexample shows a run that may violate the property of interest. The possible-topological proof in Table 1 shows that if *OFF* remains the only initial state (**TPI**), *reached* still holds in *CLEANING*, and *suck* does not hold in *OFF* and *IDLE*, while unknown in *MOVING* (**TPP**), property ϕ_1 remains possibly satisfied. In addition, all transitions must be preserved (**TPT**).[3] Note that the proof highlights portions of the model that influence the property satisfaction. For example, by inspecting the proof, the designer understands that she can change the value of the proposition *reached* in all the states of the PKS, with the exception of the state *CLEANING*, without making the property violated.

---

[3] The precise formal descriptions of x-topological proofs, **TPI**, **TPT** and **TPT** are presented in Section 4.

Table 1: Results provided by TOrPEDO for properties ϕ_1, ϕ_2, ϕ_3 and ϕ_4. $\top$, $\bot$ and ? indicate that the property is satisfied, violated and possibly satisfied.

ϕ_1 ?	**?-CE**	*OFF, IDLE, (MOVING)$^\omega$.*
	?-TP	**TPP**: $\langle CLEANING, reached, \top \rangle$ $\langle OFF, suck, \bot \rangle$, $\langle IDLE, suck, \bot \rangle$, $\langle MOVING, suck, ? \rangle$ **TPT**: $\langle OFF, \{OFF, IDLE\} \rangle$, $\langle IDLE, \{OFF, IDLE, MOVING\} \rangle$, $\quad \langle MOVING, \{MOVING, CLEANING\} \rangle$, $\langle CLEANING, \{CLEANING, IDLE\} \rangle$ **TPI**: $\langle \{OFF\} \rangle$
ϕ_2 $\top$	$\top$-**TP**	**TPP**: $\langle MOVING, on, \top \rangle$, $\langle CLEANING, on, \top \rangle$, $\langle OFF, move, \bot \rangle$, $\langle IDLE, move, \bot \rangle$ **TPT**: $\langle OFF, \{OFF, IDLE\} \rangle$, $\langle IDLE, \{OFF, IDLE, MOVING\} \rangle$, $\quad \langle MOVING, \{MOVING, CLEANING\} \rangle$, $\langle CLEANING, \{CLEANING, IDLE\} \rangle$ **TPI**: $\langle \{OFF\} \rangle$
ϕ_3 $\bot$	$\bot$-**CE**	*OFF, IDLE$^\omega$*
ϕ_4 ?	**?-CE**	*OFF, (IDLE, MOVING, CLEANING, IDLE, OFF)$^\omega$*
	?-TP	**TPP**: $\langle OFF, suck, \bot \rangle$, $\langle IDLE, suck, \bot \rangle$, $\langle MOVING, suck, ? \rangle$, $\langle MOVING, move, \top \rangle$ **TPT**: $\langle OFF, \{OFF, IDLE\} \rangle$, $\langle IDLE, \{OFF, IDLE, MOVING\} \rangle$ **TPI**: $\langle \{OFF\} \rangle$

REVISION (3). Revisions (8) can be obtained by changing some parts of the model: adding/removing states and transitions or by changing propositions labelling inside states, and are defined by considering the TP (9).

Running example. The designer may want to propose a revision that still does not violate properties ϕ_1, ϕ_2, and ϕ_4. Thus, she changes the values of some atomic propositions: *move* becomes $\top$ in state *CLEANING* and *reached* becomes $\bot$ in state *IDLE*. Since ϕ_1, ϕ_2, and ϕ_4 were previously not violated, TOrPEDO performs the RE-CHECK phase for each property.

RE-CHECK (4). The automated verification tool provided by TOrPEDO checks whether all the changes in the current model revision are compliant with the x-TPs (10), i.e., changes applied to the revised model do not include parts that had to be preserved according to the x-topological proof. If a property of interest is (possibly) satisfied in a previous model, and the revision of the model is compliant with the property x-TP, the designer has the guarantee that the property is (possibly) satisfied in the revision. Thus, she can perform another model revision round (7) or approve the current design (11). Otherwise, TOrPEDO re-executes the ANALYSIS (12).

Running example. In the vacuum-cleaner case, the revision passes the RE-CHECK and the designer proceeds to a new revision phase.

3   Background

We present background notions by relying on standard notations for the selected formalisms (see for example [26,9,10,30]).

Partial Kripke Structures (1) are state machines that can be adopted when the value of some propositions is uncertain on selected states.

Definition 1 ([9],[35]). *A* Partial Kripke Structure *(PKS) M is a tuple* $\langle S, R,$ $S_0, AP, L \rangle$, *where: S is a set of states;* $R \subseteq S \times S$ *is a left-total transition* *relation on S; S_0 is a set of initial states; AP is a set of atomic propositions; $L : S \times AP \to \{\top, ?, \bot\}$ is a function that, for each state in S, associates a truth value to every atomic proposition in AP. A* Kripke Structure *(KS) M is a PKS $\langle S, R, S_0, AP, L \rangle$, where $L : S \times AP \to \{\top, \bot\}$.*

A PKS represents a system as a set of states and transitions between these states. Uncertainty on the AP is represented through the value ?. The model in Fig. 1 is a PKS where propositions in AP are used to model actions and conditions.

LTL properties (2). For KSs we consider the classical LTL semantics $[M \models \phi]$ over infinite words that associates to a model M and a formula ϕ a truth value in the set $\{\bot, \top\}$. The interested reader may refer, for example, to [3]. Let M be a KS and ϕ be an LTL property. We assume that the function CHECK, such that $\langle res, c \rangle = \text{CHECK}(M, \phi)$, returns a tuple $\langle res, c \rangle$, where res is the model checking result in $\{\top, \bot\}$ and c is the counterexample if $res = \bot$, else an empty set.

The *three-valued LTL semantics* [9] $[M \models \phi]$ associates to a model M and a formula ϕ a truth value in the set $\{\bot, ?, \top\}$ and is defined based on the information ordering $\top > ? > \bot$. The three-valued LTL semantics is defined by considering paths of the model M. A path π is an infinite sequence of states $s_0, s_1, \ldots$ such that, for all $i \geq 0$, $(s_i, s_{i+1}) \in R$. We use the symbol π^i to indicate the infinite sub-sequence of π that starts at position i, and $Path(s)$ to indicate all the paths that start in the state s.

Definition 2 ([9]). *Let $M = \langle S, R, S_0, AP, L \rangle$ be a PKS, $\pi = s_0, s_1, \ldots$ be a path, and ϕ be an LTL formula. Then, the* three-valued semantics *$[(M, \pi) \models \phi]$ is defined inductively as follows:*

$$
\begin{aligned}
[(M, \pi) \models p] \quad &= \quad L(s_0, p) \\
[(M, \pi) \models \neg\phi] \quad &= \quad comp([(M, \pi) \models \phi]) \\
[(M, \pi) \models \phi_1 \wedge \phi_2] \quad &= \quad \min([(M, \pi) \models \phi_1], [(M, \pi) \models \phi_2]) \\
[(M, \pi) \models \mathcal{X}\,\phi] \quad &= \quad [(M, \pi^1) \models \phi] \\
[(M, \pi) \models \phi_1 \mathcal{U} \phi_2] \quad &= \quad \max_{j \geq 0}(\min(\{[(M, \pi^i) \models \phi_1] | i < j\} \cup \{[(M, \pi^j) \models \phi_2]\}))
\end{aligned}
$$

Let $M = \langle S, R, S_0, AP, L \rangle$ be a PKS, and ϕ be an LTL formula. Then $[M \models \phi] = \min(\{[(M, \pi) \models \phi] \mid \pi \in Path(s) \text{ and } s \in S_0\})$.

The conjunction (resp. disjunction) is defined as the minimum (resp. maximum) of its arguments, following the order $\bot < ? < \top$. These functions are extended to sets with $\min(\emptyset)=\top$ and $\max(\emptyset)=\bot$. The *comp* operator maps $\top$ to $\bot$, $\bot$ to $\top$, and ? to ?. The semantics of the $\mathcal{G}$ ("globally") and $\mathcal{W}$ ("weak until") operators is defined as usual [28].

Model Checking. Checking KSs with respect to LTL properties can be done by using classical model checking procedures. For example, the model checking problem of property ϕ on a KS M can be reduced to the satisfiability problem of the LTL formula $\Phi_M \wedge \neg\phi$, where Φ_M represents the behaviors of model M. If $\Phi_M \wedge \neg\phi$ is satisfiable, then $[M \models \phi] = \bot$, otherwise $[M \models \phi] = \top$.

Checking a PKS M with respect to an LTL property ϕ considering the three-valued semantics is done by performing twice the classical model checking procedure for KSs [10], one considering an optimistic approximation M_{opt} and one considering a pessimistic approximation M_{pes}. These two procedures consider the LTL formula $\phi' = F(\phi)$, where F transforms ϕ with the following steps: (i) negate ϕ; (ii) convert $\neg\phi$ in negation normal form; (iii) replace every subformula $\neg\alpha$, where α is an atomic proposition, with a new proposition $\overline{\alpha}$.

To create the optimistic and pessimistic approximations M_{opt} and M_{pes}, the PKS $M = \langle S, R, S_0, AP, L \rangle$ is first converted into its *complement-closed* version $M_c = \langle S, R, S_0, AP_c, L_c \rangle$ where the set of atomic propositions $AP_c = AP \cup \overline{AP}$ is such that $\overline{AP} = \{\overline{\alpha} \mid \alpha \in AP\}$. Atomic propositions in $\overline{AP}$ are called complement-closed propositions. Function L_c is such that, for all $s \in S$ and $\alpha \in AP$, $L_c(s, \alpha) = L(s, \alpha)$ and, for all $s \in S$ and $\overline{\alpha} \in \overline{AP}$, $L_c(s, \overline{p}) = comp(L(s, p))$. The complement-closed PKS of the vacuum-cleaner agent in Fig. 1 presents eight propositional assignments in the state $IDLE$: $move = \bot$, $\overline{move} = \top$, $suck = \bot$, $\overline{suck} = \top$, $on = \top$, $\overline{on} = \bot$, $reached =?$, and $\overline{reached} =?$.

The two model checking runs for a PKS $M = \langle S, R, S_0, AP, L \rangle$ are based respectively on an optimistic ($M_{opt} = \langle S, R, S_0, AP_c, L_{opt} \rangle$) and a pessimistic ($M_{pes} = \langle S, R, S_0, AP_c, L_{pes} \rangle$) approximation of M's related complement-closed $M_c = \langle S, R, S_0, AP_c, L_c \rangle$. Function L_{pes} (resp. L_{opt}) is such that, for all $s \in S$, $\alpha \in AP_c$, and $L_c(s, \alpha) \in \{\top, \bot\}$, then $L_{pes}(s, \alpha) = L_c(s, \alpha)$ (resp. $L_{opt}(s, \alpha) = L_c(s, \alpha)$), and, for all $s \in S$, $\alpha \in AP_c$, and $L_c(s, \alpha) =?$, then $L_{pes}(s, \alpha) = \bot$ (resp. $L_{opt}(s, \alpha) = \top$).

Let $\mathcal{A}$ be a KS and ϕ be an LTL formula, $\mathcal{A} \models^* \phi$ is true if no path that satisfies the formula $F(\phi)$ is present in $\mathcal{A}$.

Theorem 1 ([9]). *Let ϕ be an LTL formula, let $M = \langle S, R, S_0, AP, L \rangle$ be a PKS, and let M_{pes} and M_{opt} be the pessimistic and optimistic approximations of M's relative complement-closed M_c. Then*

$$[M \models \phi] \stackrel{def}{=} \begin{cases} \top & \text{if } M_{pes} \models^* \phi \\ \bot & \text{if } M_{opt} \not\models^* \phi \\ ? & \text{otherwise} \end{cases} \qquad (1)$$

We call CHECK* the function that computes the result of operator $\models^*$. It takes as input either M_{pes} or M_{opt} and the property $F(\phi)$, and returns a tuple $\langle res, c \rangle$, where res is the model checking result in $\{\top, \bot\}$, and c can be an empty set (when M satisfies ϕ), a *definitive*-counterexample (**3**, when M violates ϕ), or a *possible*-counterexample (**5**, when M possibly-satisfies ϕ).

4   Revising models

We define how models can be revised and the notion of *topological proof*, that is used to describe why a property ϕ is (possibly) satisfied in a PKS M.

Initial design and revisions (❶,❸). In the initial design a preliminary PKS is manually defined or automatically obtained from other modeling formalisms.

During a revision, a designer can add and remove states and transitions and/or change the labeling of the atomic propositions in the states of the PKS. Let $M = \langle S, R, S_0, AP, L \rangle$ and $M' = \langle S', R', S'_0, AP', L' \rangle$ be two PKSs. Then M' is a *revision* of M if and only if $AP \subseteq AP'$. Informally, the only constraint the designer has to respect during a revision is not to remove propositions from the set of atomic propositions. This condition is necessary to ensure that any property that can be evaluated on M can also be evaluated on M', i.e., every atomic proposition has a value in each of the states of the automaton. The deactivation of a proposition can instead be simulated by associating its value to $\perp$ in all the states of M'.

Topological proofs (4, 6). The pursued proof is made of a set of clauses specifying certain topological properties of M, which ensure that the property is (possibly) satisfied.

Definition 3. *Let $M = \langle S, R, S_0, AP, L \rangle$ be a PKS. A* Topological Proof clause *(TP-clause) γ for M is either:*

- *a Topological Proof Propositional clause (TPP-clause), i.e., a triad $\langle s, \alpha, v \rangle$ where $s \in S$, $\alpha \in AP$, and $v \in \{\top, ?, \perp\}$;*
- *a Topological Proof Transitions-from-state clause (TPT-clause), i.e., a pair $\langle s, T \rangle$, such that $s \in S, T \subseteq S$;*
- *a Topological Proof Initial-states clause (TPI-clause), i.e., an element $\langle S_0 \rangle$.*

These clauses indicate *topological properties* of a PKS M. Informally, TPP-clauses constrain how states are labeled (L), TPT-clauses constrain how states are connected (R), and TPI-clauses constrain from which states the runs on the model begin (S_0). For example, in Table 1, for property ϕ_1, $\langle CLEANING, reached, \top \rangle$ is a TPP-clause that constrains the atomic proposition *reached* to be labeled as true ($\top$) in the state $CLEANING$; $\langle OFF, \{OFF, IDLE\} \rangle$ is a TPT-clause that constrains the transition from OFF to OFF and from OFF to $IDLE$ to not be removed; and $\langle \{OFF\} \rangle$ is a TPI-clause that constrains the state OFF to remain the initial state of the system.

A state s' is constrained: by a TPP-clause $\langle s, \alpha, v \rangle$ if $s = s'$, by a TPT-clause $\langle s, T \rangle$ if $s = s'$ or $s' \in T$, and by a TPI-clause $\langle S_0 \rangle$ if $s' \in S_0$.

Definition 4. *Let $M = \langle S, R, S_0, AP, L \rangle$ be a PKS and let Ω be a set of TP-clauses for M. Then a PKS Ω-related to M is a PKS $M' = \langle S', R', S'_0, AP', L' \rangle$, such that the following conditions hold:*

- *$AP \subseteq AP'$;*
- *for every TPP-clause $\langle s, \alpha, v \rangle \in \Omega$, $s \in S'$, $v = L'(s, \alpha)$;*
- *for every TPT-clause $\langle s, T \rangle \in \Omega$, $s \in S', T \subseteq S', T = \{s' \in S' | (s, s') \in R'\}$;*
- *for every TPI-clause $\langle S_0 \rangle \in \Omega$, $S_0 = S'_0$.*

Intuitively, a PKS Ω-related to M is a PKS obtained from M by changing any topological aspect that does not impact on the set of TP-clauses Ω. Any transition whose source state is not the source state of a transition included in the TPT-clauses can be added or removed from the PKS and any value of a proposition that is not constrained by a TPP-clause can be changed. States can be always added and they can be removed if they are not constrained by any TPT-, TPP-, or TPI-clause. Initial states cannot be changed if Ω contains a TPI-clause.

Definition 5. *Let $M = \langle S, R, S_0, AP, L \rangle$ be a PKS, let ϕ be an LTL property, let Ω be a set of TP-clauses, and let x be a truth value in $\{\top, ?\}$. A set of TP-clauses Ω is an x-topological proof (or x-TP) for ϕ in M if: (i) $[M \models \phi] = x$; and (ii) every PKS M' Ω-related to M is such that $[M' \models \phi] \geq x$.*

Intuitively, an *x-topological proof* is a set of TP-clauses Ω such that every PKS M' that satisfies the conditions specified in Definition 4 is such that $[M' \models \phi] \geq x$. We call $\top$-TP a *definitive-topological proof* and ?-TP a *possible-topological proof*. In Definition 5, the operator $\geq$ assumes that values $\top, ?, \bot$ are ordered considering the classical information ordering $\top > ? > \bot$ among the truth values [9].

Regarding the PKS in Fig. 1, Table 1 shows two ?-TPs for properties ϕ_1 and ϕ_4, and one $\top$-TP for property ϕ_2.

Definition 6. *Let M and M' be two PKSs, let ϕ be an LTL property, and let Ω be an x-TP. Then M' is an Ω_x-revision of M if M' is Ω-related to M.*

Intuitively, since the Ω_x-revision M' of M is such that M' is Ω-related to M, it is obtained by changing the model M while preserving the statements that are specified in the x-TP. A revision M' of M is *compliant* with the x-TP for a property ϕ in M if it is an Ω_x-revision of M.

Theorem 2. *Let M be a PKS, let ϕ be an LTL property such that $[M \models \phi] = \top$, and let Ω be a $\top$-TP. Then every $\Omega_\top$-revision M' is such that $[M' \models \phi] = \top$. Let M be a PKS, let ϕ be an LTL property such that $[M \models \phi] =?$, and let Ω be an ?-TP. Then every $\Omega_?$-revision M' is such that $[M' \models \phi] \in \{\top, ?\}$.*

Proof Sketch. We prove the first statement of the Theorem; the proof of the second statement is obtained by following the same steps.

If Ω is a $\top$-TP, it is a $\top$-TP for ϕ in M', since M' is an $\Omega_\top$-revision of M (by Definition 6). Furthermore, since Ω is a $\top$-TP for ϕ in M', then $[M' \models \phi] \geq \top$ (by Definition 5). ∎

5   TOrPEDO automated support

This section describes the algorithms that support the ANALYSIS and RE-CHECK phases of TOrPEDO.

ANALYSIS (**2**). To analyze a PKS $M = \langle S, R, S_0, AP, L \rangle$ (**1**), TOrPEDO uses the three-valued model checking framework based on Theorem 1. The model checking result is provided as output by the ANALYSIS phase of TOrPEDO, whose behavior is described in Algorithm 1.

1: **function** ANALYZE(M, ϕ)
2:   $\langle res, c \rangle = $ CHECK$^*(M_{opt}, \phi)$
3:   **if** $res == \bot$ **then return** $\langle \bot, \{c\} \rangle$
4:   **else**
5:     $\langle res', c' \rangle = $ CHECK$^*(M_{pes}, \phi)$
6:     **if** $res' == \top$ **then return**
7:       $\langle \top, [\text{CTP\_KS}(M, M_{pes}, \text{F}(\phi))] \rangle$
8:     **else**
9:       **return**
10:       $\langle ?, \{c', \text{CTP\_KS}(M, M_{opt}, \text{F}(\phi))\} \rangle$
11:     **end if**
12:   **end if**
13: **end function**

Algorithm 1: The ANALYSIS algorithm.

1: **function** CTP_KS(M, $\mathcal{A}$, ψ)
2:   $\eta(C_{\mathcal{A}} \cup \{\psi\}) = $ SYS2LTL$(\mathcal{A}, \psi)$
3:   $\eta(C'_{\mathcal{A}} \cup \{\psi\}) = $ GETUC$(\eta(C_{\mathcal{A}} \cup \{\psi\}))$
4:   $TP = $ GETTP$(M, \eta(C'_{\mathcal{A}} \cup \{\psi\}))$
5:   **return** TP
6: **end function**

Algorithm 2: Compute Topological Proofs.

The algorithm returns a tuple $\langle x, y \rangle$, where x is the verification result and y is a set containing the counterexample, the topological proof or both of them. The algorithm first checks whether the optimistic approximation M_{opt} of the PKS M satisfies property ϕ (**2**, Line 2). If this is not the case, the property is violated by the PKS and the definitive-counterexample c (**3**, $\bot$-CE) is returned (Line 3). Then, it checks whether the pessimistic approximation M_{pes} of the PKS M satisfies property ϕ (Line 5). If this is the case, the property is satisfied and the value $\top$ is returned along with the definitive-topological proof (**4**, $\top$-TP) computed by the CTP_KS procedure applied on the pessimistic approximation M_{pes} and the property $\text{F}(\phi)$ (Line 7).

If this is not the case, the property is possibly satisfied and the value ? is returned along with the possible-counterexample c' (**5**, ?-CE) and the possible-topological proof (**6**, ?-TP) computed by the CTP_KS procedure applied to M_{opt} and $\text{F}(\phi)$ (Line 10).

The procedure CTP_KS (Compute Topological Proofs) to compute x-TPs is described in Algorithm 2. It takes as input a PKS M, its optimistic/pessimistic approximation, i.e., denoted generically as the KS $\mathcal{A}$, and an LTL formula ψ— satisfied in $\mathcal{A}$— corresponding to the transformed property $\text{F}(\phi)$ (see Section 3). The three steps of the algorithm are described in the following.

SYS2LTL. *Encoding of the KS $\mathcal{A}$ and the LTL formula ψ into an LTL formula* $\eta(C_{\mathcal{A}} \cup \{\psi\})$. The KS $\mathcal{A} = \langle S, R, S_0, AP_c, L_{\mathcal{A}} \rangle$ (where $L_{\mathcal{A}}$ is the optimistic or pessimistic function, L_{opt} or L_{pes}, as defined in Section 3) and the LTL formula ψ are used to generate an LTL formula

$$\eta(C_{\mathcal{A}} \cup \{\psi\}) = \bigwedge_{c \in (C_{\mathcal{A}} \cup \{\psi\})} c$$

Table 2: Rules to transform the KS in LTL formulae.

$c_i = \bigvee\limits_{s \in S_0} p(s)$
The KS is initially in one of its initial states.
$CR = \{\mathcal{G}(\neg p(s) \vee \mathcal{X}(\bigvee\limits_{(s,s') \in R} p(s'))) \mid s \in S\}$
If the KS is in state s in the current instant, in the next instant it is in one of the successors s' of s.
$CL_{\top,\mathcal{A}} = \{\mathcal{G}(\neg p(s) \vee \alpha) \mid s \in S, \alpha \in AP_c, L_{\mathcal{A}}(s,\alpha) = \top\}$
If the KS is in state s s.t. $L_{\mathcal{A}}(s,\alpha) = \top$, the atomic proposition α is true.
$CL_{\bot,\mathcal{A}} = \{\mathcal{G}(\neg p(s) \vee \neg\alpha) \mid s \in S, \alpha \in AP_c, L_{\mathcal{A}}(s,\alpha) = \bot\}$.
If the KS is in state s s.t. $L_{\mathcal{A}}(s,\alpha) = \bot$, the atomic proposition α is false.
$C_{REG} = \{\mathcal{G}(\neg p(s) \vee \neg p(s')) \mid s, s' \in S \text{ and } s \neq s'\}$
The KS is in at most one state at any time.

where $C_{\mathcal{A}}$ are sets of LTL clauses obtained from the KS $\mathcal{A}$.[4] The set of clauses that encodes the KS is $C_{\mathcal{A}} = C_{KS} \cup C_{REG}$, where $C_{KS} = \{c_i\} \cup CR \cup CL_{\top,\mathcal{A}} \cup CL_{\bot,\mathcal{A}}$ and c_i, CR, $CL_{\top,\mathcal{A}}$ and $CL_{\bot,\mathcal{A}}$ are defined as specified in Table 2. Note that the clauses in $C_{\mathcal{A}}$ are defined on the set of atomic propositions $APS = AP_c \cup \{p(s) \mid s \in S\}$, i.e., AP_S includes an additional atomic proposition $p(s)$ for each state s, which is true when the KS is in state s. The size of the encoding depends on the cardinality of $C_{\mathcal{A}}$ i.e., in the worst case, $1 + |S| + |S| \times |AP_c| + |S| \times |S|$.

GETUC. *Computation of the Unsatisfiable Core (UC)* $\eta(C'_{\mathcal{A}} \cup \{\psi\})$ *of* $\eta(C_{\mathcal{A}} \cup \{\psi\})$. Since the property ψ is satisfied on $\mathcal{A}$, $\eta(C_{\mathcal{A}} \cup \{\psi\})$ is unsatisfiable and the computation of its UC core is performed by using the PLTLMUP approach [58]. Let $C = \{\varphi_1, \varphi_2, \ldots, \varphi_n\}$ be a set of LTL formulae, such that $\eta(C) = \bigwedge\limits_{\varphi \in C} \varphi$ is unsatisfiable, then the function $\eta(C') = \text{GETUC}(\eta(C))$ returns an unsatisfiable core $\eta(C') = \bigwedge\limits_{\varphi \in C'} \varphi$ of $\bigwedge\limits_{\varphi \in C} \varphi$. In our case, since the property holds on the KS $\mathcal{A}$, $\text{GETUC}(\eta(C_{\mathcal{A}} \cup \{\psi\}))$ returns a subset of clauses $\eta(C'_{\mathcal{A}} \cup \{\psi\})$, where $C'_{\mathcal{A}} = C'_{KS} \cup C'_{REG}$ such that $C'_{KS} \subseteq C_{KS}$ and $C'_{REG} \subseteq C_{REG}$.

Lemma 1. *Let $\mathcal{A}$ be a KS and let ψ be an LTL property. Let also $\eta(C_{\mathcal{A}} \cup \{\psi\})$ be the LTL formula computed in the step* SYS2LTL *of the algorithm. Then, any unsatisfiable core $\eta(C'_{\mathcal{A}} \cup \{\psi\})$ of $\eta(C_{\mathcal{A}} \cup \{\psi\})$ is such that $C'_{\mathcal{A}} \subseteq C_{\mathcal{A}}$.*

Proof Sketch. As the property ϕ is satisfied by M, the LTL formula $\eta(C_{\mathcal{A}} \cup \{\psi\})$, where $\psi = \mathbf{F}(\phi)$ must be unsatisfiable as discussed in the Section 3. Indeed, $\mathbf{F}(\phi)$ simply perform some proposition renaming on the negation of the formula ψ. As $C_{\mathcal{A}}$ encodes a KS, $\bigwedge\limits_{c \in C_{\mathcal{A}}} c$ is satisfied. As such, the unsatisfiability is caused by the contradiction of some of the clauses in $C_{\mathcal{A}}$ and the property ψ, and as a consequence ψ must be a part of the UC.

GETTP. *Analysis of $C'_{\mathcal{A}}$ and extraction of the topological proof.* The set $C'_{\mathcal{A}}$, where $C'_{\mathcal{A}} = C'_{KS} \cup C'_{REG}$, contains clauses regarding the KS (C'_{KS} and C'_{REG})

---

[4] Note that this formula is equivalent to $\phi_M \wedge \neg\phi$ used in Section 3 as ϕ_M is generated by the clauses in $C_{\mathcal{A}}$ and $\neg\phi$ from ψ.

Table 3: Rules to extract the TP-clauses from the UC LTL formula.

LTL clause	TP clause	Type	LTL clause	TP clause	Type
$c_i = \bigvee\limits_{s \in S_0} p(s)$	$\langle S_0 \rangle$	TPI	$\mathcal{G}(\neg p(s) \vee \neg \alpha)$	$\langle s, \alpha, comp(L(s, \alpha)) \rangle$	TPP
$\mathcal{G}(\neg p(s) \vee$ $\mathcal{X}(\bigvee\limits_{(s,s') \in R} p(s')))$	$\langle s, T \rangle$ where $T = \{s' \vert (s, s') \in R\}$	TPT	$\mathcal{G}(\neg p(s) \vee \overline{\alpha})$	$\langle s, \alpha, comp(L(s, \alpha)) \rangle$	TPP
$\mathcal{G}(\neg p(s) \vee \alpha)$	$\langle s, \alpha, L(s, \alpha) \rangle$	TPP	$\mathcal{G}(\neg p(s) \vee \neg \overline{\alpha})$	$\langle s, \alpha, L(s, \alpha) \rangle$	TPP

and the property of interest (ψ) that made the formula $\eta(C'_{\mathcal{A}} \cup \{\psi\})$ unsatisfiable. Since we are interested in clauses related to the KS that caused unsatisfiability, we extract the topological proof Ω, whose topological proof clauses are obtained from the clauses in C'_{KS} as specified in Table 3. Since the set of atomic propositions of $\mathcal{A}$ is $AP_c = AP \cup \overline{AP}$, in the table we use α for propositions in AP and $\overline{\alpha}$ for propositions in $\overline{AP}$.

The elements in C'_{REG} are not considered in the TP computation as, given an LTL clause $\mathcal{G}(\neg p(s) \vee \neg p(s'))$, either state s or s' is constrained by other TP-clauses that will be preserved in the model revisions.

Lemma 2. *Let $\mathcal{A}$ be a KS and let ψ be an LTL property. Let also $\eta(C_{\mathcal{A}} \cup \{\psi\})$ be the LTL formula computed in the step SYS2LTL of the algorithm, where $C_{\mathcal{A}} = C_{REG} \cup C_{KS}$, and let $\eta(C'_{\mathcal{A}} \cup \{\psi\})$ be an unsatisfiable core, where $C'_{\mathcal{A}} = C'_{REG} \cup C'_{KS}$. Then, if $\mathcal{G}(\neg p(s) \vee \neg p(s')) \in C'_{REG}$, either:*

(i) there exists an LTL clause in C'_{KS} that constrains state s (or state s'); or
(ii) $\eta(C''_{\mathcal{A}} \cup \{\psi\})$, s.t. $C''_{\mathcal{A}} = C'_{\mathcal{A}} \setminus \{\mathcal{G}(\neg p(s) \vee \neg p(s'))\}$, is an UC of $\eta(C'_{\mathcal{A}} \cup \{\psi\})$.

Proof Sketch. We indicate $\mathcal{G}(\neg p(s) \vee \neg p(s'))$ as $\tau(s, s')$. Assume per absurdum that conditions (i) and (ii) are violated, i.e., no LTL clause in C'_{KS} constrains state s or s' and $\eta(C''_{\mathcal{A}} \cup \{\psi\})$ is not an unsatisfiable core of $\eta(C'_{\mathcal{A}} \cup \{\psi\})$. Since $\eta(C''_{\mathcal{A}} \cup \{\psi\})$ is not an unsatisfiable core of $\eta(C'_{\mathcal{A}} \cup \{\psi\})$, $\eta(C''_{\mathcal{A}} \cup \{\psi\})$ is satisfiable, as $C''_{\mathcal{A}} \subset C'_{\mathcal{A}}$. Since $\eta(C''_{\mathcal{A}} \cup \{\psi\})$ is satisfiable, $\eta(C'_{\mathcal{A}} \cup \{\psi\})$ s.t. $C'_{\mathcal{A}} = C''_{\mathcal{A}} \cup \{\tau(s, s')\}$ must also be satisfiable. Indeed, it does not exist any LTL clause that constrains state s (or state s') and, in order to generate a contradiction, the added LTL clause must generate it using the LTL clauses obtained from the LTL property ψ. This is a contradiction. Thus, conditions (i) and (ii) must be satisfied. □

The ANALYZE procedure in Algorithm 1 obtains a TP (**4**, **6**) for a PKS by first computing the related optimistic or pessimistic approximation (i.e., a KS) and then exploiting the computation of the TP for such KS.

Theorem 3. *Let $M = \langle S, R, S_0, AP, L \rangle$ be a PKS, let ϕ be an LTL property, and let $x \in \{\top, ?\}$ be an element such that $[M \models \phi] = x$. If the procedure ANALYZE, applied to the PKS M and the LTL property ϕ, returns a TP Ω, this is an x-TP for ϕ in M.*

Proof Sketch. Assume that the ANALYZE procedure returns the value $\top$ and a $\top$-TP. We show that every Ω-related PKS M' is such that $[M' \models \phi] \geq x$

(Definition 5). If ANALYZE returns the value $\top$, it must be that $M_{pes} \models^* \phi$ by Lines 5 and 7 of Algorithm 1. Furthermore, by Line 7, $\psi = \text{F}(\phi)$ and $\mathcal{A} = M_{pes}$.

Let $N = \langle S_N, R_N, S_{0,N}, AP_N, L_N \rangle$ be a PKS Ω-related to M. Let $\eta(C_\mathcal{A} \cup \{\psi\})$ be the LTL formula associated with $\mathcal{A}$ and ψ and let $\eta(C_\mathcal{B} \cup \{\psi\})$ be the LTL formula associated with $\mathcal{B} = N_{pes}$ and ψ. Let us consider an UC $\eta(C'_\mathcal{A} \cup \{\psi\})$ of $\eta(C_\mathcal{A} \cup \{\psi\})$, where $C'_\mathcal{A} = C'_{KS} \cup C'_{REG}$, $C'_{KS} \subseteq C_{KS}$ and $C'_{REG} \subseteq C_{REG}$. We show that $C'_\mathcal{A} \subseteq C_\mathcal{B}$, i.e., the UC is also an UC for the LTL formula associated with the approximation $\mathcal{B}$ of the PKS N.

- $C'_\mathcal{A} \subseteq C_\mathcal{B}$, i.e., $(C'_{KS} \cup C'_{REG}) \subseteq C_\mathcal{B}$. By Lemma 2 we can avoid considering C'_{REG}. By construction (see Line 2 of Algorithm 2) any clause $c \in C'_{KS}$ belongs to one rule among CR, $CL_{pes,\top}$, $CL_{pes,\perp}$ or $c = c_i$:
  - if $c = c_i$ then, by the rules in Table 3, there is a TPI-clause $\{S_0\} \in \Omega$. By Definition 4, $S_0 = S'_0$. Thus, $c_i \in C_\mathcal{B}$ since N is Ω-related to M.
  - if $c \in CR$ then, by rules in Table 3, there is a TPT-clause $\langle s, T \rangle \in \Omega$ where $s \in S$ and $T \subseteq R$. By Definition 4, $T = \{s' \in S' | (s, s') \in R'\}$. Thus, $c \in C_\mathcal{B}$ since N is Ω-related to M.
  - if $c \in CL_{\mathcal{A},\top}$ or $c \in CL_{\mathcal{A},\perp}$, by rules in Table 3, there is a TPP-clause $\langle s, \alpha, L(s, \alpha) \rangle \in \Omega$ where $s \in S$ and $\alpha \in AP$. By Definition 4, $L'(s, \alpha) = L(s, \alpha)$. Thus, $c \in C_\mathcal{B}$ since N is Ω-related to M.

Since N is Ω-related to M, it has preserved the elements of Ω. Thus $\eta(C'_\mathcal{A} \cup \{\psi\})$ is also an UC of $C_\mathcal{B}$. It follows that $[N \models \phi] = \top$.

The proof from the case in which ANALYZE procedure returns the value ? and a ?-TP can be derived from the first case. $\qquad\qquad\qquad\square$

RE-CHECK (④). Let $M = \langle S, R, S_0, AP, L \rangle$ be a PKS. The RE-CHECK algorithm verifies whether a revision M' of M is an Ω-revision. Let Ω be an x-TP (⑩) for ϕ in M, and let $M' = \langle S', R', S'_0, AP', L' \rangle$ be a revision of M (⑧). The RE-CHECK algorithm returns **true** if and only if the following holds:

- $AP \subseteq AP'$;
- for every TPP-clause $\langle s, \alpha, v \rangle \in \Omega$, $s \in S'$, $v = L'(s, \alpha)$;
- for every TPT-clause $\langle s, T \rangle \in \Omega$, $s \in S'$, $T \subseteq S'$, $T = \{s' \in S' | (s, s') \in R'\}$;
- for every TPI-clause $\langle S_0 \rangle \in \Omega$, $S_0 = S'_0$.

These conditions can be verified by a simple syntactic check on the PKS.

Lemma 3. *Let $M = \langle S, R, S_0, AP, L \rangle$ and $M' = \langle S', R', S'_0, AP', L' \rangle$ be two PKSs and let Ω be an x-TP. The RE-CHECK algorithm returns $\boldsymbol{true}$ if and only if M' is Ω-related to M.*

Proof Sketch. Since M' is Ω-related to M, the conditions of Definition 4 hold. Each of these conditions is a condition of the RE-CHECK algorithm. Thus, if M' is Ω-related to M, the RE-CHECK returns **true**. Conversely, if RE-CHECK returns **true**, each condition of the algorithm is satisfied and, since each of these conditions corresponds to a condition of Definition 4, M' is Ω-related to M. $\quad\square$

This Lemma allows us to prove the following Theorem.

Table 4: Properties considered in the evaluation

ϕ_1:	$\mathcal{G}(\neg OFFHOOK) \vee (\neg OFFHOOK \; \mathcal{U} \; CONNECTED)$
ϕ_2:	$\neg OFFHOOK \; \mathcal{W} \; (\neg OFFHOOK \wedge CONNECTED)$
ϕ_3:	$\mathcal{G}(CONNECTED \rightarrow ACTIVE)$
ϕ_4:	$\mathcal{G}(OFFHOOK \wedge ACTIVE \wedge \neg CONNECTED \rightarrow \mathcal{X}(ACTIVE))$
ϕ_5	$\mathcal{G}(CONNECTED \rightarrow \mathcal{X}(ACTIVE))$
ψ_1:	$\mathcal{G}(CONNECTED \rightarrow ACTIVE)$
ψ_2:	$\mathcal{G}(CONNECTED \rightarrow \mathcal{X}(ACTIVE))$
ψ_3:	$\mathcal{G}(CONNECTED) \vee (CONNECTED \; \mathcal{U} \; \neg OFFHOOK)$
ψ_4:	$\neg CONNECTED \; \mathcal{W} \; (\neg CONNECTED \wedge OFFHOOK)$
ψ_5:	$\mathcal{G}(CALLEE\_SEL \rightarrow OFFHOOK)$
η_1:	$\mathcal{G}((OFFHOOK \wedge CONNECTED) \rightarrow \mathcal{X}(OFFHOOK \vee \neg CONNECTED))$
η_2:	$\mathcal{G}(CONNECTED) \vee (CONNECTED \; \mathcal{W} \; \neg OFFHOOK)$
η_3:	$\neg CONNECTED \; \mathcal{W} \; (\neg CONNECTED \wedge OFFHOOK)$
η_4:	$\mathcal{G}(CALLEE\_FREE \vee LINE\_SEL)$
η_5:	$\mathcal{G}(\mathcal{X}(OFFHOOK) \wedge \neg CONNECTED)$

Theorem 4. *Let M be a PKS, let ϕ be a property, let Ω be an x-TP for ϕ in M where $x \in \{\top, ?\}$, and let M' be a revision of M. The* RE-CHECK *algorithm returns* **true** *if and only if M' is an Ω-revision of M.*

Proof Sketch. By applying Lemma 3, the RE-CHECK algorithm returns **true** if and only if M' is Ω-related to M. By Definition 6, since Ω is an x-TP, the RE-CHECK algorithm returns **true** if and only if M' is an Ω-revision of M. □

The ANALYSIS and RE-CHECK algorithms assume that the three-valued LTL semantics is considered. While the thorough LTL semantics [10] has been shown to provide an evaluation of formulae that better reflects the natural intuition, the two semantics coincide in the case of self-minimizing LTL formulae. In this case, our results are correct also w.r.t. the thorough semantics. Note that, as shown in [24], most practically useful LTL formulae are self-minimizing. Future work will consider how to extend the ANALYSIS and RE-CHECK to completely support the thorough LTL semantics.

6 Evaluation

We implemented TOrPEDO as a Scala stand alone application and made it available online [62]. We evaluated how the ANALYSIS helps in creating models revisions and how frequently running the RE-CHECK algorithm allows the user to avoid the re-execution of the ANALYSIS algorithm from scratch.

We considered a set of example PKSs proposed in the literature to evaluate the $\chi Chek$ [20] model checker and defined a set of properties (see Table 4) inspired by the original properties and based on the LTL property patterns [18].[5]

ANALYSIS support (❷). We checked how the size of the proofs compares w.r.t. the size of the original models. Intuitively, since the proofs represent constraints

---

[5] The original properties used in the examples were specified in Computation Tree Logic (CTL), which is currently not supported by TOrPEDO.

Table 5: Cardinalities $|S|$, $|R|$, $|AP|$, $|?|$, and $|M|$ are those of the evaluated model M. $|\Omega_p|_x$ is the size of proof Ω_p for a property p; x indicates if Ω_p is a $\top$-TP or a ?-TP.

						ANALYSIS					RE-CHECK				
Model	$\|S\|$	$\|R\|$	$\|AP\|$	$\|?\|$	$\|M\|$	$\|\Omega_{\phi_1}\|$	$\|\Omega_{\phi_2}\|$	$\|\Omega_{\phi_3}\|$	$\|\Omega_{\phi_4}\|$	$\|\Omega_{\phi_5}\|$	ϕ_1	ϕ_2	ϕ_3	ϕ_4	ϕ_5
callee-1	5	15	3	7	31	$7_?$	$9_?$	$21_?$	$23_?$	$23_?$	-	-	-	-	-
callee-2	5	15	3	4	31	$7_?$	$9_?$	$21_?$	$22_\top$	×	✓	✓	✓	✓	✗
callee-3	5	15	3	2	31	$7_?$	$9_?$	$21_?$	$23_\top$	×	✓	✓	✓	✓	-
callee-4	5	15	3	0	31	×	×	$23_\top$	$21_\top$	×	✗	✗	✓	✓	-
Model	$\|S\|$	$\|R\|$	$\|AP\|$	$\|?\|$	$\|M\|$	$\|\Omega_{\psi_1}\|$	$\|\Omega_{\psi_2}\|$	$\|\Omega_{\psi_3}\|$	$\|\Omega_{\psi_4}\|$	$\|\Omega_{\psi_5}\|$	ψ_1	ψ_2	ψ_3	ψ_4	ψ_5
caller-1	6	21	5	4	52	$28_?$	×	$2_\top$	$9_?$	$28_?$	-	-	-	-	-
caller-2	7	22	5	4	58	$30_?$	×	$2_\top$	$9_?$	$30_?$	✓	-	✓	✓	✓
caller-3	6	19	5	1	50	$26_\top$	$28_\top$	$2_\top$	$11_\top$	$26_\top$	✓	-	✓	✓	✓
caller-4	6	21	5	0	52	$28_\top$	×	$2_\top$	$9_\top$	$28_\top$	✓	✗	✓	✓	✓
Model	$\|S\|$	$\|R\|$	$\|AP\|$	$\|?\|$	$\|M\|$	$\|\Omega_{\eta_1}\|$	$\|\Omega_{\eta_2}\|$	$\|\Omega_{\eta_3}\|$	$\|\Omega_{\eta_4}\|$	$\|\Omega_{\eta_5}\|$	η_1	η_2	η_3	η_4	η_5
caller-callee-1	6	30	6	30	61	$37_?$	$2_\top$	$15_?$	$37_?$	×	-	-	-	-	-
caller-callee-2	7	35	6	36	78	$43_?$	$2_\top$	$18_?$	$43_?$	×	✓	✓	✓	✓	-
caller-callee-3	7	45	6	38	88	$53_?$	$2_\top$	$53_?$	$53_?$	$53_?$	✓	✓	✓	✓	-
caller-callee-4	6	12	4	0	42	×	×	×	$19_\top$	×	✗	✗	✗	✓	✗

that, if satisfied, ensure that the property is not violated (or possible violated), the smaller are the proofs the more flexibility the designer has, as more elements can be changed during the revision. The size of a PKS $M = \langle S, R, S_0, AP, L \rangle$ was defined as $|M| = |AP| * |S| + |R| + |S_0|$. The size of a proof Ω was defined as $|\Omega| = \sum_{c \in \Omega} |c|$ where: $|c| = 1$ if $c = \langle s, \alpha, v \rangle$; $|c| = |T|$ if $c = \langle s, T \rangle$, and $|c| = |S_0|$ if $c = \langle S_0 \rangle$. Table 5 summarizes the obtained results (columns under the label ANALYSIS). We show the cardinalities $|S|$, $|R|$ and $|AP|$ of the sets of states, transitions, and atomic propositions of each considered PKS M, the number $|?|$ of couples of a state s with an atomic proposition α such that $L(s, \alpha) =?$, the total size $|M|$ of the model, and the size $|\Omega_p|_x$ of the proofs, where p indicates the considered LTL property and x indicates whether p is satisfied ($x = \top$) or possibly satisfied ($x = ?$). Proofs are $\approx 60\%$ smaller than their respective initial models. Thus, we conclude that the proofs are significantly coincise w.r.t. the original model enabling a flexible design.

RE-CHECK support (**3**). We checked how the results output by the RE-CHECK algorithm were useful in producing PKSs revisions. To evaluate the usefulness we assumed that, for each category of examples, the designer produced revisions following the order specified in Table 5. The columns under the label RE-CHECK contain the different properties that have been analyzed for each category. A cell contains ✓ if the RE-CHECK was passed by the considered revised model, i.e., a **true** value was returned by the RE-CHECK algorithm, ✗ otherwise. The *dash* symbol - is used when the model of the corresponding line is not a revision (i.e., the first model of each category) or when the observed property was false in the previous model, i.e., an x-TP was not produced. We inspected the results produced by the RE-CHECK algorithm to evaluate their benefit in verifying if revisions were violating the proofs. Table 5 shows that, in $\approx 32\%$ of the cases, the TOrPEDO RE-CHECK notified the designer that the proposed revision violated some of the clauses contained in the Ω-proof, while in $\approx 78\%$ the RE-CHECK allowed designers to avoid re-runnning the ANALYSIS (and thus the model checker).

Scalability. The ANALYSIS phase of TOrPEDO combines three-valued model checking and UCs computation, therefore its scalability improves as the performance of frameworks enhances. Three-valued model checking is as expensive as classical model checking [9], i.e., it is linear in the size of the model and exponential in the size of the property. UCs computation is FPSPACE complete [55]. In our cases running TOrPEDO required on average 8.1s and for the callee examples, 8.2s for the caller examples, and 7.15s for the caller-callee examples.[6] However, while model checking is currently supported by very efficient techniques, UCs computation of LTL formulae is still far from being applicable in complex scenarios. For example, we manually designed an additional PKS with 10 states and 5 atomic propositions and 26 transitions and defined a property satisfied by the PKS and with a ⊤-TP proof that requires every state of the PKS to be constrained by a TPP-clause. We run TOrPEDO and measure the time required to compute this proof. Computing the proof required 1m33s. This results show that TOrPEDO has a limited scalability due to the low efficiency of the procedure that extracts the unsatisfiable core. For an analysis of the scalability of the extraction of the unsatisfiable core the interested reader can refer to [58]. We believe that reporting the current lack of FM techniques to support the proposed framework (that, as just discussed, is effective in our preliminary evaluation), is a further contribution of this paper.

7 Related work

Partial knowledge has been considered in requirement analysis and elicitation [46,45,38,13], in novel robotic planners [40,41,43], software models [66,65,22,1], and testing [15,63,67]. Several researchers analyzed the model checking problem for partially specified systems [44,12], considering both three-valued [37,25,9,10,28] and multi-valued [30,11] semantics. Other works apply model checking to incremental program development [33,6]. However, all these model checking approaches do not provide an *explanation* on why a property is satisfied, by means of a *certificate* or *proof*. Although several works have tackled this problem [4,60,50,49,29,16], differently from this work, they mostly aim to automate proof reproducibility.

Tao and Li [61] propose a theoretical solution to model repair: the problem of finding the minimum set of states in a KS which makes a formula satisfiable. However, the problem is different from the one addressed in this paper. Furthermore, the framework is only theoretical and based on complete systems.

Approaches were proposed in the literature to provide explanations by using different artifacts. For example, some works proposed using witnesses. A witness

---

[6] Processor: 2,7 GHz Quad-Core Intel Core i7, Memory: 16 GB 2133 MHz LPDDR3.

is a path of the model that satisfies a formula of interest [7,34,48]. Other works (e.g., [31,59]) studied how to enrich counterexamples with additional information in a way that allows better understanding the property violation. Work has also been done to generate abstractions of the counterexamples that are easier to understand (e.g., [21]). Alur et al. [2] analyzed the problem of synthesizing a controller that satisfies a given specification. When the specification is not realizable, a counter-strategy is returned as a witness. Pencolé et al. [51] analyzed model consistency, i.e., the problem of checking whether the system run-time behaviour is consistent with a formal specification. Bernasconi et al. [4] proposed an approach that combines model checking and deductive proofs in a multi-valued context. The notion of topological proof proposed in this work is substantially different from the notion of deductive proof.

Some works (e.g., [52,54]) considered how to understand why a property is unsatisfiable. This problem is different from the one considered in this paper.

Approaches that detect unsatisfiable cores of propositional formulae were proposed in the literature [47,39,17,32,57]. Understanding whether these approaches can be re-used to develop more efficient techniques to detect the unsatisfiable cores of LTL formulae is definitely an interesting future work direction, which deserves to be considered in a separate work since it is far from trivial.

8 Conclusions

We have proposed TOrPEDO, an integrated framework that supports the iterative creation of model revisions. The framework provides a guide for the designer who wishes to preserve slices of her model that contribute to satisfy fundamental requirements while other parts of the model are modified. For these purposes, the notion of topological proof has been formally and algorithmically described. This corresponds to a set of constraints that, if kept when changing the proposed model, ensure that the behavior of the model w.r.t. the property of interest is preserved. Our Lemmas and Theorems prove the soundness of our framework, i.e., how it preserves correctness in the case of PKS and LTL. The proposed framework can be used as baseline for other FM frameworks, and can be extended by considering other modeling formalisms that can be mapped onto PKSs.

TOrPEDO was evaluated by showing the effectiveness of the ANALYSIS and RE-CHECK algorithms included in the framework. Results showed that proofs are smaller than the original models, and can be verified in most of the cases using a simple syntactic check, paving the way for an extensive evaluation on real case scenarios. However, the scalability of existing tools, upon which TOrPEDO is based, is not sufficient to efficiently support the proposed framework when bigger models are considered.

Acknowledgments. This work has received funding from the European Research Council under the European Union's Horizon 2020 research and innovation programme (grant agreement No 694277).

References

1. A. Albarghouthi, A. Gurfinkel, and M. Chechik. From under-approximations to over-approximations and back. In *International Conference on Tools and Algorithms for the Construction and Analysis of Systems*. Springer, 2012.

2. R. Alur, S. Moarref, and U. Topcu. Counter-strategy guided refinement of GR(1) temporal logic specifications. In *Formal Methods in Computer-Aided Design*, pages 26–33, Oct. 2013.

3. C. Baier and J.-P. Katoen. *Principles of Model Checking*. The MIT Press, 2008.

4. A. Bernasconi, C. Menghi, P. Spoletini, L. D. Zuck, and C. Ghezzi. From model checking to a temporal proof for partial models. In *International Conference on Software Engineering and Formal Methods*. Springer, 2017.

5. A. Bernasconi, C. Menghi, P. Spoletini, L. D. Zuck, and C. Ghezzi. From model checking to a temporal proof for partial models: preliminary example. *arXiv preprint arXiv:1706.02701*, 2017.

6. D. Beyer, T. A. Henzinger, R. Jhala, and R. Majumdar. The software model checker blast. *International Journal on Software Tools for Technology Transfer*, 9(5-6):505–525, 2007.

7. A. Biere, A. Cimatti, E. M. Clarke, M. Fujita, and Y. Zhu. Symbolic model checking using sat procedures instead of bdds. In *Design Automation Conference*. ACM, 1999.

8. G. Brunet, M. Chechik, S. Easterbrook, S. Nejati, N. Niu, and M. Sabetzadeh. A manifesto for model merging. In *International workshop on Global integrated model management*. ACM, 2006.

9. G. Bruns and P. Godefroid. Model checking partial state spaces with 3-valued temporal logics. In *International Conference on Computer Aided Verification*. Springer, 1999.

10. G. Bruns and P. Godefroid. Generalized model checking: Reasoning about partial state spaces. In *International Conference on Concurrency Theory*. Springer, 2000.

11. G. Bruns and P. Godefroid. Model checking with multi-valued logics. In *International Colloquium on Automata, Languages and Programming*. Springer, 2004.

12. M. Chechik, B. Devereux, S. Easterbrook, and A. Gurfinkel. Multi-valued symbolic model-checking. *Transactions on Software Engineering and Methodology*, 12(4):1–38, 2004.

13. M. Chechik, R. Salay, T. Viger, S. Kokaly, and M. Rahimi. Software assurance in an uncertain world. In R. Hähnle and W. van der Aalst, editors, *Fundamental Approaches to Software Engineering*, pages 3–21, Cham, 2019. Springer.

14. A. Cimatti, E. Clarke, E. Giunchiglia, F. Giunchiglia, M. Pistore, M. Roveri, R. Sebastiani, and A. Tacchella. Nusmv 2: An opensource tool for symbolic model checking. In *International Conference on Computer Aided Verification*. Springer, 2002.

15. P. Daca, T. A. Henzinger, W. Krenn, and D. Nickovic. Compositional specifications for ioco testing. In *International Conference on Software Testing, Verification and Validation*, pages 373–382. IEEE, 2014.

16. C. Deng and K. S. Namjoshi. Witnessing network transformations. In *International Conference on Runtime Verification*. Springer, 2017.

17. N. Dershowitz, Z. Hanna, and A. Nadel. A scalable algorithm for minimal unsatisfiable core extraction. In *International Conference on Theory and Applications of Satisfiability Testing*, pages 36–41. Springer, 2006.

18. M. B. Dwyer, G. S. Avrunin, and J. C. Corbett. Patterns in property specifications for finite-state verification. In *International Conference on Software engineering*. ACM, 1999.

19. S. Easterbrook and M. Chechik. A framework for multi-valued reasoning over inconsistent viewpoints. In *International conference on software engineering*. IEEE, 2001.

20. S. Easterbrook, M. Chechik, B. Devereux, A. Gurfinkel, A. Lai, V. Petrovykh, A. Tafliovich, and C. Thompson-Walsh. χChek: A model checker for multi-valued reasoning. In *International Conference on Software Engineering*, pages 804–805, 2003.

21. N. Een, A. Mishchenko, and N. Amla. A single-instance incremental SAT formulation of proof- and counterexample-based abstraction. In *Conference on Formal Methods in Computer-Aided Design*, FMCAD, pages 181–188. FMCAD Inc, 2010.

22. M. Famelis, R. Salay, and M. Chechik. Partial models: Towards modeling and reasoning with uncertainty. In *International Conference on Software Engineering*. IEEE, 2012.

23. H. Foster, S. Uchitel, J. Magee, and J. Kramer. Ltsa-ws: a tool for model-based verification of web service compositions and choreography. In *International conference on Software engineering*. ACM, 2006.

24. P. Godefroid and M. Huth. Model checking vs. generalized model checking: Semantic minimizations for temporal logics. In *Logic in Computer Science*. IEEE, 2005.

25. P. Godefroid, M. Huth, and R. Jagadeesan. Abstraction-based model checking using modal transition systems. In *International Conference on Concurrency Theory*. Springer, 2001.

26. P. Godefroid and R. Jagadeesan. On the expressiveness of 3-valued models. In *International Workshop on Verification, Model Checking, and Abstract Interpretation*. Springer, 2003.

27. P. Godefroid and N. Piterman. LTL generalized model checking revisited. In *Verification, Model Checking, and Abstract Interpretation*, pages 89–104. Springer, 2009.

28. P. Godefroid and N. Piterman. LTL generalized model checking revisited. *International journal on software tools for technology transfer*, 13(6):571–584, 2011.

29. A. Griggio, M. Roveri, and S. Tonetta. Certifying proofs for LTL model checking. In *Formal Methods in Computer Aided Design (FMCAD)*, pages 1–9. IEEE, 2018.

30. A. Gurfinkel and M. Chechik. Multi-valued model checking via classical model checking. In *International Conference on Concurrency Theory*. Springer, 2003.

31. A. Gurfinkel and M. Chechik. Proof-like counter-examples. In *International Conference on Tools and Algorithms for the Construction and Analysis of Systems*, pages 160–175. Springer, 2003.

32. O. Guthmann, O. Strichman, and A. Trostanetski. Minimal unsatisfiable core extraction for SMT. In *Formal Methods in Computer-Aided Design (FMCAD)*, pages 57–64. IEEE, 2016.

33. T. A. Henzinger, R. Jhala, R. Majumdar, and M. A. Sanvido. Extreme model checking. In *Verification: Theory and Practice, Essays Dedicated to Zohar Manna on the Occasion of His 64th Birthday*. Springer, 2003.

34. H. S. Hong, I. Lee, O. Sokolsky, and H. Ural. A temporal logic based theory of test coverage and generation. In *International Conference on Tools and Algorithms for the Construction and Analysis of Systems*. Springer, 2002.

35. S. A. Kripke. Semantical considerations on modal logic. *Acta Philosophica Fennica*, 16(1963):83–94, 1963.

36. O. Kupferman and M. Y. Vardi. From complementation to certification. *Theoretical computer science*, 345(1):83–100, 2005.
37. K. G. Larsen and B. Thomsen. A modal process logic. In *Logic in Computer Science*. IEEE, 1988.
38. E. Letier, J. Kramer, J. Magee, and S. Uchitel. Deriving event-based transition systems from goal-oriented requirements models. *Automated Software Engineering*, 2008.
39. M. H. Liffiton and K. A. Sakallah. Algorithms for computing minimal unsatisfiable subsets of constraints. *Journal of Automated Reasoning*, 40(1):1–33, 2008.
40. C. Menghi, S. Garcia, P. Pelliccione, and J. Tumova. Multi-robot LTL planning under uncertainty. In *Formal Methods*. Springer, 2018.
41. C. Menghi, S. García, P. Pelliccione, and J. Tumova. Towards multi-robot applications planning under uncertainty. In *International Conference on Software Engineering: Companion Proceeedings*. ACM, 2018.
42. C. Menghi, P. Spoletini, M. Chechik, and C. Ghezzi. Supporting verification-driven incremental distributed design of components. In *Fundamental Approaches to Software Engineering*. Springer, 2018.
43. C. Menghi, P. Spoletini, M. Chechik, and C. Ghezzi. A verification-driven framework for iterative design of controllers. *Formal Aspects of Computing*, Jun 2019.
44. C. Menghi, P. Spoletini, and C. Ghezzi. Dealing with incompleteness in automata-based model checking. In *Formal Methods*. Springer, 2016.
45. C. Menghi, P. Spoletini, and C. Ghezzi. COVER: Change-based Goal Verifier and Reasoner. In *International Conference on Requirements Engineering: Foundation for Software Quality: Companion Proceeedings*. Springer, 2017.
46. C. Menghi, P. Spoletini, and C. Ghezzi. Integrating goal model analysis with iterative design. In *International Working Conference on Requirements Engineering: Foundation for Software Quality*. Springer, 2017.
47. A. Nadel. Boosting minimal unsatisfiable core extraction. In *Conference on Formal Methods in Computer-Aided Design*, pages 221–229. FMCAD Inc, 2010.
48. K. S. Namjoshi. Certifying model checkers. In *Computer Aided Verification*. Springer, 2001.
49. D. Peled, A. Pnueli, and L. Zuck. From falsification to verification. In *Foundations of Software Technology and Theoretical Computer Science*. Springer, 2001.
50. D. Peled and L. Zuck. From model checking to a temporal proof. In *International SPIN Workshop on Model Checking of Software*. Springer, 2001.
51. Y. Pencolé, G. Steinbauer, C. Mühlbacher, and L. Travé-Massuyès. Diagnosing discrete event systems using nominal models only. In *DX*, pages 169–183, 2017.
52. I. Pill and T. Quaritsch. Behavioral diagnosis of LTL specifications at operator level. In *Twenty-Third International Joint Conference on Artificial Intelligence*, 2013.
53. S. Rajan, N. Shankar, and M. K. Srivas. An integration of model checking with automated proof checking. In *Computer Aided Verification*. Springer, 1995.
54. V. Raman, C. Lignos, C. Finucane, K. C. Lee, M. P. Marcus, and H. Kress-Gazit. Sorry Dave, I'm Afraid I Can't Do That: Explaining Unachievable Robot Tasks Using Natural Language. In *Robotics: Science and Systems*, volume 2, pages 2–1, 2013.
55. L. Saïs, M. Hacid, and F. Hantry. On the complexity of computing minimal unsatisfiable LTL formulas. *Electronic Colloquium on Computational Complexity (ECCC)*, 19:69, 2012.

56. V. Schuppan. Enhancing unsatisfiable cores for LTL with information on temporal relevance. *Theoretical Computer Science*, 655(Part B):155 – 192, 2016. Quantitative Aspects of Programming Languages and Systems (2013-14).

57. V. Schuppan. Enhanced unsatisfiable cores for QBF: Weakening universal to existential quantifiers. In *International Conference on Tools with Artificial Intelligence (ICTAI)*, pages 81–89. IEEE, 2018.

58. T. Sergeant, S. R. Goré, and J. Thomson. Finding minimal unsatisfiable subsets in linear temporal logic using BDDs, 2013.

59. S. Shoham and O. Grumberg. A game-based framework for ctl counterexamples and 3-valued abstraction-refinement. In *International Conference on Computer Aided Verification*, pages 275–287. Springer, 2003.

60. L. Tan and R. Cleaveland. Evidence-based model checking. In *International Conference on Computer Aided Verification*, pages 455–470. Springer, 2002.

61. X. Tao and G. Li. The complexity of linear-time temporal logic model repair. In *International Workshop on Structured Object-Oriented Formal Language and Method*, pages 69–87. Springer, 2017.

62. Torpedo. http://github.com/alessandrorizzi/torpedo, 2020.

63. J. Tretmans. Testing concurrent systems: A formal approach. In *International Conference on Concurrency Theory*, pages 46–65. Springer, 1999.

64. S. Uchitel. Partial behaviour modelling: Foundations for incremental and iterative model-based software engineering. In M. V. M. Oliveira and J. Woodcock, editors, *Formal Methods: Foundations and Applications*. Springer, 2009.

65. S. Uchitel, D. Alrajeh, S. Ben-David, V. Braberman, M. Chechik, G. De Caso, N. D'Ippolito, D. Fischbein, D. Garbervetsky, J. Kramer, et al. Supporting incremental behaviour model elaboration. *Computer Science-Research and Development*, 28(4):279–293, 2013.

66. S. Uchitel, G. Brunet, and M. Chechik. Synthesis of partial behavior models from properties and scenarios. *Transactions on Software Engineering*, 35(3):384–406, 2009.

67. M. van der Bijl, A. Rensink, and J. Tretmans. Compositional testing with ioco. In *Formal Approaches to Software Testing*, pages 86–100. Springer, 2004.

5

Computing Program Reliability using Forward-Backward Precondition Analysis and Model Counting

Aleksandar S. Dimovski[iD][1] and Axel Legay[2]

[1] Mother Teresa University, 12 Udarna Brigada 2a, 1000 Skopje, N. Macedonia
`aleksandar.dimovski@unt.edu.mk`
[2] Université catholique de Louvain, 1348 Ottignies-Louvain-la-Neuve, Belgium
`axel.legay@uclouvain.be`

Abstract. The goal of probabilistic static analysis is to quantify the probability that a given program satisfies/violates a required property (assertion). In this work, we use a static analysis by abstract interpretation and model counting to construct probabilistic analysis of deterministic programs with uncertain input data, which can be used for estimating the probabilities of assertions (*program reliability*).

In particular, we automatically infer necessary preconditions in order a given assertion to be satisfied/violated at run-time using a combination of forward and backward static analyses. The focus is on numeric properties of variables and numeric abstract domains, such as polyhedra. The obtained preconditions in the form of linear constraints are then analyzed to quantify how likely is an input to satisfy them. Model counting techniques are employed to count the number of solutions that satisfy given linear constraints. These counts are then used to assess the probability that the target assertion is satisfied/violated. We also present how to extend our approach to analyze non-deterministic programs by inferring sufficient preconditions. We built a prototype implementation and evaluate it on several interesting examples.

1 Introduction

Program verification is often concerned by only determining whether one assertion always holds at a given program point. However, there are many applications where we need to know a more fine-grained information about how likely a target assertion (event) is to be satisfied/violated. Examples of other target events include the invocation of a certain method, the access to confidential information, etc. In those cases, we want to distinguish between what is possible event (even with extremely low probability) and what is likely event (possible with higher probability). In this work, we show how to calculate the reliability of programs by using combination of static analysis by abstract interpretation and model counting. In particular, we are interested to learn how the presence of uncertainty in the inputs can affect the probability of assertions at the exit of the program.

This is an important problem to consider, since uncertainty is a common aspect of many real-world software systems today (e.g., medicine and aerospatial domains).

Abstract interpretation [6,7,8] is a general theory for approximating the semantics of programs. It provides safe (all answers are correct) and efficient (with a good trade-off between precision and cost) static analyses of run-time properties of real programs. It is based on the idea of *approximations* between concrete and abstract domains of program properties. Its practical success is mainly enabled by the design of numerical abstract domains, which reason on numerical properties of variables. For example, the interval domain [6], which is non-relational, infers the information about the possible values of individual variables; the octagon domain [25], which is weakly relational, infers unit binary linear constraints between program variables; and the polyhedra domain [10], which is fully relational, infers the linear constraints between all program variables. Abstract interpretation is a powerful technique for deriving approximate, albeit computable analyses, by using fully automatic algorithms. These abstract analyses pay the price for finite computability (always terminate) by an inevitable loss of precision. We use abstract analyses for automatic inference of (over-approximated) *invariants* by *forward analysis*, and (over-approximated) *necessary preconditions* by *backward analysis*. These two abstract analyses can be combined such that the results of the first analysis refine the results of the second one. In this work, we use a combination of forward and backward analyses to automatically generate the necessary preconditions on input variables that lead to the satisfaction/violation of a given assertion. If obtained preconditions are satisfied by some concrete values for input variables, then they represent input values that will allow the given assertion to be definitely satisfied/violated by all program executions branching from them. In fact, we run two backward analyses: the first one determines necessary preconditions for the given assertion to be satisfied, while the second one determines necessary preconditions for the given assertion to be violated.

Model counting is the problem of determining the number of solutions of a given constraint (formula). The LATTE tool [1] implements state-of-the-art algorithms for computing volumes, both real and integral, of convex polytopes as well as integrating functions over those polytopes. More specifically, we use the LATTE tool to estimate algorithmically the exact number of points of a bounded (possibly very large) discrete domain that satisfy given linear constraints.

In this paper, we describe a method which uses abstract interpretation-based static analysis and model counting to perform a specific type of quantitative analysis of deterministic programs, that is the calculation of *program reliability*. Calculating the program reliability involves counting the number of solutions to preconditions, which are given in the form of linear constraints between variables, i.e. elements from the polyhedra domain, that ensure satisfaction/violation of a given assertion by using model counting, and dividing it by the total space of values of the inputs. We assume that the input values are *uniformly distributed* within their finite discrete domain. Since the set of generated preconditions represents an over-approximation, we compute the reliability of programs as upper and lower bounds of exact probabilities that a given assertion is satisfied or violated. The reported uncertainty is due to the approximation inherent in abstract interpretation, which is introduced in order to obtain a scalable and fully automatic analysis.

The focus here is on programs whose input values range over finite discrete domains. Thus, we obtain a finite input domain and so we can use model counting algorithms to compute the required probabilities. We also restrict ourselves to the domain of linear integer arithmetic, since this is supported by LATTE and the polyhedra numeric domain we use.

We also consider an extension of our approach to non-deterministic programs. For non-deterministic programs, sufficient and necessary preconditions no more coincide [26]. Sufficient preconditions ensure that the target invariant holds for all sequences of non-deterministic choices made at each execution step, whereas necessary preconditions ensure that the target invariant holds for at least one sequence of non-deterministic choices made at each execution step. In effect, increasing the non-determinism will reduce the set of sufficient preconditions and enlarge the set of necessary preconditions. Hence, for non-deterministic programs we construct backward analyses for inferring (under-approximated) sufficient preconditions that lead to the satisfaction/violation of a given assertion. The calculation of reliability is then similar to the one for deterministic programs.

We have developed a prototype probabilistic static analyzer which uses the APRON library [21] to implement numeric property domains and the LATTE tool [1] to implement model counting algorithms. APRON provides a common high-level API to the most common numerical property domains, such as intervals, octagons, and polyhedra. We have implemented a combination of forward and backward analyses of deterministic (resp., non-deterministic) C programs for the automatic inference of *invariants* and *necessary* (resp. *sufficient*) *preconditions* in all program points. Our static analyzer has two components: (1) it computes the required preconditions in the input program point for a given assertion to be satisfied/violated, and (2) it then calls LATTE to count the number of solutions of those preconditions and calculates the program reliability.

The main contributions of this work are:

- We demonstrate how to calculate the program reliability of deterministic and non-deterministic programs using static analysis by abstract interpretation and model counting.
- We develop a probabilistic static analyzer, which uses numerical property domains from the APRON library and the LATTE model counting tool.
- Finally, we evaluate our method for probabilistic static analysis of C programs and show how to handle a set of small but compelling benchmarks.

2   Motivating Examples

Consider the program P_1 in Fig. 1. Suppose that the initial value of i ranges over the integer domain $[0, 19]$, and the initial value is independently and uniformly distributed across this range. When $(i \geq 10)$ the variable k is assigned to 12, otherwise k is assigned to 50. A forward invariant analysis will find the invariant

```
                                              void  main() {
                                              ① :      int j:=[0,9]; l_input :
void  main() {                                ② :      int i:=0;
① :      int i:=[0,19]; l_input :             ③ :      while (i < 100) {
② :      int k:=0;                            ④ :          i:=i+1;
③ :      if (i ≥ 10) k:=12; else k:=50;       ⑤ :          j:=j+1; }
l_final : assert (k ≤ 30);                    l_final : assert (j ≤ 105);
         }                                             }
```

Fig. 1: The program P_1 Fig. 2: The program P_2

$k = 12 \vee k = 50$ at point $l_{\texttt{final}}$. Therefore, the assertion ($k \leq 30$) can be satisfied (when $k = 12$) and can be violated (when $k = 50$). We are interested in inferring necessary preconditions on the input state at control point $l_{\texttt{input}}$, when the assertion is satisfied and when the assertion is violated. We back-propagate necessary conditions of satisfaction and violation of the assertion from point $l_{\texttt{final}}$ to $l_{\texttt{input}}$. A backward necessary condition analysis will infer the precondition $i \geq 10$ at point $l_{\texttt{input}}$ assuming that the assertion is satisfied, and the precondition $i < 10$ at point $l_{\texttt{input}}$ assuming that the assertion is violated. The size of the input domain is 20, since $i \in [0, 19]$. By calling LATTE to count the number of solutions to the above preconditions, we can calculate that the probability for the assertion to be satisfied (*success probability*) is: $\frac{10}{20} = 50\%$, and the probability for the assertion to be violated (*failure probability*) is: $\frac{10}{20} = 50\%$.

Consider the program P_2 in Fig. 2. A forward invariant analysis will find the invariant $100 \leq j \leq 109$ at point $l_{\texttt{final}}$, so the corresponding assertion can be satisfied (when $100 \leq j \leq 105$) and can be violated (when $105 < j \leq 109$). A backward necessary condition analysis will infer the precondition $0 \leq j \leq 5$ at point $l_{\texttt{input}}$ for the assertion to be satisfied, and the precondition $5 < j \leq 9$ at point $l_{\texttt{input}}$ for the assertion to be violated. Therefore, we can calculate that the *success probability* is: $\frac{6}{10} = 60\%$, and the *failure probability* is: $\frac{4}{10} = 40\%$.

3   Forward-Backward Precondition Analyses

We describe the combination of forward and backward analyses in the framework of abstract interpretation for inferring necessary preconditions that a given assertion is satisfied/violated. The principle of the combination is to use the result of the forward invariant analysis in the subsequent backward necessary condition analysis in order to get more precise results which are still sound.

Syntax. We consider a simple deterministic programming language that is a subset of C, which will be used to exemplify our work. The control point (location) before each statement and at the end of each block is associated to a unique label $l \in \mathbb{L}$. The syntax of the language is given by:

$s ::= \texttt{skip} \,|\, \texttt{x:=}e \,|\, \texttt{x:=}[n, n'] \,|\, s \,;\, s \,|\, \texttt{if } (e) \texttt{ then } s \texttt{ else } s \,|\, \texttt{while } (e) \texttt{ do } s \,|\, \texttt{assert}(e)$

$e ::= n \;|\; \texttt{x} \;|\; e \oplus e$

where n ranges over integers, $[n, n']$ ranges over integer intervals, x ranges over variable names *Var*, and $\oplus$ over arithmetic-logic operators. Non-deterministic interval assignment x:=$[n, n']$ represents an input statement which assigns to the input variable x a uniformly distributed random value from the interval $[n, n']$. This interval assignment can occur only in the *input section* of the program, and is used to model input uncertainties. The set of all generated statements s is denoted by *Stm*, whereas the set of all expressions e is denoted by *Exp*. We assume l_{input} is the location after the input statements (i.e. it denotes the end of the input section) and l_{final} is the location at the end of the program, where an assertion $\texttt{assert}(e_{\texttt{f}})$ is posed. Without loss of generality, a program is a sequence of statements followed by a single assertion.

Concrete semantics. A *program state* is given by a control location in $\mathbb{L}$ and an environment in $\mathcal{E} : Var \rightarrow \mathbb{Z}$ mapping each variable to its value (integer number). We write $\Sigma = \mathbb{L} \times \mathcal{E}$ to denote the set of all possible program states. Programs are modelled as transition systems $(\Sigma, \longrightarrow)$, where Σ is a set of states and $\longrightarrow \subseteq \Sigma \times \Sigma$ is a transition relation modelling atomic execution steps. The relation $\longrightarrow$ is defined by local rules, such as the following:

assignment $l_0 : \texttt{x:=}e; l_1 :: (l_0, \rho) \longrightarrow (l_1, \rho[\texttt{x} \mapsto [\![e]\!](\rho)])$, where $[\![e]\!](\rho) \in \mathbb{Z}$ is the result of the evaluation of e in the environment ρ, and $\rho[\texttt{x} \mapsto n]$ denotes the environment that updates ρ at variable x with the value n.
input $l_0 : \texttt{x:=}[n, n']; l_1 :: (l_0, \rho) \longrightarrow (l_1, \rho[\texttt{x} \mapsto n''])$, where $n'' \in [n, n']$.
conditional $l_0 : \texttt{if } (e) \texttt{ then } \{l_0^t : s; l_1^t\} \texttt{ else } \{l_0^f : s'; l_1^f\}; l_1 :: (l_0, \rho) \longrightarrow (l_0^t, \rho)$ if $[\![e]\!](\rho) \neq 0$ [3], $(l_0, \rho) \longrightarrow (l_0^f, \rho)$ if $[\![e]\!](\rho) = 0$, $(l_1^t, \rho) \longrightarrow (l_1, \rho)$, and $(l_1^f, \rho) \longrightarrow (l_1, \rho)$.
loop $l_0 : \texttt{while } (e) \texttt{ do } \{l_0^t : s; l_1^t\}; l_1 :: (l_0, \rho) \longrightarrow (l_0^t, \rho)$ if $[\![e]\!](\rho) \neq 0$, $(l_0, \rho) \longrightarrow (l_1, \rho)$ if $[\![e]\!](\rho) = 0$, and $(l_1^t, \rho) \longrightarrow (l_0, \rho)$. [4]

Let $\mathbb{E} \subseteq \mathcal{E}$ be the set of input environments obtained after executing the input statements. The set of input states is $\mathcal{I} = \{(l_{\text{input}}, \rho) \mid \rho \in \mathbb{E}\}$. The invariant inference (reachability) problem consists of finding out the possible environments (values of all variables) that may arise at each control location. The concrete semantic domain is the complete lattice of the powerset of states $(\mathcal{P}(\Sigma), \subseteq, \cup, \cap, \emptyset, \Sigma)$, and the concrete semantics in the form of invariant states encountered branching from $\mathcal{I}$, denoted $\texttt{inv}(\mathcal{I})$, is:

$$\texttt{inv}(\mathcal{I}) = \texttt{lfp}_{\mathcal{I}} \lambda X.X \cup \texttt{post}(X)$$

where $\texttt{post}(X) = \{\sigma \in \Sigma \mid \exists \sigma' \in X.\sigma' \longrightarrow \sigma\}$ and $\texttt{lfp}_{\mathcal{I}} f$ is the least fixed point of the function f greater than $\mathcal{I}$.

In this work, we consider the problem of inferring necessary preconditions. Assume that a program exits with $l_{\text{final}} : \texttt{assert}(e_{\texttt{f}})$. We want to distinguish

---

[3] Following the convention popularized by C, we model Boolean values as integers, with zero interpreted as false and everything else as true.
[4] Note that control moves from the final label l_1^t of s to the initial label l_0 of $\texttt{while}$.

between program termination that leads to the satisfaction of the final assertion at $l_{\texttt{final}}$ from the one that leads to the violation of the final assertion at $l_{\texttt{final}}$. Let $\mathcal{F}_{sat} = \{(l, \rho) \in \texttt{inv}(\mathcal{I}) \mid l = l_{\texttt{final}} \implies [\![e_{\texttt{f}}]\!](\rho) \neq 0\}$ and $\mathcal{F}_{viol} = \{(l, \rho) \in \texttt{inv}(\mathcal{I}) \mid l = l_{\texttt{final}} \implies [\![e_{\texttt{f}}]\!](\rho) = 0\}$ be the invariant sets which enforce the assertion at the point $l_{\texttt{final}}$ to be satisfied and violated, respectively, and coincide with $\texttt{inv}(\mathcal{I})$ everywhere else. In the following, $\mathcal{F}$ may represent either $\mathcal{F}_{sat}$ or $\mathcal{F}_{viol}$. Given an invariant set $\mathcal{F}$ to obey, we want to infer the set of input states $\texttt{cond}(\mathcal{F})$ that guarantee that all program executions stay in $\mathcal{F}$:

$$\texttt{cond}(\mathcal{F}) = \texttt{gfp}_{\mathcal{F}} \lambda X. X \cap \texttt{pre}(X)$$

where $\texttt{pre}(X) = \{\sigma \in \Sigma \mid \exists \sigma' \in X. \sigma \longrightarrow \sigma'\}$ is the set of predecessors of X, and $\texttt{gfp}_{\mathcal{F}} f$ is the greatest fixed point of the function f smaller than $\mathcal{F}$. The above two fixed points ($\texttt{lfp}$ and $\texttt{gfp}$) exist according to Tarski, as the corresponding functions are monotone and continuous in the complete lattice of state sets.

Given a set of input environments $\mathbb{E} \subseteq \mathcal{E}$, we can compute the subsets $\mathbb{E}_{sat}$ and $\mathbb{E}_{viol}$ of input environments that lead to satisfaction and violation of the final assertion as:

$$\mathbb{E}_{sat} = \mathbb{E} \cap \{\rho \mid (l_{\texttt{input}}, \rho) \in \texttt{cond}(\mathcal{F}_{sat})\}, \mathbb{E}_{viol} = \mathbb{E} \cap \{\rho \mid (l_{\texttt{input}}, \rho) \in \texttt{cond}(\mathcal{F}_{viol})\}$$

Abstract semantics. Transition systems can become large or infinite for real programs, so that neither $\texttt{inv}(\mathcal{I})$ nor $\texttt{cond}(\mathcal{F})$ can be computed at all. Therefore, we seek for sound approximations. The actual computable abstract analyses can be defined as over-approximations of the concrete semantics. A static analyzer will infer over-approximated necessary preconditions so that all program executions that lead to satisfaction (resp., violation) of the final assertion are taken into account, thus computing an over-approximation of $\mathbb{E}_{sat}$ (resp., $\mathbb{E}_{viol}$).

We consider an abstract domain $(\mathbb{D}, \sqsubseteq_{\mathbb{D}})$, such that there exist a Galois connection [5] $\langle \mathcal{P}(\mathcal{E}), \subseteq \rangle \xleftarrow{\gamma_{\mathbb{D}}}_{\alpha_{\mathbb{D}}} \langle \mathbb{D}, \sqsubseteq_{\mathbb{D}} \rangle$. We assume that the abstract domain $\mathbb{D}$ is equipped with sound operators for ordering $\sqsubseteq_{\mathbb{D}}$, least upper bound (join) $\sqcup_{\mathbb{D}}$, greatest lower bound (meet) $\sqcap_{\mathbb{D}}$, bottom $\perp_{\mathbb{D}}$, top $\top_{\mathbb{D}}$, widening $\triangledown_{\mathbb{D}}$, and narrowing $\triangle_{\mathbb{D}}$, as well as sound transfer functions for assignments $\overrightarrow{\texttt{assign}}_{\mathbb{D}} : Var \times Exp \times \mathbb{D} \to \mathbb{D}$, tests $\texttt{filter}_{\mathbb{D}} : Exp \times \mathbb{D} \to \mathbb{D}$, and backward assignments $\overleftarrow{\texttt{b-assign}}_{\mathbb{D}} : Var \times Exp \times \mathbb{D} \times \mathbb{D} \to \mathbb{D}$. We let $\texttt{lfp}^{\#}$ (resp., $\texttt{gfp}^{\#}$) denote an abstract post-fixpoint (resp., pre-fixpoint) operator, derived using widening $\triangledown_{\mathbb{D}}$ and narrowing $\triangle_{\mathbb{D}}$, that over-approximates the concrete $\texttt{lfp}$ (resp., $\texttt{gfp}$) [8]. Finally, the concrete domain on which concrete semantics is defined $(\mathcal{P}(\Sigma), \subseteq)$ is abstracted using a Galois connection $\langle \mathcal{P}(\Sigma), \subseteq \rangle \xleftarrow{\gamma}_{\alpha} \langle \mathbb{L} \to \mathbb{D}, \dot{\sqsubseteq} \rangle$ where $\alpha(R) = \lambda l \in \mathbb{L}. \sqcup_{\mathbb{D}} \{d \in \mathbb{D} \mid (l, \rho) \in R, \alpha_{\mathbb{D}}(\rho) = d\}$. Hence, each control point $l \in \mathbb{L}$ is associated with an element $d \in \mathbb{D}$ in the abstract semantics.

---

[5] $\langle L, \leq_L \rangle \xleftarrow{\gamma}_{\alpha} \langle M, \leq_M \rangle$ is a *Galois connection* between complete lattices L and M iff α and γ are total functions that satisfy: $\alpha(l) \leq_M m \iff l \leq_L \gamma(m)$ for all $l \in L, m \in M$. Here $\leqslant_L$ and $\leqslant_M$ are the pre-order relations for L and M, respectively.

We define a family of forward transfer functions $\overrightarrow{\delta}_{l,l'} : \mathbb{D} \to \mathbb{D}$ that compute the effect of any concrete transition at the abstract level. The definition of $\overrightarrow{\delta}_{l,l'}$ for some statements is:

assignment $l_0 : \mathtt{x:=}e; l_1 :: \overrightarrow{\delta}_{l_0,l_1}(d) = \overrightarrow{\mathtt{assign}}_{\mathbb{D}}(\mathtt{x}, e, d)).$

conditional $l_0 : \mathtt{if}\ (e)\ \mathtt{then}\ \{l_0^t : s; l_1^t\}\ \mathtt{else}\ \{l_0^f : s'; l_1^f\}; l_1 :: \overrightarrow{\delta}_{l_0,l_0^t}(d) = \overrightarrow{\mathtt{filter}}_{\mathbb{D}}(e, d), \overrightarrow{\delta}_{l_0,l_0^f}(d) = \overrightarrow{\mathtt{filter}}_{\mathbb{D}}(\neg e, d), \overrightarrow{\delta}_{l_1^t, l_1}(d) = d, \overrightarrow{\delta}_{l_1^f, l_1}(d) = d.$

loop $l_0 : \mathtt{while}\ (e)\ \mathtt{do}\ \{l_0^t : s; l_1^t\}; l_1 :: \overrightarrow{\delta}_{l_0,l_0^t}(d) = \overrightarrow{\mathtt{filter}}_{\mathbb{D}}(e, d), \overrightarrow{\delta}_{l_0,l_1}(d) = \overrightarrow{\mathtt{filter}}_{\mathbb{D}}(\neg e, d),$ and $\overrightarrow{\delta}_{l_1^t, l_0}(d) = d.$

The soundness of $\{\overrightarrow{\delta}_{l,l'} \mid l, l' \in \mathbb{L}\}$ is written as: $\forall d \in \mathbb{D}, \forall \rho \in \gamma_{\mathbb{D}}(d), (l, \rho) \longrightarrow (l', \rho') \implies \rho' \in \gamma_{\mathbb{D}}(\overrightarrow{\delta}_{l,l'}(d)).$

Suppose that the abstract element $\alpha_{\mathbb{D}}(\mathbb{E}) = d_{\mathtt{input}} \in \mathbb{D}$ is at the input control point $l_{\mathtt{input}}$. We can collect the abstractions of possible environments at each program control point using the following forward interpreter:

$$\overrightarrow{F}^{\#} = \lambda I . \lambda (l \in \mathbb{L}). \sqcup_{\mathbb{D}} \{\overrightarrow{\delta}_{l',l}(I(l')) \mid l' \in \mathbb{L}\}$$

such that the result of the forward analyzer is $\overrightarrow{\mathcal{I}}^{\#} = \mathtt{lfp}_{I_0}^{\#} \overrightarrow{F}^{\#}$, where $I_0(l_{\mathtt{input}}) = d_{\mathtt{input}}$. Assume that $\mathtt{lfp}_{I_0}^{\#} \overrightarrow{F}^{\#}(l_{\mathtt{final}}) = d_{\mathtt{final}}$. Let $d_{\mathtt{final}}^{sat} = \overrightarrow{\mathtt{filter}}_{\mathbb{D}}(e, d_{\mathtt{final}})$ and $d_{\mathtt{final}}^{viol} = \overrightarrow{\mathtt{filter}}_{\mathbb{D}}(\neg e, d_{\mathtt{final}})$. We want to design two backward abstract interpreters that propagate backwards the invariants ensuring that the final assertion is satisfied $d_{\mathtt{final}}^{sat}$ and violated $d_{\mathtt{final}}^{viol}$, respectively. The backward interpreters refine the invariants found by $\overrightarrow{F}^{\#}$. Thus, they take two elements of $\mathbb{D}$ as inputs: an invariant to refine and an invariant to propagate backwards. They are based on a family of backward transfer functions $\overleftarrow{\delta}_{l,l'} : \mathbb{D} \times \mathbb{D} \to \mathbb{D}$, which map a precondition to refine and a postcondition into a refined precondition. The definition of $\overleftarrow{\delta}_{l,l'}$ for some statements is:

assignment $l_0 : \mathtt{x:=}e; l_1 :: \overleftarrow{\delta}_{l_0,l_1}(d, d') = \overleftarrow{\mathtt{b-assign}}_{\mathbb{D}}(\mathtt{x}, e, d, d').$

conditional $l_0 : \mathtt{if}\ (e)\ \mathtt{then}\ \{l_0^t : s; l_1^t\}\ \mathtt{else}\ \{l_0^f : s'; l_1^f\}; l_1 :: \overleftarrow{\delta}_{l_0,l_0^t}(d, d') = d \sqcap d',$ $\overleftarrow{\delta}_{l_0,l_0^f}(d, d') = d \sqcap d', \overleftarrow{\delta}_{l_1^t,l_1}(d, d') = d \sqcap d', \overleftarrow{\delta}_{l_1^f,l_1}(d, d') = d \sqcap d'.$

loop $l_0 : \mathtt{while}\ (e)\ \mathtt{do}\ \{l_0^t : s; l_1^t\}; l_1 :: \overleftarrow{\delta}_{l_0,l_0^t}(d, d') = d \sqcap d', \overleftarrow{\delta}_{l_0,l_1}(d, d') = d \sqcap d',$ and $\overleftarrow{\delta}_{l_1^t,l_0}(d, d') = d \sqcap d'.$

The soundness of $\{\overleftarrow{\delta}_{l,l'} \mid l, l' \in \mathbb{L}\}$ is written as: $\forall d, d' \in \mathbb{D}, \forall \rho \in \gamma_{\mathbb{D}}(d), \rho' \in \gamma_{\mathbb{D}}(d'), (l, \rho) \longrightarrow (l', \rho') \implies \rho \in \gamma_{\mathbb{D}}(\overleftarrow{\delta}_{l,l'}(d, d')).$ That is, d is refined into a stronger precondition by taking into account the postcondition d'.

Suppose that $F_{\mathbb{D}}^{sat}(l_{\mathtt{final}}) = d_{\mathtt{final}}^{sat}$, $F_{\mathbb{D}}^{viol}(l_{\mathtt{final}}) = d_{\mathtt{final}}^{viol}$, and $F_{\mathbb{D}}^{sat}(l) = F_{\mathbb{D}}^{viol}(l) = \overrightarrow{\mathcal{I}}^{\#}(l)$ for $l \neq l_{\mathtt{final}}$. The backward interpreters are defined as:

$$\overleftarrow{F}^{\#} = \lambda(I, F).\lambda(l \in \mathbb{L}). \sqcap_{\mathbb{D}} \{\overleftarrow{\delta}_{l,l'}(I(l), F(l')) \mid l' \in \mathbb{L}\}$$

such that the results of the two backward analyzers are: $\overleftarrow{C}^{\#}_{sat} = \mathtt{gfp}^{\#}_{(\overleftarrow{\mathcal{I}}^{\#}, F_{\mathbb{D}}^{sat})} \overleftarrow{F}^{\#}$
and $\overleftarrow{C}^{\#}_{viol} = \mathtt{gfp}^{\#}_{(\overleftarrow{\mathcal{I}}^{\#}, F_{\mathbb{D}}^{viol})} \overleftarrow{F}^{\#}$. The necessary preconditions that the final assertion is satisfied and violated are $d^{sat}_{\mathtt{input}} = \overleftarrow{C}^{\#}_{sat}(l_{\mathtt{input}})$ and $d^{viol}_{\mathtt{input}} = \overleftarrow{C}^{\#}_{viol}(l_{\mathtt{input}})$,
respectively. We can now compute the over-approximated sets $\mathbb{E}^{\#}_{sat}$ and $\mathbb{E}^{\#}_{viol}$ of
input environments $\mathbb{E}_{sat}$ and $\mathbb{E}_{viol}$ that lead to satisfaction and violation of the
final assertion as:

$$\mathbb{E}^{\#}_{sat} = \mathbb{E} \cap \gamma_{\mathbb{D}}(d^{sat}_{\mathtt{input}}), \quad \mathbb{E}^{\#}_{viol} = \mathbb{E} \cap \gamma_{\mathbb{D}}(d^{viol}_{\mathtt{input}})$$

such that $\mathbb{E}^{\#}_{sat} \supseteq \mathbb{E}_{sat}$ and $\mathbb{E}^{\#}_{viol} \supseteq \mathbb{E}_{viol}$.

Polyhedra numeric abstract domain. Although, the abstract domain $\mathbb{D}$ can be
instantiated with different property domains, in the following, we will use the
polyhedra numerical abstract domain for $\mathbb{D}$. This is due to the fact that only for
the polyhedra domain all necessary abstract operations and transfer functions,
such as $\overrightarrow{\mathtt{assign}}_{\mathbb{D}}$, $\overleftarrow{\mathtt{b\text{-}assign}}_{\mathbb{D}}$, $\overleftarrow{\mathtt{b\text{-}assign\text{-}under}}_{\mathbb{D}}$ (see Section 5), are implemented
in the APRON library. The *Polyhedra domain* [10], denoted as $\langle P, \sqsubseteq_P \rangle$, is a fully
relational numerical property domain, which allows manipulating conjunctions
of linear inequalities of the form $\alpha_1 x_1 + \ldots + \alpha_n x_n \geq \beta$, where $x_1, \ldots, x_n$ are
program variables and $\alpha_i, \beta \in \mathbb{R}$ (reals). The abstract operations of the *Polyhedra
domain* are defined in [10]. Polyhedra analysis is expensive but also very precise.

A property element is represented as a conjunction of linear constraints given
in the matrix form $\langle \mathbf{A}, \mathbf{b} \rangle$ that consists of a matrix $\mathbf{A} \in \mathbb{R}^{m \times n}$ and a vector
$\mathbf{b} \in \mathbb{R}^m$, where n is the number of variables and m is the number of constraints.
This is called the constraint representation of polyhedra elements, and there is
another so-called generator representation. One representation can be converted
to the other one using the Chernikova's algorithm [5]. Some domain operations
can be performed more efficiently using the generator representation only, others
based on the constraint representation, and some making use of both. We now
present some operations that can be defined using the constraint representation.

The concretization function is: $\gamma_P(\langle \mathbf{A}, \mathbf{b} \rangle) = \{\mathbf{v} \in \mathbb{R}^n \mid \mathbf{A} \cdot \mathbf{v} \geq \mathbf{b}\}$. The meet
$\sqcap_P$ is defined as: $\langle \mathbf{A_1}, \mathbf{b_1} \rangle \sqcap_P \langle \mathbf{A_2}, \mathbf{b_2} \rangle = \langle \left(\begin{smallmatrix} \mathbf{A_1} \\ \mathbf{A_2} \end{smallmatrix}\right), \left(\begin{smallmatrix} \mathbf{b_1} \\ \mathbf{b_2} \end{smallmatrix}\right) \rangle$. We also need widening
since the polyhedra domain has infinite strictly increasing chains.

$$\langle \mathbf{A_1}, \mathbf{b_1} \rangle \nabla_P \langle \mathbf{A_2}, \mathbf{b_2} \rangle = \{c \in \langle \mathbf{A_1}, \mathbf{b_1} \rangle \mid \langle \mathbf{A_2}, \mathbf{b_2} \rangle \sqsubseteq_P \{c\}\}$$

where c represents one constraint from $\langle \mathbf{A_1}, \mathbf{b_1} \rangle$. The transfer function $\overrightarrow{\mathtt{filter}}_P$
abstracts affine inequality expressions by adding them to the input polyhedra.

$$\overrightarrow{\mathtt{filter}}_P(\sum_i \alpha_i x_i \geq \beta, \langle \mathbf{A}, \mathbf{b} \rangle) = \langle \left(\begin{smallmatrix} \mathbf{A} \\ \alpha_1 \ldots \alpha_n \end{smallmatrix}\right), \left(\begin{smallmatrix} \mathbf{b} \\ \beta \end{smallmatrix}\right) \rangle$$

Example 1. Consider the program P_1 from Fig. 1. Assume that $\mathbb{D}$ is the polyhedra
domain. The input abstract element is $d_{\mathtt{input}} = (0 \leq i \leq 19)$. Using the forward
analyzer $\overrightarrow{F}^{\#}$, we obtain $d_{\mathtt{final}} = (k = 12 \vee k = 50)$, and so $d^{sat}_{\mathtt{final}} = (k = 12)$ and
$d^{viol}_{\mathtt{final}} = (k = 50)$. Using backward analyzers $\overleftarrow{F}^{\#}$, we obtain $d^{sat}_{\mathtt{input}} = (i \geq 10)$
and $d^{viol}_{\mathtt{input}} = (i < 10)$. □

4   Computing Success and Failure Probabilities

The overall goal of our approach is to answer questions about the probability of assertions at the exit of a deterministic program P. We define the *success probability* as the probability that a program terminates successfully with the target assertion being satisfied. The *failure probability* is the probability that a program hits a failure caused by the target assertion being violated.

The combination of forward and two backward analyses infers the necessary preconditions, denoted $d_{\text{input}}^{sat} = \overleftarrow{C}_{sat}^{\#}(l_{\text{input}})$ and $d_{\text{input}}^{viol} = \overleftarrow{C}_{viol}^{\#}(l_{\text{input}})$, that the target assertion is satisfied and violated, respectively. Calculating the likelihood of satisfying/violating the given assertion involves counting the number of solutions to $d_{\text{input}}^{sat}/d_{\text{input}}^{viol}$ and dividing it by the total space of possible values in its input domain $\mathbb{E}$. In particular, we use model counting techniques and LATTE tool [1] to estimate algorithmically the exact number of points of a bounded (possibly very large) discrete domain $\mathbb{E}$ that satisfy the (linear) constraints d_{input}^{sat} and d_{input}^{viol}. We restrict our attention on programs that have *finite input domains* $\mathbb{E}$ and on numeric abstract elements from the polyhedra domain expressed as *linear integer arithmetic* (LIA) constraints over program variables whose values are *uniformly distributed* over their input domain.

We use the LATTE tool to compute the number of elements of $\mathbb{E}$ that satisfy d_{input}^{sat} and d_{input}^{viol}, denoted $\#(d_{\text{input}}^{sat})$ and $\#(d_{\text{input}}^{viol})$. The size of $\mathbb{E}$, denoted $\#(\mathbb{E})$, is the product of domain's sizes of all input variables in program P. Thus, we have: $\#(\mathbb{E}) = \prod_{\mathbf{x}:=[n,n']\in P} |n'-n+1|$. Note that the exact sets of input states that lead to satisfaction and violation of the given assertion are $\mathbb{E}_{sat}$ and $\mathbb{E}_{viol}$, and their sizes are denoted $\#(\mathbb{E}_{sat})$ and $\#(\mathbb{E}_{viol})$. Since the found necessary preconditions d_{input}^{sat} and d_{input}^{viol} are over-approximations of $\mathbb{E}_{sat}$ and $\mathbb{E}_{viol}$ respectively, we have $\#(\mathbb{E}_{sat}) \leq \#(d_{\text{input}}^{sat})$ and $\#(\mathbb{E}_{viol}) \leq \#(d_{\text{input}}^{viol})$. Moreover, the input environments which are not in $\gamma_{\mathbb{D}}(d_{\text{input}}^{sat})$, that is they are in $\mathbb{E}\backslash\gamma_{\mathbb{D}}(d_{\text{input}}^{sat})$, definitely lead to the violation of the assertion. Therefore, we have $\#(\mathbb{E}) - \#(d_{\text{input}}^{sat}) \leq \#(\mathbb{E}_{viol}) \leq \#(d_{\text{input}}^{viol})$. By similar reasoning as above, we can also establish that: $\#(\mathbb{E}) - \#(d_{\text{input}}^{viol}) \leq \#(\mathbb{E}_{sat}) \leq \#(d_{\text{input}}^{sat})$. Finally, we calculate the *success* and *failure probability* of a program P as follows:

$$\begin{aligned}\frac{\#(\mathbb{E})-\#(d_{\text{input}}^{viol})}{\#(\mathbb{E})} \leq \mathbf{Pr^s}(\mathbf{P}) = \frac{\#(\mathbb{E}_{sat})}{\#(\mathbb{E})} \leq \frac{\#(d_{\text{input}}^{sat})}{\#(\mathbb{E})}\\[2mm]\frac{\#(\mathbb{E})-\#(d_{\text{input}}^{sat})}{\#(\mathbb{E})} \leq \mathbf{Pr^f}(\mathbf{P}) = \frac{\#(\mathbb{E}_{viol})}{\#(\mathbb{E})} \leq \frac{\#(d_{\text{input}}^{viol})}{\#(\mathbb{E})}\end{aligned} \tag{1}$$

Note that $Pr^s(P) + Pr^f(P) = 1$.

Example 2. Consider the program P_1 from Fig. 1. We have $\mathbb{E} = \{[\mathbf{i} \mapsto n] \mid n \in [0, 19]\}$, and so $\#(\mathbb{E}) = 20$. Using forward and two backward analyses, we obtain $d_{\text{input}}^{sat} = (\mathbf{i} \geq 10)$ and $d_{\text{input}}^{viol} = (\mathbf{i} < 10)$, and so $\#(d_{\text{input}}^{sat}) = 10$ and $\#(d_{\text{input}}^{viol}) = 10$. Thus, the success and failure probabilities are:

$$Pr^s(P_1) = \frac{10}{20} \, (50\%), \quad \text{and} \quad Pr^f(P_1) = \frac{10}{20} \, (50\%) \qquad \square$$

We use model counting and the LATTE tool [1] to determine the number of solutions of a given constraint. LATTE accepts LIA constraints expressed as a system of linear inequalities each of which defines a hyperplane encoded as the matrix inequality: $Ax \leq B$, where A is an $m \times n$ matrix of coefficients and B is an $m \times 1$ column vector of constants. Most LIA constraints can easily be converted into the form: $a_1 x_1 + \ldots + a_n x_n \leq b$. For example, $\geq$ and $>$ can be flipped by multiplying both sides by -1, and strict inequalities $<$ can be converted by decrementing the constant b. In LATTE, equalities $=$ can be expressed directly. If we have disequalities $\neq$, they can be handled by counting a set of constraints that encode all possible solutions. For example, the constraint $\alpha \wedge (x_1 \neq x_2)$ is handled by finding the sum of solutions for $\alpha \wedge (x_1 \leq x_2 - 1)$ and $\alpha \wedge (x_1 \geq x_2 + 1)$. For a system $Ax \leq B$, where A is an $m \times n$ matrix and B is an $m \times 1$ column vector, the input LATTE file is:

$$\begin{array}{cc} m & n+1 \\ B & -A \end{array}$$

where the first line indicates the matrix size: the number of inequalities m by the number of variables n plus one. The following lines encode all inequalities.

5 Extension to non-deterministic programs

Let us reconsider the program P_2 from Fig. 2, where the assignment in point ⑤ is now replaced with: j:=j+[0,1]. That is, the variable j is incremented by a uniformly distributed random integer between 0 and 1 at each iteration. We denote this non-deterministic program as P_3 (taken from [26]), given below:

```
void  main() {
①:     int j:=[0,9]; l_input :
②:     int i:=0;
③:     while (i < 100) {
④:         i:=i+1;
⑤:         j:=j+[0,1]; }
l_final : assert (j ≤ 105); }
```

A forward invariant analysis will find that at l_{final} holds: $0 \leq j \leq 109$, and so the assertion $(j \leq 105)$ can be both satisfied and violated. A backward necessary condition analysis for assertion satisfaction will infer the precondition $0 \leq j \leq 9$ at l_{input}, since for any value $j \in [0, 9]$ there exists an program execution satisfying the assertion (e.g., consider the executions where the random integer from $[0, 1]$ always evaluates to 0 in the body of while). However, a *backward sufficient condition analysis* for assertion satisfaction computes the set of input states such that all program executions branching from them satisfy the assertion. In this case, the sufficient condition analysis will infer the precondition $0 \leq j \leq 5$ at l_{input}, since even if the random integer from $[0, 1]$ always evaluates to 1 in the body of while, the assertion will always hold. As a result of this, we can conclude that the success probability is greater or equal to: $\frac{6}{10} = 60\%$.

We can see that necessary and sufficient preconditions are different in the presence of non-determinism [26]. Note that, if the non-determinism is increased in a program, then the set of sufficient preconditions will be reduced, while the set of necessary preconditions will be enlarged. For non-deterministic programs, $\mathbb{E}_{sat}$ and $\mathbb{E}_{viol}$ are subsets of input environments $\mathbb{E}$ that definitely lead to satisfaction and violation of the final assertion for all possible non-deterministic choices, respectively. We define the *success probability* $Pr^s(P)$ as the probability that a program terminates successfully with the target assertion being satisfied for all possible non-deterministic choices taken at each step. The *failure probability* $Pr^f(P)$ is the probability that a program hits a failure caused by the target assertion being violated for all possible non-deterministic choices taken at each step. We now show how to compute the success and failure probabilities for non-deterministic programs using sufficient conditions.

Remark. Note that in case of deterministic programs, $\mathbb{E}_{sat}$ and $\mathbb{E}_{viol}$ form a partition of the set of input environments $\mathbb{E}$ ($\mathbb{E}_{sat} \cup \mathbb{E}_{viol} = \mathbb{E}$), thus we have $Pr^s(P) + Pr^f(P) = 1$ for any deterministic program P. However, for non-deterministic programs this is not true anymore. That is, $\mathbb{E}_{sat} \cup \mathbb{E}_{viol} \subseteq \mathbb{E}$ and $Pr^s(P) + Pr^f(P) \leq 1$ for any non-deterministic program P. This means that there exist input environments for which it is possible the target assertion to be both satisfied and violated depending on non-deterministic choices made at each step of the given execution. For example, in the above program P_3, for input environments that satisfy $6 \leq j \leq 9$, the target assertion is satisfied (when $[0, 1]$ in the body of `while` always evaluates to 0) and violated (when $[0, 1]$ in the body of `while` always evaluates to 1), so those input environments are neither in $\mathbb{E}_{sat}$ nor in $\mathbb{E}_{viol}$. We have, $\mathbb{E}_{sat} = \{\rho \mid 0 \leq [\![j]\!]\rho \leq 5\}$ and $\mathbb{E}_{viol} = \emptyset$, thus $Pr^s(P_3) = 60\%$ and $Pr^f(P_3) = 0\%$.

Syntax. The extended non-deterministic programming language includes the same expression and statement productions as previously (see Section 3), but we add a support for non-deterministic expressions by using integer intervals $[n, n']$:

$$e ::= \ldots \mid [n, n']$$

The integer interval $[n, n']$ denotes a uniformly distributed random integer from the interval $[n, n']$ (non-deterministic choice of an integer). Note that the interval assignment `x:=`$[n, n']$ can now be freely used everywhere in programs, not only in the input section as in deterministic programs.

Concrete semantics. We now consider the problem of backward sufficient condition inference. Given an invariant set $\mathcal{F}$ to obey, we want to infer the set of input states $\mathtt{cond}(\mathcal{F})$ that guarantee that all program executions branching from them for all possible non-deterministic choices taken at each step stay in $\mathcal{F}$:

$$\mathtt{cond}(\mathcal{F}) = \mathtt{gfp}_{\mathcal{F}} \lambda X. X \cap \widetilde{\mathtt{pre}}(X)$$

where $\widetilde{\mathtt{pre}}(X) = \{\sigma \in \Sigma \mid \forall \sigma' \in \Sigma. \sigma \longrightarrow \sigma' \implies \sigma' \in X\}$ is the set of states which represent predecessors only of states in X. Note that the function $\widetilde{\mathtt{pre}}(X)$

differs from the function $\mathtt{pre}(X)$ used in Section 3, that is $\widetilde{\mathtt{pre}}(X) \neq \mathtt{pre}(X)$, if the transition system is non-deterministic (i.e. some states have several successors or none). Using $\widetilde{\mathtt{pre}}(X)$ ensures that the invariant set $\mathcal{F}$ holds for all sequences of non-deterministic choices made at each execution step, while $\mathtt{pre}(X)$ ensures that the invariant set $\mathcal{F}$ holds for at least one sequence of non-deterministic choices. Note that $\widetilde{\mathtt{pre}}(X) = \mathtt{pre}(X)$ for deterministic programs, since $|\mathtt{post}(\{\sigma\})| = 1$ for every state $\sigma \in \Sigma$ in this case.

Abstract semantics. In order to compute an *under-approximating set of sufficient preconditions*, we require an abstract domain $\mathbb{D}$ with the following backward abstract operators: meet $\sqcap_{\mathbb{D}}^{\mathtt{under}}$, backward assignment $\overleftarrow{\mathtt{b\text{-}assign\text{-}under}}_{\mathbb{D}} : Var \times Exp \times \mathbb{D} \times \mathbb{D} \to \mathbb{D}$, backward tests $\overleftarrow{\mathtt{b\text{-}filter\text{-}under}}_{\mathbb{D}} : Exp \times \mathbb{D} \times \mathbb{D} \to \mathbb{D}$, and a lower widening $\underline{\triangledown}_{\mathbb{D}}$ [26]. The above abstract operators represent a sound under-approximation of the corresponding concrete operators. We let $\mathtt{gfp}^{\#\mathtt{under}}$ denote an abstract pre-fixpoint operator, derived using lower widening $\underline{\triangledown}_{\mathbb{D}}$, that under-approximates the concrete $\mathtt{gfp}$.

We design two backward sufficient condition abstract interpreters that propagate backwards the invariants ensuring that the final assertion is satisfied $d_{\mathtt{final}}^{sat}$ and violated $d_{\mathtt{final}}^{viol}$, respectively. They are based on a family of backward transfer functions $\overleftarrow{\delta}_{l,l'}^{\,\mathtt{under}} : \mathbb{D} \times \mathbb{D} \to \mathbb{D}$, which for some statements are defined as:

- assignment $l_0 : \mathtt{x}\!:=\!e; l_1$: $\overleftarrow{\delta}_{l_0,l_1}^{\,\mathtt{under}}(d, d') = \overleftarrow{\mathtt{b\text{-}assign\text{-}under}}_{\mathbb{D}}(\mathtt{x}, e, d, d')$
- if statement $l_0 : \mathtt{if}\ (e)\ \mathtt{then}\ \{l_0^t : s; l_1^t\}\ \mathtt{else}\ \{l_0^f : s'; l_1^f\}; l_1$: $\overleftarrow{\delta}_{l_0,l_0^t}(d, d') = \overleftarrow{\mathtt{b\text{-}filter\text{-}under}}_{\mathbb{D}}(e, d, d')$, $\overleftarrow{\delta}_{l_0,l_0^f}(d, d') = \overleftarrow{\mathtt{b\text{-}filter\text{-}under}}_{\mathbb{D}}(\neg e, d, d')$, and $\overleftarrow{\delta}_{l_1^t,l_1}(d, d') = d \sqcap d'$, $\overleftarrow{\delta}_{l_1^f,l_1}(d, d') = d \sqcap d'$
- $l_0 : \mathtt{while}\ (e)\ \mathtt{do}\ \{l_0^t : s; l_1^t\}; l_1$: $\overleftarrow{\delta}_{l_0,l_0^t}(d, d') = \overleftarrow{\mathtt{b\text{-}filter\text{-}under}}_{\mathbb{D}}(e, d, d')$, $\overleftarrow{\delta}_{l_0,l_1}(d, d') = \overleftarrow{\mathtt{b\text{-}filter\text{-}under}}_{\mathbb{D}}(\neg e, d, d')$, and $\overleftarrow{\delta}_{l_1^t,l_0}(d, d') = d \sqcap d'$.

The soundness of $\{\overleftarrow{\delta}_{l,l'}^{\,\mathtt{under}} \mid l, l' \in \mathbb{L}\}$ is written as: $\forall d, d' \in \mathbb{D}, \forall \rho \in \gamma_{\mathbb{D}}(d), \rho' \in \gamma_{\mathbb{D}}(d'), \rho \in \gamma_{\mathbb{D}}(\overleftarrow{\delta}_{l,l'}(d, d')) \implies (l, \rho) \longrightarrow (l', \rho')$.

The backward sufficient condition interpreters are defined as:

$$\overleftarrow{F}^{\#\mathtt{under}} = \lambda(I, F).\lambda(l \in \mathbb{L}).\sqcap_{\mathbb{D}}^{\mathtt{under}}\{\overleftarrow{\delta}_{l,l'}^{\,\mathtt{under}}(I(l), F(l')) \mid l' \in \mathbb{L}\}$$

such that results of backward analyzers are: $\overleftarrow{C}_{sat}^{\#\mathtt{under}} = \mathtt{gfp}_{(\overrightarrow{\mathcal{I}}\#, F_{\mathbb{D}}^{sat})}^{\#\mathtt{under}} \overleftarrow{F}^{\#\mathtt{under}}$ and $\overleftarrow{C}_{viol}^{\#\mathtt{under}} = \mathtt{gfp}_{(\overrightarrow{\mathcal{I}}\#, F_{\mathbb{D}}^{viol})}^{\#\mathtt{under}} \overleftarrow{F}^{\#\mathtt{under}}$. The sufficient preconditions that the final assertion is satisfied and violated are $d_{\mathtt{input}}^{sat,\mathtt{under}} = \overleftarrow{C}_{sat}^{\#\mathtt{under}}(l_{\mathtt{input}})$ and $d_{\mathtt{input}}^{viol,\mathtt{under}} = \overleftarrow{C}_{viol}^{\#\mathtt{under}}(l_{\mathtt{input}})$, respectively. We can now compute the under-approximated sets $\mathbb{E}_{sat}^{\#\mathtt{under}}$ and $\mathbb{E}_{viol}^{\#\mathtt{under}}$ of input environments $\mathbb{E}_{sat}$ and $\mathbb{E}_{viol}$ that definitely lead to satisfaction and violation of the final assertion as:

$$\mathbb{E}_{sat}^{\#\mathtt{under}} = \mathbb{E} \cap \gamma_{\mathbb{D}}(d_{\mathtt{input}}^{sat,\mathtt{under}}), \quad \mathbb{E}_{viol}^{\#\mathtt{under}} = \mathbb{E} \cap \gamma_{\mathbb{D}}(d_{\mathtt{input}}^{viol,\mathtt{under}})$$

such that $\mathbb{E}_{sat}^{\#\mathtt{under}} \subseteq \mathbb{E}_{sat}$ and $\mathbb{E}_{viol}^{\#\mathtt{under}} \subseteq \mathbb{E}_{viol}$.

Computing success and failure probabilities. As before, we instantiate $\mathbb{D}$ with the polyhedra numeric abstract domain, since all under-approximating sound backward operators for it have been implemented in the APRON library [26]. The sufficient preconditions $d_{\text{input}}^{sat,\text{under}}$ and $d_{\text{input}}^{viol,\text{under}}$ are under-approximations of $\mathbb{E}_{sat}$ and $\mathbb{E}_{viol}$ respectively, so $\#(d_{\text{input}}^{sat,\text{under}}) \leq \#(\mathbb{E}_{sat})$ and $\#(d_{\text{input}}^{viol,\text{under}}) \leq \#(\mathbb{E}_{viol})$. Moreover, the input environments which are not in $\gamma_{\mathbb{D}}(d_{\text{input}}^{sat,\text{under}})$, that is they are in $\mathbb{E}\backslash\gamma_{\mathbb{D}}(d_{\text{input}}^{sat,\text{under}})$, may lead to the violation of the assertion. Therefore, we have $\#(d_{\text{input}}^{viol,\text{under}}) \leq \#(\mathbb{E}_{viol}) \leq \#(\mathbb{E}) - \#(d_{\text{input}}^{sat,\text{under}})$. By similar reasoning, we can also establish that: $\#(d_{\text{input}}^{sat,\text{under}}) \leq \#(\mathbb{E}_{sat}) \leq \#(\mathbb{E}) - \#(d_{\text{input}}^{viol,\text{under}})$. We calculate the *success* and *failure probability* of a program P as follows:

$$\begin{aligned}
\frac{\#(d_{\text{input}}^{sat,\text{under}})}{\#(\mathbb{E})} &\leq \mathbf{Pr^s(P)} = \frac{\#(\mathbb{E}_{sat})}{\#(\mathbb{E})} \leq \frac{\#(\mathbb{E})-\#(d_{\text{input}}^{viol,\text{under}})}{\#(\mathbb{E})} \\
\frac{\#(d_{\text{input}}^{viol,\text{under}})}{\#(\mathbb{E})} &\leq \mathbf{Pr^f(P)} = \frac{\#(\mathbb{E}_{viol})}{\#(\mathbb{E})} \leq \frac{\#(\mathbb{E})-\#(d_{\text{input}}^{sat,\text{under}})}{\#(\mathbb{E})}
\end{aligned} \tag{2}$$

Example 3. Consider the program P_3 from the beginning of this section. Using two backward sufficient condition analyses, we obtain $d_{\text{input}}^{sat,\text{under}} = (0 \leq j \leq 5)$ and $d_{\text{input}}^{viol,\text{under}} = (\perp_{\mathbb{D}})$, and so $\#(d_{\text{input}}^{sat,\text{under}}) = 6$ and $\#(d_{\text{input}}^{viol,\text{under}}) = 0$. Thus, the success and failure probabilities are:

$$(60\%)\frac{6}{10} \leq Pr^s(P_3) \leq 1\,(100\%) \quad \text{and} \quad (0\%)\,0 \leq Pr^f(P_1) \leq \frac{4}{10}\,(40\%) \qquad \Box$$

6   Implementation

We now describe the implementation and evaluation of the ideas presented so far. The evaluation aims to show the following objectives:

O1: The probabilistic analysis can be used to analyze the behaviour of various interesting programs;

O2: The probabilistic analysis gives exact results (with no precision loss) in many cases, especially for deterministic programs;

O3: The performance time of probabilistic analysis is largely insensitive to domain sizes of input variables;

O4: We can find practical application scenarios of using our probabilistic analysis to efficiently analyze C programs.

Implementation. We have implemented a prototype probabilistic static analyzer that accepts programs written in a subset of C. It does not support `struct` and union types, and provides only a limited support of arrays and pointers. The only basic data types considered are integers. As output, the tool reports the upper and lower bounds of probabilities that the target assertion is satisfied or violated. The prototype tool is written in OCAML. As the abstract analysis domain $\mathbb{D}$ for encoding program properties, we use the polyhedra numeric abstract domain [10]. All abstract operators and sound transfer functions for the polyhedra domain are provided by the APRON library [21,26]. The tool performs one forward reachability analysis and two backward necessary/sufficient condition analyses (one for satisfaction and one for violation of the assertion). The tool calls a model counter, LATTE [1], to determine the number of solutions to discovered preconditions for satisfaction or violation of the assertion. Note that if an input state satisfies the discovered precondition for satisfaction (resp., violation) of the assertion, then all program executions branching from that state will satisfy (resp., violate) the given assertion. The analysis proceeds by structural induction on the program syntax, iterating while-s until a fixed point is reached. They compute the unique solution which to every program point assigns an element from the abstract domain $\mathbb{D}$.

Experimental setup and benchmarks. All experiments are executed on a 64-bit Intel®Core^{TM} i5 CPU, Lubuntu VM, with 8 GB memory. The reported times represent the average runtime of five independent executions. We report TIME_{an} to perform all static analyses tasks (one forward plus two backward static analyses), TIME_{pr} to compute the needed probability bounds (call to LATTE plus additional calculations), and TIME to complete the overall probabilistic analysis task. The implementation, benchmarks, and all results obtained are available from: https://aleksdimovski.github.io/probab-analysis.html (or, https://github.com/aleksdimovski/probab_analyzer).

For our experiment, we use a dozen of C programs taken from several folders (categories) of the 8th International Competition on Software Verification (SV-COMP 2019) [6], as well as from the abstract interpretation community [26,30]. The folders from SV-COMP 2019 we consider are: loops, loop-lit, termination-crafted (which is denoted ter-crafted for short), as well as termination-restricted-15 (which is denoted ter-restricted for short). We have selected some numeric programs with integers that our tool can handle. We have manually added input sections, and in some of the programs we have also defined target assertions. Then, we have analyzed those programs using our prototype static analyzer. Table 1 summarizes relevant characteristics for each benchmark: the folder (source) where it is taken from, the number of lines of code (LOC), and the number of integer variables (#var). There are two classes of benchmarks in Table 1 separated by a double horizontal line. The first (upper) class of benchmarks consists of deterministic programs for which backward necessary condition analysis is performed, while the second (lower) class of benchmarks are non-deterministic programs for which backward sufficient condition analysis is performed.

Performances Table 1 shows the performance of our technique on a set of small and compelling examples (addresses Objective (**O1**)). We can note that for most of our deterministic benchmarks, the technique gives exact results without any approximation (which are marked with ✓ in the EXACT column of Table 1). This means that the lower and upper bounds for success and failure probabilities

---

[6] https://sv-comp.sosy-lab.org/2019/

coincide. This is due to the fact that we use the expressive and very precise polyhedra abstract domain (addresses Objective (**O2**)). For the remaining cases, the technique gives approximate results (which are marked with $\approx$ in the EXACT column of Table 1), since the abstraction was too coarse to calculate exact results. We can also see that the time for static analysis TIME_{an} dominates in the overall probabilistic analysis time TIME, whereas the probability computation time TIME_{pr} is a smaller fraction of the total time. The small probability computation times indicate that preconditions obtained from our analyses are relatively simple, and so LATTE can handle them very efficiently. We have also experimented with different domain sizes n of input variables (for $n = 10$ and $n = 1000$). Thus, n denotes the number of possible values per input variable. We observe that we obtain similar time performance results for $n = 10$ and $n = 1000$, which means that the performance is not affected by the fact that inputs come from a bigger pool of possible values. This is mostly due to the fact that LATTE and APRON are largely insensitive to those values in terms of time (addresses Objective (**O3**)). In general, the obtained probability bounds provide non-trivial information about the behaviour of these programs and are quite hard to estimate by hand even if the programs in question are small.

Application scenarios. Consider the following program (called `Waldkirch.c` from `termination-crafted` folder of SV-COMP 2019):

①: `int x:=`$[-5,4]$; l_{input}:
②: `while` $(\text{x} \geq 0)\,\{$
③: `x:=x-1;` $\}$
l_{final}: `assert` $(\text{x} \geq -1)$;

We want to prove this assertion, since, for example, later on in the program there are references to an array using the index `x+1` (e.g. `a[x+1]:=0`). In this way, we want to verify that there are no array-out-of-bounds references. The tool will find that the necessary precondition for assertion satisfaction is: $-1 \leq \text{x} \leq 4$, thus computing the success probability of 60%. The found necessary precondition for assertion violation is: $-5 \leq \text{x} \leq -2$, so the failure probability is 40% (addresses Objective (**O4**)).

Approximate results We now give an example where we obtain a precision loss in practice due to the approximation inherent in abstract analyses. Consider the following program (taken from [30]):

①: `int x:=`$[0,9]$, `y:=`$[0,9]$; l_{input}:
②: `int s:=x-y`;
③: `if` $(\text{s} \geq 2)$ `y:=y+2`;
l_{final}: `assert` $(\text{y} > 3)$;

The forward analysis will infer that the program can both satisfy and violate the assertion. The backward necessary condition analysis for assertion satisfaction will discover the constraint: $\text{x} + 2\text{y} \geq 8 \wedge 0 \leq \text{x} \leq 9 \wedge 2 \leq \text{y} \leq 9$, thus we

Table 1: Experimental evaluation for probabilistic static analyses of C programs. This table contains the following columns: (1) *benchmark* - the name of the analyzed program; (2) *source* - the source (folder) where the benchmark is taken from; (3) *LOC* - the number of lines of code; (4) *#var* - the number of integer variables; (5) TIME_{an}^{10} - the static analysis time in seconds for input domains of size 10; (6) TIME_{pr}^{10} - the probability computation time in seconds for input domains of size 10; (7-8) TIME^{10} and TIME^{1000} - the overall times in seconds required to completely analyze a benchmark which has input domain of size 10 and size 1000, respectively; (9) *Exact* - the preciseness of the reported result ($\checkmark$ - result is exact, $\approx$ - result is approximate). Benchmarks above the double horizontal line are deterministic programs, while those below are non-deterministic programs.

Bench.	source	LOC	#var	TIME_{an}^{10}	TIME_{pr}^{10}	TIME^{10}	TIME^{1000}	EXACT
count_up_down*.c	loops	20	3	0.043	0.001	0.004	0.049	$\checkmark$
hhk2008.c	loop-lit	20	4	0.103	0.001	0.104	0.113	$\checkmark$
gsv2008.c	loop-lit	20	2	0.027	0.001	0.028	0.030	$\checkmark$
Log.c	ter-restricted	30	4	0.194	0.001	0.195	0.197	$\approx$
Mono3-1.c	loops-crafted-1	15	2	0.044	0.001	0.045	0.046	$\approx$
Waldkirch.c	ter-crafted	20	1	0.010	0.001	0.011	0.012	$\checkmark$
bwd-loop1a.c	[26]	15	1	0.008	0.001	0.009	0.010	$\checkmark$
bwd-loop2.c	[26]	15	2	0.020	0.002	0.022	0.022	$\checkmark$
example1a.c	[30]	10	1	0.008	0.001	0.009	0.008	$\checkmark$
example7a.c	[30]	15	2	0.023	0.001	0.024	0.026	$\checkmark$
for-bounded*.c	loops	30	4	0.049	0.002	0.051	0.053	$\approx$
bwd-loop7.c	[26]	15	2	0.027	0.001	0.029	0.030	$\approx$
bwd-loop10.c	[26]	20	2	0.046	0.001	0.047	0.048	$\approx$
example7b.c	[30]	15	2	0.039	0.001	0.040	0.048	$\approx$

find that the upper bound probability for assertion satisfaction is 74%. The backward necessary condition analysis for assertion violation will discover the constraint: $x + 5y \leq 23 \land 0 \leq x \leq 9 \land 0 \leq y \leq 3$, thus we find that the upper bound probability for assertion violation is 32%. In this way, we conclude that the success probability is between 68% and 74%, while the failure probability is between 26% and 32%. On the other hand, we can calculate by hand that the success probability is exactly 71%, while the failure probability is exactly 29%.

7   Related work

Probabilistic analysis of imperative programs based on symbolic execution has been introduced before [18,17,3,29]. They calculate path probabilities by counting the number of solutions to a path condition, which represents a constraint on inputs. The analyses in [18,17] address programs with integer domains and linear constraints, whereas the analyses in [3] address programs with linear and complex floating-point computations. While the previous analyses are restricted to discrete, uniform random variables that take on a finite set of values, the probabilistic analysis in [29] can also handle non-uniform distributions over the reals and integers using a branch-and-bound technique over polyhedra. However, in presence of loops all above analyses based on symbolic execution lose precision, since they cannot enumerate all program paths. The solution is to consider bounded exploration of loops and only a finite number of feasible program paths. Thus, they also define a measure of *confidence* on the obtained probabilistic estimations in order to take into account the contribution from the unexplored feasible paths. For example, if we set the exploration bound of the loop of program P_2 in Fig. 2 to any number less than 100, both success and failure probabilities will be 0% and the confidence will be also 0. This is due to the fact that the while loop in Fig. 2 has to be unrolled at least 100 times in order to obtain a feasible path on which it can be decided whether the assertion at point l_{final} is satisfied or violated. In this work, instead of symbolic execution we use abstract interpretation to analyze programs and infer preconditions for success and failure. Thus, our approach for computing program reliability represents one of the pioneering works that provides a complete and fast treatment of while loops. In particular, the strength of our approach is being an abstract interpretation of a complete semantics for computing program reliability. This is stronger than fixing a priori an incomplete reasoning approach that can miss some feasible program paths (executions). The work [13] performs a probabilistic analysis of open programs using symbolic game semantics [12] and model counting. It uses game semantics to model open programs with undefined identifiers (e.g. calls to library functions), such that the model takes into account all possible contexts in which those programs can be placed. In the presence of loops and undefined functions, bounded exploration in the model is also used to obtain a feasible analysis. Probabilistic model checking [2] is yet another approach to perform probabilistic analysis on a high-level design of software. However, such high-level models are difficult to maintain and may abstract important details that impact the chance of property satisfaction. So the goal is to do probabilistic analysis directly on source code as here, not on high-level models.

Backward precondition analyses by abstract interpretation have also been used in practice for a long time [4,9,26,28]. Sufficient preconditions have been first introduced by Bourdoncle [4] in his work on abstract debugging of deterministic programs. He uses a combination of forward-backward analyses to find preconditions for invariant and intermittent assertions to always hold. Cousot et. al. [9] propose a method for automatically inferring contract preconditions for intermittent assertions. The preconditions extracted by their method are necessary preconditions, i.e. they do not exclude unsafe executions. Mine [26] presents a method for automatically inferring sufficient preconditions of non-deterministic programs by using a polyhedral backward analysis. The under-approximating sound abstract operators for this backward analysis are implemented as part of the APRON library. Rival [28] uses forward-backward analysis to inspect more closely reported alarms by ASTREE, which are then classified as true errors (bugs) or false alarms. Urban and Mine [30] use forward-backward analysis for the automatic inference of sufficient preconditions for program termination. The elements of the analysis domain are decision trees, where decision nodes are labeled with linear numerical constraints and leaf nodes are affine ranking functions for proving program termination. Forward-backward analysis schemes have been used in [20] for the inference of safety properties of declarative synchronous programs. In this work, for the first time we employ forward-backward precondition analysis for estimating program reliability.

Static analysis of probabilistic programs by abstract interpretation has also been a topic of research [27,11]. Monniaux [27] proposes a probabilistic analysis that annotates abstract domains with upper bounds on the probability measure associated with abstract objects. However, the measure bound is associated with the entire abstract object, without tracking how it is distributed amongst the individual states present in the concretization. This restriction makes the analysis quite conservative. Cousot and Monerau [11] provide a general framework that encompasses a variety of probabilistic interpretation schemes. However, no concrete implementation of the above probabilistic abstract interpretations is provided yet. A backward abstract interpretation for probabilistic programs [23] uses expectations that are real-valued functions of the program state and quantitative loop invariants. The automatic inference of such quantitative loop invariants was proposed in the recent work of Katoen et al [22].

8 Conclusion

We have presented a new static, abstract interpretation-based approach for computing program reliability, which allows to calculate upper and lower bounds of probabilities that a given assertion is satisfied or violated. We construct a combination of forward-backward abstract analyses, in order to find an approximation of a set of input states which lead to definite satisfaction (resp., violation) of the given assertion. Our approach to calculating program reliability is semantics-based and approximate in a provably sound way. Still, it often yields very precise results, especially for deterministic programs.

We currently support only uniform distribution of input values within their finite discrete domains. In future, we plan to model imprecision in the input by different non-uniform distributions, such as Binomial, Poisson, etc [29]. The current implementation of LATTE is limited in handling non-uniform distributions, so we will explore the use of statistical sampling techniques in those cases. Our focus here is on estimating probability for safety properties. We also plan to consider liveness properties (such as termination) and expectation queries [30]. An interesting direction for future work would also be to consider general probabilistic programs [19], as well as program families implemented with #ifdef-s from the C-preprocessor where we can use lifted static analyses to efficiently analyze all variants of the family simultaneously at once [14,24,15,16].

References

1. Latte integrale. UC Davis, Mathematics.
2. Christel Baier and Joost-Pieter Katoen. *Principles of model checking*. MIT Press, 2008.
3. Mateus Borges, Antonio Filieri, Marcelo d'Amorim, Corina S. Pasareanu, and Willem Visser. Compositional solution space quantification for probabilistic software analysis. In *ACM SIGPLAN Conference on Programming Language Design and Implementation, PLDI'14*, page 15. ACM, 2014.
4. François Bourdoncle. Abstract debugging of higher-order imperative languages. In *Proceedings of the ACM SIGPLAN'93 Conference on Programming Language Design and Implementation (PLDI)*, pages 46–55. ACM, 1993.
5. N. V. Chernikova. Algorithm for finding a general formula for the non-negative solutions of a system of linear inequalities. *USSR Computational Mathematics and Mathematical Physics*, 5(2):228—-233, 1965.
6. Patrick Cousot and Radhia Cousot. Abstract interpretation: A unified lattice model for static analysis of programs by construction or approximation of fixpoints. In *Conference Record of the Fourth ACM Symposium on Principles of Programming Languages (POPL'77)*, pages 238–252. ACM, 1977.
7. Patrick Cousot and Radhia Cousot. Systematic design of program analysis frameworks. In *6th Annual ACM Symposium on Principles of Programming Languages, POPL '79*, pages 269–282, 1979.
8. Patrick Cousot and Radhia Cousot. Abstract interpretation and application to logic programs. *J. Log. Program.*, 13(2–3):103–179, 1992.
9. Patrick Cousot, Radhia Cousot, and Francesco Logozzo. Precondition inference from intermittent assertions and application to contracts on collections. In *Verification, Model Checking, and Abstract Interpretation - 12th International Conference, VMCAI 2011. Proceedings*, volume 6538 of *LNCS*, pages 150–168. Springer, 2011.
10. Patrick Cousot and Nicolas Halbwachs. Automatic discovery of linear restraints among variables of a program. In *Conference Record of the Fifth Annual ACM Symposium on Principles of Programming Languages (POPL'78)*, pages 84–96. ACM Press, 1978.
11. Patrick Cousot and Michael Monerau. Probabilistic abstract interpretation. In *Programming Languages and Systems - 21st European Symposium on Programming, ESOP 2012, Held as Part of the European Joint Conferences on Theory and Practice of Software, ETAPS 2012. Proceedings*, volume 7211 of *LNCS*, pages 169–193. Springer, 2012.
12. Aleksandar S. Dimovski. Program verification using symbolic game semantics. *Theor. Comput. Sci.*, 560:364–379, 2014.
13. Aleksandar S. Dimovski. Probabilistic analysis based on symbolic game semantics and model counting. In *Proceedings Eighth International Symposium on Games, Automata, Logics and Formal Verification, GandALF 2017, Roma, Italy, 20-22 September 2017.*, volume 256 of *EPTCS*, pages 1–15, 2017.
14. Aleksandar S. Dimovski. Lifted static analysis using a binary decision diagram abstract domain. In *Proceedings of the 18th ACM SIGPLAN International Conference on Generative Programming: Concepts and Experiences, GPCE 2019*, pages 102–114. ACM, 2019.
15. Aleksandar S. Dimovski, Claus Brabrand, and Andrzej Wasowski. Variability abstractions: Trading precision for speed in family-based analyses. In *29th European Conf. on Object-Oriented Programming, ECOOP 2015*, volume 37 of *LIPIcs*, pages 247–270. Schloss Dagstuhl - Leibniz-Zentrum fuer Informatik, 2015.

16. Aleksandar S. Dimovski, Claus Brabrand, and Andrzej Wasowski. Finding suitable variability abstractions for lifted analysis. *Formal Asp. Comput.*, 31(2):231–259, 2019.

17. Antonio Filieri, Corina S. Pasareanu, and Willem Visser. Reliability analysis in symbolic pathfinder. In *35th International Conference on Software Engineering, ICSE'13*, pages 622–631. IEEE / ACM, 2013.

18. Jaco Geldenhuys, Matthew B. Dwyer, and Willem Visser. Probabilistic symbolic execution. In *International Symposium on Software Testing and Analysis, ISSTA 2012*, pages 166–176. ACM, 2012.

19. Andrew D. Gordon, Thomas A. Henzinger, Aditya V. Nori, and Sriram K. Rajamani. Probabilistic programming. In *Proceedings of the on Future of Software Engineering, FOSE 2014*, pages 167–181. ACM, 2014.

20. Bertrand Jeannet. Dynamic partitioning in linear relation analysis: Application to the verification of reactive systems. *Formal Methods in System Design*, 23(1):5–37, 2003.

21. Bertrand Jeannet and Antoine Miné. Apron: A library of numerical abstract domains for static analysis. In *Computer Aided Verification, 21st International Conference, CAV 2009. Proceedings*, volume 5643 of *LNCS*, pages 661–667. Springer, 2009.

22. Joost-Pieter Katoen, Annabelle McIver, Larissa Meinicke, and Carroll C. Morgan. Linear-invariant generation for probabilistic programs: - automated support for proof-based methods. In *Static Analysis - 17th International Symposium, SAS 2010. Proceedings*, volume 6337 of *LNCS*, pages 390–406. Springer, 2010.

23. Annabelle McIver and Carroll Morgan. *Abstraction, Refinement and Proof for Probabilistic Systems*. Monographs in Computer Science. Springer, 2005.

24. Jan Midtgaard, Aleksandar S. Dimovski, Claus Brabrand, and Andrzej Wasowski. Systematic derivation of correct variability-aware program analyses. *Sci. Comput. Program.*, 105:145–170, 2015.

25. Antoine Miné. The octagon abstract domain. *Higher-Order and Symbolic Computation*, 19(1):31–100, 2006.

26. Antoine Miné. Backward under-approximations in numeric abstract domains to automatically infer sufficient program conditions. *Sci. Comput. Program.*, 93:154–182, 2014.

27. David Monniaux. An abstract monte-carlo method for the analysis of probabilistic programs. In *Conference Record of POPL 2001: The 28th ACM SIGPLAN-SIGACT Symposium on Principles of Programming Languages*, pages 93–101. ACM, 2001.

28. Xavier Rival. Understanding the origin of alarms in astrée. In *Static Analysis, 12th International Symposium, SAS 2005, Proceedings*, volume 3672 of *LNCS*, pages 303–319. Springer, 2005.

29. Sriram Sankaranarayanan, Aleksandar Chakarov, and Sumit Gulwani. Static analysis for probabilistic programs: inferring whole program properties from finitely many paths. In *ACM SIGPLAN Conference on Programming Language Design and Implementation, PLDI '13*, pages 447–458. ACM, 2013.

30. Caterina Urban and Antoine Miné. A decision tree abstract domain for proving conditional termination. In *Static Analysis - 21st International Symposium, SAS 2014. Proceedings*, volume 8723 of *LNCS*, pages 302–318. Springer, 2014.

An Empirical Study on the Use and Misuse of Java 8 Streams

Raffi Khatchadourian[1,2], Yiming Tang[2], Mehdi Bagherzadeh[3], and
Baishakhi Ray[4]

[1] CUNY Hunter College, New York, NY USA
[2] CUNY Graduate Center, New York, NY USA
{raffi.khatchadourian,ytang3}@{hunter,gradcenter}.cuny.edu
[3] Oakland University, Rochester, MI USA
mbagherzadeh@oakland.edu
[4] Columbia University, New York, NY USA
rayb@cs.columbia.edu

Abstract. Streaming APIs allow for big data processing of native data
structures by providing MapReduce-like operations over these structures.
However, unlike traditional big data systems, these data structures typically reside in shared memory accessed by multiple cores. Although popular, this emerging hybrid paradigm opens the door to possibly detrimental
behavior, such as thread contention and bugs related to non-execution
and non-determinism. This study explores the use and misuse of a popular
streaming API, namely, Java 8 Streams. The focus is on how developers
decide whether or not to run these operations sequentially or in parallel
and bugs both specific and tangential to this paradigm. Our study involved analyzing 34 Java projects and 5.53 million lines of code, along
with 719 manually examined code patches. Various automated, including
interprocedural static analysis, and manual methodologies were employed.
The results indicate that streams are pervasive, parallelization is not
widely used, and performance is a crosscutting concern that accounted
for the majority of fixes. We also present coincidences that both confirm
and contradict the results of related studies. The study advances our
understanding of streams, as well as benefits practitioners, programming
language and API designers, tool developers, and educators alike.

Keywords: empirical studies · functional programming · Java 8 · streams
· multi-paradigm programming · static analysis.

1 Introduction

Streaming APIs are widely-available in today's mainstream Object-Oriented
programming (MOOP) languages and platforms [5], including Scala [14], Java-
Script [44], C# [33], F# [47], Java [39], and Android [27]. These APIs allow for
"big data"-style processing of *native* data structures by incorporating MapReduce-
like [10] operations. A "sum of even squares" example in Java, where a `stream` of
numbers is derived from a `list`, `filter`ed for evens, `map`ped to its squared, and
summed [5] is: `list.stream().filter(x -> x % 2 == 0).map(x -> x * x).sum().`

Traditional big data systems, for which MapReduce is a popular backbone [3], minimize the complexity of writing massively distributed programs by facilitating processing on multiple nodes using succinct functional-like constructs. This makes writing parallel code easier, as writing such code can be difficult due to possible data races, thread interference, and contention [1,4,28]. The code above, e.g., can execute in parallel simply by replacing `stream()` with `parallelStream()`.

However, unlike traditional big data systems, data structures processed by streaming APIs like Java 8 Streams typically reside in shared memory accessed by multiple cores. Therefore, issues may arise from the close intimacy between shared memory and the operations being performed, especially for developers not previously familiar with functional programming. Streams are not just an API but rather an emerging, hybrid paradigm. To obtain the expressiveness, speed, and parallelism that streams have to offer, developers must adopt the paradigm as well as the API [6, Ch. 7]. This requires determining whether running stream code in parallel yields an efficient yet interference-free program [24] and ensuring that no operations on different threads interleave [42].

Despite the benefits [53, Ch. 1], misusing streams may result in detrimental behavior, and the ∼4K questions related to streams on Stack Overflow [48], of which ∼5% remain unanswered, suggest that there is ample confusion surrounding the topic. Bugs related to thread contention (due to λ-expressions, i.e., units of computation, side-effects, buffering), non-execution (due to deferred execution), non-determinism (due to non-deterministic operations), operation sequencing (ordering of stream operations), and data ordering (ordering of stream data) can lead to programs that undermine concurrency, underperform, are incorrect, and are inefficient. Worse yet, these problems may increase over time as streams rise in popularity, with Mazinanian et al. [32] finding a two-fold increasing trend in the adoption of λ-expressions, an essential part of streams.

This study explores the use and misuse of a popular and representative streaming API, namely, Java 8 Streams. We set out to understand the *usage* and *bug* patterns involving streams in real software. Particularly, we are interested in discovering (i) how developers decide whether to run streams *sequentially* or in *parallel*, (ii) common stream *operations*, (iii) common stream *attributes* and whether they are amenable to safe and efficient parallelization, (iv) *bugs* both specific and tangential to streams, (v) how often *incorrect* stream APIs were used, and (vi) how often stream APIs were *misused* and in which ways?

Knowing the kinds of bugs typically associated with streams can, e.g., help improve (automated) bug detection. Being aware of the typical usage patterns of streams can, e.g., improve code completion in IDEs. In general, the results (i) advance our understanding of this emerging hybrid paradigm, (ii) provide feedback to language and API designers for future API versions, (iii) help tool designers comprehend the struggles developers have with streams, (iv) propose preliminary *best practices* and *anti-patterns* for practitioners to use streaming APIs effectively, (v) and assist educators in teaching streaming APIs.

We analyzed 34 Java projects and 5.53 million lines of source code (SLOC), along with 140,446 code patches (git commits), of which 719 were manually

---

Listing 1 Snippet of `Widget` collection processing using Java 8 streams [24,39].

```
1   Collection<Widget> unorderedWidgets = new HashSet<>(); // populate ...
2   Collection<Widget> orderedWidgets = new ArrayList<>(); // populate ...
3   List<Widget> sortedWidgets = unorderedWidgets.stream()
4       .sorted(Comparator.comparing(Widget::getWeight)).collect(Collectors.toList());
5   // collect weights over 43.2 into a set in parallel.
6   Set<Double> heavyWidgetWeightSet = orderedWidgets.parallelStream().map(Widget::getWeight)
7       .filter(w -> w > 43.2).collect(Collectors.toSet());
8   // sequentially collect into a list, skipping first 1000.
9   List<Widget> skippedWidgetList = orderedWidgets.stream().skip(1000)
10      .collect(Collectors.toList());
```

---

examined. The methodologies varied depending on the research questions and encompassed both automated, including interprocedural static analysis, and manual processes aided by automated software repository mining. Our study indicates that (i) streams have become widely used since their inception in 2014, (ii) developers tend to reduce streams back to iterative-style collections, favor simplistic, linear reductions, and prefer deterministic operations, (iii) stream parallelization is not widely used, yet streams tend not to have side-effects, (iv) performance is the largest category of stream bugs and is crosscutting.

This work makes the following contributions:

Stream usages patterns A large-scale analysis of stream and collector method calls and an interprocedural static analysis on 1.65 million lines source code is performed, reporting on attributes essential to efficient parallel execution.

Stream bug hierarchical taxonomy From the 719 git patches from 22 projects manually examined using 140 identifying keywords, we build a rich hierarchical, crosscutting taxonomy of common stream bugs and fixes.

Best practices and anti-patterns We propose preliminary best practices and anti-patterns of using streams in particular contexts from our statistical results as well as an in-depth analysis of first-hand conversations with developers.

2   Motivating Example and Conceptual Background

Lst. 1 portrays code that uses the Java 8 Stream API to process collections of `Widgets` (class not shown) with `colors` and `weights`. A `Collection` of `Widgets` is declared (line 1) that does not maintain element ordering as `HashSet` does not support it [38]. Note that ordering is dependent on the run time type.

A `stream` (a view representing element sequences supporting MapReduce-style operations) of `unorderedWidgets` is created on line 3. It is sequential, i.e., its operations will execute serially. Streams may also have an *encounter order* that may depend on its source. Here, it is unordered since `HashSets` are unordered.

On line 4, the stream is `sorted` by the corresponding *intermediate* operation, the result of which is a stream with the encounter order rearranged. `Widget::getWeight` is a method *reference* denoting the comparison scheme. Intermediate operations are deferred until a *terminal* operation is executed like `collect()` (line 4). The `collect()` operation is a (mutable) reduction that aggregates results of prior intermediate operations into a given `Collector`. In this case, it is one that yields a `List`. The result is a `Widget List` sorted by `weight`.

To potentially improve performance, this stream's "pipeline" (sequence of operations) may be executed in parallel. Note, however, that had the stream been *ordered*, running the pipeline in parallel may result in worse performance due to the multiple passes or data buffering required by *stateful* intermediate operations (SIOs) like `sorted()`. Because the stream is *unordered*, the reduction can be done more efficiently as the run time can use divide-and-conquer [39].

In contrast, line 2 instantiates an `ArrayList`, which maintains element ordering. Furthermore, a parallel stream is derived from this collection (line 6), with each `Widget` mapped to its weight, each weighted filtered (line 7), and the results `collect`ed into a `Set`. Unlike the previous example, however, no optimizations are available here as an SIO is not included in the pipeline and, as such, the parallel computation does not incur possible performance degradation.

Lines 9–10 create a list of `Widgets` gathered by (sequentially) skipping the first thousand from `orderedWidgets`. Like `sorted()`, `skip()` is also an SIO. Unlike the previous example, executing this pipeline in parallel could be counterproductive because the stream is ordered. It may be possible to unorder the stream (via `unordered()`) so that its pipeline would be more amenable to parallelization. In this situation, however, unordering could alter semantics as the data is assembled into a structure maintaining ordering. As such, the stream *correctly* executes sequentially as element ordering must be preserved.

This simplified example demonstrates that using streams effectively is not always straight-forward and can require complex (and interprocedural due to aliasing) analysis. It necessitates a thorough understanding of API intricacies, a problem that can be compounded in more extensive programs. As streaming APIs become more pervasive, it would be extremely valuable to MOOP developers not familiar with functional programming if statistical insight can be given on how best to use streams efficiently and how to avoid common bugs.

3   Study Subjects

At the core of our study is 34 open source Java projects that use streams. They vary widely in their domain and application, as well as size and popularity. All the subjects have their sources publicly available on GitHub and include popular libraries, frameworks, and applications. Many subjects were selected from previous studies [20,21,22,24], others because they contained relatively diverse stream operations and exhibited non-trivial metrics, including stars, forks, and number of collaborators. It was necessary to use different subjects for different parts of the study due to the computationally intensive nature of some of the experiments. For such experiments, subjects were chosen so that the analysis could be completed in a reasonable time period with reasonable resources.

4   Stream Characteristics

We explore the typical usage patterns of streams, including the frequency of parallel vs. sequential streams and amenability to safe and efficient parallelism, by examining stream characteristics. This has important implications for understanding the use of this incredibly expressive and powerful language feature. It also offers insight into developers' perceived risks concerning parallel streams.

Table 1. Stream characteristics.

subject	KLOC	age	eps	k	str	seq	para	ord	unord	se	SIO
bootique	4.91	4.18	362	4	14	14	0	11	3	4	0
cryptomator	7.99	6.05	148	3	12	12	0	11	1	2	0
dari	64.86	5.43	3	2	18	18	0	15	3	0	0
elasticsearch	585.71	10.03	78	6	210	210	0	165	45	10	0
htm.java	41.14	4.53	21	4	190	188	2	189	1	22	5
JabRef	138.83	16.36	3,064	2	301	290	11	239	62	9	0
JacpFX	23.79	4.71	195	4	12	12	0	9	3	1	0
jdp*	19.96	5.53	25	4	38	38	0	35	3	11	1
jdk8-exp*	3.43	6.35	34	4	49	49	0	47	2	5	0
jetty	354.48	10.93	106	4	57	57	0	47	10	8	0
JetUML	20.95	5.09	660	2	7	7	0	4	3	0	0
jOOQ	154.01	8.58	43	4	23	23	0	22	1	2	0
koral	7.13	3.47	51	3	8	8	0	8	0	0	0
monads	1.01	0.01	47	2	3	3	0	3	0	0	0
retrolambda	5.14	6.52	1	4	11	11	0	8	3	0	0
spring*	188.46	11.62	5,981	4	61	61	0	60	1	21	0
streamql	4.01	0.01	92	2	22	22	0	22	0	2	18
threeten*	27.53	7.01	36	2	2	2	0	2	0	0	0
Total	1,653.35	116.40	11,047	6	1,038	1,025	13	897	141	97	24

*jdp is java-design-patterns, jdk8-exp is jdk8-experiments, spring is a portion of spring-framework, and threeten is threeten-extra.

4.1 Methodology

For this part of the study, we examined 18 projects that use streams,[5] spanning ~1.65 million lines of Java source code. The subjects are depicted in tab. 1. Column **KLOC** corresponds to thousands of source lines of code, which ranges from ~1K for monads to ~586K for elasticsearch. Column **age** is the age of the subject project in years, averaging 6.47 years per subject. Column **str** is the total number of streams analyzed. The remaining columns are discussed in § 4.2.

Stream Pipeline Tracking Several factors contribute to determining stream attributes. First, streams are typically derived from a source (e.g., a collection) and take on its characteristics (e.g., ordering), as seen in lst. 1. There are several ways to create streams, including being derived from `Collections`, being created from arrays (e.g., `Arrays.stream()`), and via static factory methods (e.g., `IntStream.range()`). Second, stream attributes can change by the invocation of various intermediate operations in the building of the stream pipeline. Such attributes must be tracked, as it is possible to have arbitrary assignments of stream references to variables, as well as be data-dependent.

Our study involved tracking streams and their attributes (i.e., state) using a series of labeled transition systems (LTSs). The LTSs are fed into the static analysis portion of a refactoring tool [23] based on typestate analysis [16,49] Stream pipelines are tracked and stream state when a terminal operation is issued is determined by the tool. Typestate analysis is a program analysis that augments the type system with "state" information and has been traditionally used for prevention of program errors such as those related to resource usage. It works by assigning each variable an initial (⊥) state. Then, method calls transition the object's state. States are represented by a lattice and possible transitions

---

[5] Recall from § 3 that it was necessary to use different subjects for different parts of the study due to the computationally intensive nature of some of the experiments.

are represented by LTSs. If each method call sequence on the receiver does not eventually transition the object back to the ⊥ state, the object may be left in a nonsensical state, indicating the potential presence of a bug.

The LTSs for execution mode and ordering work as follows. The state ⊥ is a phantom initial state immediately before stream creation. Different stream creation methods may transition the newly created stream to one that is either sequential or parallel or ordered or unordered. The transition continues for each invoked intermediate operation and ends with a terminal operation.

Since the analysis is focused on client-side analysis of stream APIs, the call graph is constructed using a k-CFA, where k is the call string length. It is an analysis parameter, with $k = 2$ being the default, as it is the minimum k needed to consider client-code, for methods returning streams and $k = 1$ elsewhere. The refactoring tool includes heuristics for determining sufficient and tractable k.

Counting Streams Since stream attributes are control flow sensitive, the streams studied must be in the control flow of entry points. For non-library subjects, all main methods were chosen, otherwise, all unit tests were chosen.

Streams are counted as follows. First, every *syntactic* stream is counted, i.e., every allocation site. Streams in the control flow of the program starting from an entry point transition according to the LTSs. If a stream is not in the control flow, it is still counted but it remains at the state following ⊥. This way, more information about various stream attributes is available for the study as we do not need control flow to determine the state following ⊥.

Side-effects and Stateful Intermediate Operations Stream side-effects are determined using a ModRef analysis on stream operation parameters (λ-expressions) using WALA [52]. SIOs are obtained from the documentation [39].

4.2   Results

Tab. 1 illustrates our findings on stream characteristics. Column **eps** is the number of entry points. Column **k** is the maximum k value used (see § 4.1). Columns **seq** and **para** correspond to the number of *sequential* and *parallel* streams, respectively. Column **ord** is the number of streams that are *ordered*, i.e., those whose operations must maintain an encounter order, which can be detrimental to efficient parallel performance, while column **unord** is the number *unordered* streams. Column **se** is the number of stream pipelines that include *side-effects*, which may induce race conditions. Finally, column **SIO** is the number of pipelines that include *stateful intermediate operations*, which may also be detrimental to efficient parallel performance.

4.3   Discussion

Parallel streams are not popular (1.25%) despite their ease-of-use. Although Nielebock et al. [36] did not consider λ-expressions in stream contexts, this confirms that their findings extend into stream contexts. It may also coincide with the finding of Lu et al. [28], i.e., that developers tend to "think" sequentially.

Finding 1: Stream parallelization is not widely used.

When considering using parallel streams, it may also be important to consider the *context*. For example, many server applications deal with thread pools that span the JVM, and developers may be leery of the interactions of such pools with the underlying stream parallelization run time system. We found this to be the case with several pull requests [15,45] that were issued by Khatchadourian et al. [24] as part of their refactoring evaluation to introduce parallel streams into existing projects. It may also be the case that the locations where streams operate are already fast enough or do not process significant amounts of data [7,30]. In fact, Naftalin [35, Ch. 6] found that there is a particular threshold in data size that must be reached to compensate for overhead incurred by parallel stream processing. Lastly, developers pointed us to several blog articles [54,59] expressing that parallel streams could be problematic under certain conditions.

There were, however, two projects that use parallel streams. Particularly, JabRef used the most parallel streams at 11. We conjecture that JabRef's use of parallel streams may stem from its status as a desktop application. Such applications typically are not managed by application containers and thus may not utilize global thread pools as in more traditional server applications.

Many streams are ordered (86.42%), which can prevent optimal performance of parallel streams under certain conditions [24,35,40]. Thus, even if streams were run in parallel, they may not reap all of the benefits. This extends the findings of Nielebock et al. [36] that λ-expressions do not appear in contexts amenable to parallelization to streams for the case of ordering. Streams may still be amenable to parallelization, as § 5.2 shows that many streams are traversed using API that *ignores* ordering (e.g., `forEach()` vs. `forEachOrdered()`).

Finding 2: Streams are largely *ordered*, possibly hindering parallelism.

That only ~10% of streams have side-effects and only 2.31% have SIOs contradict the findings of Nielebock et al. [36] in the context of streams. This suggests that streams may run efficiently in parallel as, although they are largely ordered, they include minimal side-effects and SIOs. streamql had the most streams with SIOs ($18/22$), which may be due to its querying features using aggregate operations that are manifested as SIOs in the Java 8 Streaming API (e.g., `distinct()`).

Finding 3: Streams tend *not* to have side-effects.

5   Stream Usage

We discover the common operations on streams and the underlying reasons by examining stream method calls. This has important implications in understanding how streams are used, and studying language feature usage has been shown to be beneficial [11,43]. It provides valuable insight to programming language API designers and tool-support engineers on where to focus their evaluation efforts. We may also comprehend contexts where developers struggle with using streams.

5.1   Methodology

We examined 34 projects that use streams, spanning ~5.53 million lines of source code. To find method calls, we parsed ASTs with source-symbol bindings using the Eclipse Java Developer Tools (JDT) [12]. Then, method invocation nodes were extracted whose compile-time targets are declared in types residing in the `java.util.stream` package. This includes types such as `Streams` and `Collectors`.

While stream creation is interesting and a topic for future work, our focus is on operations *on* streams as our scope is stream *usage*. We also combined methods with similar functionalities, e.g., `mapToLong()` with `map()` but not `forEach()` and `forEachOrdered()`. Additionally, only the method name is presented, resulting in a comparison of methods from both streams and collectors. The type is clear from the method name (e.g., `map()` is for `Streams`, while `groupingBy()` is for `Collectors`). We then proceeded to count the number of method calls in each project.

5.2   Results

Fig. 1 depicts the result of our analysis.[6] A full table is available in our dataset [25]. The horizontal axis lists the method name, and the legend depicts projects analyzed. The chart is sorted by the total number of calls in descending order. Calls per project range from 4 for threeten-extra to 4,635 for cyclops. Calls per method range from 2 for `characteristics()`, which returns stream attributes such as whether it is ordered or parallel, and 3,161 for `toList()`.

5.3   Discussion

The number of method calls in fig. 1 is substantial. There are 14,536 calls to methods operating on streams in 34 projects. This is impressive considering that Android, which uses the Java syntax, did not adopt streams immediately.

It is not surprising that the four most used stream methods are `toList()`, `collect()`, `map()`, and `filter()`, as these are the core MapReduce data transformation operations. `collect()` is a specialized reduction that reduces to a non-scalar type (e.g., a map) as opposed to the traditional scalar type. The `toList()` method is a static method of `Collectors`, which are pre-made reductions, in this case, to an `ArrayList`. This informs the `collect()` operation of the non-scalar type to use. It is peculiar that there are more calls to `toList()` than `collect()`. This is due to cyclops. We conjecture that it has some unorthodox usages of `Collectors` as it is a platform for writing functional-style programs in Java $\geq$ 8 [2].

That `collect()` and `toList()`, along with other terminal operations such as `forEach()`, `iterator()`, `toSet()`, and `toArray()`, appear towards the top to the list suggest that, although developers are writing functional-style code to process data in a "big data" processing style, they are not staying there. Instead, they are "bridging" back to imperative-style code, either by collecting data into imperative-style collections or processing the data further iteratively.

There can be various reasons for this, such as unfamiliarity with functional programming, the need to introduce side-effects, or the need to interoperate with legacy code. Further investigation is necessary, yet, Nielebock et al. [36] mention that developers tend to introduce side-effects into λ-expressions, which is related.

> ***Finding 4***: Although stream usage is high, developers tend to reduce streams back to iterative-style collections.

We infer that developers tend to favor more simplistic (linear) rather than more specialized (higher-dimensionality) non-scalar reductions. It is surprising that more of the advanced reductions, such as those that return maps (e.g., `toMap()`,

---

[6] Similar conclusions hold when normalizing with subject KLOC.

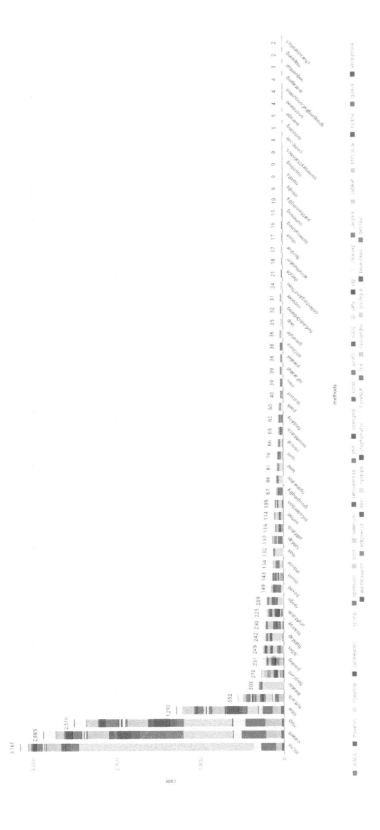

Fig. 1. Stream method calls

groupingBy()) are not used more frequently as these are highly expressive operations that can save substantial amounts of imperative-style code. For example, one may group Widgets by their Color as Map<Color, List<Widget>> widgetsByColor = widgets.stream().collect(Collectors.groupingBy(Widget::getColor)). Although these advanced reductions are powerful and expressive, developers may be leery of using them, perhaps due to unfamiliarity or risk adversement. This motivates future tools that refactor to uses of advanced reductions to save developers time and effort while possibly mitigating errors.

> **Finding 5**: Developers favor simplistic, linear reductions.

Another powerful stream feature is its non-determinism. For instance, findAny() returns any stream element. However, this operation has only 62 calls, while its deterministic counterpart, findFirst(), has 270, suggesting that developers tend to favor determinism. Yet, in contrast, developers overwhelmingly favor the *non-deterministic* forEach() operation (552) over the *deterministic* forEachOrdered() (32). We conjecture that although forEach() does not guarantee a particular ordering [41], in practice, since developers are inclined to use sequential over parallel streams, as suggested by § 4 and mirrored by Nielebock et al. [36] in terms of λ-expressions, the difference does not play out.

It could also be that traversal order is largely unimportant for many streams. This is curious because, as demonstrated in § 4, the majority of streams are *ordered*, an attribute detrimental to efficient parallelism [24,35,40]. As such, there may exist opportunities to alleviate the burden of stream ordering maintenance to make parallel streams more efficient. It may also entice developers to use more parallel streams as the performance gains may be significant.

> **Finding 6**: Developers prefer deterministic operations.

Lastly, there is a minimal amount of calls to parallel stream APIs. Of particular concern is that there are only 4 calls to groupingByConcurrent() in contrast to the 87 calls to groupingBy(). This suggests that either advanced reductions to maps are not being used on parallel streams or that they are not used safely as the concurrent version provides synchronization [37]. Furthermore, not using groupingByConcurrent() on a parallel stream may produce inefficient results [40].

6   Stream Misuses

This section is focused on discovering stream bug patterns. We are interested in bugs both specific and tangential to streams, i.e., bugs that occur in stream contexts. Understanding this can, e.g., help improve (automated) bug detection and other tool-support for writing optimal stream code. We may also begin to understand the kinds of errors developers make with streams, which may positively influence how future API and language feature versions are implemented.

6.1   Methodology

Here, we explore 22 projects that use streams, comprising ~4.68 million lines of source code and 140,446 git commits.[7] Tab. 2 summarizes the subjects used.

---

[7] Recall from § 3 that it was necessary to use different subjects for different parts of the study due to the computationally intensive nature of some of the experiments.

Table 2. Studied subjects.

subject	KLOC	studied periods	cmts	kws	exe
binnavi	328.28	2015-08-19 to 2019-07-17	286	4	4
blueocean-plugin	49.70	2016-01-23 to 2019-07-24	4,043	118	25
bootique	15.47	2015-12-10 to 2019-08-08	1,106	5	5
che	189.24	2016-02-11 to 2019-08-19	8,093	75	75
cryptomator	9.83	2014-02-01 to 2019-08-08	1,443	50	10
dari	72.46	2012-09-26 to 2018-03-02	2,466	18	6
eclipse.jdt.core	1,527.89	2001-06-05 to 2019-08-07	24,085	234	106
eclipse.jdt.ui	712.01	2001-05-02 to 2019-08-09	28,176	140	72
error-prone	165.85	2011-09-14 to 2019-08-15	3,893	71	71
guava	393.47	2009-06-18 to 2019-08-15	5,031	36	36
htm.java	41.63	2014-08-09 to 2019-02-19	1,507	40	1
JacpFX	24.06	2013-08-12 to 2018-04-27	365	37	14
jdk8-experiments	3.47	2013-08-03 to 2018-03-10	8	1	1
java-design-patterns	33.52	2014-08-09 to 2019-07-31	2,192	37	12
jetty	400.26	2009-03-16 to 2019-08-02	17,051	835	219
jOOQ	184.25	2011-07-24 to 2019-07-31	7,508	94	4
qbit	52.27	2014-08-25 to 2018-01-18	1,717	65	9
retrolambda	5.10	2013-07-20 to 2018-11-30	522	17	4
selenium	234.12	2004-11-03 to 2019-08-09	24,145	114	57
streamql	4.26	2014-04-27 to 2014-04-29	27	2	2
threeten-extra	31.26	2012-11-17 to 2019-07-14	559	28	2
WALA	203.84	2006-11-22 to 2019-07-24	6,263	52	24
Total	4,683.12		140,446	2,082	719

To find changesets (patches) corresponding to stream fixes, we compiled 140 keywords from the API documentation [39] that match stream operations and related method names from the `java.util.stream` package. We then randomly selected a subset of these commits whose changesets included these keywords and were likely to be bug fixes to manually examine.

Commit Mining To discover commits that had changesets including stream API keywords, we used `gitcproc` [9], a tool for processing and classifying git commits, which has been used in previous work [17,50]. Due to the keyword-based search used, not all of the examined commits pertained to streams (e.g., "map" has a broad range of applications outside of streams). To mitigate this, we focused more on keywords that were specific to stream contexts, e.g., "Collector." Also to reduce false positives, we only considered commits after the Java 8 release date of March 18, 2014, which is when streams were introduced.

Finding Bug Fixes We used a feature of `gitcproc` that uses heuristics based on commit log messages to identify commits that are bug fixes. Natural language processing (NLP) is used to determine which commits fall in this category. This helps us to focus on the likely bug-fix commits for further manual examination.

Next, the authors manually examine these commits to determine if the commits were indeed related to stream-related bugs. Three of the authors are software engineering and programming language professors with extensive expertise in streaming and parallel systems, concurrent systems, and empirical software engineering. The authors also have several years of industrial experience working as software engineers. As the authors did not always have expertise in the subject domains, only changes where a bug fix was extremely likely were marked as such. The authors also used commit comments and referenced bug databases to ascertain whether a change was a bug fix. This is a common practice [8,26,28].

Table 3. Stream bug/patch category legend.

name	description	acronym
Bounds	Incorrect/Missing Bounds Check	BC
Exceptions	Incorrect/Missing Exception Handling	EH
Other	Other change (e.g., syntax, refactoring)	Other
Perf	Poor Performance	PP
Concur	Concurrency Issue	CI
Stream Source	Incorrect/Missing Stream Source	SS
Intermediate Operations	Incorrect/Missing Intermediate Operations	IO
Data Ordering	Incorrect Data Ordering	DO
Operation Sequencing	Incorrect Operation Sequencing	OS
Filter Operations	Incorrect/Missing Filter Operations	FO
Map Operations	Incorrect/Missing Map Operations	MO
Terminal Operations	Incorrect/Missing Terminal Operations	TO
Reduction Operations	Incorrect Reduction Operations	RO
Collector Operations	Incorrect/Missing Collector Operations	CO
Incorrect Action	Incorrect Action (e.g., λ-expression)	IA

Classifying Bug Fixes Once bug fixes were identified, the authors studied the code changes to determine the category of bug fixes and whether the category relates to streams. Fortunately, we found that many commits reference bug reports or provide more details about the fix. Such information proved highly valuable in understanding the fixes. When in doubt, we also sent emails to developers for clarification purposes as git commits include email addresses.

6.2   Results

Quantitative Column **kws** of tab. 2 is the number of commits where occurrences of keywords were found and correspond to possible stream bug fixes. Column **exe** depicts the number of commits manually examined. From these 719 commits, we found 61 stream client code bug fixes. This is depicted in column **total** of tab. 4. Finding these bugs and understanding their relevance required a significant amount of manual labor that may not be feasible in more larger-scale, automated studies. Nevertheless, as streams become more popular (they were only introduced in 2014), we expect the usage and number of bugs related to streams to grow.

From the manual changes, we devised a set of common problem categories. Fixes were then grouped into these categories as shown in fig. 2 and tab. 4. A category legend appears in tab. 3, where column **name** is the "short" name of the bug category and is used in fig. 2. Column **description** is the categories extended name and column **acronym** is used in tab. 4.

Fig. 2 presents a hierarchical categorization of the 61 stream-related bug fixes. Bugs are represented by their category name (column **name** in tab. 3) and their bug counts. Categories with no count are *abstract*, i.e., those grouping categories.

Bugs are separated into two top-level categories, namely, bugs specifically related to stream API usage (stream-specific) and those tangentially related, i.e., bugs appearing in stream contexts but not specifically having to do with streams (generic). Generic bugs were further categorized into related to exception handling (EH), bounds checking (BC), poor performance (PP), and "other." Generic exception handling bugs (6) include those where, e.g., λ-expressions passed to stream operations threw exceptions that were not handled properly. Generic bounds checking bugs (2) included those where λ-expressions missed traversal boundary checks, and generic performance bugs (2) were those involving,

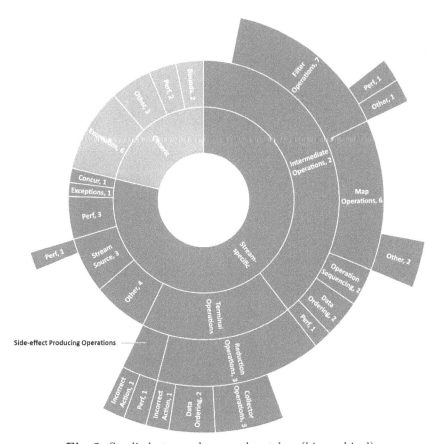

Fig. 2. Studied stream bugs and patches (hierarchical).

e.g., local variables holding stream computation results. The "other" category (3) is aligned with a similar one used by Tian and Ray [50] and involved syntactic corrections, e.g., incorrect types, and refactorings. Generally, "other" bugs can either be stream-specific or generic.

Stream-specific bugs are further divided into several categories corresponding to whether they involved intermediate operations (IO), terminal operations (TO), the stream source (SS), concurrency (CI), and performance and exception handling bugs specific to streams. IO-specific bugs (2) are related to intermediate operations other than filter operations (FO, 7) and map operations (MO, 6), e.g., `distinct()`. IO bugs are additionally partitioned into those involving incorrect operation sequencing (OS, 2), e.g., `map()` before `filter()`, data ordering (DO, 2), e.g., operating on a stream that should have been sorted, and performance bugs appearing in intermediate operations other than `map()` and `filter()` (1).

Terminal operations are split into two categories, namely, reduction operations (RO), e.g., `collect()`, `reduce()`, and side-effect producing operations, e.g., `forEach()`, `iterator()`. RO-specific bugs (3) were those related to scalar reductions, e.g., `anyMatch()`, `allMatch()`. RO-specific bugs related to collector operations (CO, 3), on the other hand, involve non-scalar reductions, e.g., a collector malfunction. RO-specific data ordering bugs (DO, 2) correspond to ordering of data related to scalar reductions, e.g., using `findAny()` instead of

Table 4. Studied stream bugs and patches (nonhierarchical).

subject	BC	CI	CO	DO	EH	FO	IA	IO	MO	OS	PP	RO	SS	Other	Total
binnavi														1	1
blueocean-plugin														1	1
bootique											1				1
che			1	1	1						1				4
cryptomator	1										2		1	2	6
dari														2	2
eclipse.jdt.core														1	1
eclipse.jdt.ui												1			1
error-prone					2	1	1		3		1	1	2	1	12
guava														1	1
JacpFX		1		1						2					4
jdp												1			1
jetty				1	2	1					3				7
jOOQ									1						1
selenium			2	1	2	5	1	2	2		1			1	17
threeten-extra	1														1
Total	2	1	3	4	7	7	2	2	6	2	9	3	3	10	61

`findFirst()`. RO-specific incorrect actions (IA, 1) is where there is a problematic λ in a scalar reduction, e.g., an incorrect predicate in `noneMatch()`. Side-effect producing operation bugs also include incorrect actions (IA, 1), e.g., a problematic λ in `forEach()`. Such operations can also exhibit poor performance (PO, 1).

Some bug categories are crosscutting, appearing under *multiple* categories. An example is performance. For this reason, tab. 4 portrays a nonhierarchical view of fig. 2, which is also broken down by **subject**, including a column for each bug category regardless of its parent category (acronyms correspond to tab. 3).

> ***Finding 7***: Bugs, e.g., performance, *crosscut* concerns, affecting multiple categories, both specifically and tangentially, associated with streams.

Performance issues dominate the functional (excluding "other") bugs depicted in tab. 4, making up the categories "Performance/API misuse" and "Performance," accounting for 14.75% (9/61) of the bugs found. While some of these fixes were more cleaning-based (e.g., superfluous operations), others affected central parts of the system and were found during performance regression testing [56].

> ***Finding 8***: Although streams feature performance improving parallelism, developers tend to struggle with using streams efficiently.

Despite widespread performance issues, concurrency issues (CI), on the other hand, were not prevalent (1.64%). The one concurrency bug was where a stream operation involved non-atomic variable access, which resulted in improper initialization [34]. Given that such a variable is accessed in a stream operation, however, it does indicate a possible side-effect and a need to consider refactoring such accesses to remove side-effects. This would make streams more amenable to efficient parallelization and perhaps promote more usage of parallel streams.

> ***Finding 9***: Concurrency issues were the *least* common streams bugs. However, concurrent variable access can cause thread contention, motivating future refactoring approaches that may promote more parallel streams.

The subjects selenium and error-prone had the most stream bugs with 27.87% and 19.67%, respectively. We hypothesize that this is due to the relatively large size of these projects, as well as their high usage of streams. Specifically, they fell into the top ten in terms of KLOC and stream method calls in tab. 2 and fig. 1, respectively, with $\sim$400 combined KLOC and 1,414 combined calls. Naturally, projects that use streams more are likely to have more bugs involving streams.

Qualitative We highlight several of the most common bug categories with examples, summarize common fixes, and propose preliminary best practices (**BP**) and anti-patterns (**AP**). Due to space limitations, only a single example of each BP/AP is shown; a complete set is available in our dataset [25]. Although some APs may seem applicable beyond streams, e.g., avoiding superfluous operations, we conjecture that streams are more prone to such patterns, e.g., due to the ease in which operations can be chained and the deferred execution they offer.

$SS{\rightarrow}PP$ Performance issues dominated the number of stream bugs found and also crosscut multiple categories. Consider the following performance regression [56]:

```
      Project: jetty
  Commit ID: 70311fe98787ffb8a74ad296c9dd2ba9ac431c9c
      Log: Issue #3681
1 - List<HttpField> cookies = preserveCookies ? _fields.stream().filter(f ->
2 -     f.getHeader() == HttpHeader.SET_COOKIE).collect(Collectors.toList()) : null;
3 + List<HttpField> cookies = preserveCookies?_fields.getFields(HttpHeader.SET_COOKIE):null;
```

The stream field is replaced with `getFields()`, which performs an iterative traversal, effectively replacing streams with iteration. The developer found that using iteration was faster than using streams [57] and wanted more "JIT-friendly" code. The developer further admitted that using streams can make code more easy to read but can also be associated with "allocation/complexity cost [55]."

> **BP1**: Use performance regression testing to verify that streams in *critical* code paths perform efficiently.

In the following, a pair of superfluous operations are removed:

```
      Project: JacpFX
  Commit ID: 4f0d62d3a0987e47a4cbdf8e056bdf89713e6aac
      Log: fixed class scanning
1       final Stream<String> componentIds = CommonUtil
2          .getStringStreamFromArray(annotation.perspectives());
3       final Stream<Injectable> perspectiveHandlerList =
4 -         componentIds.parallel().sequential().map(this::mapToInjectable);
5 +         componentIds.map(this::mapToInjectable);
```

`getStringStreaFromArray()` returns a sequential stream, which is then converted to `parallel` and then to `sequential`. The superfluous operations are then removed.

> **AP1**: Avoid superfluous intermediate operations.

Fix: Generally, fixes for performance problems varied widely. They ranged from replacing stream code with iterative code, as seen above, to removing operations, to changing the stream source representations. Depending on context, the bugs' effect can be either innocuous and cause server performance degradation.

$SS{\rightarrow}TO{\rightarrow}RO{\rightarrow}CO$ The stream API provides several ready-made `Collectors` for convenience. However, the API does not guarantee a *specific* non-scalar used during the reduction. On one hand, this is convenient as developers may not need a specific collection type; on the other hand, however, developers must be careful to ensure that the specific subclass returned by the API meets their needs.

In the following, the developer does not realize, until an incorrect program output, that the `Map` returned by `Collectors.toMap()` does not support nulls:

```
     Project: selenium
  Commit ID: 91eb004d230d8d78ec97180e66bcc7055b16130f
        Log: Fix wrapping of maps with null values. Fixes #3380
1 if (result instanceof Map) {
2 -   return ((Map<String, Object>) result).entrySet().stream().collect(Collectors.toMap(
3 -     e -> e.getKey(), e -> wrapResult(e.getValue())));
4 +   return ((Map<String, Object>) result).entrySet().stream().collect(HashMap::new,
5 +     (m, e) -> m.put(e.getKey(), e.getValue()), Map::putAll);
```

The ready-made collector (line 2) is replaced with a direct call to `collect()` with a particular `Map` implementation specified (line 4), i.e., `HashMap`.

> **BP2**: Use collectors *only* if client code is *agnostic* to particular container implementations. Otherwise, use the *direct* form of `collect()`.

Fix: Collector-related bugs are typically corrected by not using a `Collector` (as above), changing the `Collector` used, or altering the `Collector` arguments. They often adversely affect program behavior but are also caught by unit tests.

SS→IO In the ensuing commit, `distinct()` is called on a concatenated stream to ensure that no duplicates are created as a result of the concatenation:

```
     Project: selenium
  Commit ID: eb7d9bf9cea19b8bc1759c4de1eb495829489cbe
        Log: Fix tests failing because of ProtocolHandshake
1 -     return Stream.concat(fromOss, fromW3c);
2 +     return Stream.concat(fromOss, fromW3c).distinct();
```

> **BP3**: Ensure concatenated streams have distinct elements.

Fix: SS→IO bugs tend to be fixed by adding *additional* operations.

SS→IO→Other Developers "bridged" back to an imperative-style performed an operation, then switched back to streams to continue a more functional-style:

```
     Project: jetty
  Commit ID: 91e9e7b76a08b776be21560d7ba20f9bfd943f04
        Log: Issue #984 Improve module listing
1 -   List<String> ordered = _modules.stream()
2 -     .map(m->{return m.getName();}).collect(Collectors.toList());
3 -   Collections.sort(ordered);
4 -   ordered.stream().map(n->{return get(n);}).forEach(module->
5 +   _modules.stream().filter(m->...).sorted().forEach(module->
```

Each module is `mapped` to its name and `collected` into a list. Then, `ordered` is sorted via a non-stream `Collections` API. Another stream is then derived from `ordered` to perform further operations. However, on line 5, the bridge to a collection and subsequent sort operation is removed, and the computation remains within the stream API. It is now more amenable to parallelization.

> **AP2**: Avoid "bridging" between stream API and legacy collection APIs.

Using a long λ-expression in a single `map()` operation may make stream code less "functional," more difficult to read [29], and less amenable to parallelism. Consider the abbreviated commit below that returns the occupied drive letters on Windows systems by `collecting` the first uppercase character of the path:

```
     Project: cryptomator
  Commit ID: b691e374eb2dad0284e13927e7c3fc1fdccae9bf
        Log: fixes #74
1 - return rootDirs.stream().map(path -> path.toString().toUpperCase()
2 -     .charAt(0)).collect(toSet());
3 + return rootDirs.stream().map(Path::toString).map(CharUtils::toChar)
4 +     .map(Character::toUpperCase).collect(toSet());
```

The λ-expression has been replaced with method references, however, there are more subtle yet import changes. Firstly, as `CharUtils.toChar()` returns the first character of a `String`, there is a small performance improvement as the entire string is no longer turned to uppercase but rather only the first character. Also, the new version is written in more of a functional-style by replacing the single λ-expression passed to `map()` with multiple `map()` operations. How data is transformed in the pipeline is easily visible, and future data transformations can be easily integrated by simply adding operations.

AP3: Avoid too many operations within a single `map()` operation.

Fix: "Other" non-type correcting fixes, e.g., refactorings, included introducing streams, sometimes from formerly iterative code (3), replacing `map()` with `mapToInt()` [20], and dividing "larger" operations into smaller ones.

7 Threats to Validity

Subjects may not be representative. To mitigate this, subjects were chosen from diverse domains and sizes. They have also been used in previous studies (e.g., [20,22]). Although java-design-patterns is artificial, it is a reference implementation similar to that of JHotDraw, which has been studied extensively (e.g., [31]). Also, as streams are relatively new, we expect a larger selection of subjects as they grow in popularity.

Entry points may not be correct, which could affect how stream attributes are calculated. Since standard entry points were chosen, these represent a superset of practically true entry points. Furthermore, there may be custom streams or collectors outside the standard API that we are not considered. As we aim to understand stream usage and misuse in the large, we hypothesize that the vast majority of projects using streams use ones from the standard libraries.

Our study involved many hours of manual validation, which can be subject to bias. However, we investigated referenced bug reports and other comments from developers to help us understand changes more fully. We also reached out to several developers via email correspondence when in doubt. All but one returned the correspondence. The NLP features of `gitcproc` may have missed changesets that were indeed bug fixes. Nevertheless, we were still able to find 61 bugs that contributed to a rich bug categorization, best practices, and anti-patterns. Furthermore, `gitcproc` has been used previously in other studies.

8 Related Work

Previous studies [29,32,36,46,51] have focused specifically on λ-expressions. While λ-expressions are used as arguments to stream operations, our focus is on stream *operations* themselves. Such operations transition streams to different states, which can be detrimental to parallel performance [24,35]. Also, since streams can be aliased, we use a tool [24] based on typestate analysis to obtain stream attributes more reliably than AST-based approaches. We also study bugs related to stream usage and present developer feedback—fixing bugs related to streams may not involve changing λ-expressions; bugs can be caused by, e.g., an incorrect sequence of stream operations. Lastly, although Nielebock et al. [36] consider λ-expressions in "concurrency contexts," such contexts do not include streams, where λ-expressions can easily execute in parallel with minimal syntactical effort.

Khatchadourian et al. [24] report on some stream characteristics as part of their refactoring evaluation but do so on a much smaller-scale, as their focus was on the refactoring algorithm. The work presented here goes significantly above in beyond by reporting on a richer set of stream characteristics (e.g., execution mode, ordering), with a noteworthy larger and updated corpus. We also include a comprehensive categorization of stream-related bug fixes, with 719 commits *manually* analyzed. Preliminary best practices and anti-patterns are also proposed.

Zhou et al. [60] conduct an empirical study on 210 service quality issues of a big data platform at Microsoft to understand their common symptoms, causes, and mitigations. They identify hardware faults, systems, and customer side effects as major causes of quality issues. There are also empirical studies on data-parallel programs. Kavulya et al. [19] study failures in MapReduce programs. Jin et al. [18] study performance slowdowns caused by system side inefficiencies. Xiao et al. [58] conduct a study on commutativity, nondeterminism, and correctness of data-parallel programs, revealing that non-commutative reductions lead to bugs. Though related, our work specifically focuses on stream APIs as a language feature and programming paradigm, which pose special considerations due to its shared memory model, i.e., interactions between the operations and local memory. Bloch [6, Ch. 7] also puts-forth stream best practices and anti-patterns. However, ours are based on a statistical analysis of real-world software and first-hand interactions with real-world developers.

Others also study language features. Parnin et al. [43] study the adoption of Java generics. Dyer et al. [11] build an expansive infrastructure for studying the use of language features over time. Khatchadourian and Masuhara [22] employ a proactive approach in empirically assessing new language features and present a case study on default methods. There are also many studies regarding bug analysis. For example, Engler et al. [13] present a general approach to inferring errors in systems code, and Tian and Ray [50] study error handling bugs in C.

9   Conclusion & Future Work

This study advances our understanding of stream usage and bug patterns. We have surveyed common stream operations, attributes, and bugs specific and tangentially related to streams. A hierarchical taxonomy of stream bugs was devised, preliminary best practices and anti-patterns were proposed, and first-hand developer interactions were detailed. In the future, we will explore stream creation, use our findings to devise automated error checkers, and explore topics that interest stream developers. Lastly, we will investigate applicability to other streaming frameworks and languages.

Acknowledgments We would like to thank Krishna Desai and Robert Dyer for work on data summarization and discussions, respectively. Support for this project was provided by PSC-CUNY Award #617930049, jointly funded by The Professional Staff Congress and The City University of New York. This material is based upon work supported by the National Science Foundation under Grant No. CCF 1845893, CNS 1842456, and CCF 1822965.

References

1. Ahmed, S., and Bagherzadeh, M.: What Do Concurrency Developers Ask About?: A Large-scale Study Using Stack Overflow. In: International Symposium on Empirical Software Engineering and Measurement, 30:1–30:10 (2018). DOI: 10.1145/3239235.3239524

2. AOL: AOL/cyclops: An advanced, but easy to use, platform for writing functional applications in Java 8. (2019). http://git.io/fjxzF (visited on 08/29/2019)

3. Bagherzadeh, M., and Khatchadourian, R.: Going Big: A Large-scale Study on What Big Data Developers Ask. In: Joint Meeting on European Software Engineering Conference and Symposium on the Foundations of Software Engineering. ESEC/FSE 2019, pp. 432–442. ACM, Tallinn, Estonia (2019). DOI: 10.1145/3338906.3338939

4. Bagherzadeh, M., and Rajan, H.: Order Types: Static Reasoning About Message Races in Asynchronous Message Passing Concurrency. In: International Workshop on Programming Based on Actors, Agents, and Decentralized Control, pp. 21–30 (2017). DOI: 10.1145/3141834.3141837

5. Biboudis, A., Palladinos, N., Fourtounis, G., and Smaragdakis, Y.: Streams a la carte: Extensible Pipelines with Object Algebras. In: European Conference on Object-Oriented Programming, pp. 591–613 (2015). DOI: 10.4230/LIPIcs.ECOOP.2015.591

6. Bloch, J.: Effective Java. Prentice Hall, Upper Saddle River, NJ, USA (2018)

7. Bordet, S.: Pull Request #2837 • eclipse/jetty.project, Webtide. (2018). http://git.io/JeBAF (visited on 10/20/2019)

8. Casalnuovo, C., Devanbu, P., Oliveira, A., Filkov, V., and Ray, B.: Assert Use in GitHub Projects. In: International Conference on Software Engineering. ICSE '15, pp. 755–766. IEEE Press, Florence, Italy (2015). http://dl.acm.org/citation.cfm?id=2818754.2818846

9. Casalnuovo, C., Suchak, Y., Ray, B., and Rubio-González, C.: GitcProc: A Tool for Processing and Classifying GitHub Commits. In: International Symposium on Software Testing and Analysis. ISSTA 2017, pp. 396–399. ACM, Santa Barbara, CA, USA (2017). DOI: 10.1145/3092703.3098230

10. Dean, J., and Ghemawat, S.: MapReduce: Simplified Data Processing on Large Clusters. Commun. ACM 51(1), 107–113 (2008). DOI: 10.1145/1327452.1327492

11. Dyer, R., Rajan, H., Nguyen, H.A., and Nguyen, T.N.: Mining Billions of AST Nodes to Study Actual and Potential Usage of Java Language Features. In: International Conference on Software Engineering. ICSE 2014, pp. 779–790. ACM, Hyderabad, India (2014)

12. Eclipse Foundation: Eclipse Java development tools (JDT), Eclipse Foundation. (2019). http://eclipse.org/jdt (visited on 10/19/2019)

13. Engler, D., Chen, D.Y., Hallem, S., Chou, A., and Chelf, B.: Bugs As Deviant Behavior: A General Approach to Inferring Errors in Systems Code. In: Symposium on Operating Systems Principles. SOSP '01, pp. 57–72. ACM, Banff, Alberta, Canada (2001). DOI: 10.1145/502034.502041

14. EPFL: Collections–Mutable and Immutable Collections–Scala Documentation, (2017). http://scala-lang.org/api/2.12.3/scala/collection/index.html (visited on 08/24/2018)

15. Erdfelt, J.: Pull Request #2837 • eclipse/jetty.project, Eclipse Foundation. (2018). http://git.io/JeBAM (visited on 10/20/2019)

16. Fink, S.J., Yahav, E., Dor, N., Ramalingam, G., and Geay, E.: Effective Typestate Verification in the Presence of Aliasing. ACM Transactions on Software Engineering and Methodology 17(2), 91–934 (2008). DOI: 10.1145/1348250.1348255

17. Gharbi, S., Mkaouer, M.W., Jenhani, I., and Messaoud, M.B.: On the Classification of Software Change Messages Using Multi-label Active Learning. In: Symposium on Applied Computing. SAC '19, pp. 1760–1767. ACM, Limassol, Cyprus (2019). DOI: 10.1145/3297280.3297452

18. Jin, H., Qiao, K., Sun, X.-H., and Li, Y.: Performance Under Failures of MapReduce Applications. In: International Symposium on Cluster, Cloud and Grid Computing. CCGRID '11, pp. 608–609. IEEE Computer Society, Washington, DC, USA (2011). DOI: 10.1109/ccgrid.2011.84

19. Kavulya, S., Tan, J., Gandhi, R., and Narasimhan, P.: An Analysis of Traces from a Production MapReduce Cluster. In: International Conference on Cluster, Cloud and Grid Computing. CCGrid 2010, pp. 94–103. IEEE, Melbourne, Australia (2010). DOI: 10.1109/CCGRID.2010.112

20. Ketkar, A., Mesbah, A., Mazinanian, D., Dig, D., and Aftandilian, E.: Type Migration in Ultra-large-scale Codebases. In: International Conference on Software Engineering. ICSE '19, pp. 1142–1153. IEEE Press, Montreal, Quebec, Canada (2019). DOI: 10.1109/ICSE.2019.00117

21. Khatchadourian, R., and Masuhara, H.: Automated Refactoring of Legacy Java Software to Default Methods. In: International Conference on Software Engineering, pp. 82–93 (2017). DOI: 10.1109/ICSE.2017.16

22. Khatchadourian, R., and Masuhara, H.: Proactive Empirical Assessment of New Language Feature Adoption via Automated Refactoring: The Case of Java 8 Default Methods. In: International Conference on the Art, Science, and Engineering of Programming, 6:1–6:30 (2018). DOI: 10.22152/programming-journal.org/2018/2/6

23. Khatchadourian, R., Tang, Y., Bagherzadeh, M., and Ahmed, S.: A Tool for Optimizing Java 8 Stream Software via Automated Refactoring. In: International Working Conference on Source Code Analysis and Manipulation, pp. 34–39 (2018). DOI: 10.1109/SCAM.2018.00011

24. Khatchadourian, R., Tang, Y., Bagherzadeh, M., and Ahmed, S.: Safe Automated Refactoring for Intelligent Parallelization of Java 8 Streams. In: International Conference on Software Engineering. ICSE '19, pp. 619–630. IEEE Press (2019). DOI: 10.1109/ICSE.2019.00072

25. Khatchadourian, R., Tang, Y., Bagherzadeh, M., and Ray, B.: *An Empirical Study on the Use and Misuse of Java 8 Streams*, (2020). DOI: 10.5281/zenodo.3677449. Feb. 2020.

26. Kochhar, P.S., and Lo, D.: Revisiting Assert Use in GitHub Projects. In: International Conference on Evaluation and Assessment in Software Engineering. EASE'17, pp. 298–307. ACM, Karlskrona, Sweden (2017). DOI: 10.1145/3084226.3084259

27. Lau, J.: Future of Java 8 Language Feature Support on Android. Android Developers Blog (2017). http://android-developers.googleblog.com/2017/03/future-of-java-8-language-feature.html (visited on 08/24/2018)

28. Lu, S., Park, S., Seo, E., and Zhou, Y.: Learning from Mistakes: A Comprehensive Study on Real World Concurrency Bug Characteristics. In: International Conference on Architectural Support for Programming Languages and Operating Systems, pp. 329–339. ACM (2008). DOI: 10.1145/1346281.1346323

29. Lucas, W., Bonifácio, R., Canedo, E.D., Marcílio, D., and Lima, F.: Does the Introduction of Lambda Expressions Improve the Comprehension of Java Programs? In: Brazilian Symposium on Software Engineering. SBES 2019, pp. 187–196. ACM, Salvador, Brazil (2019). DOI: 10.1145/3350768.3350791

30. Luontola, E.: Pull Request #140 • orfjackal/retrolambda, Nitor Creations. (2018). http://git.io/JeBAQ (visited on 10/20/2019)

31. Marin, M., Moonen, L., and Deursen, A. van: An Integrated Crosscutting Concern Migration Strategy and its Application to JHotDraw. In: International Working Conference on Source Code Analysis and Manipulation (2007)

32. Mazinanian, D., Ketkar, A., Tsantalis, N., and Dig, D.: Understanding the Use of Lambda Expressions in Java. Proc. ACM Program. Lang. 1(OOPSLA), 85:1–85:31 (2017). DOI: 10.1145/3133909

33. Microsoft: LINQ: .NET Language Integrated Query, (2018). http://msdn.microsoft.com/en-us/library/bb308959.aspx (visited on 08/24/2018)

34. Moncsek, A.: allow OnShow when Perspective is initialized, fixed issues with OnShow/OnHide in perspective • JacpFX/JacpFX@f2d92f7, JacpFX. (2015). http://git.io/Je0X8 (visited on 10/24/2019)

35. Naftalin, M.: Mastering Lambdas: Java Programming in a Multicore World. McGraw-Hill (2014)

36. Nielebock, S., Heumüller, R., and Ortmeier, F.: Programmers Do Not Favor Lambda Expressions for Concurrent Object-oriented Code. Empirical Softw. Engg. 24(1), 103–138 (2019). DOI: 10.1007/s10664-018-9622-9

37. Oracle: Collectors (Java Platform SE 10 & JDK 10)–groupingByConcurrent, (2018). http://docs.oracle.com/javase/10/docs/api/java/util/stream/Collectors.html#groupingByConcurrent(java.util.function.Function) (visited on 08/29/2019)

38. Oracle: HashSet (Java SE 9) & JDK 9, (2017). http://docs.oracle.com/javase/9/docs/api/java/util/HashSet.html (visited on 04/07/2018)

39. Oracle: java.util.stream (Java SE 9 & JDK 9), (2017). http://docs.oracle.com/javase/9/docs/api/java/util/stream/package-summary.html (visited on 02/22/2020)

40. Oracle: java.util.stream (Java SE 9 & JDK 9)–Parallelism, (2017). http://docs.oracle.com/javase/9/docs/api/java/util/stream/package-summary.html#Parallelism (visited on 02/22/2020)

41. Oracle: Stream (Java Platform SE 10 & JDK 10)–forEach, (2018). http://docs.oracle.com/javase/10/docs/api/java/util/stream/Stream.html#forEach(java.util.function.Consumer) (visited on 08/29/2019)

42. Oracle: Thread Interference, (2017). http://docs.oracle.com/javase/tutorial/essential/concurrency/interfere.html (visited on 04/16/2018)

43. Parnin, C., Bird, C., and Murphy-Hill, E.: Adoption and Use of Java Generics. Empirical Softw. Engg. 18(6), 1047–1089 (2013). DOI: 10.1007/s10664-012-9236-6

44. Refsnes Data: JavaScript Array map() Method, (2015). http://w3schools.com/jsref/jsref_map.asp (visited on 02/22/2020)

45. Rutledge, P.: Pull Request #1 • RutledgePaulV/monads, Vodori. (2018). http://git.io/JeBAZ (visited on 10/20/2019)

46. Sangle, S., and Muvva, S.: On the Use of Lambda Expressions in 760 Open Source Python Projects. In: Joint Meeting on European Software Engineering Conference and Symposium on the Foundations of Software Engineering. ESEC/FSE 2019, pp. 1232–1234. ACM, Tallinn, Estonia (2019). DOI: 10.1145/3338906.3342499

47. Shilkov, M.: Introducing Stream Processing in F#, (2016). http://mikhail.io/2016/11/introducing-stream-processing-in-fsharp (visited on 07/18/2018)

48. Stack Overflow: Newest 'java-stream' Questions, (2018). http://stackoverflow.com/questions/tagged/java-stream (visited on 03/06/2018)

49. Strom, R.E., and Yemini, S.: Typestate: A programming language concept for enhancing software reliability. IEEE Transactions on Software Engineering SE-12(1), 157–171 (1986). DOI: 10.1109/tse.1986.6312929

50. Tian, Y., and Ray, B.: Automatically Diagnosing and Repairing Error Handling Bugs in C. In: Joint Meeting on European Software Engineering Conference and

Symposium on the Foundations of Software Engineering. ESEC/FSE 2017, pp. 752–762. ACM, Paderborn, Germany (2017). DOI: 10.1145/3106237.3106300

51. Uesbeck, P.M., Stefik, A., Hanenberg, S., Pedersen, J., and Daleiden, P.: An empirical study on the impact of C++ lambdas and programmer experience. In: International Conference on Software Engineering. ICSE '16, pp. 760–771. ACM, Austin, Texas (2016). DOI: 10.1145/2884781.2884849

52. WALA Team: T.J. Watson Libraries for Analysis, (2015). http://wala.sf.net (visited on 01/18/2017)

53. Warburton, R.: Java 8 Lambdas: Pragmatic Functional Programming (2014)

54. Weiss, T.: Java 8: Behind The Glitz and Glamour of The New Parallelism APIs. OverOps Blog (2014). http://blog.overops.com/new-parallelism-apis-in-java-8-behind-the-glitz-and-glamour (visited on 10/20/2019)

55. Wilkins, G.: Issue #3681 • eclipse/jetty.project@70311fe, Webtide, LLC. (2019)

56. Wilkins, G.: Jetty 9.4.x 3681 http fields optimize by gregw • Pull Request #3682 • eclipse/jetty.project, Webtide, LLC. (2019). http://git.io/JeBAq (visited on 09/18/2019)

57. Wilkins, G.: Jetty 9.4.x 3681 http fields optimize by gregw • Pull Request #3682 • eclipse/jetty.project. Comment, Webtide, LLC. (2019). http://git.io/Je0MS (visited on 10/24/2019)

58. Xiao, T., Zhang, J., Zhou, H., Guo, Z., McDirmid, S., Lin, W., Chen, W., and Zhou, L.: Nondeterminism in MapReduce Considered Harmful? An Empirical Study on Non-commutative Aggregators in MapReduce Programs. In: ICSE Companion, pp. 44–53 (2014). DOI: 10.1145/2591062.2591177

59. Zhitnitsky, A.: How Java 8 Lambdas and Streams Can Make Your Code 5 Times Slower. OverOps Blog (2015). http://blog.overops.com/benchmark-how-java-8-lambdas-and-streams-can-make-your-code-5-times-slower (visited on 10/20/2019)

60. Zhou, H., Lou, J.-G., Zhang, H., Lin, H., Lin, H., and Qin, T.: An Empirical Study on Quality Issues of Production Big Data Platform. In: International Conference on Software Engineering. ICSE 2015, pp. 17–26. ACM, Florence, Italy (2015)

7

Improving Symbolic Automata Learning with Concolic Execution*

Donato Clun[1] , Phillip van Heerden[2] , Antonio Filieri[1] , and Willem Visser[2]

[1] Imperial College London
[2] Stellenbosch University

Abstract. Inferring the input grammar accepted by a program is central for a variety of software engineering problems, including parsers verification, grammar-based fuzzing, communication protocol inference, and documentation. Sound and complete active learning techniques have been developed for several classes of languages and the corresponding automaton representation, however there are outstanding challenges that are limiting their effective application to the inference of input grammars. We focus on active learning techniques based on L^* and propose two extensions of the *Minimally Adequate Teacher* framework that allow the efficient learning of the input language of a program in the form of symbolic automata, leveraging the additional information that can extracted from concolic execution. Upon these extensions we develop two learning algorithms that reduce significantly the number of queries required to converge to the correct hypothesis.

1 Introduction

Inferring the input grammar of a program from its implementation is central for a variety of software engineering activities, including automated documentation, compiler analyses, and grammar-based fuzzing.

Several learning algorithms have been investigated for inferring a grammar from examples of accepted and rejected input words, with active learning approaches achieving the highest data-efficiency and strong convergence guarantees. Active learning is a theoretical framework enabling a *learner* to gather information about a target language by interacting with a *teacher* [1]. A minimally adequate teacher that can guarantee the convergence of an active language learning procedure for regular language is an oracle that can answer membership and equivalence queries. Membership queries check whether a word indicated by the learner is accepted by the target language and equivalence queries can confirm that a hypothesis language proposed by the learner is equivalent to the target language, or provide a counterexample word otherwise.

However, when learning the input language accepted by a program from its code implementation, it is unrealistic to assume the availability of a complete equivalence oracle, because such an oracle would need to check the equivalence between the hypothesis language and arbitrary software code.

In this paper, we explore the use of concolic execution to design active learning procedures for inferring the input grammar of a program in the form of a symbolic finite automaton. In particular, we extend two state of the art active learning frameworks for symbolic learning by enabling the teacher to 1) provide more informative answers for membership queries by pairing the accept/reject outcome with a path condition describing all the input words that would result in the same execution as the word indicated by the learner, and 2) provide a partial equivalence oracle that may produce counterexamples for the learner hypothesis. The partial equivalence oracle would rely on the exploration capabilities of the concolic execution engine to identify input words for which the acceptance outcome differs between the target program and the learner's hypothesis. To guarantee the termination of the concolic execution for equivalence queries, we set a bound on the length of the inputs the engine can generate during its exploration. While necessarily incomplete, such equivalence oracle may effectively guide the learning process and guarantee the correctness of the learned language for inputs up to the set input bound. Finally, we propose a new class of symbolic membership queries that build on the constraint solving capabilities of the concolic engine to directly infer complete information about the transitions between states of the hypothesis language.

In our preliminary evaluation based on Java implementations of parsers for regular languages from the Automatark benchmark suite, the new active learning algorithms enabled by concolic execution learned the correct input language for 76% of the subject, despite the lack of a complete equivalence oracle and achieving a reduction of up to 96% of the number of membership and equivalence queries produced by the learner.

The remaining of the paper is structured as follows: Section 2 introduces background concepts and definitions concerning symbolic finite state automata, active learning, and concolic execution. Section 3 describes in details the data structures and learning algorithms of two state of the art approaches – Λ^* [11] and MAT* [3] – that will be the base for active learning strategies based on concolic execution formalized in Section 4. Section 5 will report on our preliminary experiments on the effectiveness and query-efficiency capabilities of the new strategies. Finally, Section 6 discusses related work and Section 7 presents our concluding remarks.

2   Preliminaries

2.1   Symbolic finite state automata

Symbolic finite state automata (SFA) are an extension of finite state automata where a transitions can be labeled with a predicate identifying a subset of the input alphabet [28]. The set of predicates allowed on SFA transitions should constitute an *effective Boolean algebra* [3], which guarantees closure with respect to boolean operations according to the following definition:

Definition 1. *Effective Boolean algebra [3]. An effective Boolean algebra $\mathcal{A}$ is a tuple $(\mathcal{D}, \Psi, \llbracket \_ \rrbracket, \bot, \top, \vee, \wedge, \neg)$ where $\mathcal{D}$ is the set of domain elements; Ψ is the set of predicates, including $\bot$ and $\top$; $\llbracket \_ \rrbracket : \Psi \rightarrow 2^{\mathcal{D}}$ is a denotation function such that $\llbracket \bot \rrbracket = \emptyset$, $\llbracket \top \rrbracket = \mathcal{D}$, and for all $\phi, \psi \in \Psi$, $\llbracket \phi \vee \psi \rrbracket = \llbracket \phi \rrbracket \cup \llbracket \psi \rrbracket$, $\llbracket \phi \wedge \psi \rrbracket = \llbracket \phi \rrbracket \cap \llbracket \psi \rrbracket$, and $\llbracket \neg \phi \rrbracket = \mathcal{D} \setminus \llbracket \phi \rrbracket$.*

Given an effective Boolean algebra $\mathcal{A}$, an SFA is formally defined as:

Definition 2. *Symbolic Finite Automaton (SFA) [3] A symbolic finite automaton $\mathcal{M}$ is a tuple $(\mathcal{A}, Q, q_{init}, F, \Delta)$ where $\mathcal{A}$ is an effective Boolean algebra, called the* alphabet*; Q is a finite set of states; $q_{init} \in Q$ is the* initial *state; $F \subseteq Q$ is the set of* final *states; and $\Delta \subseteq Q \times \Psi_{\mathcal{A}} \times Q$ is the transition relation* consisting of a finite set of *moves or transitions.*

Given a linearly ordered finite alphabet Σ, through the rest of the paper we will assume $\mathcal{A}$ to be the Boolean algebra over the union of intervals over Σ, with the canonical interpretations of union, intersection, and negation operators. With an abuse of notation, we will write $\psi \in \mathcal{A}$ to refer to a predicate ψ in the set Ψ of $\mathcal{A}$. A *word* is a finite sequence of alphabet symbols (*characters*) $w = w_0 w_1 \ldots w_n$ ($w_i \in \Sigma$), whose *length* $len(w) = n - 1$. We indicate with $w[: i]$ the prefix of w up to the i element excluded, and with $w[i :]$ the suffix of w starting from element i. We will use the notation w_i and $w[i]$ interchangeably. The language accepted by an SFA $\mathcal{M}$ will be indicated as $L_{\mathcal{M}}$, or only L when the SFA M can be inferred by the context. For an SFA $\mathcal{M}$ and a word w, $\mathcal{M}(w) = true$ if $\mathcal{M}$ accepts w; $false$ otherwise.

Similarly to finite state automata, SFAs are closed under language intersection, union, and complement, and admit a minimal form [3]. Compared to non-symbolic automata, SFAs can produce more compact representations over large alphabets (e.g., Unicode), allowing a single transition predicate to account for a possibly large set of characters, instead of explicitly enumerating all of them.

2.2   Active learning and minimally adequate teachers

Active learning encompasses a set of techniques enabling a learning algorithm to gather information interacting with a suitable oracle, referred to as *teacher*. Angluin [1] proposed an exact, active learning algorithm for a regular language L named L^*. In L^* the learner can ask the oracle two types of queries, namely *membership* and *equivalence* queries. In a membership query, the learner selects a word $w \in \Sigma^*$ and the oracle answers whether the $w \in L$ (formally, the membership oracle is a function $\mathcal{O}_m : \Sigma^* \rightarrow \mathbb{B}$, where $\mathbb{B} = \{true, false\}$). In an equivalence query, the learner selects an hypothesis finite state automaton (FSA) $\mathcal{H}$ and asks the oracle whether $L_{\mathcal{H}} \equiv L$; if $L_{\mathcal{H}} \not\equiv L$, the oracle returns a *counterexample*, i.e., a word w in which L differs from L_H (formally, the equivalence oracle is a function $\mathcal{O}_e : FSA \rightarrow \Sigma^* \cup \{true\}$). A teacher providing both $\mathcal{O}_m$ and $\mathcal{O}_e$, and able to produce a counter example as result from $\mathcal{O}_e$ is called a *minimally adequate teacher*. Given a minimally adequate teacher, L^* is guaranteed to learn the target language L with a number of queries polynomial in the number of states of a minimal deterministic automaton accepting L and in the size of the largest counterexample returned by the teacher [1].

Discovering FSA states. Consider an FSA $\mathcal{M}$. Given two words u and v such that $\mathcal{M}(u) \neq \mathcal{M}(v)$ (i.e., one accepted and one rejected), it can be concluded that u and v reach different states of $\mathcal{M}$. Moreover, if u and v share a suffix s (i.e., $u = a.s$ and $v = b.s$ with $a, b, s \in \Sigma^*$ and the dot representing word concatenation), a and b necessarily reach two different states q_a and q_b of $\mathcal{M}$. The suffix s is a *discriminator suffix* for the two states because its parsing starting from q_a and q_b leads to difference acceptance outcomes. The words a and b are instead *access words* of q_a and q_b, respectively, because their parsing from the initial state reaches q_a and q_b. This observation can be generalized to a set of words by considering all the unordered pairs of words in the set. Because $\mathcal{M}$ is a finite state automaton, there can be only a finite number of discriminable words in Σ^* and, correspondingly, a finite number of distinct access string identifying the automaton's states.

State reached parsing a word. For a word w, consider a known discriminator suffix s and access word a. If $\mathcal{O}_m(w.s) \neq \mathcal{O}_m(a.s)$, the state reached parsing w cannot be the one identified by a. Throughout the learning process, it is possible that none of the already discovered access words identifies the state reached by w. In this case, w would be a suitable candidate for discovering a new FSA state as described in the previous paragraph.

Discovering FSA transitions. For each access string a and symbol $\sigma \in \Sigma$, a transition should exist between the states reached parsing a and $a.\sigma$, respectively.

2.3 Concolic execution

Concolic execution [14,27] combines concrete and symbolic execution of a program, allowing to extract for a given concrete input a set of constraints on the input space that uniquely characterize the corresponding execution path. To this end, the target program is instrumented to pair each program input with a symbolic input variable and to record along an execution path the constraints on the symbolic inputs induced by the encountered conditional branches. The conjunction of the constraints recorded during the execution of the instrumented program on a concrete input is called *path condition* and characterize the equivalence class of all the inputs that would follow the same execution path (in this paper, we focus on sequential program, whose execution is uniquely determined by the program inputs).

Explored path conditions can be stored in a prefix tree (*symbolic execution tree*), which captures all the paths already covered by at least one executed input. A concolic engine can traverse the symbolic execution tree to find branches not yet explored. The path condition corresponding to the selected unexplored branch is then solved using a constraint solver (e.g., an SMT solver [26]) generating a concrete input that will cover the branch. The traversal order used to find the next branch to be covered is referred to as *search strategy* of the concolic executor.

2.4 From path conditions to SFA

In this paper, we consider only terminating programs that can either accept or reject a finite input word $w \in \Sigma^*$ (e.g., either parsing it correctly or throwing a parsing exception). Furthermore, we assume for a given input word w, the resulting path condition to be expressible using a subset of the string constraint language defined in [5]. This allows the translation of the resulting path condition into a finite state automaton [5]. The adaptation of this translation procedure to produce SFAs is straightforward. In particular, we will focus on constraints F recursively defined as:

$$F \to C \mid \neg F \mid F \wedge F \mid F \vee F$$
$$C \to E \; O \; E \mid len(w) \; O \; E \mid w[n] \; O \; \sigma \mid w[len(w) - n] \; O \; \sigma$$
$$E \to n \mid n + n \mid n - n$$
$$O \to < \mid = \mid >$$

with $n \in \mathbb{Z}$ is an integer constant and $\sigma \in \Sigma$. Informally, the path condition corresponding to processing a symbolic input word w should be reducible to a combination of interval constraints on the linearly ordered alphabet Σ for each of the symbols $w[i]$ composing the input. Despite its restriction, this constraint language is expressive enough to capture the path conditions obtained from the concolic execution of a variety of programs that accept regular languages (which will be described in the evaluation section). The extension to support the entire string constraint language proposed in [5] is left as future work.

3   Active learning for SFA

Several active learning algorithms have been defined for SFAs. In this section, we recall and formalize the core routines of two extensions of L^* proposed in [11] and [3], named Λ^* and MAT^*, respectively. We will then extend and adapt these routines to improve their efficiency and resilience to incomplete oracles based on partial concolic execution.

Running example. To demonstrate the functioning of the algorithms discussed in this section and their extensions later one, we introduce here as running example the SFA accepting the language corresponding to regular expression `.*\w[^\w]\d[^\d].*`, where `\w` matches any letter, digit, or underscore (i.e., `[a-zA-Z0-9_]`), `\d` matches any digit, and `.*` matches any sequence of symbols. The regular expression is evaluated over the 16bit unicode symbols. The corresponding SFA is represented in Figure 1, where transitions are labeled by the union of disjoint intervals and each interval is represented as $\sigma_i - \sigma_j$, or σ if it is composed by a single element; intervals are separated by a semicolon.

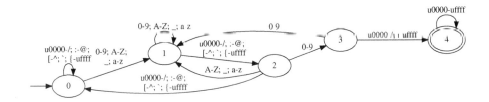

Fig. 1. SFA accepting the language for the running example.

This example highlights the conciseness of symbolic automata. It was chosen because the benefits of the methodologies discussed in this paper increase as the transitions are labeled with predicates representing larger set of characters, and the intervals used in this example are representative of commonly used ones.

3.1   Learning using observation tables

Λ^* is an adaptation of L^* for learning SFAs. In both algorithms, the learner stores and process the information gathered by the oracle in an *observation table* (we adapt here the notation defined in [11]):

Definition 3. *Observation table [11]. An observation table T for an SFA $\mathcal{M}$ is a tuple (Σ, S, R, E, f) where Σ is a potentially infinite set called the* alphabet; $S, R, E \subset \Sigma^*$ *are finite subsets of words called, respectively,* prefixes, boundary, *and* suffixes. $f : (S \cup R) \times E \to \{true, false\}$ *is a Boolean* classification *function such that for word $w \in (S \cup R)$ and $e \in E$, $f(w.e) = true$ iff $\mathcal{M}(w.e)$. Additionally, the following invariants hold: (i) $S \cap R = \emptyset$, (ii) $S \cup R$ is prefix-closed, and the empty word $\epsilon \in S$, (iii) for all $s \in S$, there exists a character $\sigma \in \Sigma$ such that $s.\sigma \in R$, and (iv) $\epsilon \in E$.*

Figure 2a shows an example observation table (**T**) according to the notation in [11]. The rows are indexed by elements of $S \cup R$, with the elements of S reported above the horizontal line and those of R below it. The columns instead are indexed by elements of E. An element in $s \in S$ represent the access word to a state q_s, i.e., the state that would be reached by parsing s from the initial state. Elements in the boundary set R provide information about the SFA transitions. The elements of $e \in E$ are discrimination suffixes in that, if there exist $s_i, s_j \in S$ and $e \in E$ such that $f(s_i.e) \neq f(s_j.e)$, s_i and s_j reach different states of $\mathcal{M}$. The cell corresponding to a row index $w \in S \cup R$ and column index $e \in E$ contains the result of $f(w.e)$, which, for compactness, is represented as $+$ or $-$ when the f evaluates to *true* or *false*, respectively. For an element $w \in S \cup R$, we use $row(w)$ to indicate the vector of $+/-$ in the row of the table indexed by w.

An observation table is: *closed* if for each $r \in R$ there exists $s \in S$ such that $row(r) = row(s)$; *reduced* if for all $s_i, s_j \in S$, $s_i \neq s_j \Rightarrow row(s_i) \neq row(s_j)$; *consistent* if for all $w_i, w_j \in S \cup R$ and $\sigma \in \Sigma$, if $w_i.\sigma, w_j.\sigma \in S \cup R$ and $row(w_i) = row(w_j)$ then $row(w_i.\sigma) = row(w_j.\sigma)$; *evidence-closed* if for all $e \in E$ and $s \in S$, $s.e \in S \cup R$. An observation table is *choesive* if it is closed, reduced, consistent, and evidence-closed. Informally, closed means that every element of R corresponds to a state identified by an element of S; reduced, that every state is identified by a unique access string in S; consistent, that if two words w_i and w_j are equivalent according to f and E, then also $w_i.\sigma$ and $w_j.\sigma$ should be equivalent for any symbol $\sigma \in \Sigma$.

Induced SFA. A cohesive observation table **T** induces an SFA that accepts or reject words consistently with its classification function f. Such induced SFA $\mathcal{M}_\mathbf{T} = (\mathcal{A}, Q, q_{init}, F, \Delta)$, where $\mathcal{A}$ is assumed to be the effective Boolean algebra over the union of intervals of Σ, is constructed as follows. For each $s \in S$ a corresponding state $q_s \in Q$ is defined, with the initial state q_{init} being q_ϵ. The final states F are all the states q_s such that $f(s) = true$. Since **T** is cohesive, a function $g : S \cup R \to S$ can be defined such that $g(w) = s$ iff $row(w) = row(s)$. Given g, for $w \in \Sigma^*$ and $\sigma \in \Sigma$, if $w.\sigma \in S \cup R$ then $(q_{g(w)}, \sigma, q_{g(w.\sigma)}) \in \Delta$. However, this intuitive construction of the transition relation Δ would result in

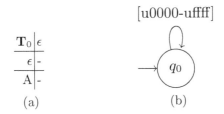

Fig. 2. Example of a cohesive observation table and its induced automata.

the construction of a FSA, where each transition is labeled with a single element $\sigma \in \Sigma$. To obtain an equivalent SFA, an additional step is required to learn the transition predicates of the SFA $\mathcal{M}_{\mathbf{T}}$.

Transition predicates. Given a Boolean algebra $\mathcal{A}$ with domain $\mathcal{D} = \Sigma$, a *partition function* can be defined that generalizes the concrete evidence for a transition of the induced automaton into a predicate of $\mathcal{A}$. Intuitively, the resulting predicate for a transition from state q_i to state q_j should evaluate positively for all the elements $\sigma_j \in \Sigma$ that would label a transition from q_i to q_j according to the function g defined in the previous paragraph, and negatively for all the elements σ_k that would label a transition from q_i to a state other than q_j. Because the function g is by construction a partial function (defined only for words $w.\sigma \in S \cup R$), the partition function can arbitrarily assign the symbols σ not classified by g. This produces a natural generalization of the induced SFA from an observation table.

In this paper, we assume $\mathcal{A}$ to be the Boolean algebra over the union of intervals over Σ, with Σ being a linearly ordered finite alphabet, such as the ascii or unicode symbols. For this algebra, a partition function can be trivially defined by constructing for each transition an interval union predicate characterizing all the concrete evidence symbols that would label the transition according to g. Then, for a given state, the symbols for which g is not defined can be arbitrarily added to any of the predicates labeling an outgoing transition. A more efficient definition of a partition function for this algebra is beyond the scope of this section. The interested reader is instead referred to [11].

The introduction of a partition function to abstract concrete transition symbols into predicates of a Boolean algebra is the key generalization of Λ^* over L^* that allow learning SFAs instead of FSA. Going back to the observation table in Figure 2a, the induced SFA is shown in Figure 2b. The observation table provides concrete evidence for labeling the transition from ϵ to itself with the symbol A. The partition function generalized this concrete evidence into the predicate [u0000-uffff], which assigned all the elements of the unicode alphabet to the sole outgoing transition from q_0.

Learning algorithm. Initially, the learner assumes an observation table corresponding to the empty language, with $S = E = \{\epsilon\}$ and $R = \{\sigma\}$ for an arbitrary $\sigma \in \Sigma$, like the one in Figure 2a. The corresponding induced SFA $\mathcal{M}_{\mathbf{T}}$ is the hypothesis the learner proposes to the equivalence oracle $\mathcal{O}_e$. If the hypothesis does not correspond to the target language, the equivalence oracle returns a counterexample $c \in \Sigma^*$. There are two possible reasons for a counterexample: either a new state should be added to the current hypothesis or one of the predicates in the hypothesis SFA needs refinement. Both cases will be handled updating the observation table to include new evidence from the counterexample c, with the partition function automatically refining the transition predicates according to the new evidence in the table.

To update the observation table, first all the prefixes of c (including c itself) are added to R, except those already present in S. (We assume every time an element is added to R, the corresponding row is filled by issuing membership queries to determine the value of $f(r.e)$, $e \in E$, for each cell.) If for a word $r \in R$ there is no word $s \in S$ such that $row(r) = row(s)$, the word r identifies a newly discovered state and it is therefore moved to S; a word $r.\sigma$ for an arbitrary $\sigma \in \Sigma$ is then added to R to trigger the exploration of outgoing transitions from the newly discovered state. To ensure the updated observation table is evidence-closed, for all $s \in S$ and $e \in E$ $s.e$ and all its prefixes are added to R, if not already present. Finally, the observation table should be made consistent. To this end, if there exist and element $\sigma \in \Sigma$ such that $w_i, w_j, w_i.\sigma, w_j.\sigma \in S \cup R$ with $row(w_i) = row(w_j)$ but $row(w_i.\sigma) \neq row(w_j.\sigma)$, then w_i and w_j should lead to different states. Since $row(w_i.\sigma) \neq row(w_j.\sigma)$, there exist $e \in E$ such that $f(w_i.\sigma.e) \neq f(w_j.\sigma.e)$. Therefore, $a.e$ can discriminate between the states reached parsing w_i and w_j and as such $a.e$ should be added to E. The observation table is now cohesive and its induced SFA can be checked against the equivalence oracle, repeating this procedure until no counterexample can be found.

Running example. We demonstrate the first three iterations of the Λ^* learning procedure invoked on the automaton in Figure 1. The initial table (Figure 2a) is cohesive, so an SFA is induced (Figure 2b) and an equivalence query is issued. The oracle returns the counter example $A!0B$. The counter example and its prefixes are added to the table (Figure 3a), and the table becomes open. The table is closed (Figure 3b), and becomes cohesive. An SFA is induced (Figure 3.1), and the equivalence query returns the counter example B. The counter example is added to the evidence (Figure 3c), and the table becomes consistent but open. The table is closed (Figure 3d), and becomes cohesive.

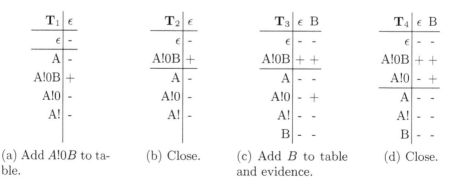

$\mathbf{T}_1$	ϵ
ϵ	-
A	-
A!0B	+
A!0	-
A!	-

(a) Add $A!0B$ to table.

$\mathbf{T}_2$	ϵ
ϵ	-
A!0B	+
A	-
A!0	-
A!	-

(b) Close.

$\mathbf{T}_3$	ϵ	B
ϵ	-	-
A!0B	+	+
A	-	-
A!0	-	+
A!	-	-
B	-	-

(c) Add B to table and evidence.

$\mathbf{T}_4$	ϵ	B
ϵ	-	-
A!0B	+	+
A!0	-	+
A	-	-
A!	-	-
B	-	-

(d) Close.

Fig. 3. Observation tables for two iterations of Λ^*.

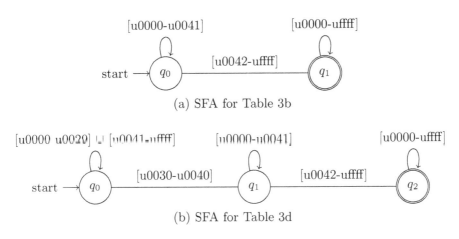

(a) SFA for Table 3b

(b) SFA for Table 3d

Fig. 4. Hypothesis automata for the learning iterations in Figure 3.

3.2 Learning using discrimination trees

A discrimination tree (DT) is a binary classification tree used by the learner to store the information gathered from the teacher. Introduced in [23], it is the core data structure of several learning algorithms, including TTT [20] and MAT^* [3]. We formalize its structure and main routines that will be the baseline for extensions presented in the next section.

Recalling from Section 2.2, each state q_a of an SFA $\mathcal{M}$ is identified by the learner using a unique *access word* $a \in \Sigma^*$. Given two states q_a and q_b, $s \in \Sigma^*$ is a *discriminator suffix* for q_a and q_b if parsing s starting from the two states leads to different outcomes (accept or reject). In terms of the state access words, this is equivalent to stating $\mathcal{M}(a.s) \neq \mathcal{M}(b.s)$. A discrimination tree stores the access words and discriminator suffixes learned for an SFA as per the following definition:

Definition 4. *Discrimination tree (adapted from [3]). A discrimination tree $\mathcal{T}$ is a tuple (N, L, T) where N is a set of nodes, $L \subseteq N$ is a set of leaves, and $T \subset N \times N \times \mathbb{B}$ is the transitions relation. Each leaf $l \in L$ is associated with a corresponding access word $(aw(l))$. Each internal node $i \in N \backslash L$ is associated with a discriminator suffix $d(i)$. For each element $(p, n, b) \in T$, p is the parent node of n and if $b = true$ (respectively $b = false$) we say that n is the accept (respectively, reject) child of p.*

For a leaf $l \in L$ and inner node $n \in N \backslash L$, if l is in the subtree of n rooted in its accept child, then $\mathcal{M}(aw(l).d(n)) = true$. Similarly, if l is in the reject subtree of n, $\mathcal{M}(aw(l).d(n)) = false$. In other words, the concatenation of $aw(l)$ with the discriminator suffix of any of its ancestor nodes is accepted iff l is in the accept subtree of the ancestor node. For any two leaves $l_i, l_j \in L$ let $n_{i,j}$ be their lowest common ancestor in the DT. Then the discriminator suffix $d(n_{i,j})$ allows to discriminate the two states corresponding to l_i and l_j since $\mathcal{M}(aw(l_i).d(n_{i,j})) \neq \mathcal{M}(aw(l_j).d(n_{i,j}))$, with $aw(l_i).d(n_{i,j})$ being the accepted word if l_i is in the accept subtree of $n_{i,j}$, or the rejected word otherwise.

Learning algorithm. We will here refer to the functioning of MAT^* [3], although the main concepts apply to DT-based learning in general. To initialize the DT, the learner performs a membership query on the empty string ϵ. The initial discrimination tree will be composed of two nodes: the root and a leaf node, both labeled with ϵ. Depending on the outcome of the membership query, the leaf will be either the accept or the reject child of the root.

Given a word $w \in \Sigma^*$, to identify the state reached by parsing it according to the DT, the learner performs an operation called *sift*. Sift traverses the tree starting from its root r. For each internal node n it visits, it executes the membership query $\mathcal{O}_m(w.d(n))$ to check whether w concatenated with the discriminator suffix of d is accepted by the target language. If it is accepted, sift continues visiting the accept child of n, and the reject child otherwise. If a leaf is reached, the learner concludes that parsing w the target SFA reaches the state identified by the leaf's access word. If instead the child node sift should traverse next does not exist, a new leaf is created in its place with access word w. Membership queries of the form $a.\sigma$, where a is an access string in the DT and $\sigma \in \Sigma$ are then issued to discover transitions of the SFA, possibly leading to the discovery of new states.

Induced SFA. A discrimination tree DT induces an SFA $\mathcal{M}_{DT} = (\mathcal{A}, Q, q_{init}, F, \Delta)$. In this paper, we assume $\mathcal{A}$ to be the Boolean algebra over the union of disjoint intervals over Σ. Q is populated with one state q_l for each leaf $l \in L$ of DT. The state q_ϵ is the initial state. If $\mathcal{O}_m(aw(l)) = true$, then $q_l \in F$ is a final state of $\mathcal{M}_{DT}$. To construct the transition relation Δ, sifts of the form $aw(l).\sigma$ for $\sigma \in \Sigma$ are issued for the states q_l and the concrete evidence for a transition between two states q_i and q_j is summarized into a consistent predicate of $\mathcal{A}$ using a partition function, as described for Λ^*.

Counterexamples. The equivalence query $\mathcal{O}_e(\mathcal{M}_{DT})$ will either confirm the learner identified the target language or produce a counterexample $c \in \Sigma^*$. As for Λ^*, the existence of c implies that either a transition predicate is incorrect or that there should be a new state. To determine the cause of c, the first step is to identify the longest prefix $c[: i]$ before the behavior of the hypothesis SFA diverged from the target language. To localize the divergence point, the learner analyzes the prefixes $c[: i]$ for $i \in [0, len(c)]$. Let a_i be the access string of the state of $\mathcal{M}_{DT}$ reached parsing $c[: i]$. If $\mathcal{O}_m(a_i.w[i :]) \neq \mathcal{O}_m(c)$, i is the divergence point, which implies that the transition taken from q_{a_i} is incorrect. Let q_j be the state corresponding to the leaf reached when sifting $a_i.c[i :]$. The predicate guarding the transition between q_{a_i} and q_j is incorrect if $c[i]$ does not satisfy the corresponding transition predicate. This is possible because the partition function assigns the symbols in Σ for which no concrete evidence is available to any of the outgoing transitions of q_{a_i}. In this case, the transition predicates should be recomputed to account for the new evidence from c. If instead $c[i]$ satisfies the transition predicate between q_{a_i} and q_j, a new state should be added such that parsing $c[i]$ from q_{a_i} reaches it. To add the new state, the leaf labeled with a_i is replaced by a subtree composed of three nodes: an internal node with discriminator suffix $c[i :]$ having as children the leaf a_i and a new leaf labeled by the access string $j.c[i]$, where j is the access string of the state q_j obtainened by sifting $a_i.c[i :]$. This procedure is called *split* (for more details, see, e.g., [3]). The updated DT will then be the base for the next learning iteration.

Running example. A DT corresponding to the running example introduced in Section 3 is shown below. While the specific structure of the learned DT depends on the order in which words are added to it, all the DT resulting from the learning process induce the same classification of the words $w \in \Sigma^*$, being them consistent representations of the same target language.

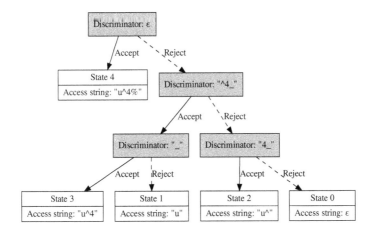

Fig. 5. Discrimination tree learned for the example of Section 3.

4   Active learning with concolic execution

The state-of-the-art active learning algorithms formalized in the previous sections are of limited use when trying to infer (an approximation of) the input language accepted by a program. Their main limitation is the reliance on a complete equivalence oracle, which is unavailable in this case.

In this section, we will propose several extensions of the Λ^* and MAT^* algorithms formalized in Sections 3.1 and 3.2 that make use of a concolic execution engine to 1) gather enhanced information from membership queries thanks to the path condition computed by the concolic engine, and 2) mitigate the lack of an equivalence oracle using the concolic engine to find counterexamples for a hypothesis. While it is usually unrealistic to assume a complete concolic execution of a large program (which would per se be sufficient to characterize the accepted input language), the ability of the concolic engine to execute each execution path only once brings significant benefits in our preliminary evaluation. Additionally, because the concolic engine can ask a constraints solver to produce inputs with a bounded length, it can be used to prove bounded equivalence between the learned input SFA and the target language. Finally, the availability of a partial symbolic execution tree and a constraint solver enables the definition of more effective types of membership queries.

4.1   Concolic learning with symbolic observation tables

Given a program $\mathcal{P}$ its concolic execution on a word $w \in \Sigma^*$ produces a boolean outcome (accept/reject) and a path condition capturing the properties of w that led to that outcome. In particular, we assume the path condition to be reducible to the constraint language defined in Section 2.4, i.e., the conjunction of interval predicates on the elements w_i of w and its length $len(w)$. Under this assumption, the path condition is directly translatable to a word w_Ψ over the predicates Ψ of the Boolean algebra $\mathcal{A}$ over the union of intervals over Σ. We will therefore refer to the path condition produced by the concolic execution of a word $w \in \Sigma^*$ with the Ψ-predicate as w_Ψ, where $len(w) = len(w_\Psi)$.

Symbolic observation table. The surjective relation between concrete words w and their predicates w_Ψ enables a straightforward extension of the observation table used for Λ^*, where the rows of the table can be indexed by words $w_\Psi \in \Psi^*$ instead of concrete words from Σ^*, i.e., $S \cup R \subset \Psi^*$. This allows for each row index to account for the entire equivalence class of words $w \in \Sigma^*$ that would follow the same execution path (these words will also have the same length). We describe as $[\![w_\Psi]\!]$ a concrete representative of the class w_Ψ. The set of suffixes $E \subset \Sigma^*$ will instead contain concrete elements of the alphabet.

Membership queries. Executing a membership query of the form $\mathcal{O}_m([\![w_\Psi]\!].\sigma)$, with $\sigma \in \Sigma$, will produce both the boolean outcome (accept/reject) and a word over Ψ^* that can be added to R, if not already present. As a result, the transition predicates of the induced SFA can be obtained directly from the symbolic observation table, avoiding the need for a partition function to synthesize Ψ-predicates from the collected concrete evidence, as required in Λ^*. The transition relation is then completed by redirecting every $\sigma \in \Sigma$ that does not satisfy any of the discovered transition predicates to an artificial sink state. The induced SFA is then used as hypothesis for the next equivalence query.

Equivalence queries. Because a complete equivalence oracle for the target language is not available, we will use concolic execution to obtain a bounded equivalence oracle comparing the hypothesis SFA induced by the symbolic observation table with the program under analysis. To this end, we translate the hypothesis SFA into a function in the same programming language of the target program $\mathcal{P}$ that takes as argument a word w and returns true (respectively, false) if the hypothesis SFA accepts (respectively, rejects) the word. We assume $\mathcal{P}$ to be wrapped into an analogous boolean function. We then write a program asserting that the result of the two functions is equal and use the concolic engine to find an input word that violate the assertion. If such word can be found, the counterexample is added to the symbolic observation table and the learner starts another iteration. If the concolic execution terminates without finding any assertion violation, it can be concluded that the hypothesis SFA represent the input language of $\mathcal{P}$. However, it is usually unrealistic to assume the termination of the concolic execution. Instead, we configure the solver to search for counterexamples up to a fixed length n. Assuming this input bounded concolic execution terminates without finding a counterexample, it can be concluded that the hypothesis is equivalent to $\mathcal{P}$'s input language for every word up to length n. Notably, this implies that if the target language is actually regular and the corresponding minimal automata has at most n states, the hypothesis learned the entire language.

Running example. A symbolic observation table inducing the SFA for the example introduced in Section 3 is shown in Figure 6. The use of Ψ predicates to index its rows significantly reduces the size of the table, since each row index accounts for a possibly large number of concrete elements of Σ.

T	ϵ	_$1)	$1)	1)	)
ϵ	-	+	-	-	-
0 0; [ˆ; 0 0; ·\uffff	|	|	±	±	±
0-9; [-ˆ; 0-9	-	+	+	-	+
0-9; [-ˆ	-	+	-	+	-
0-9	-	+	+	-	-
a-z; a-z	-	+	+	-	-
-; '; {-\uffff	-	+	-	-	-
-; [-ˆ	-	+	-	+	-
0-9; 0-9	-	+	+	-	-
a-z; :-@	-	+	-	+	-
-; [-ˆ; [-ˆ	-	+	-	-	-
A-Z; A-Z	-	+	+	-	-
\u0000-/	-	+	-	-	-
[-ˆ	-	+	-	-	-
A-Z; -; {-\uffff; 0-9	-	+	+	-	+
0-9; :-@; 0-9; 0-9	-	+	+	-	-
A-Z; \u0000-/; :-@	-	+	-	-	-
0-9; [-ˆ; \u0000-/	-	+	-	-	-
A-Z; :-@	-	+	-	+	-
a-z	-	+	+	-	-
A-Z; -	-	+	+	-	-
-; '	-	+	-	+	-
-	-	+	+	-	-
0-9; :-@; 0-9	-	+	+	-	+
A-Z; :-@; A-Z	-	+	+	-	-
'	-	+	-	-	-
A-Z; '; 0-9; :-\uffff	+	+	+	+	+
:-@	-	+	-	-	-
0-9; {-\uffff	-	+	-	+	-
{-\uffff	-	+	-	-	-
A-Z; \u0000-/	-	+	-	+	-
A-Z; -; {-\uffff; 0-9; \u0000-/	+	+	+	+	+
-; [-ˆ; a-z	-	+	+	-	-
A-Z	-	+	+	-	-
A-Z; '; 0-9; :-\uffff; \u0000-\uffff	+	+	+	+	+
A-Z; :-@; '	-	+	-	-	-
a-z; :-@; -	-	+	+	-	-

Fig. 6. Symbolic observation table for the example of Section 3.

4.2 Concolic learning with a symbolic membership oracle

In the previous section, we used the concolic engine to extract the path conditions corresponding to the execution of membership queries produced by the learner. This enabled reducing the number of queries – each query gathering information about a set of words instead of a single one – and keeping the observation table more compact. In this section, we introduce an oracle that answers a new class of *symbolic membership queries (SMQs)* using the constraint solving capabilities of the concolic engine to directly compute predicates characterizing all the accepted words of the form $p.\sigma.s$, where $p, s \in \Sigma^*$ and $\sigma \in \Sigma$. This oracle will enable a more efficient learning algorithm based on an extension of the discrimination tree data structure.

Definition 5. *Symbolic Membership Oracle ($\mathcal{O}_s$). Given a Boolean algebra $\mathcal{A}$ with predicate set Ψ, a symbolic membership oracle $\mathcal{O}_s : \Sigma^* \times \Sigma^* \to \Psi$ takes as input a pair (p, s) and returns a predicate $\psi \in \Psi$ such that for a symbol $\sigma \in \Sigma$,* *the target program accepts p.σ.s iff σ $\models$ ψ. p and s are called* prefix *and* suffix, *respectively.*

An SMQ query can be solved by issuing a membership query for each $\sigma \in \Sigma$. However, this operation would be costly for large alphabets, such as unicode. On the other hand, the concolic execution of $w = p.\sigma.s$ for a concrete symbol σ returns via the path condition the entire set of symbols that wold follow the same execution path, in turn leading to the same execution outcome. A constraint solver can then be used to generate a new concrete input outside of such set, which is guaranteed to cover a new execution path. This procedure is summarized in Algorithm 1, where we use $pathCondition[\sigma]$ to represent the projection of the path condition on the element of the input string $w = p.\sigma.s$ corresponding to the position of σ.

Input: SMQ $Q = (p, \psi, s)$; *concolic* : $\Sigma^* \rightarrow$(accepted, pathCondition)
Result: ψ such that $\forall \sigma \in \Sigma : p.\sigma.s$ is accepted iff $\sigma \models \psi$

$\psi \leftarrow \bot$;
unknown $\leftarrow \Sigma$;
while *unknown* $\neq \emptyset$ **do**
    $\sigma \leftarrow$ pickElementFrom(*unknown*);
    accepted, pathCondition $\leftarrow$ concolic(p.σ.s);
    if *accepted* **then**
        | $\psi \leftarrow \psi \vee pathCondition[\sigma]$;
    end
    unknown $\leftarrow$ *unknown* $\wedge \neg pathCondition[\sigma]$;
end
return ψ;

Algorithm 1: Answering SMQ queries.

Learning transition predicates with $\mathcal{O}_s$. Consider the learning algorithm using discrimination tree introduced in Section 3.2, MAT^*. After each iteration, the discrimination tree DT contains in its leaves all the discovered states (identified by the respective access words) and organized according to their discrimination suffixes (labeling the internal nodes of DT). To construct the transition relation of the induced SFA, the algorithm executes for each leaf l and $\sigma \in \Sigma$ a sift operation to determine the state reached when parsing $aw(l).\sigma$. Each such sift operation requires as many membership query as the depth of the reached state to be determined. Therefore, the number of sift operations needed to construct the complete transition relation is proportional to the number of states times the size of the input alphabet, with each sift operation issuing a number of membership queries proportional to the depth of DT.

Using the symbolic membership oracle, we can instead define a procedure that traversing DT directly synthesize the transition predicate between a source state q_s and a destination state q_t of the induced SFA. This procedure is formalized in Algorithm 2.

Input: $DT = (N, L, T)$; $\mathcal{O}_s : \Sigma^* \to \psi$; source state q_s; target state q_t
Result: The transition predicate π between q_s and q_t
$n \leftarrow$ root of DT;
$\pi \leftarrow \top$;
while $n \in N \backslash L$ **do**
    $\psi \leftarrow \mathcal{O}_s(aw(q_s), d(n))$;
    if q_t *in the accept subtree of* n **then**
        $\pi \leftarrow \pi \wedge \psi$;
        $n \leftarrow acceptChild(n)$;
    else
        $\pi \leftarrow \pi \wedge \neg\psi$;
        $n \leftarrow rejectChild(n)$;
    end
end
return π;

Algorithm 2: Learning transition predicates with $\mathcal{O}_s$.

Algorithm 2 allows to construct the induced SFA by computing for each ordered pair of leaves of DT the transition predicate of the corresponding transition. This results in the direct construction of the complete transition relation of the induced SFA. In practice, the implementation of Algorithm 2 can be improved by observing that π_i computed in the i-th iteration of the loop is by construction a subset of π_{i-1}. The symbolic membership oracle $\mathcal{O}_s$ can make use of this observation to limit the search procedure for the construction of the predicate *psi* during the i-th iteration to only symbols that satisfy π_{i-1}, significantly improving its efficiency. Finally, for the same reason, the loop in Algorithm 2 can terminate as soon as $\pi = \bot$, which indicates that no transition exists between the source and destination states.

Example. Referring to the discrimination tree in Figure 5 for the example introduced in Section 3, assume we want to learn transition predicate from State 2 to State 3. Initially, $\pi_0 = \top$. The access string of State 2 is "u^". The suffix of the root node is ϵ. Invoking the symbolic membership oracle, we obtain $\psi = \mathcal{O}_s(\text{"u^"}, \epsilon) = \bot$ (no string of length 3 are accepted by the target language). Because State 3 is in the reject subtree, $\pi_1 = \pi_0 \wedge \neg\bot = \top$ and the execution moves to the internal node labeled with the discriminator suffix "^4_". The corresponding SMQ query returns $\psi = \mathcal{O}_s(\text{"u^"}, \text{"^4_"}) = \{0 \ldots 9, A \ldots Z, \_, a \ldots z\}$. Because State 3 is in the accept subtree of the current node, $\pi_2 = \pi_1 \wedge \psi = \{0 \ldots 9, A \ldots Z, \_, a \ldots z\}$ and the execution moves to the internal node with discriminator prefix "_", where $pi_3 = [0 \ldots 9]$ is finally computed as the transition predicate from State 2 to State 3.

Decorated discrimination tree. For every leaf l and internal node n of a discrimination tree DT, Algorithm 2 issues a SMQ query $(aw(l), d(n))$. The corresponding intermediate value of the transition predicate π is intersected with the result of the SMQ query or its negation depending on whether l is in the accept or the reject subtree of n. Notably, the addition of a newly discovered state to DT does not change the relative positioning of a leaf l with respect to an internal node n, i.e., if l is initially in the accept (respectively, reject) subtree of n, it will remain in that subtree also after a new state is added. This observation implies that the results of the SMQ queries performed through Algorithm 2 remain valid between different executions of the algorithm. Therefore, when a new state is discovered and added to the discrimination tree via the *split* operation defined in Section 3.2, only the membership queries involving the new internal node and the new leaf added by *split* would require an actual execution of the symbolic membership oracle.

To enable the reuse of previous SMQ queries issued through Algorithm 2, we decorate the DT adding to each node a map from the set of leaves L to the value of π computed when traversing the node. We refer to this map as *predicate map*. Every predicate in the root node map is $\top$, as this is the initial value of π in Algorithm 2. The maps in the children nodes are then computed as follows. Let n be a parent node and n_a, n_r its accept and reject children respectively, m be a leaf of DT, and π_n^m, $\pi_{n_a}^m$, $\pi_{n_r}^m$ the predicates for m stored in n, n_a, and n_r, respectively. Then $\pi_{n_a}^m = \mathcal{O}_s(aw(m), d(n)) \wedge \pi_n^m$ and $\pi_{n_r} = \neg\mathcal{O}_s(aw(m), d(n)) \wedge \pi_n^m$. Proceeding recursively a leaf l will be decorated with a predicate map assigning to each leaf l_i in DT the predicate of the transition going from q_{l_i} to q_l.

Figure 7 shows the decorated version of the discrimination tree of Figure 5, constructed for the same example language introduced in Section 3.

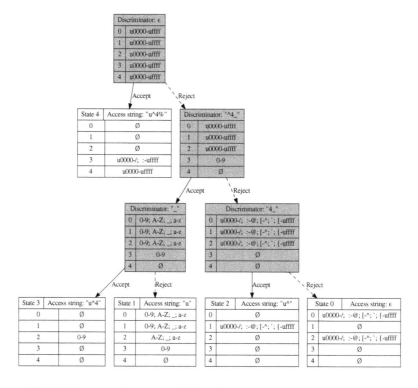

Fig. 7. Decorated version of the discrimination tree in Figure 5.

Induced SFA and number of equivalence queries. Notice that, by construction, for every node n with accept child n_a and reject child n_r, if π_n^l, $\pi_{n_a}^l$, and $\pi_{n_r}^l$ are the predicates the three nodes associate with a leaf l, $\pi_{n_a}^l \vee \pi_{n_r}^l = \pi_n^l$ and $\pi_{n_a}^l \wedge \pi_{n_r}^l = \bot$. As a consequence, after all the maps decorating a node in the discrimination tree are completed, the predicates in the leaves represent the complete transition relation of the induced SFA. Further more, the maps grows monotonically through the learning process, with entries computed in previous iterations remaining valid throughout the entire process. Practically, after each split operation resulting from the counterexample of an equivalence query (see Section 3.2), we traverse the discrimination tree and incrementally update all the predicate maps to include information about transitions to the new leaf, as well as populating the maps of the new internal node and new leaf added by the split.

Differently from the original algorithm MAT^* described in Section 3.2, a counterexample for the induced SFA corresponding to a decorated discrimination tree can only be returned if a new state has been discovered. This bound the number of equivalence query to be at most equal to the minimum number of states needed to represent the target language as an SFA. In our settings, a complete equivalence oracle is not available for the target program $\mathcal{P}$. Equivalence queries are instead solved using a (input bounded) concolic execution that compares the hypothesis SFA (induced by the discrimination tree) with the original program. Because this execution is computationally expensive, reducing the number of necessary equivalence queries has a significant impact on the execution time (at the cost of keeping in memory the node predicate maps).

5 Experimental evaluation

5.1 Experimental Setup

In this section we evaluate a prototype implementation of our contributions, built upon SVPAlib [9] (the symbolic automata and alphabet theory library used by MAT*) and Coastal [12], a concolic execution engine for Java bytecode. in Section 5.2 we consider our approach of using symbolic observations tables from Section 4.1 (referred to as SYMLEARN in the following presentation) and in Section 5.3 we evaluate the use of the symbolic membership queries from Section 4.2 (referred to as MAT*++). All the experiments have been executed on a server equipped with an AMD EPYC 7401P 24-Core CPU and 440Gb of memory. Coastal was configured to use at most 3 threads using its default generational exploration strategy [12] to find counterexamples for equivalence queries.

The experiments in this section are based on regular expressions taken from the AutomatArk [8] benchmark suite. To ensure a uniform difficulty distribution among the experiments, the regular expressions were converted to their automaton representation, sorted by the number of states, and 200 target automata selected by a stratified sampling (maximum number of states in an automaton is 637 and average 33; maximum number of transitions 2,495 and average 96). Each automaton is then translated into a Java program accepting the same language and compiled. The program analysis is performed on the resulting bytecode.

In the first experiment, we demonstrate the increase in query efficiency we achieve, by comparing the number of queries, using a complete oracle that can answer equivalence queries in a negligible amount of time. In this idealised setup the learner halted when the correct automaton was identified, relying on the fact that the oracle can confirm the correctness of the hypothesis. Although this setup does not represent a realistic scenario, it allowed us to reliably evaluate the number of queries of each type that are required to converge to the correct automaton, and to measure the computational requirements of the learning algorithm in isolation.

In the second experiment, we demonstrate the use of a concolic engine as a symbolic oracle, and measure the impact on the execution time of the algorithms. Providing a meaningful evaluation of the cost of the equivalence queries is difficult, as it is essentially a software verification problem over arbitrary Java code, and in principle an equivalence query could never terminate. Instead, a complete concolic analysis of each parser is performed, without using the perfect oracle for any type of query, and enforcing a timeout of ten minutes for each analysis, after which the learner yielded it's latest hypothesis. The correctness of that hypothesis is then confirmed by comparison to the known target automata. Note also that we use an input string length limit of 30 for the words to be parsed during concolic execution.

5.2   Learning with symbolic observation tables

Evaluating the algorithm with a perfect oracle. We learn 78% of the target languages within the ten minute timeout using a perfect oracle for equivalence. We see a 54% reduction in the total number of membership queries, and a 88% reduction in the total number of equivalence queries over MAT* (see Table 1).

Table 1. Number of queries and execution time with perfect oracle.

Algorithm	Membership queries	Equivalence queries	Execution time (s)
MAT*	1, 545, 255	25, 802	38.60
SYMLEARN	720, 658	3, 124	1321.70

The SYMLEARN approach requires the path conditions to be stored in the observation table, even when using a perfect oracle for equivalence. In order to achieve this, concrete counter examples from the perfect oracle are resolved to path conditions via the concolic engine. The slower execution time can be attributed to the infrastructure overhead present in our implementation, and the speed of the concolic engine when performing these resolutions.

Evaluating the algorithm with the concolic oracle. We now replace the perfect equivalence oracle with a concolic execution engine, as described in Section 4.1. We learn 30% of the target automata within the ten minute timeout. The execution time is orders of magnitude slower when compared MAT*, and in our implementation 99% of the learner's execution time is spent running symbolic equivalence queries. While the increase in bandwidth due to the path conditions returned for each query does result in a significant reduction of queries overall, the execution time of the SYMLEARN approach is orders of magnitude slower than MAT*, partly because SYMLEARN requires the actual (concolic) execution of the program implementation, instead of performing queries on an SFA representation of the regular expression. There are however a number of optimizations that can be made to improve the performance (some of which will be discussed in the following section).

5.3 Learning with symbolic membership queries

Under the assumption that the language to be learned is regular, and that the equivalence check will eventually find a counterexample if there exists one, our active learning approach guarantees that eventually the correct hypothesis will be generated. The experimental evaluation was therefore aimed at understanding what is achievable in a realistic setting, with constrained time, and how our methodology improves the outcome.

Table 2. Number of queries and execution time with perfect oracle.

	Membership queries	SMQ	Equivalence queries	Learner execution time
MAT*	3,517,474	–	47,374	137.51 s
MAT*++	42,075	81,401	1,913	1.33 s

Table 2 shows the total number of queries[3] necessary to learn the correct automaton over the 200 test cases, along with the CPU time used by the learner process alone, without considering the time required to answer the queries.

The decrease in the CPU time required by the learner process can be explained by the reduction in the number of counterexamples that the learner has to process (recall that in MAT*++, a counterexample can be caused only by a missing state in the hypothesis, while in MAT* it can be also be due to an incorrect transition predicate). To understand the balance between the benefit due to the sharp reduction in the number of membership and equivalence queries, and the cost due to the introduction of the symbolic queries, the next section will evaluate the cost of answering each type of query without the help of a perfect oracle.

Evaluating the impact of SMQ. First, observe that the impact of membership queries are negligible since it is simply a check to see if an input is accepted. However, measuring the complexity of the symbolic membership queries (SMQs) is crucial to assess the effectiveness of our approach. Answering a SMQ requires the concolic execution of the program under analysis potentially multiple times, and requires processing each resulting path condition to collect the information needed to refine the answer. In this experiment we measured the time and the

---

[3] Note that all 200 automata are included in Table 2 whereas only the results for the subset that finished before the timeout was shown in Table 1.

number of concolic executions required to answer all the SMQs of table 2. The total time required to answer the queries was 4,408s, with an average of 54.15 ms per query. The number of concolic executions per query was between 1 and 31, with an average of 3.45. Since the concolic execution requires the program under analysis to be instrumented and a symbolic state to be maintained, it is orders of magnitude slower than a standard concrete execution.

Evaluating the impact of equivalence queries. Each equivalence query is answered in the same way as in the SYMLEARN approach (see Section 4.1), by doing a concolic execution of the hypothesis and the program being analyzed on the same symbolic input to see if they give a different result; if so, we have a counter-example, otherwise we simply know none could be found before the timeout or within the input string length of 30. As a further optimization, we also maintained two automata *knownAccept* and *knownReject* that were the union of the automata translation of the path conditions of all the previously explored accepted and rejected inputs respectively.

In this experiment 1,207 equivalence queries were issued, and on average it took 56.92s to answer a query. 573 answers were generated in negligible time using the *knownAccept* and *knownReject* automata (demonstrating the usefulness of this optimization), 93 cases Coastal could not find a counter-example (within the input size limit), 107 the timeout occurred and in the rest a counter-example was found by Coastal. In 152 cases the correct automaton was learned (76%), and interestingly in 62 of these cases Coastal timed-out (but the current hypothesis at the time was in fact correct). In 3 of the cases Coastal finished exploring the complete state-space up to the 30 input before the timeout, but the correct automaton was not learned. This happened because a counter-example requiring more than 30 input characters exist.

Discussion of the results.   The benefit of the symbolic membership queries is clear: it reduces the number of equivalence queries by 96%, and the latter is by far the most expensive step in active learning without a perfect oracle. Furthermore, simple engineering optimizations, for example a caching scheme for the accepted and rejected path conditions, can have a significant impact on the execution time.

6   Related work

The problem of learning input grammars has been tackled using a variety of techniques, and with various specific goals in mind.

6.1   Active learning

The active learning algorithms most closely related to our are Λ^* [11] and MAT* [3], which have been extensively discussed in Section 3.

Argyros et al. [4] used Angluin-style active learning of symbolic automata for the analysis of finite state string sanitizers and filters. Being focused on security, their goal was not to learn exactly the filter under analysis, but to verify that it filters every potentially dangerous string. In the proposed approach each equivalence query is approximated with a single membership query, which is a string that is not filtered by the current hypothesis, but belongs to the given language of "dangerous" strings. If no such string exists, the filter is considered successfully validated. If the string exists but is successfully filtered it provides a counterexample with which the hypothesis is refined, otherwise a vulnerability in the filter has been found. This equivalence approximation is incomplete, but greatly simplifies the problem, considering the complexity of equivalence queries.

Multiple other approaches use different active learning techniques not based on L* that, compared to our solution, provide less theoretical guarantees and often rely on a corpus of valid inputs. Glade [6] generates a context free grammar starting from a set of seed inputs that the learner attempts to generalize, using a membership oracle to check whether the generalization is correct. No other information is derived from the execution of the program under analysis, and therefore the set of seed inputs is of crucial importance. Reinam [29] further extends Glade by using symbolic execution to automatically generate the seed inputs, and adding a second probabilistic grammar refinement phase in which reinforcement learning is used to select the generalization rules to be applied.

The approach proposed by Höschele et al. [19] uses a corpus of valid inputs and applies generalizations that are verified with a membership oracle. Dynamic taint analysis is used to track the flow of the various fragments of the input during the execution, extracting additional information that aids in the creation of the hypothesis and generates meaningful non-terminal symbol names. A similar approach is used by Gopinath et al. [16], with the addition of automatic generation of the initial corpus.

6.2 Passive learning

Godefroid et al. [15] use recurrent neural networks and a corpus of sample inputs to create a generative model of the input language. This approach does not learn any information from the system under test, so the sample corpus is important.

A completely different approach is used by Lin et al. [24] to tackle a related problem: reconstructing the syntax tree of arbitrary inputs. The technique is based on the analysis of an execution trace generated by an instrumented version of the program under analysis. This approach relies on the knowledge of the internal mechanisms used by different types of parsers to generate the syntax tree.

Tupni [7] is a tool to reverse engineer input formats and protocols. Starting from one or more seed inputs, it analyzes the parser execution trace together with data flow information generated using taint analysis, identifies the structure of the input format (how the data is segmented in fields of various types, aggregated in records, and some constraints that must be satisfied), and generates a context free grammar.

7 Conclusions

Most established active learning algorithms for (symbolic) finite state automata assume the availability of a minimal adequate teacher, which includes a complete equivalence oracle to produce counterexample disproving an incorrect hypothesis of the learner. This assumption is unrealistic when learning the input grammar of a program from its implementation, as such a complete oracle would need to automatically check the equivalence of the hypothesis with arbitrary software code. In this paper, we explored how the use of a concolic execution engine can improve the information efficiency of membership queries, provide a partial input-bounded oracle to check the equivalence of an hypothesis against a program, and enable the definition of a new class of symbolic membership queries that allow the learner inferring the transition predicates of a symbolic finite state automata representation of the target input language more efficiently.

Preliminary experiments with the Autmatark [8] benchmark showed that our implementations of SYMLEARN and MAT*++ achieve a significant reduction (up to 96%) in the number of queries required to actively learn the input language of a program in the form of a symbolic finite state automaton. Despite bounding the total execution time to 10 minutes, using the concolic execution engine as partial equivalence oracle, MAT*++ managed to learn the correct input language in 76% of the cases.

This results demonstrate the suitability of concolic execution as enabling tool for the definition of active learning algorithms for the input grammar of a program. However, our current solutions learn the input grammar in the form of a symbolic finite state automaton. This implies that only an approximation of non-regular input languages can be constructed. Such approximation can at best match the input language up to a finite length, but would fail in recognizing more sophisticated language features that may require, for example, a context free representation. Investigating how the learning strategies based on concolic execution we explored in this paper can generalize to more expressive language models is envisioned as a future direction for this research, as well as the use of the inferred input languages to support parsers validation and grammar-based fuzzing.

References

1. Angluin, D.: Learning regular sets from queries and counterexamples. Information and Computation **75**(2), 87–106 (1987)
2. Angluin, D.: Queries and Concept Learning. Machine Learning **2**(4), 319–342 (apr 1988)
3. Argyros, G., D'Antoni, L.: The learnability of symbolic automata. In: Chockler, H., Weissenbacher, G. (eds.) Computer Aided Verification. CAV 2018. pp. 427–445. Springer International Publishing, Cham (2018)
4. Argyros, G., Stais, I., Kiayias, A., Keromytis, A.D.: Back in Black: Towards Formal, Black Box Analysis of Sanitizers and Filters. Proceedings - 2016 IEEE Symposium on Security and Privacy, SP 2016 pp. 91–109 (2016). https://doi.org/10.1109/SP.2016.14
5. Aydin, A., Bang, L., Bultan, T.: Automata-Based Model Counting for String Constraints. In: Kroening, D., Păsăreanu, C.S. (eds.) Computer Aided Verification. pp. 255–272. Lecture Notes in Computer Science, Springer International Publishing, Cham (2015)
6. Bastani, O., Sharma, R., Aiken, A., Liang, P.: Synthesizing Program Input Grammars. In: Proceedings of the 38th ACM SIGPLAN Conference on Programming

Language Design and Implementation. pp. 95–110. ACM (2017), http://arxiv.org/abs/1608.01723

7. Cui, W., Peinado, M., Chen, K., Wang, H.J., Irun-Briz, L.: Tupni: Automatic reverse engineering of input formats. Proceedings of the ACM Conference on Computer and Communications Security pp. 391–402 (2008). https://doi.org/10.1145/1455770.1455820

8. D'Antoni, L.: AutomatArk (2018), https://github.com/lorisdanto/automatark

9. D'Antoni, L.: SVPAlib (2018), https://github.com/lorisdanto/symbolicautomata/

10. D'Antoni, L., Veanes, M.: The power of symbolic automata and transducers. Lecture Notes in Computer Science (including subseries Lecture Notes in Artificial Intelligence and Lecture Notes in Bioinformatics) **10426 LNCS**, 47–67 (2017)

11. Drews, S., D'Antoni, L.: Learning symbolic automata. Lecture Notes in Computer Science (including subseries Lecture Notes in Artificial Intelligence and Lecture Notes in Bioinformatics) **10205 LNCS**, 173–189 (2017)

12. Geldenhuys, J., Visser, W.: Coastal (2019), https://github.com/DeepseaPlatform/coastal

13. Godefroid, P., Kiezun, A., Levin, M.Y.: Grammar-based whitebox fuzzing. In: Proceedings of the 29th ACM SIGPLAN Conference on Programming Language Design and Implementation. pp. 206–215 (2008). https://doi.org/10.1145/1379022.1375607

14. Godefroid, P., Klarlund, N., Sen, K.: Dart: Directed automated random testing. In: Proceedings of the 2005 ACM SIGPLAN Conference on Programming Language Design and Implementation. p. 213–223. PLDI '05, Association for Computing Machinery, New York, NY, USA (2005). https://doi.org/10.1145/1065010.1065036, https://doi.org/10.1145/1065010.1065036

15. Godefroid, P., Peleg, H., Singh, R.: Learn&Fuzz: Machine Learning for Input Fuzzing. In: Proceedings of the 32nd IEEE/ACM International Conference on Automated Software Engineering. pp. 50–59. IEEE Press, Urbana-Champaign, IL, USA (2017)

16. Gopinath, R., Mathis, B., Höschele, M., Kampmann, A., Zeller, A.: Sample-Free Learning of Input Grammars for Comprehensive Software Fuzzing (2018). https://doi.org/arXiv:1810.08289v1, http://arxiv.org/abs/1810.08289

17. Heinz, J., Sempere, J.M.: Topics in grammatical inference (2016)

18. de la Higuera, C.: Grammatical Inference: Learning Automata and Grammars. Cambridge University Press, New York, NY, USA (2010)

19. Höschele, M., Kampmann, A., Zeller, A.: Active Learning of Input Grammars (2017), http://arxiv.org/abs/1708.08731

20. Isberner, M.: Foundations of Active Automata Learning: an Algorithmic Perspective. Ph.D. thesis (2015)

21. Isberner, M., Howar, F., Steffen, B.: The TTT Algorithm: A Redundancy-Free Approach to Active Automata Learning. In: Bonakdarpour, B., Smolka, S.A. (eds.) Runtime Verification. pp. 307–322. Springer International Publishing, Cham (2014), http://link.springer.com/10.1007/978-3-319-11164-3{_}26

22. Isberner, M., Steffen, B.: An Abstract Framework for Counterexample Analysis in Active Automata Learning. JMLR: Workshop and Conference Proceedings (1993), 79–93 (2014)

23. Kearns, M.J., Vazirani, U.: Learning Finite Automata by Experimentation. In: An Introduction to Computational Learning Theory, pp. 155–158. The MIT Press (1994)

24. Lin, Z., Zhang, X., Xu, D.: Reverse engineering input syntactic structure from program execution and its applications. IEEE Transactions on Software Engineering **36**(5), 688–703 (2010). https://doi.org/10.1109/TSE.2009.54

25. Maler, O., Mens, I.E.: Learning Regular Languages over Large Alphabets. In: Abraham, E., Havelund, K. (eds.) Tools and Algorithms for the Construction and Analysis of Systems. TACAS 2014. pp. 485–499. Springer Berlin Heidelberg, Berlin, Heidelberg (2014)

26. de Moura, L., Bjørner, N.: Z3: An efficient smt solver. In: Ramakrishnan, C.R., Rehof, J. (eds.) Tools and Algorithms for the Construction and Analysis of Systems. pp. 337–340. Springer Berlin Heidelberg, Berlin, Heidelberg (2008)

27. Sen, K., Marinov, D., Agha, G.: Cute: A concolic unit testing engine for c. SIGSOFT Softw. Eng. Notes **30**(5), 263–272 (Sep 2005). https://doi.org/10.1145/1095430.1081750, https://doi.org/10.1145/1095430.1081750

28. Veanes, M., De Halleux, P., Tillmann, N.: Rex: Symbolic regular expression explorer. ICST 2010 - 3rd International Conference on Software Testing, Verification and Validation pp. 498–507 (2010). https://doi.org/10.1109/ICST.2010.15

29. Wu, Z., Johnson, E., Bastani, O., Song, D.: REINAM: Reinforcement Learning for Input-Grammar Inference. In: Proceedings of the 2019 27th ACM Joint Meeting on European Software Engineering Conference and Symposium on the Foundations of Software Engineering. pp. 488–498. ACM (2019)

8

LLVM-based Hybrid Fuzzing with LibKluzzer (Competition Contribution)

Hoang M. Le[ID]

Insitute of Computer Science
University of Bremen, Germany
hle@uni-bremen.de

Abstract. LibKluzzer is a novel implementation of hybrid fuzzing, which combines the strengths of coverage-guided fuzzing and dynamic symbolic execution (a.k.a. whitebox fuzzing). While coverage-guided fuzzing can discover new execution paths at nearly native speed, whitebox fuzzing is capable of getting through complex branch conditions. In contrast to existing hybrid fuzzers, that operate directly on binaries, LibKluzzer leverages the LLVM compiler framework to work at the source code level. It employs LibFuzzer as the coverage-guided fuzzing component and KLUZZER, an extension of KLEE, as the whitebox fuzzing component.

Keywords: Hybrid Fuzzing · Coverage-guided Fuzzing · Symbolic Execution · LLVM.

1 Test Generation Approach

LibKluzzer is based on hybrid fuzzing which tries to combine the strengths of coverage-guided fuzzing and whitebox fuzzing. Most existing advanced hybrid fuzzers, e.g. [6,7,8], employ coverage-guided fuzzing as the main search algorithm and only apply whitebox fuzzing selectively on the most promising inputs. While such advanced approach is also being under development and evaluation for LibKluzzer, for simplicity and given the short time frame available for adapting to Test-Comp, the participating version of LibKluzzer combines coverage-guided fuzzing and whitebox fuzzing in a very simple way. Without any intrinsic integration, multiple instances of coverage-guided fuzzing and whitebox fuzzing are scripted to run in parallel in their own OS process. They operate on a common corpus to enable sharing the individual progresses. Each instance keeps an in-memory set of inputs it has generated, together with the code coverage achieved so far. Whenever an instance discovers an input that covers new code, it writes this input as a file to the common corpus. The corpus is scanned periodically by the instances to check for newly added files. Despite of (or thanks to) its simplicity, LibKluzzer managed to perform very well in Test-Comp 2020.

2   Software Architecture

Two major components of LibKluzzer are LibFuzzer [1] for coverage-guided fuzzing and KLUZZER [5] for whitebox fuzzing. As mentioned earlier, KLUZZER is an extension of KLEE [2]. While it uses most of the KLEE infrastructure including the underlying SMT solver STP [3], KLUZZER provides several signicant enhancements that make it more suitable for hybrid fuzzing (see [5] for more details). For Test-Comp, both LibFuzzer and KLUZZER have been extended to support its specific requirements. The extension involves writing test cases in XML format, glue logic to convert the random byte array needed for the fuzzers into a sequence of calls to *nondet* functions, and implementing a fuzzing target as described later.

Workflow First, the C program under test undergoes a set of source-to-source program transformations to enable *in-process* coverage-guided fuzzing. The transformed program is then compiled using Clang to create an LLVM bitcode file and an executable. The compilation involves, among others, code coverage instrumentation and linking with LibFuzzer. Finally, the LLVM bitcode file is fed to KLUZZER to perform whitebox fuzzing, while the executable is started in two instances to perform coverage-guided fuzzing. These three fuzzing instances run concurrently until terminated by the Test-Comp BenchExec runner due to time limit exceeded. They share generated inputs via a common corpus of files as mentioned earlier and write XML test cases to the test suite on-the-fly.

Transformations for in-process fuzzing While the main components of LibKluzzer are implemented in C++, the program transformations, that are required to enable *in-process* coverage-guided fuzzing, consist of a set of Bash and Python scripts. This form of fuzzing is much faster than traditional out-of-process fuzzing, which forks a new process for each execution of the *main* function, but requires the global state of the fuzzing target to remain largely unchanged or to be resetted between executions. The transformations esssentially perform the following steps for each benchmark:

1. rename the existing *main* function to *FuzzMe*;
2. identify and duplicate global variables;
3. insert additional functions: *FuzzerSaveCtx* to capture the initial global state into the duplicated variables and *FuzzerRestoreCtx* to restore this state before each new execution of the *FuzzMe* function;
4. redirect calls to *exit* and *abort* to custom functions to prevent unwanted early exit from the fuzzing loop.

The current script-based implementation of these transformations is very fragile and might not work out-of-the-box for non-Test-Comp benchmarks. The next version of LibKluzzer will replace these with proper Clang-based source-to-source transformations.

```
int nondet_int() {                      int LLVMFuzzerTestOneInput(
  int Value = 0;                            uint8_t *Data, size_t Size) {
  if (Used + 4 <= Size) {               FuzzerRestoreCtx();
    memcpy(&Value, Data + Used, 4);     MakeGlobalCopy(Data, Size);
    Used += 4;                          Used = 0;
  }                                     FuzzMe();
  return Value;                       }
}
```

Fig. 1. Implementation of *nondet* functions and fuzzing target for Test-Comp

Test-Comp fuzzing target and *nondet* functions Both KLUZZER and LibFuzzer require the definition of a fuzzing target, i.e. an implementation of the declared *LLVMFuzzerTestOneInput* function. The *main* function provided by the fuzzers will repeatedly call *LLVMFuzzerTestOneInput* with fuzz inputs in a loop to perform fuzzing. Each fuzz input consists of an array of random bytes and its size. Fig. 1 shows a conceptual implementation of *LLVMFuzzerTestOneInput* on the right hand side. First, the initial global execution state is restored. Then, the given fuzz input is copied into a global array and the number of bytes already consumed for fuzzing is set to zero; Finally, *FuzzMe* is invoked. During its execution, each time a *nondet* function is called to provide input, a corresponding number of bytes from the global byte array will be consumed to create the requested value, as exemplarily shown on the left hand side of Fig. 1 for *int*. With this conversion from random bytes, no changes are needed in the core algorithms of KLUZZER and LibFuzzer for Test-Comp.

3   Strengths and Weaknesses

The main strength of LibKluzzer lies in achieving high code coverage as demonstrated by winning the branch coverage category of Test-Comp. Multiple factors contribute to this success including the extremely high throughput of in-process coverage-guided fuzzing implemented by LibFuzzer and the use of generational search in KLUZZER, a coverage-maximizing search heuristic for dynamic symbolic execution/whitebox fuzzing first proposed by SAGE [4]. The individual contribution of each single component is to be analyzed more thoroughly in a further detailed study.

The main conceptual weakness of LibKluzzer is that the same coverage-maximizing search strategy is used for reaching error calls. It is a big surprise that LibKluzzer has still achieved the second place in the corresponding category. We expect that adapting the search heuristics of both LibFuzzer and KLUZZER to be directed by the distance to the location of error calls should improve the performance significantly.

Especially, the big ECA benchmarks have proven to be problematic for both LibFuzzer and KLUZZER and hence also for LibKluzzer. The sequence of *nondet* values required to reach the error calls is very specific and nearly impossible to find with coverage-guided fuzzing, while KLUZZER suffers from path explosion.

In addition to error-directed search, path/state merging might be required to efficiently deal with these benchmarks.

A further weakness is that LibKluzzer makes little effort on minimizing the test suite with respect to both the size of the test suite and the size of each test case. Too many redundant test cases might cause the validator to timeout. Furthermore, some produced test cases are too big hitting a corner case in the validator and forcing it to exceed the given memory limit. In these cases, the validator crashes prematurely, leaving the remaining test cases uncounted.

4   Tool Setup and Configuration

Installation The LibKluzzer archive submitted to Test-Comp 2020 (version 0.6) can be downloaded from https://gitlab.com/sosy-lab/test-comp/archives-2020/ blob/testcomp20/2020/libkluzzer.zip. After unpacking, the main executable script LibKluzzer can be found in the *bin* folder.

Configuration The main script has been configured to reflect the resource restrictions of Test-Comp 2020. LibKluzzer treats every benchmark as 64-bit and always tries to maximize code coverage, and thus is agnostic to the property and architecture specification. The only meaningful parameter is the path to the source code file of the benchmark.

Participation LibKluzzer participates in both available categories of Test-Comp 2020: *Finding Bugs* and *Code Coverage*.

5   Software Project and Contributors

LibKluzzer and KLUZZER are being developed by the author at University of Bremen, Germany. This research and development are supported by the Central Research Development Fund, University of Bremen, Germany within the project SYMVIR. The source code of LibKluzzer will be made available at https:// github.com/hoangmle/LibKluzzerTestComp2020Submission. Much of the credits should go to the respective development teams of LibFuzzer and KLEE, which lay the foundation for LibKluzzer.

References

1. LibFuzzer - a library for coverage-guided fuzz testing. Available at https://llvm. org/docs/LibFuzzer.html.
2. C. Cadar, D. Dunbar, and D. R. Engler. KLEE: unassisted and automatic generation of high-coverage tests for complex systems programs. In *USENIX OSDI*, pages 209–224, 2008.
3. V. Ganesh and D. L. Dill. A decision procedure for bit-vectors and arrays. In *CAV*, pages 519–531, 2007.

4. P. Godefroid, M. Y. Levin, and D. A. Molnar. Automated whitebox fuzz testing. In *NDSS*, 2008.
5. H. M. Le. KLUZZER: Whitebox fuzzing on top of LLVM. In *ATVA*, pages 246–252.
6. N. Stephens, J. Grosen, C. Salls, A. Dutcher, R. Wang, J. Corbetta, Y. Shoshitaishvili, C. Kruegel, and G. Vigna. Driller: Augmenting fuzzing through selective symbolic execution. In *NDSS*, 2016.
7. I. Yun, S. Lee, M. Xu, Y. Jang, and T. Kim. QSYM : A practical concolic execution engine tailored for hybrid fuzzing. In *USENIX Security*, pages 745–761, 2018.
8. L. Zhao, Y. Duan, H. Yin, and J. Xuan. Send hardest problems my way: Probabilistic path prioritization for hybrid fuzzing. In *NDSS*, 2019.

9

Extracting Semantics from Question-Answering Services for Snippet Reuse

Themistoklis Diamantopoulos📷, Nikolaos Oikonomou📷, and Andreas Symeonidis📷

Electrical and Computer Engineering Dept., Aristotle University of Thessaloniki
Thessaloniki, Greece
`thdiaman@issel.auth.gr, nikooiko@ece.auth.gr, asymeon@eng.auth.gr`

Abstract. Nowadays, software developers typically search online for reusable solutions to common programming problems. However, forming the question appropriately, and locating and integrating the best solution back to the code can be tricky and time consuming. As a result, several mining systems have been proposed to aid developers in the task of locating reusable snippets and integrating them into their source code. Most of these systems, however, do not model the semantics of the snippets in the context of source code provided. In this work, we propose a snippet mining system, named StackSearch, that extracts semantic information from Stack Overlow posts and recommends useful and in-context snippets to the developer. Using a hybrid language model that combines Tf-Idf and fastText, our system effectively understands the meaning of the given query and retrieves semantically similar posts. Moreover, the results are accompanied with useful metadata using a named entity recognition technique. Upon evaluating our system in a set of common programming queries, in a dataset based on post links, and against a similar tool, we argue that our approach can be useful for recommending ready-to-use snippets to the developer.

Keywords: Code Search · Snippet Mining · Code Semantic Analysis · Question-Answering Systems.

1   Introduction

Lately, the widespread use of the Internet and the introduction of the open-source development initiative have given rise to a new way of developing software. Developers nowadays rely more than ever on online services in order to solve common problems arising during development, including e.g. developing a component, integrating an API, or even fixing a bug. This new reuse paradigm has been greatly supported by search engines, code hosting facilities, programming forums, and question-answering communities, such as Stack Overflow[1]. One could even argue that software today is built using reusable components, which are found in software libraries and are exposed via APIs.

---
[1] https://stackoverflow.com/

As a result, the challenge lies in properly integrating these APIs/components in order to support the required functionality. This process is typically performed via *snippets*, i.e. small code fragments that usually perform clearly defined tasks (e.g. reading a CSV file, connecting to a database, etc.). Given the vastness of data in the services outlined in the previous paragraph (e.g. Stack Oveflow alone has more than 18 million question posts[2]), locating the most suitable snippet to perform a task and integrating it to one's own source code can be hard. In this context, developers often have to leave the IDE, form a query in an online tool and navigate through several solutions before finding the most suitable one.

To this end, several systems have been proposed. Some of these systems focus on the *API usage mining* problem [5,9,13,14,17,18,27,30] and extract examples for specific library APIs, while others offer more generic *snippet mining* solutions [3,6,28,29] and further allow queries for common programming problems (e.g. how to read a file in Java). Both types of systems usually employ an indexing mechanism that allows developers to form a query and retrieve relevant snippets.

These systems, however, have important limitations. First of all, several of them do not allow queries in natural language and may require the developer to spend time in order to form a query in some specialized format. Secondly, most systems index only information extracted from source code, without accounting for the semantics that can be extracted from comments or even from the surrounding text in the context (web location) that each snippet is found. Furthermore, most tools employ some type of lexical (term frequency) indexing, thus not exploiting the benefits of embeddings that can lead to semantic-aware retrieval. Finally, the format and the presentation of the results is most of the time far from optimal. There are systems that return call sequences as opposed to ready-to-use snippets, while, even when snippets are retrieved, they are sometimes provided as-is without any additional information concerning their APIs.

In this paper, we design and develop StackSearch, a system that receives queries in natural language and employs an indexing mechanism on Stack Overflow data in order to retrieve useful snippets. The indexing mechanism takes advantage of all possible information about a snippet by extracting semantics from both the textual (title, tags, body) and the source code part of Stack Overflow posts. The information is extracted using lexical matching as well as embeddings in order to produce a hybrid model and retrieve the most useful results, even when taking into account the possible ambiguities of natural language. Finally, the snippets retrieved by StackSearch are accompanied by relevant labels that provide an interpretation of the semantics of the posts and the employed APIs.

2   Related Work

As already mentioned, we focus on snippet mining systems that recommend solutions to typical programming problems. Some of the first systems proposed in this area were Prospector [16] and PARSEWeb [25]. These systems focus on

---

[2] Source: https://data.stackexchange.com/

recommending snippets that form a path between a source object to a target object. For Prospector, these paths are called jungloids and the program flow is a jungloid graph. Though interesting, the system has a local database, which limits its applicability. PARSEWeb, on the other hand, uses the Google search engine and produces better results in most scenarios [25]). However, both systems have important limitations; they require the developer to know which API calls to use and further receive queries in a specialized format, and not in natural language.

Another popular category of systems in current research involves those focusing on the challenge of API usage mining, such as MAPO [30], UP-Miner [27] or PAM [9]. The problem is typically defined as extracting common usage patterns from client source code, i.e. source code that uses the relevant API. To do so, MAPO employs frequent sequence mining, while UP-Miner uses graphs and mines frequent closed API call paths. PAM, on the other hand, employs probabilistic machine learning to extract sequences that exhibit higher coverage of the API under analysis and are more diverse [9]. Though quite effective, these systems are actually limited to the API under analysis and cannot support more generic queries. Furthermore, they too do not accept queries in natural language, while their output is in the form of sequences, instead of ready-to-use snippets.

Similar conclusions can be drawn for API mining systems that output snippets. For example, APIMiner [17] performs code slicing in order to generate common API usage examples, while eXoaDocs [14] further performs semantic clustering (using the DECKARD code clone detection algorithm [11]) to group them according to their functionality. CLAMS [13] also clusters the snippets and further generates the most representative (medoid) snippet of each cluster using slicing and code summarization techniques. Another interesting approach is MUSE [18], which employs a novel ranking scheme for the recommended snippets based on metrics such as the ease of reuse, a metric computed by determining whether a snippet has custom object types, and thus requires external dependencies. As with the previous approaches, these systems are effective for mining API usage examples, however they do not generalize to the problem of receiving natural language queries and retrieving API-agnostic reusable solutions.

This more generic snippet mining scenario is supported by several contemporary systems. One such system is SnipMatch [29], which employs pattern-based code search to retrieve useful snippets. SnipMatch, however, relies on a local index that has to be updated from the developer. More advanced systems in this aspect usually connect to online search engines and process their results to extract and recommend snippets. For example, Blueprint [3] and CodeCatch [6] employ the Google search engine, while Bing Code Search [28] employs Bing. Due to the integration with strong engines, these systems tend to offer effective natural language understanding features and their results are adequate even in less common queries. However, the text surrounding the code is not parsed for semantic information, so the quality of the retrieved snippets is bound only to the semantics introduced by the search engines. Moreover, the agnostic web search that these systems perform may often be suboptimal compared to issuing the queries to a better focused question-answering service.

These limitations have led to more specialized tools that employ Stack Overflow in order to recommend snippets that are proposed by the community and are accompanied by useful metadata. One of the first such systems is Example Overflow [35], an online code search engine that uses Tf-Idf as a scoring mechanism and retrieves snippets relevant to the jQuery framework. Two other systems in this area, which are built as plugins of the Eclipse IDE, are Prompter [22] and Seahawk [21]. Prompter employs a sophisticated ranking mechanism based not only on the code of each snippet, but also on metadata, such as the score of the post or reputation of the user that posted it on Stack Overflow. Seahawk also uses similar metadata upon building a local index using Apache Solr[3]. The main limitation of the systems in this category is their reliance on term occurrence; the lack of more powerful semantics restricts the retrieved results to cases where the query terms appear as-is within the Stack Overflow posts.

Finally, there are certain research efforts towards semantic-aware snippet retrieval. SWIM [23], for instance, which is proposed by the research team behind Bing Code Search [28], uses a natural language to API mapper that computes the probability $Pr(t|Q)$ that an API t appears as a result to a query Q. The system retrieves the most probable snippets and synthesizes them to produce valid and human-readable snippets. A limitation of SWIM, which was highlighted by Gu et al. [10], is that it follows the bag-of-words assumption, therefore it cannot distinguish among certain queries (e.g. "convert number to string" and "convert string to number). The authors instead propose DeepAPI [10], a system that defines snippet recommendation as a machine translation problem, where natural language is the source language and source code is the target language. DeepAPI employs a model with three recurrent neural networks (one for the text of the query as-is, one for the same text reversed, and one to combine them) that retrieves the most relevant API call sequence given a query. The system, however, is largely based on code comments, so its performance depends on whether there is sufficient documentation in the snippets of its index. A similar approach is followed by T2API [20], another Eclipse plugin that uses a graph-based translation approach to translate query text into API usages. This system, however, is also largely based on synthesizing API calls and does not focus on semantic retrieval. Finally, an even more recent system is CROKAGE [24], which employs embeddings and further expands the query with relevant API classes from Stack Overflow. The final results are ranked according to multiple factors, including their lexical and semantic similarity with the query and their similar API usage.

In conclusion, the systems analyzed in the above paragraphs have the limitations that were discussed also in the introduction of this work. Several of them are focused only on APIs without generalizing to common programming problems. And while there are certain systems that allow queries in natural language, most of them rely on term frequency indexing and do not incorporate semantics extracted by the context of the snippets. In this work, we design a hybrid system that employs both a lexical (term frequency) and a word embeddings model on Stack Overflow posts' data. Note that, compared to source code comments that

---

[3] https://lucene.apache.org/solr/

may be incomplete or sometimes even non-existent, the text of Stack Overflow posts is a more complete source of information as it is the outcome of the explanation efforts of different members of the community [7]. As a result, our system can extract the semantic meaning of natural language queries and retrieve useful snippets, which are accompanied by semantic-aware labels.

3 StackSearch: A Semantic-aware Snippet Recommender

3.1 Overview

The architecture of StackSearch is shown in Figure 1. The left part of the figure refers to building the index while the right one refers to answering user queries.

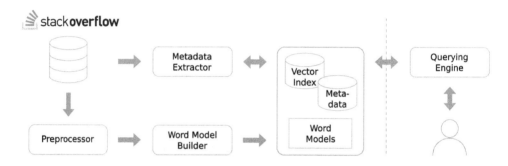

Fig. 1. Architecture of StackSearch

At first, our system retrieves information from Stack Overflow[4] and builds an SQLite[5] database of all Java posts. Note that our methodology is mostly language agnostic, however we use Java here as a proof of concept[6]. We created four tables in order to store question posts, answer posts, comments, and post links (to be used for evaluation, see subsection 4.2). For each of these tables we kept all information, i.e. title, tags, body, score, etc., as well as all connections of the data dump as foreign keys (e.g. any answer has a foreign key towards the corresponding question), so that we fully take into account the post context.

Upon storing the data in a suitable format, the Preprocessor receives as input all question posts, answer posts, and comments and extracts a corpus of texts. The corpus is then given to the Word Model Builder, which trains different models to transform the text to vector form. Finally, the system includes a vector index, where each set of vectors corresponds to to the title, tags, and body of one question post, the produced word models, and certain metadata for each question, which are extracted by the Metadata Extractor.

---

[4] We used the latest official data dump provided by Stack Overflow, which is available at https://archive.org/details/stackexchange

[5] https://www.sqlite.org/

[6] Applying our methodology to a different language requires only providing a preprocessor in order to extract the relevant source code elements from the post snippets.

When the developer issues a query, the Querying Engine initially extracts a vector for the query given the stored vector models, and then computes the similarity between the query vector and each vector in the vector index. The engine then ranks the results and presents them to the user along with their metadata. The steps required to build the index as well as the issuing of queries are discussed in detail in the following subsections.

3.2 Preprocessor

Upon creating our database, the next step is to preprocess the data in order to build the corpus that will be used to train our models. We extract the text and the code of each post by parsing the <pre> and <code> tags. We further remove all html tags from text and then perform a series of preprocessing steps. At first, the code is parsed to extract its semantic information. The posts are then filtered to remove the ones that introduce noise to the dataset and, finally, the texts are tokenized. These steps are outlined in the following paragraphs.

Extracting Semantics from Source Code Upon extracting the code from each question post, we parse it using an extension of the parser described in [8]. The parser checks if the snippets are compilable and also drops any snippets that are not written in Java. Upon making these checks, our parser extracts the AST of each snippet and takes two passes over it, one to extract type declarations, and one to extract method invocations (i.e. API calls). For example, in the snippet of Figure 2, the parser initially extracts the declarations is: InputStream, br: BufferedReader, and sb: StringBuilder (strings and exceptions are excluded). After that, it extracts the relevant API calls, which are highlighted in Figure 2.

```
// initialize an InputStream
InputStream is = new ByteArrayInputStream ("sample".getBytes());
// convert InputStream to String
BufferedReader br = null;
StringBuilder sb = new StringBuilder ();
String line;
try {
    br = new BufferedReader (new InputStreamReader (is));
    while ((line = br. readLine ()) != null) { sb. append (line); }
} catch (IOException e) {
    e.printStackTrace();
} finally {
    if (br != null) {
        try { br. close (); } catch (IOException e) { e.printStackTrace(); }
    }
}
```

Fig. 2. Example snippet for "How to read a file line by line" (API calls highlighted)

Finally, the calling object of each API call is replaced by its type and the text of comments is also retrieved to produce the sequence shown in Figure 3.

---

initialize an InputStream, InputStream, ByteArrayInputStream, convert InputStream to String, BufferedReader, StringBuilder, StringBuilder, BufferedReader, InputStreamReader, BufferedReader.readLine, StringBuilder.append, BufferedReader.close

---

Fig. 3. Extracted sequence for the snippet of Figure 2

Filtering the Posts Filtering is performed using a classifier that rules out any posts that are considered by our system as noise. We used the regional CNN-LSTM model of Wang et al. [26], a model shown in Figure 4 that combines the CNN and LSTM architectures and achieves in capturing the characteristics of text considering also its order. Our classifier is binary; it receives as input the data of each post and its output determines whether a post is *useful* or *noisy.*

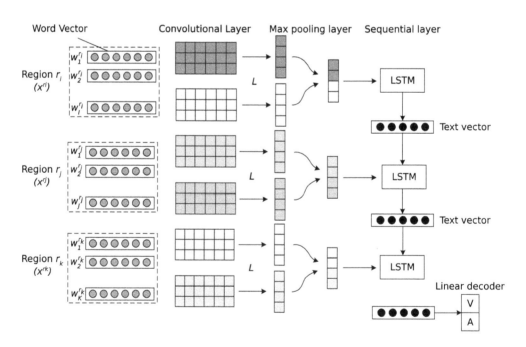

Fig. 4. Architecture of Regional CNN-LSTM model by Wang et al. [26]

The input embedding layer receives a one-hot encoding that corresponds to the concatenation of the title, body and tags of each post. Tokenization and one-hot encoding are performed before the text is given as input so no rules are given other than splitting on spaces and punctuation (this tokenization process is only used here on-the-fly to filter the posts, while we fully tokenize the text afterwards as described in the next paragraph). Punctuation marks are also kept as each of them is actually a token. After that, the classifier includes a CNN layer, which extracts and amplifies the terms (including punctuation) that cause noise. The CNN layer is followed by a max pooling layer that is used to reduce the number of parameters that have to be optimized by the model. Finally, the next layer is the LSTM that captures semantic information from nearby terms, which is finally given to the output to provide the binary decision.

To train our classifier, we have annotated a set of 2500 posts. For each post, we consider it noisy if it has error logs, debug logs or stack traces. Though useful in other contexts, in our case these posts would skew our models, as they contain a lot of generic data. Furthermore we deem noisy any posts with large amounts of numeric data (usually in tables) and any posts with code snippets in languages other than Java. The training was performed with accuracy as the metric to optimize, while we also used dropout to avoid overfitting. Upon experimenting with different parameter values, we ended up using the Adagrad optimizer, while the dropout and recurrent dropout parameters were set to 0.6 and 0.05 respectively. Setting the embedding length to 35 and the number of epochs to 5 proved adequate, as our classifier achieved accuracy equal to 0.94.

Text Tokenization Upon filtering, we now have a set of texts that must be tokenized before they are given as input to the models. Since tokenization might split Java terms (e.g. method invocations), we excluded these from tokenizing using regular expressions. After that, we removed all URLs and all non-alphabetical characters (i.e. numbers and special symbols) and tokenized the text.

3.3 Word Model Builder

We build two models for capturing the semantics of posts, a Tf-Idf model and a FastText embedding. These models are indicative of lexical matching and semantic matching, respectively. They will serve as baselines and at the same time be used to build a more powerful hybrid model (see subsection 3.5). Both models are executed three times, one for the titles of the question posts, one for their bodies, and one for their tags. As already mentioned the code snippets are replaced by their corresponding text sequences, so they now are textual parts of the bodies. The two models are analyzed in the following paragraphs.

Tf-Idf Model We employ a vector space model to represent the texts (titles or bodies or tags) as documents and the words/terms as dimensions. The vector representation for each document is extracted using Tf-Idf vectorizer. According to Tf-Idf, the weight (vector value) of each term t in a document d is defined as:

$$tfidf(t, d, D) = tf(t, d) \cdot idf(t, D) \tag{1}$$

where $tf(t, d)$ is the term frequency of term t in document d and refers to the number of occurrences of the term t in the document (title, body or tag). Also,

$idf(t, D)$ is the inverse document frequency of term t in the set of all documents D, and is used as a normalizing factor to indicate how common the term is in the corpus. In our implementation (we used scikit-learn), $idf(t, D)$ is equal to $1 + log((1 + |D|)/(1 + d_t))$, where $|d_t|$ is the number of documents containing the term t, i.e. the number of titles, bodies or tags that include the relevant term. Intuitively, very common terms (e.g. "Java" or "Exception") may act as noise for our dataset, as they could appear to semantically different posts.

FastText Model FastText is a neural language model proposed by Facebook's AI Research (FAIR) lab [2,12]. Practically, fastText is a shallow neural network that is trained in order to reconstruct linguistic contexts of words. In our case, we transform the terms of the documents in one-hot encoding format and give the documents as input to the network during the training step. The result, i.e. the output of the hidden layer, is actually a set of word vectors. So, in this case, the resulting model is one where terms are represented as vectors. Given proper parameters, these vectors should incorporate semantic information, so that our model will have learned from the context.

We used the official implementation of fastText[7], selected the skip-gram variation of the model and we also set it up to use n-grams of size 3, 4, 5, 6, and 7. Upon experimenting with the parameters of the model, we ended up building a model with 300 dimensions and training it for 25 epochs. We used the negative sampling cost function (with number of negative samples equal to 10) and set the learning rate to 0.025 and the window size (i.e. number of terms that are within the context of a word) to 10. Also, the sampling threshold was set to 10^{-6}, while we also dropped any words with fewer than 5 occurrences. Upon extracting all word vectors, we create the vector of each document level (title, body or tags) by averaging over its word vectors.

Finally, the output of either of our two models is a set of vectors, one for the title, one for the body and one for the tags of each post. In the case of Tf-Idf the dimensions of the vector are equal to the total number of words, while in the case of fastText there are 300 dimensions. In both cases, the vectors are stored in a vector index, which also contains ids that point to the original posts.

3.4 Metadata Extractor

As metadata, we extract the named entities of each post, i.e. useful terms that may help the developer understand the semantics behind each post. To do so, we build a Conditional Random Fields (CRF) classifier [15], which performs named entity recognition based on features extracted from the terms themselves and from their context (neighboring terms). The goal is to estimate the probability that a term belongs to one of the available categories. To create a feature set for each term, we initially use two models.

At first, we employ the Brown hierarchical clustering algorithm [4] to generate a binary representation of all terms in the corpus. The algorithm clusters all

---

[7] https://github.com/facebookresearch/fastText

terms in a binary tree structure. An example fragment of such a tree is shown in Figure 5. The leaf nodes of the tree are all the terms, so by traversing the tree from the root to a leaf we are given a binary representation known as *bitstring* for the corresponding term. Semantically similar terms are expected to share more similar tree paths. For instance, in the fragment of Figure 5, the terms 'array' and 'table' have binary representations 00100000 and 00100001 respectively, which are quite similar, as is their semantic meaning. The terms 'collection' and 'list' are also similar, yet somewhat less, as their representations (001000010 and 001001 respectively) differ more.

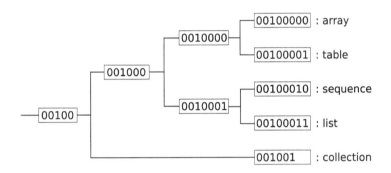

Fig. 5. Example Fragment of Binary Tree generated by the Brown Algorithm

Secondly, we use the fastText model of subsection 3.3. As already mentioned, our model extracts vector representations of terms so that semantically similar terms have vectors that are closer to each other (where proximity is computed using cosine similarity, see section 3.5). To reduce the size of these vectors (and thus avoid the curse of dimensionality), we further employ K-Means to cluster them into 5 configurations with different number of clusters (500, 1000, 1500, 2000, and 3000), an idea originating from similar natural language approaches [33,34]. Thus, instead of using the term vector, we use 5 features for each term, each one corresponding to the id of the cluster that the feature is assigned.

Upon applying the two models, we finally build the feature set for the CRF classifier. Given each term t_i, its preceding term t_{i-1} its following term t_{i+1}, we define their Brown bitstrings as b_i, b_{i-1}, and b_{i+1} respectively, and we also define their K-Means cluster assignments as k_i, k_{i-1}, and k_{i+1} respectively. Note that the k_i includes all 5 cluster configurations used, thus producing on its own five features. Using these definitions, we build the following feature set:

- the term itself (t_i), and its combination with the preceding term ($t_{i-1}t_i$), and the following term (t_it_{i+1});
- the ids of the cluster assigned by K-Means to the term (k_i), the preceding term (k_{i-1}), and the following term (k_{i+1});
- the bigram of the ids of K-Means clusters for the three terms ($k_{i-1}k_ik_{i+1}$);
- the bitstrings of the term (b_i), the preceding term (b_{i-1}), and the following term (b_{i+1});

- the bigram of the three bitstrings $(b_{i-1}b_ib_{i+1})$;
- the prefixes with length 2, 4, 6, 8, 10, 12 of each one of the three bitstrings (e.g. for a bitstring 100100 the prefixes are 10, 1001, and 100100).

Finally, our features are augmented by employing the dataset proposed by Ye et al. [31, 32]. The dataset comprises annotated entities extracted from Stack Overflow that lie in five categories: API calls, programming languages, platforms (e.g. Android), tools-frameworks (e.g. Maven), and standards (e.g. TCP). For each of these categories, we check whether the term is found in the corresponding dataset file and produce a true/false decision that is added as one more feature in our feature set. After that, we apply the CRF classifier for all terms and build a metadata index. Using this index we can produce a list of semantically rich named entities for each post in the dataset.

3.5   Querying Engine

As already mentioned in subsection 3.3, the vector index comprises a set of vectors, three for each question post, corresponding to the title, the body and the tags of the post. When a developer issues a new query, it is initially preprocessed and tokenized, and then it is vectorized using either of our models. After that, we now have to produce a similarity score between each question post p and the query q of the developer. To do so, we use the following equation:

$$sim_{model}(q,p) = \frac{csim(v_q, v_{title(p)}) + csim(v_q, v_{body(p)}) + csim(v_q, v_{tags(p)})}{3} \quad (2)$$

where v_q is the vector of the query and $v_{title(p)}$, $v_{body(p)}$, and $v_{tags(p)}$ are the vectors of the title, the body, and the tags of the question post respectively. Finally, $csim$ is the cosine similarity, which is computed for two vectors v_1 and v_2 as follows:

$$csim(v_1, v_2) = \frac{v_1 \cdot v_2}{|v_1| \cdot |v_2|} \quad (3)$$

Apart from the two models described so far, we also created a hybrid model by taking the average between the two scores computed by our models:

$$sim_{hybrid}(q,p) = \frac{sim_{Tf-Idf}(q,p) + sim_{fastText}(q,p)}{2} \quad (4)$$

This hybrid model incorporates the advantages of fastText, while giving more weight than only fastText to well-formed queries (i.e. with expected terms).

Finally, the user is presented with a list of possible results to the query, ranked according to their score. Each result contains information extracted by a question post and the corresponding answer posts. In specific, we include the title of the question post, the snippets extracted by the answer posts, the links to the question and answer posts (should the developer want to examine them), the Stack Overflow score of the answer posts, and the 8 most frequent named entities among all answer posts of the relevant question post. For example, assuming our system receives the query "How to read from text file?", an example result is shown in Table 1. The developer can obviously select to check the second most relevant snippet of this question post, or even check another question post.

Table 1. Example StackSearch Response to Query "How to read from text file?"

Type	Data
Post title	Reading a plain text file in Java
Question post link	https://stackoverflow.com/questions/4716503
Top 8 labels	FileReader, BufferedReader, FileInputStream, InputStreamReader, Scanner.hasNext, Files.readAllBytes, FileUtils.readLines, Scanner

Snippet 1	`Scanner in = new Scanner(new FileReader( "file.txt" ));`
	`StringBuilder sb = new StringBuilder();`
	`while(in.hasNext()) {`
	`        sb.append(in.next());`
	`}`
	`in.close();`
	`outString = sb.toString();`

Answer post link	https://stackoverflow.com/questions/4716556
Answer post score	117

4 Evaluation

To fully evaluate StackSearch, we perform three experiments. The first experiment involved annotating the results of common programming problems and is expected to illustrate the usefulness of our system. The second experiment relies on post links and is used to provide proof that our system is effective (and minimize possible threats to validity). Finally, for our third experiment, we compare StackSearch to the tool CROKAGE [24], which is quite similar to our system. Comparing StackSearch with other approaches was not possible, since several systems are not maintained and/or they are not publicly available (to facilitate researchers with similar challenges, we uploaded our code at https://github.com/AuthEceSoftEng/StackSearch).

4.1 Evaluation using Programming Queries

We initially evaluate StackSearch using a set of common programming queries shown in Table 2. The dataset includes certain queries that are semantically very similar, which are marked as belonging to the same group, to determine whether our method captures the semantic features of the dataset. Queries in the same group call for the same solutions, i.e. their only difference is in the phrasing.

We evaluate all three implementations of our system, the Tf-Idf model, the fastText model, and the hybrid model. For each implementation, upon giving the queries as input, we retrieve the first 20 results and annotate them as relevant or non-relevant. A result is marked as relevant if its snippet covers the functionality that is described by the query. We gathered the results of all three algorithms together and randomly permuted them, so the annotation was performed without any prior knowledge about which result corresponds to each model, in order to be as objective as possible.

Table 2. Dataset used for Semantically Evaluating StackSearch

ID	Query	Group
1	How to read a comma separated file?	1
2	How to read a CSV file?	1
3	How to read a delimited file?	1
4	How to read input from console?	2
5	How to read input from terminal?	2
6	How to read input from command prompt?	2
7	How to play an mp3 file?	3
8	How to play an audio file?	3
9	How to compare dates?	4
10	How to compare time strings?	4
11	How to dynamically load a class?	5
12	How to load a jar/class at runtime?	5
13	How to calculate checksums for files?	6
14	How to calculate MD5 checksum for files?	6
15	How to iterate through a hashmap?	7
16	How to loop over a hashmap?	7
17	How to split a string?	8
18	How to handle an exception?	9

For each query, we evaluate each implementation by computing the average precision of the results. Given a ranked list of results, the average precision is computed by the following equation:

$$AveP = \frac{\sum_{k=1}^{n} (P(k) \cdot rel(k))}{number\ of\ relevant\ results} \tag{5}$$

where $P(k)$ is the precision at k and corresponds to the percentage of relevant results in the first k, and $rel(k)$ denotes if the result in the position k is relevant. We also use the mean average precision, defined as the mean of the average precision values of all queries.

We calculated the average precision at 10 and 20 results. The values for each query are shown in Figure 6. As shown in these graphs, the fastText and the hybrid models clearly outperform the Tf-Idf model, which is expected as they incorporate semantic information. We also note that the hybrid implementation is even more effective than fastText for most queries. Interestingly, there are certain queries in which Tf-Idf outperforms one or both of the other implementations. Consider, for example, query 17; this is a very specific query with clear terms (i.e. developers would rarely form such a query without using the term 'string') so there is not really any use for semantics. For most queries, however, better results are proposed by fastText or by our hybrid model.

We note, especially, what is the case with queries in the same group (divided by gray lines in the graphs of Figure 6). Given, for instance, the second group, query 4, which refers to input from the console, returns multiple useful results using any of the three models. The results, however are quite different for queries

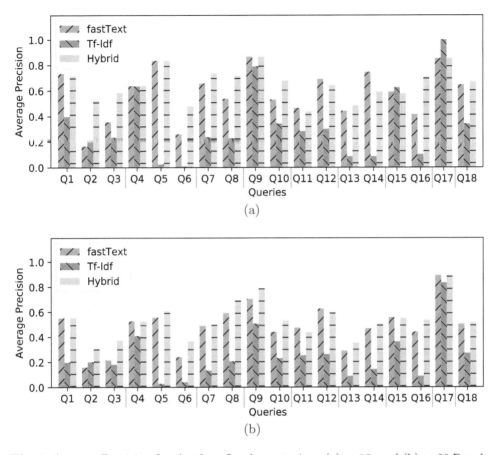

Fig. 6. Average Precision for the three Implementations (a) at 10, and (b) at 20 Results

5 and 6, which are similar albeit for the replacement of the term 'console' with 'terminal' and with 'command prompt' respectively. This indicates that our word embedding successfully captures the semantics of the text and considers the aforementioned terms as synonyms. This advantage of our system is also clear in group 1 (comma-separated vs CSV vs delimited file), group 4 (dates vs time strings), etc., and even in more difficult semantic relationships, such as the one of group 5 (i.e. loading dynamically vs at runtime).

Finally, we calculated the mean average precision for the same configurations as before. The values for the three implementations are shown in Figure 7a, where it is clear once again that the word embeddings outperform the Tf-Idf model, while our hybrid model is the most effective of the three models.

To further outline the differences among the models we also computed the mean search length. The search length is a very useful metric since it intuitively simulates the process used when searching for relevant results. The metric is defined as the number of non-relevant results that one must examine in order to find a number of relevant results. We computed the search length for all queries for finding from 1 up to 10 relevant results.

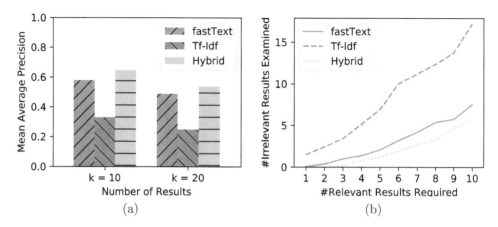

Fig. 7. Results depicting (a) the Mean Average Precision, and (b) the Mean Search Length, for the three Implementations

Averaging over all queries provides the mean search length, of which the results are shown in Figure 7b. The results are again encouraging for our proposed models. Indicatively, to find the first useful result, the developer has to examine less than 0.1 irrelevant results on average for fastText and for the hybrid model, whereas using Tf-Idf requires examining 1.5 irrelevant results. Furthermore, when the developer skims over the results of fastText, he/she will only need to view 2.11 irrelevant snippets on average, before finding the first 5 relevant. Using the hybrid model, he/she will only need to see 1.22. Tf-Idf is clearly outperformed in this case, providing on average almost 7 irrelevant results, along with the first 5 relevant. Similar conclusions can be drawn for the first 10 relevant results. In this case, the developer would need to examine around 17.5, 7.5, and 5.5 results on average, for Tf-Idf, fastText, and our hybrid model, respectively.

4.2   Evaluation using Post Links

The main goal of the previous subsection was to illustrate the potential of our word embedding models. The results, especially for the groups of queries, have shown that our models indeed capture the semantics of text. As already mentioned, the annotation process was performed in such a way to limit any threats to validity. Nevertheless, to further strengthen the objectivity of the results, we perform one more experiment, which is described in this subsection.

In the lack of a third-party annotated Stack Overflow dataset, what we decided to do is evaluate our models using the post links provided by Stack Overflow, an idea found in [8]. In Stack Overflow, the presence of a link between two questions is an indicator that the two questions are similar. Note, of course, that the opposite assumption, i.e. that any two questions that are not linked are not similar to each other, is not necessarily correct. There are many questions that are asked and perhaps not linked to similar ones. In our evaluation, however, we formulate the problem as a search/retrieval scenario, so we only use post links to determine whether our models can retrieve objectively relevant results.

To create our link evaluation dataset, we first extracted all post links of Java question posts. After that, for performance reasons, we dropped any posts without snippets and any posts with Stack Overflow score lower or equal to -3, as these are not within the scenario of a system that retrieves useful snippets. These criteria reduced the number of question posts to roughly 200000 (as opposed to the original dataset that had approximately 1.3 million question posts). These question posts have approximately 37000 links, reinforcing our assumption that non-linked questions are not necessarily dissimilar.

We execute StackSearch with all three models giving as queries the titles of all question posts of the dataset. For each query, we retrieve the first 20 results (as we may assume this is the maximum a developer would normally examine). We determine how many of these 20 results are linked to the specific question post, and compute the percentage of relevant results compared to the total number of relevant post links of the question post. By averaging over all queries (i.e. titles of question posts of the dataset), we compute the percentage of relevant links retrieved on average for each model. The results are shown in Figure 8.

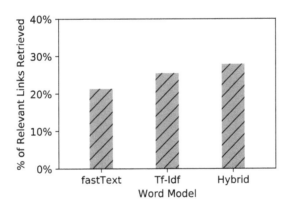

Fig. 8. Percentage of Relevant Results (compared to the number of Links of each Question Post) in the first 20 Results for the three Implementations

At first, one may note that the results for all models are below 30%, a rather low number, which is however expected, given the shortcomings of our dataset. Many retrieved results are actually relevant, however they are not linked to the question posts of the queries. In any case, we are given an objective relative comparison of the three models. And this comparison provides some interesting insights. An interesting observation is that Tf-Idf outperforms fastText. This is not totally unexpected, if we consider that the post links of Stack Overflow are created by the community, therefore it is possible that posts with similar meanings but different key terms are not linked. As a result, fastText may discover several posts that should be linked, yet they are not. On the other hand, Tf-Idf focuses on identical terms which are rather easier to discover using the Stack Overflow service. In any case, however, our hybrid model outperforms Tf-Idf and fastText, as it combines the advantages of Tf-Idf and fastText.

4.3   Comparative Evaluation

Upon demonstrating the effectiveness of StackSearch in the previous subsections, we now proceed to compare it with a similar system, the tool CROKAGE. To do so, we have employed the dataset proposed by CROKAGE [24]. The dataset involves 48 programming queries, similar to those introduced in subsection 4.1. The queries include diverse tasks, such as comparing dates, resizing images, pausing the current thread, etc.

Given that our dataset comprises Stack Overflow posts, it can be used to assess both tools. Thus, we issued the queries at both StackSearch and CROKAGE. The results of the queries had been originally annotated by two annotators (of which the results were merged) in Stack Overflow posts, marking any post as relevant if it addresses the query with a feasible amount of changes [24]. So we have used these annotations and only had to update a small part of them in order to make sure that they are on par with our dataset, which includes the latest data dump of Stack Overflow. As before, for each query we have calculated the average precision at 5 and 10 results as well as the search length for finding 1 up to 10 relevant results. The mean average precision and the mean search length results for the two tools are shown in Figures 9a and 9b, respectively (results per query are omitted due to space limitations).

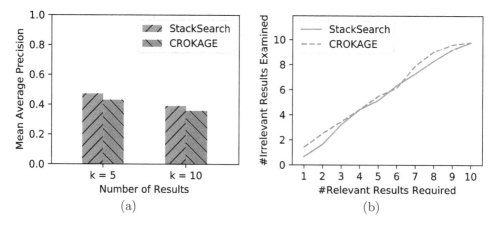

Fig. 9. Results depicting (a) the Mean Average Precision, and (b) the Mean Search Length, for StackSearch and CROKAGE

Both tools seem to be effective on the provided dataset. Concerning mean average precision, StackSearch outperforms CROKAGE both at 5 and at 10 results, indicating that it retrieves more useful results on average. Moreover, it seems that their difference is more noticeable when a fewer number of results is required, indicating that StackSearch provides a better ranking.

This difference is also illustrated by the mean search length for the two approaches. Indicatively, using StackSearch, the developer will need to examine only 0.66 irrelevant snippets on average, before finding the first relevant one (the corresponding value for CROKAGE is 1.42). Our tool also performs better for finding the second and third relevant results, while the two tools perform equally well for finding five or more results.

5 Conclusion

Although several API usage and snippet mining solutions have been proposed, most of them do not account for the semantics of the source code and the surrounding text. Furthermore, most contemporary systems do not employ word embeddings to enable semantic-aware retrieval of snippets, and are limited either by the format of their input, which is not natural language, or by their output, which is not ready-to-use snippets. In this work, we have created a novel snippet mining system that extracts snippets from Stack Overflow and employs word embeddings to model code and as well as contextual information. Given our evaluation, we conclude that the hybrid model of StackSearch effectively extracts the semantics of the data and outperforms both our baselines (Tf-Idf and fastText) as well as the snippet mining tool CROKAGE. Finally, our system accompanies the retrieved snippets with useful metadata that convey the meaning of each post.

Future work lies in several directions. At first, we may employ a more sophisticated ranking scheme using more information from Stack Overflow (e.g. the Stack Overflow score of the snippet's answer post) or even from other sources (e.g. the reuse rate of Stack Overflow snippets in GitHub [1]) and assess the influence of that information on the effectiveness of the scheme. Furthermore, we could employ different word embedding techniques or even variations of fastText, such as the combination of the In-Out vectors of fastText [19]. We could also further investigate our hybrid solution, implementing a more complex scheme other than averaging the scores of the two models. Finally, we could further assess StackSearch using a survey to ask developers whether the system actually retrieves useful snippets and whether it reduces the effort required for finding and integrating reusable snippets.

Acknowledgements

This research has been co-financed by the European Regional Development Fund of the European Union and Greek national funds through the Operational Program Competitiveness, Entrepreneurship and Innovation, under the call RESEARCH - CREATE - INNOVATE (project code: T1EDK-02347).

References

1. Baltes, S., Treude, C., Diehl, S.: SOTorrent: Studying the Origin, Evolution, and Usage of Stack Overflow Code Snippets. In: Proceedings of the 16th International Conference on Mining Software Repositories. pp. 191–194. MSR '19, IEEE Press, Piscataway, NJ, USA (2019)
2. Bojanowski, P., Grave, E., Joulin, A., Mikolov, T.: Enriching Word Vectors with Subword Information. Transactions of the Association for Computational Linguistics **5**, 135–146 (2017)
3. Brandt, J., Dontcheva, M., Weskamp, M., Klemmer, S.R.: Example-centric Programming: Integrating Web Search into the Development Environment. In: Proceedings of the SIGCHI Conference on Human Factors in Computing Systems. pp. 513–522. CHI '10, ACM, New York, NY, USA (2010)
4. Brown, P.F., deSouza, P.V., Mercer, R.L., Pietra, V.J.D., Lai, J.C.: Class-based N-gram Models of Natural Language. Computational Linguistics **18**(4), 467–479 (1992)
5. Buse, R.P.L., Weimer, W.: Synthesizing API Usage Examples. In: Proceedings of the 34th International Conference on Software Engineering. pp. 782–792. ICSE '12, IEEE Press, Piscataway, NJ, USA (2012)
6. Diamantopoulos, T., Karagiannopoulos, G., Symeonidis, A.L.: CodeCatch: Extracting Source Code Snippets from Online Sources. In: Proceedings of the 6th International Workshop on Realizing Artificial Intelligence Synergies in Software Engineering. pp. 21–27. RAISE '18, ACM, New York, NY, USA (2018)
7. Diamantopoulos, T., Sifaki, M.I., Symeonidis, A.L.: Towards Mining Answer Edits to Extract Evolution Patterns in Stack Overflow. In: Proceedings of the 16th International Conference on Mining Software Repositories. p. 215–219. MSR '19, IEEE Press (2019)
8. Diamantopoulos, T., Symeonidis, A.L.: Employing Source Code Information to Improve Question-answering in Stack Overflow. In: Proceedings of the 12th Working Conference on Mining Software Repositories. pp. 454–457. MSR '15, IEEE Press, Piscataway, NJ, USA (2015)
9. Fowkes, J., Sutton, C.: Parameter-free Probabilistic API Mining across GitHub. In: Proceedings of the 2016 24th ACM SIGSOFT International Symposium on Foundations of Software Engineering. pp. 254–265. FSE 2016, ACM, New York, NY, USA (2016)
10. Gu, X., Zhang, H., Zhang, D., Kim, S.: Deep API Learning. In: Proceedings of the 2016 24th ACM SIGSOFT International Symposium on Foundations of Software Engineering. pp. 631–642. FSE 2016, ACM, New York, NY, USA (2016)
11. Jiang, L., Misherghi, G., Su, Z., Glondu, S.: DECKARD: Scalable and Accurate Tree-Based Detection of Code Clones. In: Proceedings of the 29th International Conference on Software Engineering. pp. 96–105. ICSE '07, IEEE Computer Society, Washington, DC, USA (2007)
12. Joulin, A., Grave, E., Bojanowski, P., Mikolov, T.: Bag of Tricks for Efficient Text Classification. In: Proceedings of the 15th Conference of the European Chapter of the Association for Computational Linguistics: Volume 2, Short Papers. pp. 427–431. Association for Computational Linguistics, Valencia, Spain (2017)
13. Katirtzis, N., Diamantopoulos, T., Sutton, C.: Learning a Metric for Code Readability. In: 21th International Conference on Fundamental Approaches to Software Engineering. pp. 189–206. FASE 2018, Springer International Publishing, Boston, MA, USA (2018)

14. Kim, J., Lee, S., Hwang, S.w., Kim, S.: Towards an Intelligent Code Search Engine. In: Proceedings of the 24th AAAI Conference on Artificial Intelligence. pp. 1358–1363. AAAI '10, AAAI Press, Palo Alto, CA, USA (2010)
15. Lafferty, J.D., McCallum, A., Pereira, F.C.N.: Conditional Random Fields: Probabilistic Models for Segmenting and Labeling Sequence Data. In: Proceedings of the Eighteenth International Conference on Machine Learning. pp. 282–289. ICML '01, Morgan Kaufmann Publishers Inc., San Francisco, CA, USA (2001)
16. Mandelin, D., Xu, L., Bodík, R., Kimelman, D.: Jungloid Mining: Helping to Navigate the API Jungle. SIGPLAN Not. **40**(6), 48–61 (2005)
17. Montandon, J.E., Borges, H., Felix, D., Valente, M.T.: Documenting APIs with Examples: Lessons Learned with the APIMiner Platform. In: Proceedings of the 20th Working Conference on Reverse Engineering. pp. 401–408. WCRE 2013, IEEE Computer Society, Piscataway, NJ, USA (2013)
18. Moreno, L., Bavota, G., Di Penta, M., Oliveto, R., Marcus, A.: How Can I Use This Method? In: Proceedings of the 37th International Conference on Software Engineering - Volume 1. pp. 880–890. ICSE '15, IEEE Press, Piscataway, NJ, USA (2015)
19. Nalisnick, E., Mitra, B., Craswell, N., Caruana, R.: Improving Document Ranking with Dual Word Embeddings. In: Proceedings of the 25th International Conference Companion on World Wide Web. pp. 83–84. WWW '16 Companion, International World Wide Web Conferences Steering Committee, Republic and Canton of Geneva, Switzerland (2016)
20. Nguyen, T., Rigby, P.C., Nguyen, A.T., Karanfil, M., Nguyen, T.N.: T2API: Synthesizing API Code Usage Templates from English Texts with Statistical Translation. In: Proceedings of the 2016 24th ACM SIGSOFT International Symposium on Foundations of Software Engineering. pp. 1013–1017. FSE 2016, ACM, New York, NY, USA (2016)
21. Ponzanelli, L., Bacchelli, A., Lanza, M.: Seahawk: Stack Overflow in the IDE. In: Proceedings of the 2013 International Conference on Software Engineering. pp. 1295–1298. ICSE '13, IEEE Press, Piscataway, NJ, USA (2013)
22. Ponzanelli, L., Bavota, G., Di Penta, M., Oliveto, R., Lanza, M.l.: Mining Stack-Overflow to Turn the IDE into a Self-confident Programming Prompter. In: Proceedings of the 11th Working Conference on Mining Software Repositories. pp. 102–111. MSR 2014, ACM, New York, NY, USA (2014)
23. Raghothaman, M., Wei, Y., Hamadi, Y.: SWIM: Synthesizing What I Mean: Code Search and Idiomatic Snippet Synthesis. In: Proceedings of the 38th International Conference on Software Engineering. pp. 357–367. ICSE '16, ACM, New York, NY, USA (2016)
24. Silva, R.F.G., Roy, C.K., Rahman, M.M., Schneider, K.A., Paixao, K., de Almeida Maia, M.: Recommending Comprehensive Solutions for Programming Tasks by Mining Crowd Knowledge. In: Proceedings of the 27th International Conference on Program Comprehension. p. 358–368. ICPC '19, IEEE Press (2019)
25. Thummalapenta, S., Xie, T.: PARSEWeb: A Programmer Assistant for Reusing Open Source Code on the Web. In: Proceedings of the 22nd IEEE/ACM International Conference on Automated Software Engineering. pp. 204–213. ASE '07, ACM, New York, NY, USA (2007)
26. Wang, J., Yu, L.C., Lai, K.R., Zhang, X.: Dimensional sentiment analysis using a regional CNN-LSTM model. In: Proceedings of the 54th Annual Meeting of the Association for Computational Linguistics (Volume 2: Short Papers). pp. 225–230. Association for Computational Linguistics, Berlin, Germany (2016)

27. Wang, J., Dang, Y., Zhang, H., Chen, K., Xie, T., Zhang, D.: Mining Succinct and High-Coverage API Usage Patterns from Source Code. In: Proceedings of the 10th Working Conference on Mining Software Repositories. pp. 319–328. MSR '13, IEEE Press, Piscataway, NJ, USA (2013)
28. Wei, Y., Chandrasekaran, N., Gulwani, S., Hamadi, Y.: Building Bing Developer Assistant. Tech. Rep. MSR-TR-2015-36, Microsoft Research (2015)
29. Wightman, D., Ye, Z., Brandt, J., Vertegaal, R.: SnipMatch: Using Source Code Context to Enhance Snippet Retrieval and Parameterization. In: Proceedings of the 25th Annual ACM Symposium on User Interface Software and Technology. pp. 219–228. UIST '12, ACM, New York, NY, USA (2012)
30. Xie, T., Pei, J.: MAPO: Mining API Usages from Open Source Repositories. In: Proceedings of the 2006 International Workshop on Mining Software Repositories. pp. 54–57. MSR '06, ACM, New York, NY, USA (2006)
31. Ye, D., Xing, Z., Foo, C.Y., Ang, Z.Q., Li, J., Kapre, N.: Software-Specific Named Entity Recognition in Software Engineering Social Content. In: 2016 IEEE 23rd International Conference on Software Analysis, Evolution, and Reengineering (SANER). vol. 1, pp. 90–101. IEEE Press (2016)
32. Ye, D., Xing, Z., Foo, C.Y., Li, J., Kapre, N.: Learning to Extract API Mentions from Informal Natural Language Discussions. In: 2016 IEEE International Conference on Software Maintenance and Evolution (ICSME). pp. 389–399. IEEE Press (2016)
33. Yin, W., Kann, K., Yu, M., Schütze, H.: Comparative Study of CNN and RNN for Natural Language Processing. arXiv:1702.01923 (2017)
34. Yu, M., Zhao, T., Dong, D., Tian, H., Yu, D.: Compound Embedding Features for Semi-supervised Learning. In: Proceedings of the 2013 Conference of the North American Chapter of the Association for Computational Linguistics: Human Language Technologies. pp. 563–568. Association for Computational Linguistics, Atlanta, Georgia (2013)
35. Zagalsky, A., Barzilay, O., Yehudai, A.: Example Overflow: Using Social Media for Code Recommendation. In: Proceedings of the Third International Workshop on Recommendation Systems for Software Engineering. pp. 38–42. RSSE '12, IEEE Press, Piscataway, NJ, USA (2012)

10

Family-Based SPL Model Checking Using Parity Games with Variability

Maurice H. ter Beek[1], Sjef van Loo[2], Erik P. de Vink[2], and
Tim A. C. Willemse[2]

[1] ISTI–CNR, Pisa, Italy
[2] TU Eindhoven, Eindhoven, The Netherlands

Abstract. Family-based SPL model checking concerns the simultaneous
verification of multiple product models, aiming to improve on enumerative product-based verification, by capitalising on the common features
and behaviour of products in a software product line (SPL), typically
modelled as a featured transition system (FTS). We propose efficient
family-based SPL model checking of modal μ-calculus formulae on FTSs
based on variability parity games, which extend parity games with conditional edges labelled with feature configurations, by reducing the SPL
model checking problem for the modal μ-calculus on FTSs to the variability parity game solving problem, based on an encoding of FTSs as
variability parity games. We validate our contribution by experiments on
SPL benchmark models, which demonstrate that a novel family-based
algorithm to collectively solve variability parity games, using symbolic
representations of the configuration sets, outperforms the product-based
method of solving the standard parity games obtained by projection with
classical algorithms.

1 Introduction

Software product line engineering (SPLE) is a software engineering method for
cost-effective and time-efficient development of a family of software-intensive
configurable systems, according to which individual products (system variants)
can be distinguished by the features they provide, where a feature is typically
understood as some user-aware (difference in) functionality [1, 2]. The intrinsic
variability of SPLs challenges formal methods and analysis tools, because the
number of possible products may be exponential in the number of features and
each product may moreover exhibit a large behavioural state space.

The SPL model checking problem, first recognised in the seminal paper [3],
generalises the classical model checking problem in the following way: given a
formula, determine for each product whether it satisfies the formula (and, ideally,
provide a counterexample for each product that does not satisfy the formula). A
straightforward way to solve this problem is to provide a model for each product
and apply classical model checking. This enumerative, product-based method has
several drawbacks. Most importantly, the state-space explosion problem –typical
of model checking– is amplified with the number of products, while products of a
product line usually have a large amount of features and behaviour in common.

Therefore, Classen et al. have extended labelled transition systems (LTSs) with features to concisely describe and analyse the combined behaviour of a family of models [3–5]. Concretely, transitions in the resulting featured transition systems (FTSs) are labelled with actions and feature expressions. Given a product, a transition can be executed if the product fulfills the feature expression. Hence, an FTS incorporates all eligible product behaviour, and each individual product's behaviour can be obtained as an LTS. Moreover, FTSs cater for the simultaneous verification of multiple products, known as family-based analysis [6].

Properties of behavioural models for SPLs such as FTSs can be verified with dedicated SPL model checkers like SNIP [7], ProVeLines [8], VMC [9], ProFeat [10,11], or QFLan [12,13], or with classical model checkers like NuSMV [14, 15], SPIN [16], Maude [17], or mCRL2 [18,19]. The advantage of using established off-the-shelf model checkers for SPL analysis is obvious: it lifts the burden of maintaining dedicated model checkers in favour of highly optimised tools with a broad user base. In [19], it was shown how to perform family-based SPL model checking with mCRL2 [20, 21] of properties of FTSs expressed in a feature-oriented variant of the modal μ-calculus to deal with transitions labelled with feature expressions [22]. However, this approach is based on a decision procedure for the binary partitioning of the product space into products that do and those that do not satisfy a given formula, and it is underlined that computing suitable partitionings for the conducted experiments is a largely manual activity.

In this paper, we present efficient family-based SPL model checking of modal μ-calculus formulae on FTSs based on parity games with variability. Years after its introduction [3, 14], family-based model checking of SPLs or program families is still a popular topic [10, 16, 19, 23–26], including a few game-theoretic approaches based on solving (3-valued) model checking games on featured symbolic automata and on modal transition systems. A parity game is a 2-player turn-based graph game. It is well known that the model checking problem for modal μ-calculus formulae on LTSs is equivalent to parity game solving, for which Zielonka defined a recursive algorithm that performs well in practice [27–29].

Here we introduce variability parity games as a generalisation of parity games with conditional edges labelled with feature configurations. We then show how the SPL model checking problem for modal μ-calculus formulae on FTSs can be reduced to the variability parity game solving problem based on an encoding of FTSs as variability parity games. Finally, we show the results of implementing two different methods, product-based and family-based, to solve variability parity games and of experimenting with them on two well-known SPL case studies, the minepump and the elevator. The product-based method simply projects a variability parity game to the different configurations and independently solves all resulting parity games with existing algorithms. The family-based method, instead, is based on a novel algorithm to collectively solve variability parity games, using symbolic representations of sets of configurations. The experiments clearly show that the family-based method outperforms the product-based method.

Outline. After defining some preliminary notions in Section 2, we introduce SPL model checking in Section 3. In Section 4, we introduce variability parity games and show how they can be used to solve the SPL model checking problem.

In Section 5, we present a family-based, collective strategy for recursively solving variability parity games, which we experiment with on two SPL case studies in Section 6. Section 7 concludes the paper and provides directions for future work. Relevant related work other than the above is mentioned throughout the paper.

2 Preliminaries

We give a brief overview of *labelled transition systems* and the *modal μ-calculus*.

Definition 1. *A labelled transition system or LTS L over a non-empty set of actions $\mathcal{A}ct$ is a triple $L = (S, \rightarrow, s_0)$, where S is the set of states with $s_0 \in S$ and $\rightarrow \subseteq S \times \mathcal{A}ct \times S$ is the transition relation.*

The modal μ-calculus is an expressive logic, subsuming LTL and CTL, for reasoning about the behaviours of LTSs, among others.

Definition 2. *Formulae in the modal μ-calculus are given by the following (minimal) grammar.*

$$\phi ::= \mathsf{true} \mid \mathsf{false} \mid X \mid \phi \wedge \phi \mid \phi \vee \phi \mid \langle a \rangle \phi \mid [a]\phi \mid \mu X.\phi \mid \nu X.\phi$$

where $a \in \mathcal{A}ct$ is an action and $X \in \mathcal{X}$ is some propositional variable taken from a sufficiently large set of variables $\mathcal{X}$.

Next to the Boolean constants and the propositional connectives, the modal μ-calculus contains the existential diamond operator $\langle \, \rangle$ and its dual universal box operator $[\,]$ of modal logic as well as the least and greatest fixed point operators μ and ν that provide recursion used for 'finite' and 'infinite' looping, respectively.

Given a formula ϕ, an occurrence of a variable X in ϕ is said to be *bound* iff this occurrence is within a formula ψ, where $\mu X.\psi$ or $\nu X.\psi$ is a subformula of ϕ; an occurrence of a variable is *free* otherwise. A formula ϕ is *closed* iff all variables occurring in ϕ are bound; here we only consider closed formulae. For simplicity, we assume that the formulae that we consider are *well-named, i.e.,* formulae do not contain two fixed point subformulae binding the same variable.

Given an LTS, the semantics of a μ-calculus formula is the set of states of the LTS that satisfy the formula. Since we focus on games in this paper, we introduce two auxiliary concepts, *viz.* the *Fischer-Ladner closure* of a formula and the *alternation depth* of a formula. The Fischer-Ladner closure $FL(\phi)$ of a formula ϕ is the smallest set of formulae satisfying

- $\phi \in FL(\phi)$;
- if $\phi_1 \wedge \phi_2 \in FL(\phi)$ or $\phi_1 \vee \phi_2 \in FL(\phi)$ then $\phi_1, \phi_2 \in FL(\phi)$;
- if $\langle a \rangle \phi_1 \in FL(\phi)$ or $[a]\phi_1 \in FL(\phi)$ then $\phi_1 \in FL(\phi)$;
- if $\sigma X.\phi_1 \in FL(\phi)$ then $\phi_1[X := \sigma X.\phi_1] \in FL(\phi)$.

Note that for a closed formula ϕ, the set $FL(\phi)$ contains no variables.

The complexity of a μ-calculus formula is given by its *alternation depth*; the larger the alternation depth, the harder the formula is to solve (and, incidentally, also to understand). The alternation depth of a formula ϕ is defined as the largest alternation depth of the bound propositional variables in ϕ, defined as follows.

Definition 3. *The* dependency order *on bound variables of a formula ϕ is the smallest partial order $\leq_\phi$ satisfying $X \leq_\phi Y$ if X occurs free in $\sigma Y.\psi$. The alternation depth of a μ-variable X in ϕ, denoted $AD_\phi(X)$, is the maximal length of a chain $X_1 \leq_\phi \cdots \leq_\phi X_n$, where $X_1 = X$, variables $X_1, X_3, \ldots$ are μ-variables and $X_2, X_4, \ldots$ are ν-variables. Analogously for the alternation depth of a ν-variable.*

Definition 4. *A parity game is a tuple $G = (V, E, p, (V_0, V_1))$ where*

- *V is a finite set of vertices, partitioned into a set V_0 of vertices owned by player 0 and a set V_1 of vertices owned by player 1;*
- *$E \subseteq V \times V$ is the edge relation;*
- *$p : V \to \mathbb{N}$ is the priority function.*

We depict parity games as graphs in which diamond-shaped vertices represent vertices owned by player 0 and box-shaped vertices represent vertices owned by player 1. Edges are annotated with configurations while priorities are typically written inside vertices.

We write $v \to w$ instead of $(v, w) \in E$ and let α range over the set of players, *i.e.* $\alpha \in \{0, 1\}$. For a given vertex v, we write vE to denote the set $\{w \in V \mid v \to w\}$ of successors of v. Likewise, Ev denotes the set $\{w \in V \mid w \to v\}$ of predecessors of v. A sequence of vertices $v_1 \cdots v_n$ is a *path* if for all $1 \leqslant m < n$ we have $v_{m+1} \in v_m E$. Infinite paths are defined in a similar way. We write π_n to denote the n-th vertex in a path π and $\pi^{\leqslant n}$ to indicate the prefix $\pi_1 \cdots \pi_n$ of π.

A play, starting in a vertex $v \in V$, starts by placing a token on that vertex. Players then move the token according to a single simple rule: if a token is on a vertex $u \in V_\alpha$ and $uE \neq \emptyset$, player α pushes it to some successor vertex $w \in uE$. The finite and infinite paths thus constructed are referred to as *plays*. For an infinite play, and the infinite sequence of priorities it induces, the *parity* of the highest priority that occurs infinitely often on that play defines its *winner*: player 0 wins if this priority is even; player 1 wins otherwise. A finite play is won by the player that does *not* own the vertex on which the token is stuck.

The moves of players 0 and 1 are determined by their respective *strategies*. Informally, a strategy for a player α determines, for a vertex $\pi_i \in V_\alpha$ the next vertex π_{i+1} that will be visited if a token is on π_i, provided π_i has successors. In general, a strategy is a partial function $\sigma : V^* V_\alpha \to V$ which, for a given history of vertices of the locations of the token and a vertex on which the token currently resides, determines the next vertex by selecting an edge to that vertex. A finite or infinite path π *conforms to* a given strategy σ if for all prefixes $\pi^{\leqslant i}$ for which σ is defined, we have $\pi_{i+1} = \sigma(\pi^{\leqslant i})$.

A strategy σ for player α is *winning* from a vertex v iff α is the winner of every play starting in v that conforms to σ. Parity games are known to be *positionally determined* [30]. This means that a vertex is won by player α iff α has a winning strategy that does not depend on the history of vertices visited by the token. Such strategies can be represented by partial functions $\sigma : V_\alpha \to V$. Note that every vertex in a parity game is won by one of the two players.

Closed modal μ-calculus formulae can be interpreted by associating a game semantics to these formulae. The definition we provide below is adopted from [30].

Table 1. The game semantics for a closed modal μ-calculus formula ϕ: vertex v (1st column), its owner α (2nd column), its successors (if any) $w \in vE$ (3rd column), and priority $p(v)$ (4th column). Vertices of the form $(s, \langle a \rangle \psi)$ and $(s, [a]\psi)$ have no successors when s has no a-successors.

Vertex	Owner	Successor(s)	Priority
(s, true)	1		0
(s, false)	0		0
$(s, \psi_1 \wedge \psi_2)$	1	(s, ψ_1) and (s, ψ_2)	0
$(s, \psi_1 \vee \psi_2)$	0	(s, ψ_1) and (s, ψ_2)	0
$(s, [a]\psi)$	1	(t, ψ) for every $s \xrightarrow{a} t$	0
$(s, \langle a \rangle \psi)$	0	(t, ψ) for every $s \xrightarrow{a} t$	0
$(s, \nu X.\psi)$	1	$(s, \psi[X := \nu X.\psi])$	$2\lfloor AD_\phi(X)/2 \rfloor$
$(s, \mu X.\psi)$	1	$(s, \psi[X := \mu X.\psi])$	$2\lfloor AD_\phi(X)/2 \rfloor + 1$

Definition 5. *Let $L = (S, \rightarrow, s_0)$ be an LTS and ϕ be a closed modal μ-calculus formula. A state $s \in S$ satisfies formula ϕ, denoted by $L, s \models \phi$, iff vertex (s, ϕ) is won by player 0 in the game $G_{L,\phi} = (V, E, p, (V_0, V_1))$, where $V = S \times FL(\phi)$, and the sets E, V_0, and V_1 and priority function p are given by Table 1.*

If the context is such that no confusion can arise, we write $s \models \phi$ for $L, s \models \phi$.

For a more in-depth treatment of the modal μ-calculus, we refer to [30]. Here, we finish by illustrating the game semantics on a small example, drawing inspiration from an example in [19].

Example 1. Consider the LTS L depicted in the bottom-left corner of Fig. 1, modelling a coffee machine that after inserting one or two units of some currency (indicated by action *ins*) can dispense a standard regular coffee (indicated by action *std*) or an extra large coffee (indicted by action *xxl*), respectively.

The LTL-type formula ϕ, depicted in the top-left corner of Fig. 1, asserts that on all infinite runs of the coffee machine, it infinitely often dispenses a regular coffee. (Note, nothing is required to hold on finite runs.) The parity game that can answer whether $s_0 \models \phi$ holds is depicted on the right in Fig. 1. Each node is annotated with a pair consisting of a state of the LTS and a (sub)formula of ϕ. Note that the references to ϕ_1, ϕ_2, and ϕ_3 are meant as an indication and not to be interpreted exactly, since they lack the substitution that needs to be carried out. We remark that the parity game is *solitair*: only one player can make decisions. Vertex (s_0, ϕ) is won by player 1 by enforcing a 1-dominated infinite play, bypassing the vertex with priority 2 on the loop. Consequently, $s_0 \not\models \phi$. □

3 Software Product Lines Model Checking

Software products with variability can be modelled effectively using so-called *featured transition systems* or FTSs [3]. Fix a finite non-empty set $\mathcal{F}$ of features, with $\mathtt{f}$ as typical element. Let $\mathbb{B}[\mathcal{F}]$ denote the set of Boolean expressions over $\mathcal{F}$. Elements χ and γ of $\mathbb{B}[\mathcal{F}]$ are referred to as feature expressions. A product P is a set of features, $\mathcal{P}$ denotes the set of products, thus $\mathcal{P} \subseteq 2^{\mathcal{F}}$.

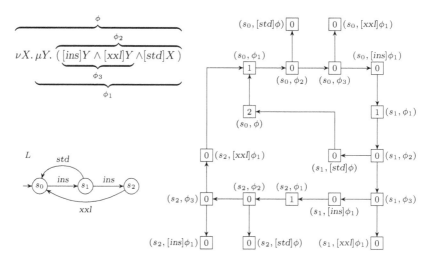

Fig. 1. Parity game encoding the model checking problem $s_0 \models \phi$

A feature expression γ, as Boolean expression over $\mathcal{F}$, can be interpreted as a set of products P_γ, *viz.* all products P for which the induced truth assignment (**true** for $f \in P$, **false** for $f \notin P$) validates γ. Reversely, for each family $P \subseteq \mathcal{P}$ we fix a feature expression γ_P to represent it. The constant $\top$ denotes the feature expression that is always true. We now recall FTSs from [4] as a model for software product lines, using the notation of [19, 22].

Definition 6. *An FTS F over $\mathcal{A}ct$ and $\mathcal{F}$ is a triple $F = (S, \theta, s_0)$, where S is the set of states with $s_0 \in S$ and $\theta : S \times \mathcal{A}ct \times S \to \mathbb{B}[\mathcal{F}]$ is the transition constraint function.*

For states $s, t \in S$, we write $s \xrightarrow{a|\gamma}_F t$ if $\theta(s, a, t) = \gamma$ and $\gamma \neq \bot$. The projection of F onto a product $P \in \mathcal{P}$ is the LTS $F|P = (S, \to_{F|P}, s_0)$ over $\mathcal{A}ct$ with $s \xrightarrow{a}_{F|P} t$ iff $P \in P_\gamma$ for a transition $s \xrightarrow{a|\gamma}_F t$ of F.

Example 2. Assume that the coffee machine from Example 1 is to model a family of coffee machines for different countries, depending on whether a coffee machine accepts the insertion of dollars or euros, or both. Let P be a product line of coffee machines, with the independent features $\$$ and $\in$, representing the presence of a coin slot accepting dollars or euros, respectively, leading to a set of four products: $\{\varnothing, \{\$\}, \{\in\}, \{\$, \in\}\}$. The FTS F below models the family behaviour of P.

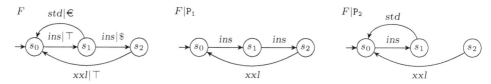

The idea is that extra large coffee is exclusively available for 2 dollars, whereas 1 euro or dollar suffices for a standard regular coffee. The behaviour of products $P_1 = \{\$\}$ and $P_2 = \{\in\}$ is modelled by the LTSs $F|P_1$ and $F|P_2$ depicted above.

Note that coffee machine $F|\mathrm{P}_1$ accepting only dollars lacks the transition from s_1 to s_0 requiring feature €, while coffee machine $F|\mathrm{P}_2$ accepting only euros lacks the one from s_1 to s_2 requiring feature \$. The behaviour of product $\mathrm{P}_3 = \{\$, €\}$ is modelled by the LTS $L = F|\{\$, €\}$ depicted in Fig. 1. Finally, the product without any features is not depicted, but it deadlocks at state s_1.   □

Definition 7. *The* SPL *model checking problem is to compute, for a given FTS $F = (S, A, s_0)$ and closed modal μ-calculus formula ϕ, the largest subsets P^+ and P^- of $\mathcal{P}$ such that $F|\mathrm{P}, s_0 \models \phi$ for all $\mathrm{P} \in P^+$ and $F|\mathrm{P}, s_0 \not\models \phi$ for all $\mathrm{P} \in P^-$.*

Sets P^+ and P^- partition $\mathcal{P}$: a formula either does or does not hold in a state.

Example 3. It is not difficult to see that the formula ϕ from Example 1 does not hold for all products. In fact, $P^+ = \{\varnothing, \{€\}\}$ and $P^- = \{\{\$\}, \{\$, €\}\}$. For products with feature \$, there is an infinite run that avoids action *std* altogether, whereas for products not containing feature \$, either all runs are finite, or all infinite runs contain an infinite number of *std* actions.   □

4   Variability Parity Games and SPL Model Checking

In practice, the model checking problem for LTSs, yielding a *yes/no* answer, can efficiently be decided using parity game solving algorithms [27,30]. The SPL model checking problem can be solved in a similar fashion by constructing parity games associated with the formula and with each individual product separately. Such an approach, however, does not take full advantage of the efficient, compact representation of the variation points in the individual product LTSs represented by an FTS. The *variability parity games* we introduce in Section 4.1, exploit constructs similar to those in FTSs to compactly encode variation points in the parity games they represent. We show in Section 4.2 that the SPL model checking problem can be solved by solving such variability parity games.

4.1   Variability Parity Games

A variability parity game is a generalisation of a parity game. It is a two-player game, again played by players *odd*, denoted by 1, and *even*, denoted by 0, on a finite directed graph. Contrary to parity games, an edge in a variability parity game is associated with a set of *configurations*.

Definition 8 (Variability Parity Game). *A variability parity game $\mathcal{G}$ is a sextuple $\mathcal{G} = (V, E, \mathfrak{C}, p, \theta, (V_0, V_1))$, where*

- *V is a finite set of vertices, partitioned into sets V_0 and V_1 of vertices owned by player 0 and player 1, respectively;*
  $E \subseteq V \times V$ is the edge relation;
- *$\mathfrak{C}$ is a finite set of configurations;*
- *$p : V \to \mathbb{N}$ is the priority function that assigns priorities to vertices;*
- *$\theta : E \to 2^{\mathfrak{C}} \setminus \{\emptyset\}$ is the configuration mapping.*

In line with our depiction of parity games, we visualise variability parity games as graphs with diamond-shaped and box-shaped vertices, and directed edges connecting vertices. Moreover, edges are annotated with configurations. A variability parity game $\mathcal{G} = (V, E, \mathfrak{C}, p, \theta, (V_0, V_1))$ is called *total* if, for all $u \in V$, it holds that $\bigcup \{ \theta(u, v) \mid v \in V, (u, v) \in E \} = \mathfrak{C}$.

As before, we write $v \to w$ for $(v, w) \in E$, and we use α to range over $\{0, 1\}$. We use $v \xrightarrow{c} w$ to denote $v \to w$ and $c \in \theta(v, w)$ and say that the edge between v and w is *compatible* with c. The notions of a finite and infinite path from parity games carry over to variability parity games, and we use similar notation to denote the prefixes of a path and the vertices along a path. A finite path $v_1 \cdots v_n$ is *admitted* for a configuration $c \in \mathfrak{C}$ iff for all $m < n$, $c \in \theta(v_m, v_{m+1})$. In a similar vein, an infinite path can be said to be admitted for a given configuration.

A play starts by placing a *configured* token $c \in \mathfrak{C}$ on vertex $v \in V$. The players move configured token c in the game according to the following rule: if token $c \in \mathfrak{C}$ is on some vertex $v \in V_\alpha$, player α pushes c, if possible, to some adjacent vertex w along an edge compatible with c, *i.e.* $c \in \theta(v, w)$. The finite and infinite paths thus constructed are admitted by c, and are again referred to as *plays*; the conditions for players 0 and 1 for winning such plays are identical to those for parity games.

For a configuration $c \in \mathfrak{C}$, a strategy is a partial function $\sigma_c : V^* V_\alpha \to V$ which, when defined for $\pi^{\leqslant i}$, yields a vertex π_{i+1} that is reachable from π_i via an edge that is compatible with c. A path π, admitted by configuration c, *conforms to* a given strategy σ_c iff for all prefixes $\pi^{\leqslant i}$ for which σ is defined, we have $\pi_{i+1} = \sigma_c(\pi^{\leqslant i})$. Strategy σ_c for player α and configuration c is *winning* from a vertex v iff α is the winner of every play starting in v that conforms to σ_c.

Definition 9. *The* variability parity game solving problem *for a vertex v is the problem of computing the largest set of configurations $C_0, C_1 \subseteq \mathfrak{C}$ such that:*

- *player 0 has a winning strategy for v for each $c \in C_0$;*
- *player 1 has a winning strategy for v for each $c \in C_1$.*

For a given variability parity game $\mathcal{G}$ and a configuration $c \in \mathfrak{C}$, we define the projection of $\mathcal{G}$ onto c, denoted $\mathcal{G}|c$ as the parity game obtained by retaining only those edges from $\mathcal{G}$ that are compatible with c. We note that it follows rather immediately that variability parity games are also *positionally determined*: player 0 (player 1, respectively) has a winning strategy σ_c for vertex v for configuration c iff she has a winning strategy for v in the projection of the variability parity game onto configuration c. Since parity games are positionally determined, so are variability parity games. Consequently, the variability parity game solving problem asks for the computation of a partition of the set of configurations $\mathfrak{C}$.

4.2 Solving SPL Model Checking Using Variability Parity Games

If we ignore the representation of the sets of configurations decorating the edges, a variability parity game is a compact representation of a set of parity games. The

Table 2. Transformation of the SPL model checking problem to the variability parity game solving problem. For a given vertex v (1st column), its owner α (2nd column), successors $w \in vE$ (3rd column) and configuration mapping $\theta(v, w)$ (3rd column), and priority $p(v)$ (4th column) are given.

Vertex	Owner	Successor(s) | Configurations	Priority
(s, true)	1		0
(s, false)	0		0
$(s, \psi_1 \wedge \psi_2)$	1	$(s, \psi_1) \mid \mathcal{P}$ and $(s, \psi_2) \mid \mathcal{P}$	0
$(s, \psi_1 \vee \psi_2)$	0	$(s, \psi_1) \mid \mathcal{P}$ and $(s, \psi_2) \mid \mathcal{P}$	0
$(s, [a]\psi)$	1	$(t, \psi) \mid P_\gamma$ for every $s \xrightarrow{a\mid\gamma}_F t$	0
$(s, \langle a \rangle \psi)$	0	$(t, \psi) \mid P_\gamma$ for every $s \xrightarrow{a\mid\gamma}_F t$	0
$(s, \nu X.\psi)$	1	$(s, \psi[X := \nu X.\psi]) \mid \mathcal{P}$	$2\lfloor AD_\phi(X)/2 \rfloor$
$(s, \mu X.\psi)$	1	$(s, \psi[X := \mu X.\psi]) \mid \mathcal{P}$	$2\lfloor AD_\phi(X)/2 \rfloor + 1$

next definition shows how to exploit these configurations to efficiently encode the SPL model checking problem as a variability parity game solving problem, based on the game-based semantics of the modal μ-calculus we presented in Section 2.

Definition 10. *Let $F = (S, \theta_F, s_0)$ be an FTS, let $\mathcal{P}$ be the set of all products, and let ϕ be a closed modal μ-calculus formula. The variability parity game $F_\phi = (V, E, \mathfrak{C}, p, \theta, (V_0, V_1))$ associated with F and ϕ, with $V = S \times FL(\phi)$ and $\mathfrak{C} = \mathcal{P}$, is defined by the rules given in Table 2.*

Note that the size of the graph underlying variability parity game F_ϕ, measured in terms of $|V| + |E|$, is linear in the size of formula ϕ and the FTS F, measured in terms of $|S| + |\{(s, a, t) \in S \times \mathcal{A}ct \times S \mid \theta(s, a, t) \neq \bot\}|$. Hence, the structural information in an FTS is compactly reflected in the variability parity game which encodes the SPL model checking problem for the FTS. The correctness of the encoding is expressed by the Theorem 1.

Theorem 1. *For a given FTS F, a closed modal μ-calculus formula ϕ, and a product P, we have $F|P, s \models \phi$ iff player 0 wins the vertex (s, ϕ) for configuration P in the variability parity game F_ϕ associated to F and ϕ.*

Proof (sketch). Fix an FTS F and a closed modal μ-calculus formula ϕ. Let P be a product. It is not hard to show that the parity game we obtain by encoding the model checking problem $F|P, s \models \phi$ (cf. Definition 5) is isomorphic to the projection of F_ϕ onto P, *viz.* $F_\phi|P$. □

We revisit the SPL model checking problem of Example 3, illustrating the encoding of Definition 10. By abuse of notation, we write feature expressions instead of sets of configurations in variability parity games associated to SPL model checking problems.

Example 4. Consider the FTS F of Example 2 and the modal μ-calculus formula ϕ of Example 1, both for convenience repeated in Fig. 2. The variability parity game F_ϕ encoding the SPL model checking problem for F and ϕ is depicted on the right in Fig. 2 (ignoring all dashed self loops for now). We omitted most state annotations to yield a more readable figure.

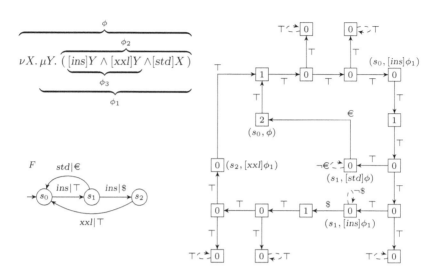

Fig. 2. Variability parity game encoding the SPL model checking problem for F and ϕ.

Observe that the graph structure of the variability parity game F_ϕ is the same as that of the parity game of Example 1 in Fig. 1. The construction leading to the variability parity game only differs in the construction of the parity game with respect to the edge annotations. Furthermore, note that vertex (s_0, ϕ) is won by player 0 for the set of configurations $\neg\$$, whereas player 1 wins the set of configurations $\$$: for configurations containing the feature $\$$, player 1 can essentially reuse the strategy of Example 1, avoiding the vertex with priority 2. For configurations not containing the feature $\$$, this option is not available, since the vertex $(s_1, [ins]\phi_1)$ is a sink. For products with feature $\in$ but not $\$$, the only infinite play infinitely often visits vertex (s_0, ϕ). For products without features $\in$ and $\$$ all plays starting in (s_0, ϕ) are finite. Hence, by Theorem 1, the solution to the SPL model checking problem is the pair $(\neg\$, \$)$, as expected.   □

5   Recursively Solving Variability Parity Games

Given a variability parity game $\mathcal{G}$ and a vertex v of $\mathcal{G}$, a straightforward way of solving the variability parity game problem for v is by simply solving the standard parity game problem $\mathcal{G}|c$ for every $c \in \mathfrak{C}$. In doing so, however, we ignore that players can potentially use (parts of) a single strategy for possibly many different configurations. As opposed to the above solving strategy, to which we refer as the *individual solving strategy*, we investigate an alternative for variability parity games, called the *collective solving strategy*.

We provide an algorithm, Algorithm 1, for solving variability parity games inspired by the classical *recursive* algorithm for solving parity games [27]. The recursive algorithm is, despite its unappealing theoretical worst-case complexity, in practice one of the most effective algorithms for solving parity games [28,29]. It is a divide-and-conquer algorithm that relies on two building blocks, *viz.* the concept of a *subgame computation* and of an *attractor computation*. We generalise and adapt these concepts to the setting of variability parity games.

Fix a variability parity game $\mathcal{G} = (V, E, \mathfrak{C}, p, \theta, (V_0, V_1))$. For simplicity we assume that $\mathcal{G}$ is total. This is not a limitation; any variability parity game can be turned into a total one. The auxiliary notion of a *restriction* is a mapping $\varrho : V \to 2^{\mathfrak{C}}$ which, for a variability parity game $\mathcal{G}$, indicates which configurations are under consideration for a vertex. Given such a restriction ϱ, we say that a vertex v for configuration $c \in \mathfrak{C}$ is won by player α in the game $\mathcal{G}$ restricted to ϱ iff $c \in \varrho(v)$ and the winning strategy for α only passes through vertices v' for which $c \in \varrho(v')$. We say that $\mathcal{G}$ is *total* with respect to ϱ iff for all $v \in V$ and all $c \in \varrho(v)$, there is a vertex w such that $w \in vE$ and $c \in \theta(v, w) \cap \varrho(w)$.

Let $U, U' : V \to 2^{\mathfrak{C}}$ be arbitrary mappings. The union of U and U', denoted $U \cup U'$, is defined point-wise, *i.e.* $(U \cup U')(v) = U(v) \cup U(v')$. We say that mapping U is a *sub-mapping* of ϱ iff for all $v \in V$ we have $U(v) \subseteq \varrho(v)$. The reduction of ϱ with respect to a sub-mapping U, denoted $\varrho \backslash U$, is a new restriction defined as $(\varrho \backslash U)(v) = \varrho(v) \backslash U(v)$.

For a given sub-mapping $U : V \to 2^{\mathfrak{C}}$ of a restriction ϱ, the α-attractor towards U is a sub-mapping of ϱ which assigns those configurations to a vertex for which player α can force the play to reach some vertex v for which that configuration belongs to $U(v)$. Formally, we define $Attr_\alpha(U)$, in the context of ϱ and $\mathcal{G}$, as $Attr_\alpha(U)(v) = \bigcup_{i \geq 0} Attr_\alpha^i(U)(v)$, where

$$
\begin{aligned}
Attr_\alpha^0(U)(v) \;\; &= U(v) \\
Attr_\alpha^{i+1}(U)(v) &= Attr_\alpha^i(U)(v) \cup \\
&\quad \{\, c \in \varrho(v) \mid v \in V_\alpha \wedge \exists w \in vE : c \in \theta(v, w) \cap \varrho(w) \cap Attr_\alpha^i(U)(w) \,\} \cup \\
&\quad \{\, c \in \varrho(v) \mid v \in V_{\bar\alpha} \wedge \forall w \in vE : c \in (\mathfrak{C} \backslash (\theta(v, w) \cap \varrho(w))) \cup Attr_\alpha^i(U)(w) \,\}
\end{aligned}
$$

Thus, in case $v \in V_\alpha$ and $c \in \varrho(v)$, configuration c is in $Attr_\alpha^{i+1}(U)(v)$ if for a move by player α to some vertex w allowed for configuration c, the sub-attractor $Attr_\alpha^i(U)(w)$ can be reached. In case $v \in V_{\bar\alpha}$ and $c \in \varrho(v)$, configuration c is in $Attr_\alpha^{i+1}(U)(v)$ if all moves for player $\bar\alpha$ are not allowed for configuration c or lead to a vertex w in the sub-attractor $Attr_\alpha^i(U)(w)$ for player α for A.

Example 5. Reconsider the variability parity game of Example 4. First, observe that it is not total. In this case, the variability parity game can be made total without changing the solution by taking into account also the dashed self loops.

Let $\varrho(v) = \mathfrak{C}$ and define $U(s_0, \phi) = \mathfrak{C}$ and $U(v) = \varnothing$ for all $v \neq (s_0, \psi)$. For vertex (s_0, ϕ) we have $Attr_0(U)(s_0, \phi) = \{\varnothing, \{\$\}, \{€\}, \{\$, €\}\}$. All vertices v on the (single) path starting in $(s_0, [ins]\phi_1)$ and ending in $(s_1, [std]\phi)$ satisfy $Attr_0(U)(v') = \{\{\$, €\}\}$. The remaining vertices v' satisfy $Attr_0(U)(v') = \varnothing$. Note that for no configuration the immediate predecessor of $(s_0, [ins]\phi_1)$ is attracted to U because of the escape to the sink that player 1 can use. □

We have the following result, which can be proven by induction on i following the definition of $Attr_\alpha(U)(v) = \bigcup_{i \geq 0} Attr_\alpha^i(U)(v)$.

Algorithm 1 Recursive Algorithm for a fixed variability parity game $\mathcal{G} = (V, E, \mathfrak{C}, p, \theta, (V_0, V_1))$. Given a restriction $\varrho : V \to 2^{\mathfrak{C}}$, the algorithm returns a pair of functions (W_0, W_1) where $W_0, W_1 : V \to 2^{\mathfrak{C}}$ denote, for each vertex, which set of configurations is won by player 0 (player 1, respectively).

```
 1: function SOLVE(ϱ)
 2:     if ϱ = λv ∈ V. ∅ then
 3:         (W₀, W₁) ← (λv ∈ V. ∅, λv ∈ V. ∅)
 4:     else
 5:         m ← max{ p(v) | v ∈ V ∧ ϱ(v) ≠ ∅ }
 6:         α ← m mod 2
 7:         U ← λv ∈ V. {ϱ(v) | p(v) = m}
 8:         A ← Attrα(U)
 9:         (W₀′, W₁′) = SOLVE(ϱ\A)
10:         if W_ᾱ′ = λv ∈ V. ∅ then
11:             Wα ← Wα′ ∪ A
12:             W_ᾱ ← W_ᾱ′
13:         else
14:             B ← Attr_ᾱ(W_ᾱ′)
15:             (W₀″, W₁″) = SOLVE(ϱ\B)
16:             Wα ← Wα″
17:             W_ᾱ ← W_ᾱ″ ∪ B
18:         end if
19:     end if
20:     return (W₀, W₁)
21: end function
```

Lemma 1. *Let $\mathcal{G} = (V, E, \mathfrak{C}, p, \theta, (V_0, V_1))$ be a variability parity game, let $\varrho : V \to 2^{\mathfrak{C}}$ a restriction, and let α be an arbitrary player. Then for all sub-mappings U of ϱ, also $Attr_\alpha(U)$ is a sub-mapping of ϱ.* □

Totality of a game is preserved for the complements of attractors of sub-mappings.

Lemma 2. *Let $\mathcal{G} = (V, E, \mathfrak{C}, p, \theta, (V_0, V_1))$ be a variability parity game and let $\varrho : V \to 2^{\mathfrak{C}}$ be a restriction such that $\mathcal{G}$ is total with respect to ϱ. Then $\mathcal{G}$ is total with respect to $\varrho \backslash Attr_\alpha(U)$ for all sub-mappings U of ϱ and each player α.*

Proof. Let $\mathcal{G}$ and ϱ be as stated. Consider an arbitrary mapping $U : V \to 2^{\mathfrak{C}}$, and let $A = Attr_\alpha(U)$ be the α-attractor towards U. By Lemma 1, A is a sub-mapping of ϱ. Towards a contradiction, assume that $\mathcal{G}$ is not total with respect to $\varrho \backslash A$. Then there is some vertex $v \in V$ and some configuration $c \in (\varrho \backslash A)(v)$ such that for all $w \in vE$, if $c \in \theta(v, w)$ then $c \notin (\varrho \backslash A)(w)$. Pick such a vertex v and configuration c. Since $\mathcal{G}$ is total with respect to ϱ, we know that there is at least one $w \in vE$ with $c \in \theta(v, w)$ and $c \in \varrho(w)$. Let $w \in vE$ be such that $c \in \theta(v, w)$ and $c \in \varrho(w)$. It then follows that $c \notin (\varrho \backslash A)(w)$, and, hence, $c \in A(w)$. So, for all $w \in vE$ for which $c \in \theta(v, w)$ and $c \in \varrho(w)$ we have $c \in A(w)$. But then, by definition of α-attractor, also $c \in A(v)$. Contradiction, since $c \in (\varrho \backslash A)(v)$. □

We proceed with the following result regarding the propagation of winning with respect to a sub-mapping along an attractor.

Lemma 3. *Let $\mathcal{G} = (V, E, \mathfrak{C}, p, \theta, (V_0, V_1))$ be a variability parity game and let $\varrho : V \to 2^{\mathfrak{C}}$ be a restriction. Let α be an arbitrary player and suppose U is a sub-mapping of ϱ. If for all $v \in V$, player α wins vertex v for all configurations $c \in U(v)$, then α wins vertex v for all configurations $c \in Attr_{\alpha}(U)(v)$.*

Proof. Let ϱ, α and U be as stated. We proceed by induction on i with respect to the definition of $Attr_{\alpha}^{i}(U)$.

Base case $(i = 0)$: Follows by assumption. Induction step $(i > 0)$: Suppose player α wins vertex v for all configurations $c \in Attr_{\alpha}^{i}(U)(v)$. Pick an arbitrary vertex v' and configuration $c' \in Attr_{\alpha}^{i+1}(U)(v')$. Since $c' \in Attr_{\alpha}^{i+1}(U)(v')$, we have $c' \in \varrho(v)$. If $c' \in Attr_{\alpha}^{i}(U)(v')$, the result follows instantly by induction. If $c' \notin Attr_{\alpha}^{i}(U)(v')$, then we distinguish two cases.

Case $v' \in V_{\alpha}$: Then there must be some $w \in v'E$ such that $c' \in \theta(v', w)$ and $c' \in Attr_{\alpha}^{i}(U)(w)$. Let w be such. Then player α can play a c'-configured token from v' to w and, by induction, win vertex w for configuration c'. But then she also wins vertex v' for configuration c'.

Case $v' \in V_{\bar{\alpha}}$. Then, for all $w \in v'E$ such that $c' \in \theta(v', w)$, also $c' \in Attr_{\alpha}^{i}(U)(w)$. Since regardless of how player $\bar{\alpha}$ moves the c'-configured token from v' along an edge admitting c', she will end up in a vertex that, by induction, is won by α for configuration c'. $\qquad\square$

The next theorem captures the correctness of Algorithm 1.

Theorem 2. *Let $\mathcal{G} = (V, E, \mathfrak{C}, p, \theta, (V_0, V_1))$ be a variability parity game and let $\varrho : V \to 2^{\mathfrak{C}}$ be a restriction such that $\mathcal{G}$ is total with respect to ϱ. Then $\text{SOLVE}(\varrho)$ returns the mappings $W_0, W_1 : V \to 2^{\mathfrak{C}}$ such that for all $v \in V$, $W_0(v) \cup W_1(v) = \mathfrak{C}$ and both for player 0 and 1, for each $c \in W_{\alpha}(v)$, player α wins vertex v for configuration c.*

Proof. Fix a total variability parity game $\mathcal{G} = (V, E, \mathfrak{C}, p, \theta, (V_0, V_1))$. We prove a slightly stronger property, *viz.* for all restrictions $\varrho : V \to 2^{\mathfrak{C}}$ such that $\mathcal{G}$ is total with respect to ϱ, procedure $\text{SOLVE}(\varrho)$ returns mappings $W_0, W_1 : V \to 2^{\mathfrak{C}}$ that are sub-mappings of ϱ such that for all $v \in V$ it holds that $W_0(v) \cup W_1(v) = \varrho(v)$ and player α wins vertex v for each configuration $c \in W_{\alpha}(v)$. Let us define $|\varrho| = \sum_{v \in V} |\varrho(v)|$. The proof will proceed by induction on $|\varrho|$ and closely follows the standard proofs of correctness for parity games.

Base case: We have $\varrho(v) = \emptyset$ for all $v \in V$. Consequently, the algorithm returns the functions W_0 and W_1 satisfying $W_0(v) = W_1(v) = \emptyset$ for all $v \in V$. Trivially W_0 and W_1 satisfy the statement.

Induction step: Let ϱ be a restriction such that $\mathcal{G}$ is total with respect to ϱ. As our induction hypothesis, assume that the statement holds for all ϱ' such that $|\varrho'| < |\varrho|$. Let m be the maximal priority among those vertices in $\mathcal{G}$ for which ϱ yields a non-empty set of configurations, and let α be m mod 2. Let U be the sub-mapping of ϱ for which $U(v) = \varrho(v)$ if $p(v) = m$, and $U(v) = \emptyset$ otherwise, and let A be the sub-mapping $Attr_{\alpha}(U)$. By Lemma 2, $\mathcal{G}$ is total with respect to $\varrho \backslash A$, and hence, by induction, the functions W_0', W_1' returned by $\text{SOLVE}(\varrho \backslash A)$ satisfy the statement. Next, we distinguish two cases.

Case $W'_{\bar{\alpha}}(v) = \emptyset$ for all v. Then, by our induction hypothesis, player α wins all vertices v for configurations $c \in W'_\alpha(v)$ in the game restricted to $\varrho \backslash A$. Regarding the remaining vertices, note that for vertices $v \in V_{\bar{\alpha}}$ and configurations $c \in W'_\alpha(v)$ with an edge to a vertex w with $c \in A(w)$, player $\bar{\alpha}$ may escape to such vertices. However, then α can force the play to visit a vertex with priority m. Remaining in vertices with priority m means losing for $\bar{\alpha}$. Playing to any vertex other than those in U leads to a play that remains either in W_α or infinitely often revisits U. In either case, α wins such plays. For vertices $v \in V_\alpha$ and configurations $c \in \varrho(v)$, player α either follows the winning strategy in W'_α or the attractor strategy for A towards a vertex in U. Consequently, α wins all vertices v for all configurations $c \in \varrho(v)$, which is consistent with W_α and $W_{\bar{\alpha}}$ as returned by SOLVE.

Case $W'_{\bar{\alpha}}(v) \neq \emptyset$ for some v. Since player $\bar{\alpha}$ wins any vertex v for configuration $c \in W'_{\bar{\alpha}}(v)$ in the game restricted to $\varrho \backslash A$, and player α cannot force the play to a vertex w for which $c \in A(w)$, player $\bar{\alpha}$ also wins all such vertices and configurations in $\mathcal{G}$ restricted to ϱ. By Lemma 3, $\bar{\alpha}$ thus also wins all vertices v for configurations $c \in B = Attr_{\bar{\alpha}}(W'_{\bar{\alpha}})(v)$. By Lemma 2, $\mathcal{G}$ is total with respect to $\varrho \backslash B$, and hence, by induction, the functions W''_0, W''_1 returned by the call SOLVE$(\varrho \backslash B)$ satisfy the statement. It then follows that player α wins all vertices v for configurations $c \in W''_\alpha(v)$ and player $\bar{\alpha}$ wins all vertices v for configurations $c \in (W_{\bar{\alpha}} \cup B)(v)$ as set by SOLVE.   □

Algorithm 1 requires that the attractor $Attr_\alpha(U)$ for a sub-mapping U can be computed (cf. line 8 of the algorithm). To cater for this, the attractor computation for sub-mappings can be implemented following the pseudo-code of Algorithm 2, the correctness of which is claimed by Lemma 4.

Lemma 4. *For a restriction $\varrho : V \to 2^{\mathfrak{C}}$, a sub-mapping $U : V \to 2^{\mathfrak{C}}$ of ϱ and a player α, ATTR(α, U) terminates and returns a sub-mapping A of ϱ satisfying $A = Attr_\alpha(U)$.*   □

Algorithm 2 is actually a straightforward implementation of the definition of the attractor set computation following the high-level structure of the attractor computation for standard parity games. We forego a detailed proof of Lemma 4, which, for soundness, uses an invariant stating that the computed sub-mapping A under-approximates $Attr_\alpha(U)$ and for completeness uses an invariant that asserts for all configurations $c \in Attr_\alpha(U)(v)$ either $c \in A(v)$ or there is a vertex $v' \in Q$ and attractor strategy underlying $Attr_\alpha(U)(v)$ inducing a play for c, starting in v, visiting v' and not visiting vertices v'' with $c \in A(v'')$ in between.

Instead, we briefly explain the underlying intuition. It conducts a typical backwards reachability analysis, maintaining a queue Q of vertices that are at the frontier of the search for at least some configurations. For each vertex w in this frontier, its predecessors $v \in Ew$ are inspected in a for-loop. Either such a predecessor is owned by player α, in which case all configurations that can reach w in one step are added to the attractor set for v, or such a predecessor is owned by player $\bar{\alpha}$, in which case *all* v's successors must be inspected, and only those configurations c of v for which all their successor options are to move to some vertex w' already satisfying $c \in A(w')$ are added to its attractor.

Algorithm 2 Attractor computation. Given a variability parity game $\mathcal{G} = (V, E, \mathfrak{C}, p, \theta, (V_0, V_1))$, a restriction $\varrho : V \to 2^{\mathfrak{C}}$ and a sub-mapping U of ϱ, the algorithm computes the α-attractor towards U.

1: **function** ATTR(α, U)
2:     Queue $Q \leftarrow \{\, v \in V \mid U(v) \neq \emptyset \,\}$
3:     $A \leftarrow U$
4:     **while** Q is not empty **do**
5:         $w \leftarrow Q.\mathrm{pop}()$
6:         **for** every $v \in Ew$ such that $\varrho(v) \cap \theta(v, w) \cap A(w) \neq \emptyset$ **do**
7:             **if** $v \in V_\alpha$ **then**
8:                 $a \leftarrow \varrho(v) \cap \theta(v, w) \cap A(w)$
9:             **else**
10:                $a \leftarrow \varrho(v)$
11:                **for** $w' \in vE$ such that $\varrho(v) \cap \theta(v, w') \cap \varrho(w') \neq \emptyset$ **do**
12:                   $a \leftarrow a \cap (\mathfrak{C} \setminus (\theta(v, w') \cap \varrho(w')) \cup A(w'))$
13:                **end for**
14:             **end if**
15:             **if** $a \setminus A(v) \neq \emptyset$ **then**
16:                 $A(v) \leftarrow A(v) \cup a$
17:                 **if** $v \notin Q$ **then** $Q.\mathrm{push}(v)$
18:             **end if**
19:         **end for**
20:     **end while**
21:     **return** A
22: **end function**

---

6 Implementation and Experiments

As an initial validation of our approach we experimented with two SPL examples, *viz.* the well-known minepump and elevator case studies first recognised as SPLs in [3, 14], modelled for the mCRL2 toolset [20, 21].

A prototype for solving variability parity games connecting to the mCRL2 toolset was implemented in C++ using the BuDDy package [31, 32] for BDD operations. The prototype uses BDDs to represent product families; parity games are represented as graphs with adjacency lists for incoming and outgoing edges. For the recursive algorithm, bit vectors are used to represent sets of vertices sorted by parity then by priority. All experiments were run on a standard Linux desktop with Intel i5-4570 3.20Hz processor and 8GB DDR3 internal memory.[3]

6.1 Minepump Case Study

The minepump example of [33], in the SPL variant of [4], describes a configurable software system coordinating the sensors and actuators of a pump for mine drainage. The purpose of the system is to keep a mine shaft free from water.

---

[3] Solvers and experiments: https://github.com/SjefvanLoo/VariabilityParityGames

A controller operates a pump that may not start nor continue running in the presence of dangerously high levels of methane gas. To this end, it needs to communicate with sensors that measure the water and methane levels. The SPL model has 11 features and 128 products; the resulting FTS consists of 582 states and 1376 transitions. The mCRL2 code of this model, developed for [19], closely follows the fPROMELA code of [4] (also used in [16]) that is distributed with [8].

We verified nine properties, φ_1 to φ_9, for the minepump case study, examined also elsewhere in the SPL literature (cf., *e.g.* [3, 4, 7, 16, 19, 24, 34–36]). These induce variability parity games consisting of approximately 3000 to 9200 vertices and 2 to 4 different priorities. Specifically, for properties φ_1, φ_4, and φ_7, we used the following formulae, expressed in the mCRL2 variant of the modal μ-calculus, which allows to mix fixed points, regular expressions, and first-order constructs.

Property φ_1. Absence of deadlock: [true*] <true> true

Property φ_4. The pump cannot be switched on infinitely often:

```
( mu X. nu Y. ([pumpStart] [!pumpStop*] [pumpStop] X &&
     [!pumpStart] Y )) && ( [true*] [pumpStart] mu Z. [!pumpStop] Z )
```

Property φ_7. The controller can always eventually receive/read a message, *i.e.* return to its initial state from any state: [true*] <true*> <receiveMsg> true

While φ_4 is a common LTL-type formula, φ_7 is typical for CTL. Table 3 provides the running times for verification of properties φ_1 to φ_9 via variability parity games, and the sizes of classes (P^+, P^-) partitioning $\mathcal{P}$. The results show that the collective solving strategy for family-based SPL model checking outperforms the individual solving strategy for product-based SPL model checking.

While a full baseline comparison with other SPL model checking algorithms was not performed, our approach promises to be at least as efficient as related approaches. This conjecture is based on the running times reported for properties φ_1, φ_4, and φ_6 in [4, 16, 19] (all verified with standard computers of that time).

Table 3. Running times (**in ms**) for experiments for the product-based and family-based SPL model checking of the minepump and elevator case studies using recursive algorithm for variability parity games.

Minepump SPL				Elevator SPL			
Property	product	family	$|P^+|/|P^-|$	Property	product	family	$|P^+|/|P^-|$
φ_1	28.88	3.92	128/0	ψ_1	14335	5409	2/30
φ_2	54.79	6.76	0/128	ψ_2	14988	5744	4/28
φ_3	184.7	24.70	0/128	ψ_3	16045	5020	4/28
φ_4	145.0	37.46	96/32	ψ_4	16865	5272	4/28
φ_5	144.5	12.19	96/32	ψ_5	8954	3013	16/16
φ_6	242.9	42.79	112/16	ψ_6	4252	772	32/0
φ_7	134.3	11.71	128/0	ψ_7	4171	765	32/0
φ_8	17.44	1.058	128/0				
φ_9	110.0	6.853	0/128				

6.2 Elevator Case Study

The other configurable system we considered is the elevator example of [37] of a lift travelling between five floors. A product in the elevator system may or may not provide the features of parking, load and overload detection, cancelling on emptiness, and priority for specific floors. Absence or presence of specific features in a system configuration generally leads to different behaviour. The behaviour of the lift itself is governed by the so called single button collective control strategy, deciding which floor is visited next. Roughly speaking, and dependent on the specific feature setting, the lift operates in sweeps, only changing direction if there are no outstanding calls in the current direction. The FTS implementation in mCRL2 underlying the experiments is derived from the 120 lines of SMV code presented in [37]. Although the number of features in this SPL example is small, *viz.* only 5 independent features resulting in 32 different configurations, the FTS consists of 95591 states and 622265 transitions.

The seven properties, ψ_1 to ψ_7 for the elevator case study, also examined elsewhere in the literature (cf., *e.g.* [10–12, 14, 15, 25, 26, 35, 38]), which we experimented with were adapted from [37]. These induce variability parity games consisting of approximately 440000 to 18500000 vertices with 2 to 3 different priorities. The properties cover a proper handling of requests, correct behaviour with respect to the control strategy, proper behaviour when idling, and the possibility to stop at floors while passing. By way of illustration, properties ψ_2, ψ_3, and ψ_5 are expressed as follows in the mCRL2 variant of the modal μ-calculus.

Property ψ_2. Invariantly, if a lift button is pressed for a floor, the lift will eventually open its doors on this floor:

```
[true*] forall i:Floor. [liftButton(i)]
    ( mu X. ( [!open(i)] X && <true> true ) )
```

Property ψ_3. Invariantly, if the lift is travelling up while there are calls above the lift will not change direction:

```
[true*] ( ([ direction(up).
    (!(direction(down) || exists k:Floor. open(k)))* ]
        forall i:Floor. val(1 <= i && i <= 5) =>
            [ open(i) ] forall j:Floor. val(i < j && j <= 5) =>
                [ liftButton(j) ] mu Y. ( [!open(j)] Y &&
                    [direction(down)] false && < true > true ) ) )
```

Property ψ_5. Invariantly, if the lift is idling, it does not change floors:

```
( forall i:Floor. val(1 <= i && i <= 5) =>
    <true*.idling(i)> true ) &&
( [true*] forall i:Floor. val(1 <= i && i <= 5) =>
    [ idling(i) ] nu Y. <idling(i)> Y )
```

It is noted, in particular with regard to property ψ_5, that unlike the original SMV elevator system, our lift idles with its doors open, to prevent the situation where someone in the lift infinitely often presses the landing button for the current floor, keeping the process busy without the lift making any movement.

Also in the case of the elevator system we notice a significant difference in performance when doing product-based model checking calling the individual solving strategy or family-based model checking calling the collective solving strategy. The difference is, however, not that striking compared to the minepump case study, which, we believe, is due to the small number of different features.

As said, a full baseline comparison with other SPL model checking algorithms was not performed. For one, the efficiency of our approach with respect to related approaches is not easily measured with the elevator case study. While properties ψ_2 and ψ_5 were verified also in [14, 15, 25, 26, 35, 38], not much can be concluded from the reported running times. First, our model's mCRL2 code was developed from scratch, following the SMV code from [37], and not the fPROMELA code of [14, 15, 25, 26, 35, 38]. Moreover, the number of floors in these models ranges from 4 to 6. In [10–12], finally, the models are probabilistic, the number of floors ranges from 2 to 40, and different (probabilistic) properties were verified.

7 Conclusions

We have introduced variability parity games as a generalisation of parity games, reflecting the generalisation by FTSs of LTSs, and have defined the SPL model checking problem of modal μ-calculus formulae on FTSs as a variability parity game solving problem, for which we have provided a recursive algorithm based on a collective, family-based solving strategy. To illustrate the efficiency of the approach, we have applied it to two classical examples from the SPL literature, *viz.* the minepump and the elevator case studies. The experiments show that the collective, family-based strategy of solving variability parity games typically outperforms the individual, product-based strategy of solving the standard parity games obtained by projection from the variability parity games

Further experiments are needed to measure and pinpoint the differences in efficiency. One direction for future work is to generate a sufficient number of random variability parity games to this aim. In particular, the configuration sets that label the edges of the variability parity games for the minepump and elevator case studies obey a very specific distribution, typically admitting either 100% or 50% of the configurations. It would be interesting to see how our approach behaves in case of SPLs with more complexly structured feature diagrams.

There is a wealth of different algorithms available for parity games, of which the recursive algorithm that we have here lifted to variability parity games is one of the most competitive ones in practice. Nevertheless, we think it pays to study other algorithms and lift these to variability parity games, too. Finally, we believe that variability parity games have applications beyond SPL model checking; *e.g.* in (parameter) synthesis problems. We leave these topics for future research.

Acknowledgements Work partially supported by the MIUR PRIN 2017FTXR7S project IT MaTTerS (Methods and Tools for Trustworthy Smart Systems).

References

1. A. Classen, P. Heymans, and P.-Y. Schobbens. What's in a Feature: A Requirements Engineering Perspective. In J.L. Fiadeiro and P. Inverardi, editors, *FASE'08*, volume 4961 of *LNCS*, pages 16–30. Springer, 2008.

2. S. Apel, D. Batory, C. Kästner, and G. Saake. *Feature-Oriented Software Product Lines: Concepts and Implementation*. Springer, 2013.

3. A. Classen, P. Heymans, P.-Y. Schobbens, A. Legay, and J.-F. Raskin. Model Checking Lots of Systems: Efficient Verification of Temporal Properties in Software Product Lines. In *Proc. ICSE'10*, pages 335–344. ACM, 2010.

4. A. Classen, M. Cordy, P.-Y. Schobbens, P. Heymans, A. Legay, and J.-F. Raskin. Featured Transition Systems: Foundations for Verifying Variability-Intensive Systems and their Application to LTL Model Checking. *IEEE Trans. Softw. Eng.*, 39(8):1069–1089, 2013.

5. M. Cordy, X. Devroey, A. Legay, G. Perrouin, A. Classen, P. Heymans, P.-Y. Schobbens, and J.-F. Raskin. A Decade of Featured Transition Systems. In M.H. ter Beek, A. Fantechi, and L. Semini, editors, *From Software Engineering to Formal Methods and Tools, and Back*, volume 11865 of *LNCS*, pages 285–312. Springer, 2019.

6. T. Thüm, S. Apel, C. Kästner, I. Schaefer, and G. Saake. A Classification and Survey of Analysis Strategies for Software Product Lines. *ACM Comput. Surv.*, 47(1):6:1–6:45, 2014.

7. A. Classen, M. Cordy, P. Heymans, A. Legay, and P.-Y. Schobbens. Model checking software product lines with SNIP. *Int. J. Softw. Tools Technol. Transf.*, 14(5):589–612, 2012.

8. M. Cordy, A. Classen, P. Heymans, P.-Y. Schobbens, and A. Legay. ProVeLines: a product line of verifiers for software product lines. In *Proc. SPLC'13*, volume 2, pages 141–146. ACM, 2013.

9. M.H. ter Beek, F. Mazzanti, and A. Sulova. VMC: A Tool for Product Variability Analysis. In D. Giannakopoulou and D. Méry, editors, *Proc. FM'12*, volume 7436 of *LNCS*, pages 450–454. Springer, 2012.

10. P. Chrszon, C. Dubslaff, S. Klüppelholz, and C. Baier. Family-Based Modeling and Analysis for Probabilistic Systems – Featuring PROFEAT. In P. Stevens and A. Wąsowski, editors, *Proc. FASE'16*, volume 9633 of *LNCS*, pages 287–304, 2016.

11. P. Chrszon, C. Dubslaff, S. Klüppelholz, and C. Baier. ProFeat: feature-oriented engineering for family-based probabilistic model checking. *Form. Asp. Comp.*, 30(1):45–75, 2018.

12. M.H. ter Beek, A. Legay, A. Lluch Lafuente, and A. Vandin. A framework for quantitative modeling and analysis of highly (re)configurable systems. *IEEE Trans. Softw. Eng.*, 2018.

13. A. Vandin, M.H. ter Beek, A. Legay, and A. Lluch Lafuente. QFLan: A Tool for the Quantitative Analysis of Highly Reconfigurable Systems. In K. Havelund, J. Peleska, B. Roscoe, and E. de Vink, editors, *Proc. FM'18*, volume 10951 of *LNCS*, pages 329–337. Springer, 2018.

14. A. Classen, P. Heymans, P.-Y. Schobbens, and A. Legay. Symbolic Model Checking of Software Product Lines. In *Proc. ICSE'11*, pages 321–330. ACM, 2011.

15. A. Classen, M. Cordy, P. Heymans, A. Legay, and P.-Y. Schobbens. Formal semantics, modular specification, and symbolic verification of product-line behaviour. *Sci. Comput. Program.*, 80(B):416–439, 2014.

16. A.S. Dimovski, A.S. Al-Sibahi, C. Brabrand, and A. Wąsowski. Family-Based Model Checking Without a Family-Based Model Checker. In B. Fischer and J. Geldenhuys, editors, *Proc. SPIN'15*, volume 9232 of *LNCS*, pages 282–299. Springer, 2015.

17. M. Lochau, S. Mennicke, H. Baller, and L. Ribbeck. Incremental model checking of delta-oriented software product lines. *J. Log. Algebr. Meth. Program.*, 85(1):245–267, 2016.

18. M.H. ter Beek and E.P. de Vink. Using mCRL2 for the Analysis of Software Product Lines. In *Proc. FormaliSE'14*, pages 31–37. IEEE, 2014.

19. M.H. ter Beek, E.P. de Vink, and T.A.C. Willemse. Family-Based Model Checking with mCRL2. In M. Huisman and J. Rubin, editors, *Proc. FASE'17*, volume 10202 of *LNCS*, pages 387–405. Springer, 2017.

20. S. Cranen, J.F. Groote, J.J.A. Keiren, F.P.M. Stappers, E.P. de Vink, W. Wesselink, and T.A.C. Willemse. An Overview of the mCRL2 Toolset and Its Recent Advances. In N. Piterman and S.A. Smolka, editors, *Proc. TACAS'13*, volume 7795 of *LNCS*, pages 199–213. Springer, 2013.

21. O. Bunte, J.F. Groote, J.J.A. Keiren, M. Laveaux, T. Neele, E.P. de Vink, W. Wesselink, A. Wijs, and T.A.C. Willemse. The mCRL2 Toolset for Analysing Concurrent Systems: Improvements in Expressivity and Usability. In T. Vojnar and L. Zhang, editors, *Proc. TACAS'19*, volume 11428 of *LNCS*, pages 21–39. Springer, 2019.

22. M.H. ter Beek, E.P. de Vink, and T.A.C. Willemse. Towards a Feature mu-Calculus Targeting SPL Verification. *Electr. Proc. Theor. Comput. Sci.*, 206:61–75, 2016.

23. A.S. Dimovski. Symbolic Game Semantics for Model Checking Program Families. In D. Bošnački and A. Wijs, editors, *Proc. SPIN'16*, volume 9641 of *LNCS*, pages 19–37. Springer, 2016.

24. A.S. Dimovski and A. Wąsowski. Variability-Specific Abstraction Refinement for Family-Based Model Checking. In M. Huisman and J. Rubin, editors, *Proc. FASE'17*, volume 10202 of *LNCS*, pages 406–423. Springer, 2017.

25. A.S. Dimovski. Abstract Family-Based Model Checking Using Modal Featured Transition Systems: Preservation of CTL*. In A. Russo and A. Schürr, editors, *Proc. FASE'18*, volume 10802 of *LNCS*, pages 301–318. Springer, 2018.

26. A.S. Dimovski, A. Legay, and A. Wąsowski. Variability Abstraction and Refinement for Game-Based Lifted Model Checking of Full CTL. In R. Hähnle and W. van der Aalst, editors, *Proc. FASE'19*, volume 11424 of *LNCS*, pages 192–209. Springer, 2019.

27. W. Zielonka. Infinite games on finitely coloured graphs with applications to automata on infinite trees. *Theor. Comput. Sci.*, 200(1-2):135–183, 1998.

28. O. Friedmann and M. Lange. Solving Parity Games in Practice. In Z. Liu and A.P. Ravn, editors, *Proc. ATVA'09*, volume 5799 of *LNCS*, pages 182–196. Springer, 2009.

29. T. van Dijk. Oink: An Implementation and Evaluation of Modern Parity Game Solvers. In D. Beyer and M. Huisman, editors, *Proc. TACAS'18*, volume 10805 of *LNCS*, pages 291–308. Springer, 2018.

30. J.C. Bradfield and I. Walukiewicz. The mu-calculus and model checking. In E.M. Clarke, T.A. Henzinger, H. Veith, and R. Bloem, editors, *Handbook of Model Checking*, chapter 26, pages 871–919. Springer, 2018.

31. J. Lind-Nielsen. BuDDy: A Binary Decision Diagram package. Technical Report IT-TR 1999–028, IT University of Copenhagen, 1999.

32. H. Cohen, J. Whaley, J. Wildt, and N. Gorogiannis. BuDDy: A Binary Decision Diagram library. http://sourceforge.net/p/buddy/. Last visited October 18, 2019.

33. J. Kramer, J. Magee, M. Sloman, and A. Lister. CONIC: an integrated approach to distributed computer control systems. *IEE Proc. E*, 130(1):1–10, 1983.

34. X. Devroey, G. Perrouin, M. Papadakis, A. Legay, P.-Y. Schobbens, and P. Heymans. Featured Model-based Mutation Analysis. In *Proc. ICSE'16*, pages 655–666. ACM, 2016.

35. A.S. Dimovski, A.S. Al-Sibahi, C. Brabrand, and A. Wąsowski. Efficient family-based model checking via variability abstractions. *Int. J. Softw. Tools Technol. Transf.*, 19(5):585–603, 2017.

36. M.H. ter Beek, F. Damiani, M. Lienhardt, F. Mazzanti, and L. Paolini. Static Analysis of Featured Transition Systems. In *Proc. SPLC'19*, pages 39–51. ACM, 2019.

37. M. Plath and M. Ryan. Feature integration using a feature construct. *Sci. Comput. Program.*, 41(1):53–84, 2001.

38. A.S. Dimovski. CTL* family-based model checking using variability abstractions and modal transition systems. *Int. J. Softw. Tools Technol. Transf.*, 22(1):35–55, 2020.

11

Skill-Based Verification of Cyber-Physical Systems

Alexander Knüppel[1] ⓘ, Inga Jatzkowski[1] ⓘ, Marcus Nolte[1] ⓘ, Thomas Thüm[1,2], Tobias Runge[1], and Ina Schaefer[1]

[1] TU Braunschweig, Braunschweig, Germany
{a.knueppel, tobias.runge, i.schaefer}@tu-bs.de
{jatzkowski, nolte}@ifr.ing.tu-bs.de
[2] University of Ulm, Ulm, Germany
thomas.thuem@uni-ulm.de

Abstract. Cyber-physical systems are ubiquitous nowadays. However, as automation increases, modeling and verifying them becomes increasingly difficult due to the inherently complex physical environment. *Skill graphs* are a means to model complex cyber-physical systems (e.g., vehicle automation systems) by distributing complex behaviors among skills with interfaces between them. We identified that skill graphs have a high potential to be amenable to scalable verification approaches in the early software development process. In this work, we suggest combining skill graphs with hybrid programs. Hybrid programs constitute a program notation for hybrid systems enabling the verification of cyber-physical systems. We provide the first formalization of skill graphs including a notion of compositionality and propose SKEDITOR, an integrated framework for modeling and verifying them. SKEDITOR is coupled with the theorem prover KEYMAERA X, which is specialized in the verification of hybrid programs. In an experiment exhibiting the *follow mode* of a vehicle, we evaluate our skill-based methodology with respect to savings in verification effort and potential to find modeling defects at design time. Compared to non-compositional verification, the initial verification effort needed is reduced by more than 53%.

Keywords: Deductive verification, design by contract, formal methods, theorem proving, KEYMAERA X, hybrid systems, automated reasoning, cyber-physical systems

1 Introduction

Cyber-physical systems combine digital computations and physical processes by tightly integrating discrete and continuous dynamics [6]. The last decade has witnessed an increase in the degree of automation in *safety-critical* cyber-physical systems (e.g., such as self-driving cars and transportation in general). Furthermore, the complexity of formally modeling and verifying such systems (e.g., by means of hybrid systems models [11, 19, 30]) to reason about safety increased simultaneously. Although there is a clear desire for an early identification and

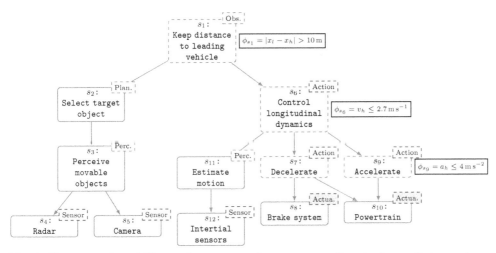

Fig. 1: Excerpt of a skill graph representing an operation to keep distance to a leading vehicle. We illustrate informal safety guarantees for the three skills s_1, s_6, and s_9.

elimination of severe mistakes [9], there is still a remarkable lack of formal methods integrated in the software development cycle [16, 17]. The challenge is to derive modeling and verification approaches that are applicable in the early development stages (e.g., requirements analysis and design time). To address this challenge, we present a model-based verification framework unifying the decomposition and modeling of cyber-physical systems by means of skill graphs [33] and a formal verifcation of these models by means of hybrid systems [2, 3, 5, 25].

A skill is a simple capability (e.g., acceleration in the context of a vehicle) *explicitly* provided by a cyber-physical system. Skills exhibit specific behaviors (i.e., control algorithms) by a mapping to some implementation unit (e.g., *source code* or interacting *software components*). Skills are assigned to a specific category (e.g., *actuator*, *sensor*, or *observable behavior*) with a defined hierarchy to prevent modeling mistakes. This categorization follows the design principle of *separation of concerns* [27], which ensures that skills only have single well-defined responsibilities. Separation of concerns is known to have a positive effect on modeling complexity, comprehensibility, functional reusability, fault localization, and artifact traceability [15, 36]. Skills can be annotated with safety guarantees obtained from a preceding requirements analysis, which enables the application of verification techniques.

Skill graphs, informally introduced by Reschka et al. [32, 33], are a promising means to model complex actions of cyber-physical systems from an architectural point of view. A skill graph [26, 32, 33, 37] is a directed acyclic graph comprising a set of *skills* (i.e., nodes) and dependencies between them (i.e., edges). To describe the properties we want to verify in a skill graph, we illustrate a skill graph representing a driving task in Figure 1. The task exhibits that a vehicle autonomously tries to keep a distance of at least 10 m to a leading vehicle. On the top level, skill **Keep distance to leading vehicle** (s_1) depends on two other skills, namely (1) the planning skill **Select target object** (s_2) and (2) the action skill ***Control the longitudinal dynamics*** (s_6). Whereas sensor-dependent skills are typically realized by software algorithms only (e.g., deep learning for detecting an obstacle), actuator-dependent skills (highlighted with a dashed border) also need to incorporate control theory, as the physical environment has to be taken into account. Skills are annotated with safety requirements (e.g., maximum acceleration or minimum distance to other vehicles). Together with the skill's realization and its dependencies to other skills, this requirement expresses the property we want to verify at design time. Successfully verifying all skills in the context of a skill graph ensures that the represented task complies to the complete set of safety requirements.

Conceptually, skill graphs as applied in this work are used for designing and organizing the architecture of a cyber-physical system. First, they facilitate the modeling of complex maneuvers built from simpler skills, which interact through explicit *interfaces*. Second, they advocate the systematic reuse of ready-to-integrate skills for multiple skill graphs, which reduces maintenance costs and increases software quality in general. Third, skill graphs are intuitive and therefore accommodate good potential for communicating with stakeholders and non-experts. Typically, skill graphs are supplied with performance measurements with the goal to enforce safety requirements at run-time. We are the first to exploit skill graphs to formally reason about the satisfiability of safety requirements at design time. Both areas of application complement each other, as they cover the full range from static analysis in the design phase to run-time verification and monitoring during operation.

As the foundation for our model-based verification approach, we propose to realize skills that interact with the physical environment by means of hybrid systems based on the *differential dynamic logic $d\mathcal{L}$* [28, 29, 31]. Hybrid systems represent complex physical systems, typically modeled as automata, where states are defined by continuous variables based on differential equations and transitions between states are discrete. Differential dynamic logic enables the deductive verification of hybrid systems, and as such is suitable for reasoning automatically about the correctness of hybrid systems. The key step of our approach is to decompose complex tasks of a cyber-physical system into skills connected by means of a skill graph and to provide a translation of skills to hybrid systems. The combination of skill graphs and hybrid systems allows the identification of severe mistakes during early design phases and also – in case of success – to generate correctness proofs, which increases trust that the system under design behaves as intended. Moreover, we propose a notion of compositionality for skill graphs, which is crucial to manage scalability during the verification phase. While skill graphs may only model simple functional aspects, they can be assembled to exhibit more complex behaviors, and verification results of skills can be reused.

We have implemented a prototype for modeling and verifying skill graphs called SKEDITOR. SKEDITOR supports the graphical modeling of skill graphs, allows to specify safety guarantees, and enables formal verification through a mapping to hybrid programs [30] (i.e., a program notation for hybrid systems as required by the theorem prover KEYMAERA X [14]). In a case study exhibiting

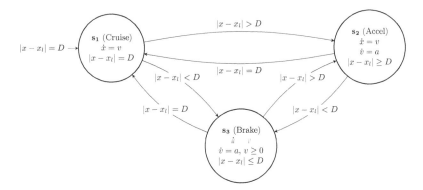

Fig. 2: Simplified hybrid system of a vehicle with automatic headway control.

the *follow mode* of an automated vehicle, we evaluate SKEDITOR with respect to its potential to find modeling defects. In particular, SKEDITOR allowed us to find conceptual defects of control algorithms early on in the design phase of our case study. To summarize, the contribution of this work is threefold.

- **Framework:** We are the first to formalize skill graphs and propose *skill-based verification*, a model-based verification technique allowing us to identify poorly defined safety requirements in early design phases by combining skill graphs with hybrid programs.
- **Tool support:** We implemented skill-based verification in a prototypical open-source tool called SKEDITOR, which paves the way for users to model and verify cyber-physical systems based on skill graphs.
- **Evaluation:** We demonstrate our approach on a realistic case study examining the *follow mode* of an automated vehicle. We show that skill-based verification decreases effort compared to monolithic modeling.

2   Background on Hybrid-System Modeling

A prominent mathematical foundation for cyber-physical systems is constituted by *hybrid systems* [2, 11, 19, 30], which enable a mixed modeling of continuous dynamics (expressed by differential equations) and discrete dynamics (expressed by automata). The states change on the basis of flow conditions.

Example 1 *Consider the example of an automatic headway control of a vehicle depicted in Figure 2. Four variables exist: the host's current position (x), the current position of the leading vehicle (x_l), the current velocity (v), and the current acceleration (a). The headway control exhibits three states: (s_1) the vehicle is in cruise mode when the current distance to the leading vehicle is equal to a defined constant D, (s_2) the vehicle accelerates when the distance is greater than D, and (s_3) the vehicle decelerates when the distance is less than D, but only until the vehicle comes to a full stop. The headway control ensures that the distance to the leading vehicle is approximately equal to D.*

Hybrid programs define an imperative-like program notation for hybrid systems [28], which support the definition of variables that evolve along a differential equation and are interpreted by tools such as KEYMAERA X [14]. The syntax of hybrid programs is as follows.

$$\alpha ::= \alpha; \beta \mid \alpha \cup \beta \mid \alpha^* \mid x := \Theta \mid x := * \mid x' = \Theta \,\&\, H \mid ?H \qquad (1)$$

$\alpha; \beta$ represents the sequential composition of two hybrid programs. $\alpha \cup \beta$ expresses the non-deterministic choice between two hybrid programs. α^* expresses that the execution of α may be repeated zero or more times. The discrete assignment to x is either a term Θ (possibly over x) or an arbitrary value represented by the wildcard $*$. The continuous evolution of a variable x along a differential equation is described by $x' = \Theta \,\&\, H$, where H is an optional evolution domain. Finally, $?H$ describes a testable condition that aborts the evolution if H is false. For instance, the program $\alpha \dot{=} (v := *; a := *; ?(-a_b \leq a \leq 0); \{v' = a \,\&\, v \geq 0\})$ sets velocity v to an arbitrary value and acceleration a to a value between $-a_b$ (i.e., maximum braking force) and zero. The execution stops nondeterministically at any time but at the latest before velocity v reaches a negative value.

Semantics of hybrid programs are based on differential dynamic logic $d\mathcal{L}$ [28, 29, 31] to specify and verify properties of hybrid programs associated with a skill in a skill graph. Models specified in $d\mathcal{L}$ can be verified with KEYMAERA X, a matured open-source theorem prover for hybrid programs. The following grammar describes all valid formulas of $d\mathcal{L}$. Symbol $\sim$ is a placeholder for a comparison operator (i.e., $\sim \in \{<, \leq, >, \geq, =, \neq\}$) between two terms Θ_1 and Θ_2. Terms are polynomials with rational coefficients over the set of continuous variables.

$$\Phi ::= \Theta_1 \sim \Theta_2 \mid \neg\Phi \mid \Phi \wedge \Psi \mid \Phi \vee \Psi \mid \Phi \rightarrow \Psi \mid \forall x\, \Phi \mid \exists x\, \Phi \mid [\alpha]\Phi \qquad (2)$$

The semantics of the logical connectives is defined as in first-order logic. Additionally, the modal formula $[\alpha]\Phi$ holds if all runs of the hybrid program α end in a state that satisfies the given condition Φ. Following the idea of Hoare-style specification in classical deductive reasoning [1, 7, 10, 18, 34], we are particularly interested to prove validity of the condition $\Psi \rightarrow [\alpha]\Phi$ with Ψ expressing assumptions we have and Φ expressing guarantees to meet by the hybrid program α.

3   A Formalization for Skill-Based Modeling

In this section, we propose the first formalization of modeling cyber-physical systems based on skill graphs. First, we define the essence of a skill. Second, we continue with the definition of a skill graph and what makes it well-formed. Third, we define how to compose skill graphs to exhibit more complex behaviors.

3.1   Formalizing Skills

In the context of cyber-physical systems, *skills* describe fine-grained executable activities inspired by human behaviors [32, 33]. For instance, a skill may represent longitudinal driving (i.e., driving with constant velocity) or even a more complex combination of longitudinal and lateral maneuvers (i.e., following the lane). To ensure that such maneuvers are executed safely, skills are associated with so-called *safety guarantees*, which they must fulfill to be considered *safe*. For example, a skill exhibiting the following of a leading vehicle should keep a minimum distance of a specified constant D (cf. Fig. 2). Informal safety guarantees are typically formulated by experts who identify numerous hazardous scenarios with respect to a maneuver and resolutions to prevent them.

The implementation of skills was only vaguely specified before. Typically, skills are implemented by software components [33]. However, our goal of early verification at design time requires to also consider a model of the physical environment. Therefore, we propose to implement skills by hybrid programs [28], which already incorporate assumptions about the physical environment and enable the verification of implementation against safety guarantees *at design time*.

To separate concerns, a skill has an associated type. We define the set Type = {observable behavior, action, perception, planning, sensor, actuator}, which categorizes the purpose of a skill. Moreover, a skill has dependency-relationships with other skills. Informally, the idea is that a hybrid program of a skill may introduce a set of continuous state variables, their computation, and their valid domains (e.g., velocity $v \in [0, 60]$ with $v' = a$), but may also require the presence of variables and their domains defined by other skills (e.g., acceleration $a \in [0, 4]$). In the following, we formally define a skill. Let $\mathcal{X}$ denote the universe of continuous variables. The syntactic domain of a skill is defined as follows.

Definition 1 (Skill). *A skill is a 5-tuple $\langle X_{\mathrm{def}}, X_{\mathrm{req}}, \alpha, \tau, \Phi \rangle$, where*
- $X_{\mathrm{def}} \subseteq \mathcal{X}$ *is a finite set of variables defined in the hybrid program α,*
- $X_{\mathrm{req}} \subseteq \mathcal{X}$ *is a finite set of variables required by the hybrid program α,*
- α *is the (possibly empty) hybrid program (cf. Eq. 1) over variables in $X_{\mathrm{def}} \cup X_{\mathrm{req}}$,*
- $\tau \in$ Type *is the associated type,*
- $\Phi = \{\phi_1, \ldots, \phi_m\}$ *is a finite set of safety guarantees in first-order logic over variables in $X_{\mathrm{def}} \cup X_{\mathrm{req}}$ (cf. Eq. 2).*

To be well-formed, we require that the sets of defined and required variables of a skill are disjoint (i.e., $X_{\mathrm{def}} \cap X_{\mathrm{req}} = \emptyset$). To access a skill's attribute, we use the '.' (dot) operator (e.g., $s.\tau$ expresses the type of skill s).

3.2 Formalizing Skill Graphs

We formalize skill graphs as directed acyclic graphs comprising a set of skills (i.e., nodes), which are connected through directed edges representing their dependencies. We denote by $\mathcal{S}$ the universe of all skills and define the syntactic domain of skill graphs as follows.

Definition 2 (Skill Graph). *A skill graph is given by $G \mathrel{\hat{=}} \langle S, r, E \rangle$, where*
- $S \subset \mathcal{S}$ *is a finite set of skills,*
- $r \in S$ *is the root skill,*
- $E \subseteq S \times S$ *is set of directed edges between skills. We denote $(s_c, s_p) \in E$ as $s_c \prec s_p$ meaning that s_c is a child of s_p.*

$\tau_s \setminus \tau_t$	observable	action	actuator	planning	perception	sensor
observable	✓	✓	-	✓	✓	-
action	-	✓	✓	✓	✓	-
planning	-	-	-	✓	✓	-
perception	-	-	-	-	✓	✓

Table 1: Valid types of a child skill t for a skill s (i.e., $t \prec s$).

A skill graph is an acyclic directed graph with exactly one root skill r. To guarantee that skill graphs are *well-formed*, we impose specific constraints. We formally introduce the *path* between two skills as follows.

Definition 3 (Path). *Let E be a set of edges and $s_1, \ldots, s_l \in S$ skills of a skill graph. A path of length $l-1$ is a (possibly empty) sequence of $l-1$ edges (s_1, s_2), (s_2, s_3), $\ldots$, $(s_{l-1}, s_l) \in E$ denoted by $\pi_{s_1 \to s_l} = [(s_1, s_2), (s_2, s_3), \ldots, (s_{l-1}, s_l)]$. We say that a path between skills $s, s' \in S$ exists if $\pi_{s \to s'}$ is non-empty, and does not exists otherwise.*

As mentioned before, each skill has an assigned type. Based on our definition of a well-formed graph, we enforce that only skills with particular types can form valid parent-child relationships (cf. Table 1). For instance, for two skills $s, s' \in S$, if $s \prec s'$ holds and skill s' is of type `perception`, then skill s is only allowed to have type `sensor` or `perception`.

Definition 4 (Well-Formed Skill Graph). *Let $G = \langle S, r, E \rangle$ be a skill graph. G is* well-formed *if and only if*
- *each skill $s \in S \setminus \{r\}$ in a skill graph has at least one parent skill $s' \in S$ (i.e., $\{s' \in S \mid s \prec s'\} \neq \emptyset$) and there exists at least one path from skill s to root skill r,*
- *for each edge $(s, s') \in E$, skills s, s' satisfy the typing restriction depicted in Table 1,*
- *for each skill $s \in S$ and variable $x \in s.X_{\mathtt{req}}$ there exists a path $\pi_{s' \to s'}$ from a skill $s' \in S$ that introduces variable x (i.e., $x \in s'.X_{\mathtt{def}}$),*
- *for each pair of skills $s, s' \in S$, the sets of defined variables are disjoint (i.e., $s.X_{\mathtt{def}} \cap s'.X_{\mathtt{def}} = \emptyset$).*
- *for each skill s in G, formula $\bigwedge_{\phi \in s'.\Phi \wedge s' \prec s} \phi$ must be satisfiable.*

Remark. Unlike behavioral models, skill graphs as defined here do not suggest an execution order of skills on the same level (i.e., child skills). The reason is twofold. First, the information needed for the scheduling may be incomplete at design time (i.e., concrete hardware and scheduling parameters). Second, the intent of skill graphs is to abstract away from implementation details, while providing guarantees about the correctness of defined safety requirements. In Section 4.2, we illustrate how to assemble the decomposed hybrid programs of a skill graph to a complete hybrid program, while being safe with respect to our chosen level of abstraction.

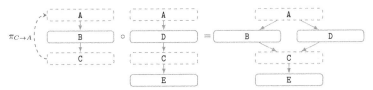

Fig. 3: Example of a composition of two skill graphs.

3.3 Composition of Skill Graphs

From the perspective of software engineering practices, an advantage of skill graphs is their modular nature. Multiple skill graphs can be designed in isolation, but may also share the same skills. To model and verify more complex skill graphs and to prevent unnecessary redundancy, the idea is to adequately *reuse* previously designed skill graphs and subsequently compose them together. This method further supports the identification and location of design mistakes, maintenance of skill graphs in general, and also enables the distribution of modeling tasks in multi-team software development.

Our composition technique of skill graphs is inspired by *superimposition* [8], a simple process that composes two graphs recursively together by merging their substructures. Starting from the root skill of one of the skill graphs, skills at the same level fulfilling defined criteria can then be composed to form a new resulting skill. Starting from a joint root skill of two different skill graphs $G_1 = \langle S_1, r, E_1 \rangle$ and $G_2 = \langle S_2, r, E_2 \rangle$, two skills $s_1 \in S_1$ and $s_2 \in S_2$ are composed to a new skill s if:

- both paths, $\pi_{s_1 \to s_1'}$ and $\pi_{s_2 \to s_2'}$, exist and s_1', s_2' are already composed,
- s_1 and s_2 have an equal type and equal sets of defined and required variables,
- and either any of the two hybrid programs is empty or both are identical.

For illustration, Fig. 3 depicts an abstraction of the composition of two skill graphs. Both skill graphs share the identical skills A and C. First, the root skill A of both skill graphs is superimposed, and second, skill C is superimposed after identifying that in both skill graphs there exists a path to a skill already subject to composition (i.e., A). In the following, we call two skills from different skill graphs *composable* if they are subject to the composition as explained here. The resulting skill s receives all the properties (i.e., variables, type, and hybrid program) from the composable skills and additionally the union of their safety guarantees:

Definition 5 (Composition of Skills). *Let $s_1 \in S_1$ and $s_2 \in S_2$ be two composable skills. The binary composition of s_1 and s_2 then produces the skill*

$$s_1 \oplus s_2 = \langle s_1.X_{\text{def}}, s_1.X_{\text{req}}, s_1.\alpha, s_1.\tau, s_1.\Phi \cup s_2.\Phi \rangle. \tag{3}$$

The binary composition of two skill graphs is then formally defined as follows, where $M = \{(s_1, s_2) \in S_1 \times S_2 \mid s_1 \text{ and } s_2 \text{ are composable}\}$ is the set of composable skills and f is a function that maps every skill in $(S_1 \cup S_2) \setminus \{s_1, s_2 \in S_1 \cup S_2 \mid (s_1, s_2) \in M\}$ to itself and maps all skills s_1, s_2 with $(s_1, s_2) \in M$ to a new skill $s = s_1 \oplus s_2$.

Definition 6 (Composition of Skill Graphs). *Let $G_1 = \langle S_1, r_1, E_1 \rangle$ and G_2 $= \langle S_2, r_2, E_2 \rangle$ be two well-formed skill graphs with $r_2 \in S_1$. The composition of G_1 and G_2 then produces the skill graph*

$$G_1 \circ G_2 = \langle S, f(r_1), E \rangle \tag{4}$$

where

- $S = \{f(s) \mid s \in S_1 \cup S_2\}$,
- *for every $s, s' \in (S_1 \cup S_2)$, there exists an edge $(f(s), f(s')) \in E$ if and only if there exists an edge $(s, s') \in (E_1 \cup E_2)$.*

A mathematical convenience of our definition of composition is that it requires the root skill of one skill graph to be present in the second skill graph. This is not a severe limitation, as it is always possible to add an artificial root to one skill graph (or both) with respect to well-formedness.

4 Compositional Verification of Skill Graphs

In this section, we formalize the generation of verification conditions to check correctness of skills in the context of a skill graph, show how correctness results transfer to the composition of skill graphs, and discuss how this methodology can be integrated into the development process for cyber-physical systems.

4.1 Verification Condition Generation

Our verification procedure relies on assume-guarantee reasoning. Thus, to verify whether a skill s in the context of a skill graph adheres to its safety guarantees $s.\Phi$, we have to construct two logical conditions: (1) necessary assumptions on a skill's behavior denoted by $\texttt{assume}_s$ and (2) the overall safety condition in the context of the skill graph denoted by $\texttt{safe}_s$. For instance, $\texttt{assume}_s$ for leaf skills valuates trivially to $\texttt{true}$, but child skills impose constraints on their parent skills through their safety guarantees. Both conditions can be computed automatically based on the skill's dependencies and by the manually defined safety guarantees $s.\Phi$. The overall verification condition then becomes $\texttt{assume}_s \rightarrow [s.\alpha]\texttt{safe}_s$ (cf. Sec. 2). In the following, we describe how both conditions are constructed.

In the context of a skill graph, a particularity to deal with is that a skill may *require* variables introduced in a *distant* skill (i.e., path length greater than one), possibly with numerous updates along the path. These variables may be unknown in direct children, so it is not possible to only define the assumption (i.e., $\texttt{assume}_s$) of a skill s as the conjunction of the safety guarantees of all children (i.e., $\bigwedge \texttt{safe}_{s'}$ with $s' \prec s$). In Fig. 4, we illustrate this problem and its solution on a simple skill graph comprising three skills.

$\texttt{Skill \#1}$ introduces variables $\texttt{A}$ and $\texttt{B}$ including safety guarantees on them in ϕ_1. Typical for assume-guarantee reasoning, ϕ_1 becomes the assumption for all parent skills (i.e., $\texttt{Skill \#2}$ in this case). However, the safety guarantee of $\texttt{Skill \#2}$ (i.e., ϕ_2) states only a modification of variable A and not B, but $\texttt{Skill}$

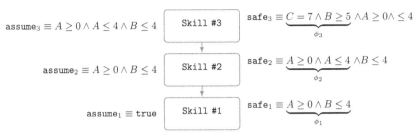

Fig. 4: Computation of $\texttt{assume}_t$ and $\texttt{safe}_t$.

#3 may indeed need the information of the current domain of variable B to be verifiable. To keep assume-guarantee propagation intact, we resolve this issue by additionally encoding all safety guarantees that *remain valid* for a skill in its safety guarantee $\texttt{safe}_s$ (highlighted in blue). In the following, we introduce our formalization.

The definitions of both formulas, $\texttt{assume}_s$ and $\texttt{safe}_s$, are mutually recursive. The logical formula $\texttt{assume}_s$ for a skill s results from the conjunction of the overall safety guarantees $\texttt{safe}_{s'}$ of all children $s' \prec s$. The assumption for skills with no children valuates trivially to $\texttt{true}$.

$$\texttt{assume}_s \equiv \bigwedge_{s' \prec s} \texttt{safe}_{s'} \tag{5}$$

To compute the overall safety guarantee $\texttt{safe}_s$, we exploit that $\texttt{assume}_s$ exhibits an overapproximation on the current state of the required variables for a skill s prior to executing the hybrid program $s.\alpha$. As the behavior of a skill may change the initial state, we discard all clauses in $\texttt{assume}_s$ sharing a variable with one of the user provided safety guarantees in $s.\Phi$. The remaining clauses become part of $\texttt{safe}_s$. For instance, in Fig. 4, $\texttt{Skill \#3}$ guarantees a change of variable B in ϕ_1. Thus, only clauses of $\texttt{assume}_3$ without mentioning B transfer to $\texttt{safe}_3$. For mathematical convenience, we denote the conjunction of all safety guarantees of a skill by the logical formula $\phi_s \equiv \bigwedge_{\phi \in s.\Phi} \phi$ and the set of assumptions of a skill in a skill graph by the set $\mathcal{A}_s = \{\psi_1, \ldots, \psi_n \mid \texttt{assume}_s \equiv \psi_1 \wedge \cdots \wedge \psi_n\}$. Furthermore, set $\texttt{var}(\cdot)$ denotes the set of variables of a logical formula. The overall safety guarantee of a skill is then computed as follows.

$$\texttt{safe}_s \equiv \phi_s \wedge \Big(\bigwedge_{\substack{\psi \in \mathcal{A}_s \wedge \\ \texttt{var}(\phi_s) \cap \texttt{var}(\psi) = \emptyset}} \psi \Big) \tag{6}$$

We can now define the *validity* of a skill graph as follows.

Definition 7 (Valid Skill Graph). *Let $G = \langle S, r, E \rangle$ be a well-formed skill graph. We say that skill graph G is valid if and only if $\forall s \in S$ formula $\texttt{assume}_s$ is satisfiable and formula $\texttt{assume}_s \to [s.\alpha]\texttt{safe}_s$ is valid. We denote by $s \models_G s.\Phi$ the validity of a skill s in a skill graph G with respect to its safety guarantees and by $\models G$ the validity of the entire skill graph (i.e., $\models G \equiv \forall s \in S, s \models_G s.\Phi$).*

The upcoming important theorem states that the individual validity of two skill graphs also transfers to the validity of their composition. However, based on

Def. 6, composition may also lead to an invalid skill graph if the assumption of a skill in the new skill graph is not satisfiable (e.g., possible in case of diamond structures). Therefore, we require satisfiability checks for the computed assumptions and define the *compatibility* between two skill graphs as follows.

Definition 8 (Compatible Skill Graphs). *Let G_1 and G_2 be two well-formed skill graphs. We say that G_1 and G_2 are* compatible *if the following holds.*

- *$G_1 \circ G_2$ is a well-formed skill graph,*
- *for each skill s in $G_1 \circ G_2$, formula $\mathtt{assume}_s$ is satisfiable.*

Theorem 1 (Composition of Skill Graphs Retains Validity). *Let G_1 and G_2 be two compatible skill graphs and $G = G_1 \circ G_2$ their composition. Then, G is valid if G_1 and G_2 are valid (i.e., $\models G$ if $\models G_1$ and $\models G_2$).*

Proof. Let s_1 and s_2 be two composed skills and $s = s_1 \oplus s_2$ their composition. Following Def. 6, the verification condition for s becomes

$$(\mathtt{assume}_{s_1} \wedge \mathtt{assume}_{s_2}) \to [s.\alpha](\mathtt{safe}_{s_1} \wedge \mathtt{safe}_{s_2}).$$

Based on the semantics of $d\mathcal{L}$ [31], condition $\Psi \to [\alpha]\Phi_1 \wedge \Psi \to [\alpha]\Phi_2 \leftrightarrow \Psi \to [\alpha](\Phi_1 \wedge \Phi_2)$ holds. As the hybrid programs of s_1 and s_2 are identical (or at least one of them is empty), the resulting two conditions to check are the following:

$$(1) \quad (\mathtt{assume}_{s_1} \wedge \mathtt{assume}_{s_2}) \to [s_1.\alpha](\mathtt{safe}_{s_1})$$
$$(2) \quad (\mathtt{assume}_{s_1} \wedge \mathtt{assume}_{s_2}) \to [s_2.\alpha](\mathtt{safe}_{s_2})$$

Satisfiability of $(\mathtt{assume}_{s_1} \wedge \mathtt{assume}_{s_2})$ follows from Def. 8. Then, validity of both conditions follow from Def. 7 and, consequently, $\models G$ holds. $\qquad\square$

4.2 Assembling Hybrid Programs in a Skill graph

Skill graphs decompose the system into smaller parts. Likewise, the hybrid program that represents the complete behavior is also distributed over the skill graph. Now that we have defined the structure and behavior of single skills in the context of a skill graph, we define how we can construct the complete behavior of a skill as a single monolithic hybrid program. The resulting hybrid program is then a complete representation of the skill's behavior while also retaining all safety guarantees without the need of re-verifying skills or even entire skill graphs. We start by giving a definition on *how* hybrid programs of skills are assembled together.

Definition 9 (Hybrid Program Assembly). *Let $G = \langle S, r, E \rangle$ be a skill graph, HP the set of all hybrid programs, and let $s \in S$ denote an arbitrary skill of G. A hybrid program assembly of s is a function $\rho : S \to HP$, which is recursively defined as follows.*

$$\rho(s) = \begin{cases} s.\alpha & \text{if } s \text{ has no children (i.e., } \neg \exists s' \in S : s' \prec s) \\ (\bigcup_{s' \prec s} \rho(s')); s.\alpha & \text{otherwise} \end{cases}$$

The motivation is that such assemblies are safe to be used in other contexts, such as code generation for the validation of prototypes or monitor generation. Assuming a valid skill graph G, the following theorem guarantees that any hybrid program assembly over skills in G retains the respective safety guarantees.

Theorem 2 (Safety Compliance of Hybrid Program Assemblies). *Let $G = \langle S, r, E \rangle$ be a valid skill graph and let $s \in S$ denote an arbitrary skill of G. Then, formula $[\rho(s)]\mathtt{safe}_s$ is valid*

Proof. We proceed by induction on the skills of skill graph G. For the basis step, we assume that s has no children (i.e., $\neg \exists s' \in S : s' \prec s$). Because $[\rho(s)]\mathtt{safe}_s \equiv [s.\alpha]\mathtt{safe}_s$ and G is a valid skill graph, it follows from Def. 7 that formula $[\rho(s)]\mathtt{safe}_s$ is valid. From now on, we assume that s has children. Our induction hypothesis is that if for each skill $s' \prec s$ program assembly $\rho(s')$ satisfies $\mathtt{safe}_{s'}$, then hybrid program assembly $\rho(s)$ satisfies $\mathtt{safe}_s$:

$$\textbf{(IH)} \qquad (\bigwedge_{s' \prec s} [\rho(s')]\mathtt{safe}_{s'}) \to [\rho(s)]\mathtt{safe}_s$$

$$(1) \quad \leftrightarrow \quad (\bigwedge_{s' \prec s} [\rho(s')]\mathtt{safe}_{s'}) \to [\bigcup_{s' \prec s} \rho(s'); s.\alpha]\mathtt{safe}_s$$

$$(2) \quad \leftrightarrow \quad (\bigwedge_{s' \prec s} [\rho(s')]\mathtt{safe}_{s'}) \to [\bigcup_{s' \prec s} \rho(s')][s.\alpha]\mathtt{safe}_s$$

$$(3) \quad \leftrightarrow \quad (\bigwedge_{s' \prec s} [\rho(s')]\mathtt{safe}_{s'}) \to \bigwedge_{s' \prec s} [\rho(s')][s.\alpha]\mathtt{safe}_s$$

$$(4) \quad \leftrightarrow \quad (\bigwedge_{s' \prec s} \mathtt{safe}_{s'}) \to [s.\alpha]\mathtt{safe}_s$$

$$(5) \quad \leftrightarrow \quad \mathtt{assume}_s \to [s.\alpha]\mathtt{safe}_s$$

Transformation step (1) follows from substituting $\rho(s)$ with its definition given in Def. 9. Steps (2)–(4) are again based on the semantics of $d\mathcal{L}$ [31]. Step (2) follows from the *sequential composition axiom* $[a; b]P \leftrightarrow [a][b]P$, step (3) from the *nondeterministic choice axiom* $[a \cup b]P \leftrightarrow [a]P \wedge [b]P$, and step (4) from *monotonicity*. Because G is a valid skill graph, validity of $\mathtt{assume}_s \to [s.\alpha]\mathtt{safe}_s$ follows again from Def. 7. Consequently, $[\rho(s)]\mathtt{safe}_s$ is valid. □

4.3   Integration into the Software Development Process

In Figure 5, we summarize the methodology for modeling and verifying skill graphs. The main idea is that the safety verification of skill graphs modeled in isolation transfers to the composition of compatible skill graphs. This (a) eases the modeling process, as smaller models tend to be less complex and easier to repair, (b) fosters reusability, which is known to be cost-effective and less error-prone, and (c) is promising for scaling the verification to large skill graphs.

In particular, the methodology consists of five major parts. In the first part (*1*), practitioners define and model skills together with their hybrid programs and relevant safety guarantees in isolation and subsequently connect them to form well-formed skill graphs (if possible). In the second part (*2*), for each

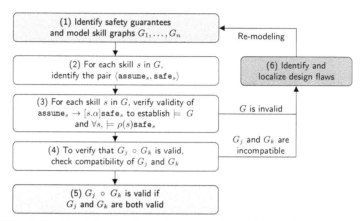

Fig. 5: Methodology of modeling and verifying skill graphs.

skill s in a skill graph, the assumption $\mathtt{assume}_s$ and safety guarantee $\mathtt{safe}_s$ are computed by evaluating the context of the skill in the skill graph. The third part (3) uses the identified assumptions and the safety guarantee to validate each skill in a skill graph individually. If each skill is proven valid (cf. Theorem 1), the complete skill graph is proven valid and can be put into a repository to be reused. Following Theorem 2, all program assemblies over skills in this skill graph retain the respective safety guarantees. The fourth part (4) becomes relevant, if two skill graphs are composed together to represent a more complex task of a cyber-physical system. In this case, compatibility of the skill graphs is checked and, if successful, the validity of the composed skill graph is established (5). The final part (6) is relevant in the presence of unsuccessful proof attempts. If validity of a skill graph or the composition of multiple skill graphs cannot be established, practitioners need to identify and fix mistakes in their models. Typically, the complexity of localizing design mistakes is reduced with our methodology, as it is explicitly known which exact skills in a skill graph with respect to their safety guarantees could not be verified.

5   Evaluation and Discussion

We evaluate our skill-based verification approach on a case study to answer the following two research questions.

RQ-1 *How does the skill-based methodology compare to monolithic modeling and verification?*

RQ-2 *To what extent can skill-based compositional verification reduce the verification effort?*

5.1   Open-Source Implementation

We implemented skill-based verification in a tool with the name SKEDITOR. The implementation is written in JAVA as an Eclipse plug-in based on Graphiti [13],

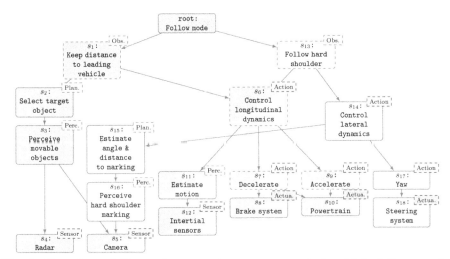

Fig. 6: Complete skill graph expressing an automated vehicle follow mode.

a framework for developing diagram editors in the context of model-driven development. The prototype allows practitioners to model and annotate well-formed skill graphs with safety guarantees as described in Section 3.

Thereupon, we implemented our compositional verification approach as described in Section 4. SKEDITOR allows to synthesize hybrid programs of specific skills with respect to their dependencies in the skill graph. Compliance checks of the provided safety guarantees are performed by employing the deductive theorem prover KEYMAERA X [14] in version 4.7.3. SKEDITOR and all experimental results can be found online.[3] We use the SKEDITOR to answer research questions *RQ-1* and *RQ-2*.

5.2   Case Study: Vehicle Follow Mode

To illustrate the practicality of our approach, we model and verify the *vehicle follow mode* of an automated protective vehicle as adopted from Nolte et al. [26] and depicted in Figure 6. The aim of was to develop an unmanned protective vehicle which is able to drive on the hard shoulder autonomously (i.e., without any human interaction). On the lowest level, the skill graph consists of three sensors (i.e., **Radar**, **Camera**, and **Inertial sensor**) to perceive information from the environment. Additionally, three actuators (i.e., **Brake system**, **Powertrain**, and **Steering system**) represent concrete technical aspects. These skills propagate information about typical properties of a concrete model of a vehicle (e.g., the *maximal deceleration*). As highlighted with two shades of gray, this skill graph is dividable into two separate skill graphs, which we refer to as G_1 and G_2. G_1 has **Keep distance to leading vehicle** as the root skill, which is responsible for ensuring a minimum distance to a leading vehicle. G_2 has **Follow hard shoulder** as root skill, which is responsible for ensuring the vehicle's position inside the lane markings on a road. Skills shared by both skill graphs are highlighted with both shades.

---

[3] https://github.com/TUBS-ISF/Skeditor

Skill	Requirement
Follow hard shoulder	Vehicle deviates from the center of the lane by at most half the lane width
Control lateral dynamics	Lateral controller must guarantee overshoot of less than 25 cm
Yaw	Vehicle yaw rate must not exceed $0.3\,\mathrm{rad\,s^{-1}}$
Control longitudinal dynamics	Vehicle speed must not exceed $2.7\,\mathrm{m\,s^{-1}}$
Accelerate	Acceleration must not exceed $4\,\mathrm{m\,s^{-2}}$
Decelerate	Vehicle must at least provide a deceleration of $5\,\mathrm{m\,s^{-2}}$
Keep distance to leading vehicle	Vehicle must keep a minimum distance of 10 m to leading vehicle
Select target object	Object recognition must always select an object of lateral position of x > 10 m
Perceive movable objects	Object recognition must track vehicles of relative speeds between 0 and $60\,\mathrm{m\,s^{-1}}$
Estimate angle and distance to marking	Angle to lanemarking must be extracted with maximum error of ±0.5 degrees and distance to lanemarking must be extracted with maximum error of ±3 cm
Perceive hard shoulder	Image processing must extract right edge of shoulder marking with a maximum error of 20 cm
Estimate motion	Vehicle velocity must be estimated with a maximal error of $\pm0.03\,\mathrm{m\,s^{-1}}$

Table 2: Specified safety requirements for the vehicle follow mode as adopted from Nolte et al. [26].

The overall procedure ***Follow mode*** (i.e., the composition $G_1 \circ G_2$) requires a combination of autonomously following a leading vehicle (i.e., skill s_1) and following the lane marking (i.e., skill s_{13}). The informal safety guarantees for the skill graph of our case study are adopted from Nolte et al. [26] and illustrated in Table 2. Requirements are typically given informally, which is why we translated them to their formal counterpart. For our case study, we focus on four particular skills, as these are the only non-trivial skills in our case study that comprise both, the vehicle's dynamics and a control algorithm. Namely, these skills are ***Control longitudinal dynamics*** (s_6), ***Control lateral dynamics*** (s_{14}), ***Follow hard shoulder*** (s_{13}), and ***Keep distance to leading vehicle*** (s_1).

Example 2 *Consider skill* **Control longitudinal dynamics** *(s_6) in the context of the overall skill graph. Skill s_6 comprises the dynamic system for the longitudinal motion of the vehicle while depending on skills* **Accelerate** *and* **Decelerate** *as well as the perception skill* **Estimate motion**. *The control algorithm of this skill as part of the hybrid program complies with the safety requirements as given in Table 2 (e.g., velocity (v_s) must not exceed $2.7\,\mathrm{m\,s^{-1}}$). Preconditions for this skill are propagated from skills* **Estimate motion**, **Accelerate**, *and* **Decelerate**, *and guarantee that the vehicle provides a maximal deceleration of $5\,\mathrm{m\,s^{-2}}$ (B) and a maximal acceleration of $4\,\mathrm{m\,s^{-2}}$ (A). Table 3 summarizes all attributes of skill s_6.*

$X_{\mathrm{def}} = \{x, v, v_{\max}\}$
$X_{\mathrm{req}} = \{a, A, B, ep, t\}$
$\alpha ::= \begin{cases} \text{init} \rightarrow [(ctrl; dyn)*](\text{guar}) \\ \quad \text{init} \equiv v \geq 0 \wedge v \leq v_{\max} \wedge A > 0 \wedge A \leq 4 \wedge B \geq 5 \wedge v_{\max} = 2.7 \\ \quad ctrl \equiv (?v_{\max} - v \leq \text{margin}); a = *; -B \leq a \leq 0; \\ \qquad \cup ?v_{\max} - v \geq \text{margin}); a = *; -B \leq a \leq A;) \\ \text{margin} \equiv ep * A \\ \quad dyn \equiv t := 0; x' = v, v' = a, t' = 1 \& v \geq 0 \wedge t \leq ep \\ \text{guar} \equiv v \leq v_{\max} \end{cases}$
$\tau = \text{action}$
$\Phi = \{v_s \leq v_{\max} \ (2.7\,\mathrm{m\,s}^{-1})\}$

Table 3: Attributes for skill *Control longitudinal dynamics (s_6).*

5.3 Results

All measurements were conducted on an Intel i7-6600U CPU @ 2.60GHz with 12 GB RAM and Z3 [12] in version 4.6.0 was used as the underlying solver for KEYMAERA X in version 4.7.3.

RQ-1: How does the skill-based methodology compare to monolithic modeling and verification? We modeled the overall behavior of $G_1 \circ G_2$ as a monolithic model (i.e., following the hard shoulder and following a leading vehicle in concert) as described in Section 4.2. As mentioned before, the skill-based approach has a high reuse potential. Each skill needs to be verified only once, and the verification results can be reused in other skill graphs (cf. Theorem 1). While in case of a change of parameters or an update of control algorithms the monolithic model has to be re-modeled and re-verified completely, a change impact analysis identifying only affected skills may reduce the re-verification effort even further for the compositional approach. Importantly, skill s_{13} and the monolithic model could only be verified interactively, whereas skills s_1, s_{14}, and s_6 were verified fully automatically with the automatic proof search of KEYMAERA X. Chances of an automatic re-verification are thus higher with the skill-based methodology.

An important hypothesis of ours is that skill-based verification is more effective in discovering modeling defects compared to a monolithic model. To get some insights into this hypothesis, we developed three initial experiments to render the verification attempt invalid. We (1) changed the safety guarantee of skills, (2) changed the control algorithm of skills, and (3) did a combination of both and compared these results to the same changes performed in the monolithic model. Following our methodology helped to trace and resolve defects effectively with respect to this case study, whereas identifying multiple modeling defects in the monolithic model became quickly intractable. During the resolution of Scenario 3, re-verification had to be performed several times for the monolithic model (i.e., resolving one conflict at a time), which emphasizes the advantage of our compositional approach over the monolithic modeling. However, we do not want to overclaim the importance of our insights, as more complex experiments

	Verified Skill				Proof steps				Σ	Σ_{reuse}
	s_1	s_6	s_{13}	s_{14}	s_1	s_6	s_{13}	s_{14}		
G_1	✓	✓			4,746	3,769			8,515	8,515
G_2		✓	✓	✓		3,769	16,924	7,223	27,916	24,147
$G_1 \circ G_2$	✓	✓	✓	✓	4,746	3,769	16,924	7,223	32,662	0*
Σ_{total}									**69,093**	**32,662**

*No re-verification of skills with Theorem 1

Table 4: Comparison of the verification effort for skill-based compositional verification.

and a larger evaluation have to be conducted to adequately test whether our hypothesis is significant.

RQ-2: To what extent can skill-based compositional verification reduce the verification effort? To answer RQ-2, we measured the verification effort in proof steps for each of the three skills mentioned before per skill graph. In Table 4, we summarize the results. Column *Verified Skill* describes which skill is part of which skill graph and column *Proof steps* compares the number of proof steps needed for each skill individually. A common scenario is to model and verify each maneuver individually (i.e., each skill graph). The total verification effort Σ_{total} would then cumulate to 69,093 proof steps. Instead, our skill-based approach allows to reuse verification results for skill s_6 in skill graph G_2 and per Theorem 1 even the verification results for all skills in skill graph $G_1 \circ G_2$. Entries highlighted in gray indicate that the respective skill could be reused instead of re-verification. The compositional approach needs approximately 53% less proof steps in our case study.

6　Related Work

Skill Graphs. Maurer [23] pioneered the concept of skills by introducing so-called *abilities* in vehicle guidance systems. Abilities are similar to skills, as they concisely describe the capabilites of a vehicle, and are intended to be permanently monitored at run-time to enforce safety mechanics. Reschka et al. [32, 33] introduced skill graphs informally in their work giving definitions for skills and abilities in relation to autonomous vehicles. Nolte et al. [26] built upon this approach by employing the informal concept of skill graphs for the development of self-aware automated road vehicles. We adopted their case study to evaluate our skill-based verification approach.

Hybrid Systems and Verification of Cyber-Physical Systems. Hybrid systems [3] are a generalization of timed automata [4] and well-suited for modeling and verifying cyber-physical systems. Krishna et al. [20] show that using hybrid automata to model and verify cyber-physical systems is, in principle, feasible. Typically, hybrid systems are verified employing reachability analyses and model checking [2, 21, 22, 35]. However, these technqiues are not compositional in general (i.e., modular verification of individual parts to establish correctness of the entire systems is not possible). It is also not intended to generate and reuse proofs to increase trust in the system's correctness, as, for instance, possible with theorem proving. To address this issue, we built our methodology upon the notion of *hybrid programs* [30] and the theorem prover KEYMAERA X [14], which helped us to also satisfy the important property of compositionality in the modeling and formal verification of hybrid systems. We further extend this concept with skill graphs by modularizing the verification of complex driving tasks, such that the verification of the entire behavior is reduced to simpler sub-tasks and compatibility checks.

Finally, there exists a seamless connection to the work conducted by Müller et al. [24], who present a compositional component-based approach for the verification of hybrid systems based on hybrid programs. Skill graphs provide an abstract and organized view of the system and are applied (1) in the verification and validation phase of the *requirements analysis* and (2) the early stages of the *design phase*. Subsequently, a skill may be implemented by a set of multiple interacting components to take more necessary specifics into account, such as communication protocols and resource consumption. To conclude, the process of refining skill graphs including their safety requirements to formally specified component-based systems exhibits a high level of quality assurance at the level of both, requirement engineers and software architects.

7 Conclusion and Future Work

In this work, we proposed skill-based verification of cyber-physical systems with the notion of skill graphs that (1) encourages the modular development of small and reusable actions in isolation, and (2) enables the identification of poorly defined requirements in early software development processes by considering formal verification of hybrid systems. We provide the first formalization of skill graphs, showed how skill graphs and hybrid programs can be combined, and also introduced a proved notion of compositionality for skills. The investigated case study on a *vehicle follow mode* showcases that the compositionality property of skill graphs is important for scaling, as the verification effort is reduced by more than 53%. Compositionality is particularly important for model and software evolution, as costly re-verification of a skill's requirement can be minimized.

For the future, we want to enable the composition of skills with dissimilar hybrid programs, for which the theoretical groundwork partially exists. Moreover, our current focus is on the integration of skill graphs into software engineering practices for cyber-physical systems to amplify the utilization of formal methods from the start of new software projects.

Acknowledgements. We are grateful to Enis Belli and Arne Windeler for their help with the implementation of SKEDITOR. This work was supported by the DFG (German Research Foundation) under the Researcher Unit FOR1800: Controlling Concurrent Change (CCC).

References

1. Ahrendt, W., Beckert, B., Bubel, R., Hähnle, R., Schmitt, P.H., Ulbrich, M.: Deductive Software Verification–The KeY Book: From Theory to Practice. Springer (2016)
2. Alur, R.: Formal Verification of Hybrid Systems. In: Embedded Software (EMSOFT), 2011 Proceedings of the International Conference on. pp. 273–278. IEEE (2011)
3. Alur, R., Courcoubetis, C., Henzinger, T.A., Ho, P.H.: Hybrid Automata: An Algorithmic Approach to the Specification and Verification of Hybrid Systems. In: Hybrid systems, pp. 209–229. Springer (1993)
4. Alur, R., Dill, D.L.: A Theory of Timed Automata. Theoretical computer science **126**(2), 183–235 (1994)
5. Alur, R., Henzinger, T.A., Sontag, E.D.: Hybrid Systems III: Verification and Control, vol. 3. Springer Science & Business Media (1996)
6. Baheti, R., Gill, H.: Cyber-physical Systems. The impact of control technology **12**(1), 161–166 (2011)
7. Barnett, M., Fähndrich, M., Leino, K.R.M., Müller, P., Schulte, W., Venter, H.: Specification and Verification: The Spec# Experience. Communications of the ACM **54**, 81–91 (Jun 2011)
8. Batory, D., Sarvela, J.N., Rauschmayer, A.: Scaling Step-Wise Refinement. IEEE Transactions on Software Engineering (TSE) **30**(6), 355–371 (2004)
9. Broy, M.: Yesterday, Today, and Tomorrow: 50 Years of Software Engineering. IEEE Software **35**(5), 38–43 (2018)
10. Burdy, L., Cheon, Y., Cok, D.R., Ernst, M.D., Kiniry, J., Leavens, G.T., Leino, K.R.M., Poll, E.: An Overview of JML Tools and Applications **7**(3), 212–232 (Jun 2005)
11. Cuijpers, P.J.L., Reniers, M.A.: Hybrid Process Algebra. The Journal of Logic and Algebraic Programming **62**(2), 191–245 (2005)
12. De Moura, L., Bjørner, N.: Z3: An Efficient SMT Solver. In: Proceedings of the International Conference on Tools and Algorithms for the Construction and Analysis of Systems. pp. 337–340. Springer (2008)
13. Foundation, T.E.: Graphiti - a Graphical Tooling Infrastructure, [Available at https://www.eclipse.org/graphiti/; accessed 22-January-2018
14. Fulton, N., Mitsch, S., Quesel, J.D., Völp, M., Platzer, A.: KeYmaera X: An Axiomatic Tactical Theorem Prover for Hybrid Systems. In: International Conference on Automated Deduction. pp. 527–538. Springer (2015)
15. Garcia, A., Sant'Anna, C., Chavez, C., da Silva, V.T., de Lucena, C.J., von Staa, A.: Separation of Concerns in Multi-agent Systems: An Empirical Study. In: International Workshop on Software Engineering for Large-Scale Multi-agent Systems. pp. 49–72. Springer (2003)
16. Gleirscher, M., Foster, S., Woodcock, J.: Opportunities for Integrated Formal Methods. CoRR **abs/1812.10103** (2018), http://arxiv.org/abs/1812.10103
17. Gleirscher, M., Marmsoler, D.: Formal Methods: Oversold? Underused? A Survey. arXiv preprint arXiv:1812.08815 (2018)
18. Hatcliff, J., Leavens, G.T., Leino, K.R.M., Müller, P., Parkinson, M.: Behavioral Interface Specification Languages **44**(3), 16:1–16:58 (Jun 2012)
19. Henzinger, T.A.: The Theory of Hybrid Automata. In: Verification of Digital and Hybrid Systems, pp. 265–292. Springer (2000)

20. Krishna, S.N., Trivedi, A.: Hybrid Automata for Formal Modeling and Verification of Cyber-Physical Systems (Mar 2015)
21. Lunze, J., Lamnabhi-Lagarrigue, F.: Handbook of Hybrid Systems Control: Theory, Tools, Applications. Cambridge University Press (2009)
22. Maler, O.: Algorithmic Verification of Continuous and Hybrid Systems. arXiv preprint arXiv:1403.0952 (2014)
23. Maurer, M.: Flexible Automatisierung von Straßenfahrzeugen mit Rechnersehen (2000)
24. Müller, A., Mitsch, S., Retschitzegger, W., Schwinger, W., Platzer, A.: Tactical Contract Composition for Hybrid System Component Verification. International Journal on Software Tools for Technology Transfer **20**(6), 615–643 (2018)
25. Nerode, A., Kohn, W.: Models for Hybrid Systems: Automata, Topologies, Controllability, Observability. In: Hybrid systems, pp. 317–356. Springer (1993)
26. Nolte, M., Bagschik, G., Jatzkowski, I., Stolte, T., Reschka, A., Maurer, M.: Towards a Skill-and Ability-based Development Process for Self-aware Automated Road Vehicles. In: Intelligent Transportation Systems (ITSC), 2017 IEEE 20th International Conference on. pp. 1–6. IEEE (2017)
27. Parnas, D.L.: On the Criteria to be used in Decomposing Systems into Modules. Communications of the ACM **15**(12), 1053–1058 (Dec 1972). https://doi.org/10.1145/361598.361623
28. Platzer, A.: Differential Dynamic Logic for Hybrid Systems. Journal of Automated Reasoning **41**(2), 143–189 (2008)
29. Platzer, A.: Logics of Dynamical Systems. In: Proceedings of the 2012 27th Annual IEEE/ACM Symposium on Logic in Computer Science. pp. 13–24. IEEE Computer Society (2012)
30. Platzer, A.: The Complete Proof Theory of Hybrid Systems. In: Proceedings of the 2012 27th Annual IEEE/ACM Symposium on Logic in Computer Science. pp. 541–550. IEEE Computer Society (2012)
31. Platzer, A.: A Complete Uniform Substitution Calculus for Differential Dynamic Logic. Journal of Automated Reasoning **59**(2), 219–265 (2017)
32. Reschka, A.: Fertigkeiten- und Fähigkeitengraphen als Grundlage des sicheren Betriebs von automatisierten Fahrzeugen im öffentlichen Straßenverkehr in städtischer Umgebung. Ph.D. thesis (Jul 2017)
33. Reschka, A., Bagschik, G., Ulbrich, S., Nolte, M., Maurer, M.: Ability and Skill Graphs for System Modeling, Online Monitoring, and Decision Support for Vehicle Guidance Systems. In: Intelligent Vehicles Symposium (IV), 2015 IEEE. pp. 933–939. IEEE (2015)
34. Schumann, J.M.: Automated Theorem Proving in Software Engineering. Springer Science & Business Media (2001)
35. Tabuada, P.: Verification and Control of Hybrid Systems: A Symbolic Approach. Springer Science & Business Media (2009)
36. Tarr, P., Ossher, H., Harrison, W., Sutton, Jr., S.M.: N Degrees of Separation: Multi-Dimensional Separation of Concerns. In: Proceedings of the International Conference on Software Engineering (ICSE). pp. 107–119. ACM (1999)
37. Ulbrich, S., Reschka, A., Rieken, J., Ernst, S., Bagschik, G., Dierkes, F., Nolte, M., Maurer, M.: Towards a Functional System Architecture for Automated Vehicles. arXiv preprint arXiv:1703.08557 (2017)

Combining Partial Specifications using Alternating Interface Automata*

Ramon Janssen

Radboud University, Nijmegen, The Netherlands
ramonjanssen@cs.ru.nl

Abstract. To model real-world software systems, modelling paradigms should support a form of compositionality. In interface theory and model-based testing with inputs and outputs, *conjunctive* operators have been introduced: the behaviour allowed by composed specification $s_1 \wedge s_2$ is the behaviour allowed by both partial models s_1 and s_2. The models at hand are non-deterministic *interface automata*, but the interaction between non-determinism and conjunction is not yet well understood. On the other hand, in the theory of *alternating automata*, conjunction and non-determinism are core aspects. Alternating automata have not been considered in the context of inputs and outputs, making them less suitable for modelling software interfaces. In this paper, we combine the two modelling paradigms to define *alternating interface automata* (AIA). We equip these automata with an observational, trace-based semantics, and define testers, to establish correctness of black-box interfaces with respect to an AIA specification.

1 Introduction

The challenge of software verification is to ensure that software systems are correct, using techniques such as model checking and model-based testing. To use these techniques, we assume that we have an abstract specification of a system, which serves as a description of what the system should do. A popular approach is to model a specification as an automaton. However, the huge number of states in typical real-world software systems quickly makes modelling with explicit automata infeasible. A form of compositionality is therefore usually required for scalability, so that a specification can be decomposed into smaller and understandable parts. Parallel composition is based on a structural decomposition of the modelled system into components, and it thus relies on the assumption that components themselves are small and simple enough to be modelled. This assumption is not required for logical composition, in which partial specification models of the same component or system are combined in the manner of logical conjunction. Formally, for a composition to be conjunctive, the behaviour allowed by $s_1 \wedge s_2$ is the behaviour allowed by both partial specifications s_1 and

s_2. Such a composition is important for scalability of modelling, as it allows writing independent partial specifications, sometimes called view modelling [3]. On a fundamental level, specifications can be seen as logical statements about software, and the existence of conjunction on such statements is only natural. Conjunctive operators have been defined in many language-theoretic modelling frameworks, such as for regular expressions [12] and process algebras [5].

1.1 Conjunction for Inputs and Outputs

A conjunctive operator $\wedge$ has also been introduced in many automata frameworks for formal verification and testing, such as interface theory [8], ioco theory [3] and the theory of substitutivity refinement [7]. Within these theories, systems are modelled as *labelled transition systems* [15] or *interface automata* [1] (IA), and actions are divided into inputs and outputs.

An informal example of some (partial) specification models, as could be expressed in these theories, is shown by the automata in Figure 1, in which inputs are labelled with question marks, and outputs with exclamation marks. The specifications represent a vending machine with two input buttons (?a and ?b), which provides coffee (!c) and tea (!t) as outputs, optionally with milk (!c+m and !t+m). The first model, p, specifies that after pressing button ?a, the machine dispenses coffee. The second model, q, specifies that after pressing button ?b, the machine has a choice between dispensing tea, or tea with milk. The third model, r, is similar, but uses non-determinism to specify that button ?b results in coffee with milk or tea with milk.

The fourth model, $p \wedge q \wedge r$, states that all former three partial models should hold. Here, we use the definition of $\wedge$ from [3], but the definition from [7] is similar. An input is specified in the combined model if it is specified in any partial model, making both buttons ?a and ?b specified. Additionally, an output is allowed in the combined model if it is allowed by all partial models, meaning that after button ?b, only tea with milk is allowed.

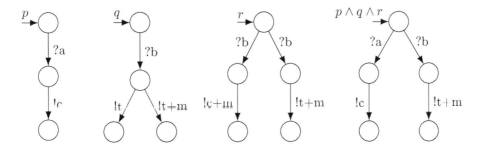

Fig. 1. Three independent specifications for a vending machine, and their conjunction.

1.2 Conjunctions of states

This form of conjunctive composition acts as an operator on entire models. However, a partial specification could also describe the expected behaviour of a particular state of the system, other than the initial state. For example, suppose that the input ?on turns the vending machine on, after which the machine should behave as specified by p, q and r from Figure 1. This, by itself, is also a specification, illustrated by s in Figure 2. However, the formal meaning of this model is unclear: transitions connect states, whereas $p \wedge q \wedge r$ is not a state but an entire automaton. A less trivial case is partial specification t, also in Figure 2: after obtaining any drink by input ?take, we should move to a state where we can obtain a drink as described by specifications p, q, r and t. Thus, we combine conjunctions with a form of recursion. This cannot easily be formalized using $\wedge$ as an operator on automata, like in [3,7,8]. Defining conjunction as a composition on individual states would provide a formal basis for these informal examples.

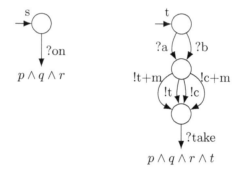

Fig. 2. Two specifications with transitions to a conjunction.

Conjunctions of states are a main ingredient of *alternating automata* [6], in which conjunctions and non-determinism alternate. Here, non-determism acts as logical disjunction, dually to conjunction. Because of this duality, both conjunction and disjunction are treated analogously: both are encoded in the transition relation of the automaton. This contrasts the approach of defining conjunction directly on IAs, where non-determinism is encoded in the transition relation of the IA, whereas conjunction is added as an operator on IAs, leaving the duality between the two unexploited. In fact, the conjunction-operator in [3] even requires that any non-determinism in its operands is removed first, by performing an exponential determinization step. For example, model r in Figure 1 is non-deterministic, and must be determinized to the form of model q before $p \wedge q \wedge r$ is computed. This indicates that it is hard to combine conjunction and non-determinism in an elegant way, without understanding their interaction.

Despite their inherent support for conjunction, alternating automata are not entirely suitable for modeling the behaviour of software systems, since they lack the distinction between inputs and outputs. In this respect, alternating automata are similar to deterministic finite automata (DFAs). Distinguishing inputs and outputs in an IA allows modelling of software systems in a less abstract way than with the homogeneous alphabet of actions of DFAs and alternating automata.

1.3 Contributions

We combine concepts from the worlds of interface theory and alternating automata, leading to Alternating Interface Automata (AIAs), and show how these can be used in the setting of a trace semantics for observable inputs and outputs. We provide a solid formal basis of AIAs, by

- combining alternation with inputs and outputs (Section 3.1),
- defining a trace semantics for AIAs (Section 3.2), by lifting the *input-failure refinement* semantics for non-deterministic interface automata [11] to AIAs,
- providing insight into the semantics of an AIA, by defining a determinization operator (Section 3.3) and a transformation between IAs and AIAs (Section 3.4), and
- defining testers (Section 4), which represent practical testing scenarios for establishing input-failure refinement between a black-box implementation IA and a specification AIA, analogously to ioco test case generation [15].

The definition of input-failure refinement [11] is based upon the observation that, for a non-deterministically reached set of states Q, the observable outputs of that set are the union of the outputs of the individual states in Q, whereas the specified inputs for Q are the intersection of the inputs specified in individual states in Q. For conjunction, we invert this: outputs allowed by a conjunction of states are captured by the intersection, whereas specified inputs are captured by the union. In this way, our AIAs seamlessly combine the duality between conjunction and non-determinism with the duality between inputs and outputs.

Proofs can be found in the extended technical report [10].

2 Preliminaries

We first recall the definition of interface automata [1] and input-failure refinement [11]. The original definition of IAs [1] allows at most one initial state, but we generalize this to sets of states. Moreover, [1] supports internal actions, which we do not need. Transitions are commonly encoded by a relation, whereas we use a function.

Definition 1. *An Interface Automaton (IA) is a 5-tuple (Q, I, O, T, Q^0), where*

- *Q is a set of states,*
- *I and O are disjoint sets of input and output actions, respectively,*
- *$T : Q \times (I \cup O\}) \to \mathcal{P}(Q)$ is an image-finite transition function (meaning that $T(q, \ell)$ is finite for all q and ℓ), and*
- *$Q^0 \subseteq Q$ is a finite set of initial states.*

The domain of IAs is denoted $\mathcal{IA}$. For $s \in \mathcal{IA}$, we refer to its respective elements by Q_s, I_s, O_s, T_s, Q_s^0. For $s_1, s_2, \ldots, s_A, s_B, \ldots$ a family of IAs, we write Q_j, I_j, O_j, T_j and Q_j^0 to refer to the respective elements, for $j = 1, 2, \ldots, A, B, \ldots$.

In examples, we represent IAs graphically as in Figure 1. For the remainder of this paper, we assume fixed input and output alphabets I and O for IAs, with $L = I \cup O$. For (sets of) sequences of actions, $*$ denotes the Kleene star, and ϵ denotes the empty sequence. We define auxiliary notation in the style of [15].

Definition 2. *Let $s \in \mathcal{IA}$, $Q \subseteq Q_s$, $q, q' \in Q_s$, $\ell \in L$ and $\sigma \in L^*$. We define*

$$q \xrightarrow{\epsilon}_s q' \Leftrightarrow q = q' \qquad\qquad q \xrightarrow{\sigma\ell}_s q' \Leftrightarrow \exists r \in Q_s : q \xrightarrow{\sigma}_s r \wedge q' \in T_s(r, \ell)$$

$$q \xrightarrow{\sigma}_s \Leftrightarrow \exists r \in Q_s : q \xrightarrow{\sigma}_s r \qquad\qquad q \not\xrightarrow{\sigma}_s \Leftrightarrow \neg(q \xrightarrow{\sigma}_s)$$

$$\mathrm{traces}_s(q) = \{\sigma \in L^* \mid q \xrightarrow{\sigma}_s\} \qquad\qquad Q \text{ after}_s\ \sigma = \{r \in Q_s \mid \exists r' \in Q : r' \xrightarrow{\sigma}_s r\}$$

$$\mathrm{traces}(s) = \bigcup_{q \in Q_s^0} \mathrm{traces}_s(q) \qquad\qquad s \text{ after } \sigma = Q_s^0 \text{ after}_s\ \sigma$$

$$\mathrm{out}_s(Q) = \{x \in O \mid \exists q \in Q : q \xrightarrow{x}_s\} \quad \mathrm{in}_s(Q) = \{a \in I \mid \forall q \in Q : q \xrightarrow{a}_s\}$$

$$q \text{ is a sink-state of } s \iff \forall \ell \in L : T_s(q, \ell) \subseteq \{q\}$$
$$s \text{ is input-enabled} \iff \forall q \in Q_s : \mathrm{in}_s(q) = I$$
$$s \text{ is deterministic} \iff \forall \sigma \in L^*, |s \text{ after } \sigma| \leq 1$$

We omit the subscript for interface automaton s when clear from the context.

We use IAs to represent black-box systems, which can produce outputs, and consume or refuse inputs from the environment. This entails a notion of observable behaviour, which we define in terms of *input-failure traces* [11].

Definition 3. *For any input action a, we denote the* input-failure *of a as $\overline{a}$. Likewise, for any set of inputs A, we define $\overline{A} = \{\overline{a} \mid a \in A\}$. The domain of* input-failure traces *is defined as $\mathcal{FT}_{I,O} = L^* \cup L^* \cdot \overline{I}$. For $s \in \mathcal{IA}$, we define*

$$\mathrm{Ftraces}(s) = \mathrm{traces}(s) \cup \{\sigma\overline{a} \mid \sigma \in L^*, a \in I, a \notin \mathrm{in}(s \text{ after } \sigma)\}$$

Thus, a trace $\sigma\overline{a}$ indicates that σ leads to a state where a is not accepted, e.g. a greyed-out button which cannot be clicked.

Any such set of input-failure traces is prefix-closed. Input-failure traces are the basis of *input-failure refinement*, which we will now explain briefly. This refinement relation was introduced in [11] to bridge the gap between alternating refinements [1,2] and ioco theory [15]. Similarly to normal trace inclusion, the idea is that an implementation may only show a trace if a specification also shows this trace. Moreover, the most permissive treatment of an input is to fail it, so if a specification allows an input failure, then it also must allow acceptance of that input, as expressed by the *input-failure closure*.

Definition 4. *Set $S \subseteq \mathcal{FT}_{I,O}$ of input-failure traces is* input-failure closed *if, for all $\sigma \in L^*$, $a \in I$ and $\rho \in \mathcal{FT}_{I,O}$, $\sigma\overline{a} \in S \implies \sigma a \rho \in S$. The* input-failure closure *of S is the smallest input-failure closed superset of S, that is, $\mathrm{fcl}(S) = S \cup \{\sigma a \rho \mid \sigma\overline{a} \in S, \rho \in \mathcal{FT}_{I,O}\}$.*

Input-failure refinement *and* input-failure equivalence *on IAs are respectively defined as*

$$s_1 \leq_{if} s_2 \iff \text{Ftraces}(s_1) \subseteq \text{fcl}(\text{Ftraces}(s_2)), \text{ and}$$
$$s_1 \equiv_{if} s_2 \iff s_1 \leq_{if} s_2 \land s_2 \leq_{if} s_1.$$

The input-failure closure of the Ftraces serves as a canonical representation of the behaviour of an IA. That is, two models are input failure equivalent if and only if the closure of their input-failure traces is the same, as stated in Proposition 5.

Proposition 5. *[11] Let $s_1, s_2 \in \mathcal{IA}$. Then*

$$s_1 \leq_{if} s_2 \iff \text{fcl}(\text{Ftraces}(s_1)) \subseteq \text{fcl}(\text{Ftraces}(s_2))$$
$$s_1 \equiv_{if} s_2 \iff \text{fcl}(\text{Ftraces}(s_1)) = \text{fcl}(\text{Ftraces}(s_2))$$

Proposition 5 implies that relation $\leq_{if}$ is reflexive ($s \leq_{if} s$) and transitive ($s_1 \leq_{if} s_2 \land s_2 \leq_{if} s_3 \implies s_1 \leq_{if} s_3$). Formally, it is thus a preorder, making it suitable for stepwise refinement.

3   Alternating Interface Automata

Real software systems are always in a single state, but the precise state of a system cannot always be derived from an observed trace. Due to non-determinism, a trace may lead to multiple states. In IAs, this is modelled as a set of states, such as the set of initial states, the set $T(q, \ell)$ for state q and action ℓ, and the set s after σ for IA s and trace σ. The domain of such non-deterministic views on an IA with states Q is thus the powerset of states, $\mathcal{P}(Q)$. In set of states Q, traces from any individual state in Q may be observed.

3.1   Alternation

Alternation generalizes this view on automata: a system may not only be non-deterministically in multiple states, but also conjunctively. When conjunctively in multiple states, only traces which are in *all* these states may be observed. Alternation is formalized by exchanging the domain $\mathcal{P}(Q)$ for the domain $\mathcal{D}(Q)$. Formally, $\mathcal{D}(Q)$ is the *free distributive lattice*, which exist for any set Q [14].

Definition 6. *For any set Q, $\mathcal{D}(Q)$ denotes the* free distributive lattice *generated by Q. That is, $\mathcal{D}(Q)$ is the domain of equivalence classes of terms, inductively defined by the the grammar*

$$e \quad = \quad \top \mid \bot \mid \langle q \rangle \mid e_1 \lor e_2 \mid e_1 \land e_2 \qquad \text{with } q \in Q,$$

where equivalence of terms is completely defined by the following axioms:

$$e_1 \vee e_2 = e_2 \vee e_1 \qquad\qquad e_1 \wedge e_2 = e_2 \wedge e_1 \qquad [Commutativity]$$

$$e_1 \vee (e_2 \vee e_3) = (e_1 \vee e_2) \vee e_3 \quad e_1 \wedge (e_2 \wedge e_3) = (e_1 \wedge e_2) \wedge e_3 \ [Associativity]$$

$$e_1 \vee (e_1 \wedge e_2) = e_1 \qquad\qquad e_1 \wedge (e_1 \vee e_2) = e_1 \qquad [Absorption]$$

$$e \vee e = e \qquad\qquad\qquad e \wedge e = e \qquad\qquad [Idempotence]$$

$$e_1 \vee (e_2 \wedge e_3) = (e_1 \vee e_2) \wedge (e_1 \vee e_3) \qquad e_1 \wedge (e_2 \vee e_3) = (e_1 \wedge e_2) \vee (e_1 \wedge e_3)$$

$$[Distributivity]$$

$$e \vee \top = \top \qquad\qquad\qquad e \wedge \bot = \bot \qquad\qquad [Identity]$$

In short, $(\mathcal{D}(Q), \vee, \wedge, \bot, \top)$ forms a distributive lattice. Expression $\langle q \rangle$ is named the embedding of q in $\mathcal{D}(Q)$, and operators $\vee$ and $\wedge$ are named disjunction and conjunction, respectively. For the remainder of this paper, we make no distinction between expressions and their equivalence classes.

For finite n, we introduce the shorthand n-ary operators $\bigvee$ and $\bigwedge$, as follows:

$$\bigvee \{e_1, e_2, \ldots e_n\} = e_1 \vee e_2 \vee \ldots e_n \qquad\qquad \bigvee \emptyset = \bot$$

$$\bigwedge \{e_1, e_2, \ldots e_n\} = e_1 \wedge e_2 \wedge \ldots e_n \qquad\qquad \bigwedge \emptyset = \top$$

We distinguish the embedding $\langle q \rangle \in \mathcal{D}(Q)$ from q itself. We require this distinction only in Definition 18, where we will point this out. Otherwise, we do not need this distinction, so we write q instead of $\langle q \rangle$.

Intuitively, disjunction $q_1 \vee q_2$ replaces the non-deterministic set $\{q_1, q_2\}$. This is formalized by extending IAs with alternation.

Definition 7. *An* alternating interface automaton *(AIA) is defined as a 5-tuple (Q, I, O, T, e^0) where*

- *Q is a set of states, and elements of $\mathcal{D}(Q)$ are referred to as* configurations,
- *I and O are disjoint sets of input and output actions, respectively,*
- *$T : Q \times (I \cup O) \to \mathcal{D}(Q)$ is a transition function, with $T(q, a) \neq \bot$ for all $a \in I$, and*
- *$e^0 \in \mathcal{D}(Q)$ is the initial configuration.*

The domain of AIAs is denoted by $\mathcal{AIA}$. Notations for IAs are reused for AIAs, if this causes no ambiguity. For $\ell \in L$, we define $T_\ell : Q \to \mathcal{D}(Q)$ by $T_\ell(q) = T(q, \ell)$.

Configurations $\top$ and $\bot$ are analogous to the empty set of states in an IA s: if $T_s(q, \ell) = \emptyset$, this means that state q does not have a transition for ℓ. In terms of input-failure refinement, not having a transition for an input means that the input is underspecified, whereas not having a transition for an output means that the output is forbidden. This distinction is made explicit in AIA by using $\top$ to represent underspecification and $\bot$ to represent forbidden behaviour. We will formalize this in Section 3.2. Definition 7 also allows output transitions to $\top$, meaning that the behaviour is unspecified after that output. Automata models which do not allow distinct configurations $\top$ and $\bot$ commonly represent such underspecified behaviour with an explicit chaotic state [3,4] instead.

We graphically represent AIAs in a similar way as IAs, with some additional rules. A transition $T(q^0, \ell) = \langle q^1 \rangle$ is represented by a single arrow from q^0 to q^1. We represent $T(q^0, \ell) = q^1 \vee q^2$ by two arrows $q^0 \xrightarrow{\ell} q^1$ and $q^0 \xrightarrow{\ell} q^2$, analogous to non-determinism in IAs. Conjunction $T(q^0, \ell) = q^1 \wedge q^2$ is shown by adding an arc between the arrows. Nested expressions are represented by successive splits, as shown in Example 8. A state q without outgoing arrow for an output $\ell \in O$ represents $T(q, \ell) = \bot$, and a state without input transitions for input ℓ indicates $T(q, \ell) = \top$. For $\ell \in U$, a transition $T(q, \ell) = \top$ is shown with an arrow to $\top$, denoting underspecification, but note that $\top$ is a configuration, not a state.

Example 8. Figure 3 shows AIA s_A, with $Q_A = \{q_A^0, q_A^1, q_A^2\}$, $I = \{?a, ?b\}$, $O = \{!x, !y\}$, $e_A^0 = q_A^0$ and T given by the following table:

action state	?a	?b	!x	!y
q_A^0	$q_A^0 \wedge (q_A^1 \vee q_A^2)$	$\top$	q_A^0	q_A^0
q_A^1	$\top$	$\top$	$\top$	$\bot$
q_A^2	$\top$	q_A^0	$\bot$	q_A^2

Moreover, AIA s_B combines the partial specifications from Section 1.

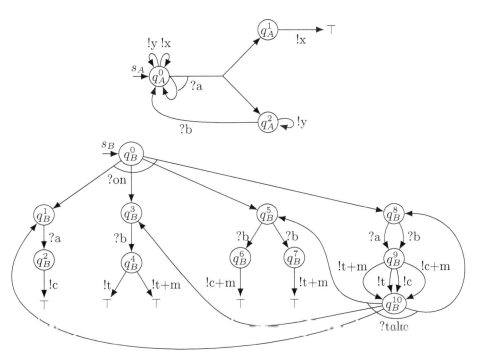

Fig. 3. Example AIAs s_A and s_B.

Before defining trace semantics for AIAs, we extend the transition function from single actions to sequences of actions, by defining an after-function on AIAs. This function transforms configurations by substituting every state according to the transition function, similarly to the approach for alternating automata in [6].

Definition 9. *Let* $f : Q \to \mathcal{D}(Q)$ *and* $e \in \mathcal{D}(Q)$. *Then* substitution $e[f]$ *is equal to* e *with all atomic propositions replaced by* $f(e)$. *Formally,* $[f] : \mathcal{D}(Q) \to \mathcal{D}(Q)$ *is a postfix operator defined by*
$$(e_1 \vee e_2)[f] = e_1[f] \vee e_2[f] \quad (e_1 \wedge e_2)[f] = e_1[f] \wedge e_2[f]$$
$$\top[f] = \top \quad \bot[f] = \bot \quad \langle q \rangle[f] = f(q)$$

Definition 10. *Let* $s \in \mathcal{AIA}$. *We define* after: $\mathcal{D}(Q_s) \times L^* \to \mathcal{D}(Q_s)$ *as*

$$e \text{ after}_s \epsilon = e \qquad e \text{ after}_s (\ell \cdot \sigma) = e[T_\ell] \text{ after}_s \sigma$$

Like before, we omit the subscript if clear from the context. We also define $(s \text{ after } \sigma) = e_s^0 \text{ after}_s \sigma$.

Example 11. Consider s_B in Figure 3. We evaluate s_B after ?on ?b !t, as follows:

$$q_B^0 \text{ after ?on ?b !t} = q_B^0[T_{?\mathrm{on}}] \text{ after ?b !t} = T(q_B^0, ?\mathrm{on}) \text{ after ?b !t}$$
$$= (q_B^1 \wedge q_B^3 \wedge q_B^5 \wedge q_B^8) \text{ after ?b !t} = (q_B^1 \wedge q_B^3 \wedge q_B^5 \wedge q_B^8)[T_{?\mathrm{b}}] \text{ after !t}$$
$$= (\top \wedge q_B^4 \wedge (q_B^6 \vee q_B^7) \wedge q_B^9) \text{ after !t} = (q_B^4 \wedge (q_B^6 \vee q_B^7) \wedge q_B^9)[T_{!\mathrm{t}}]$$
$$= (\top \wedge (\bot \vee \bot) \wedge q_B^{10}) = \bot$$

Intuitively, this means that giving a tea without milk after ?on ?b is forbidden. In contrast, tea with milk is allowed, and leads to configuration q_B^{10}:

$$q_B^0 \text{ after ?on ?b !t+m} = (q_B^4 \wedge (q_B^6 \vee q_B^7) \wedge q_B^9)[T_{!\mathrm{t+m}}] = \top \wedge (\bot \vee \top) \wedge q_B^{10} = q_B^{10}$$

3.2   Input-Failure Semantics for AIAs

IAs are equipped with input-failure semantics, based on the traces and under-specified inputs of the IA. We lift this to AIAs via the after-function, using that $\bot$ indicates forbidden behaviour, and $\top$ indicates underspecified behaviour.

Definition 12. *Let* $s, s' \in \mathcal{AIA}$, *and* $e \in \mathcal{D}(Q_s)$. *Then we define*

$$\mathrm{Ftraces}_s(e) = \{\sigma \in L^* \mid (e \text{ after}_s \sigma) \neq \bot\} \cup \{\sigma \bar{a} \in L^* \cdot \bar{I} \mid (e \text{ after}_s \sigma a) = \top\}$$
$$\mathrm{Ftraces}(s) = \mathrm{Ftraces}_s(e_s^0)$$
$$s \leq_{if} s' \iff \mathrm{Ftraces}(s) \subseteq \mathrm{Ftraces}(s')$$
$$s \equiv_{if} s' \iff \mathrm{Ftraces}(s) = \mathrm{Ftraces}(s')$$

Compare Definition 4 and Definition 12 for input-failure refinement for IAs and for AIAs. For AIAs, refinement is defined directly over their Ftraces, whereas for IA, the input-failure closure of the Ftraces is used for the right-hand model (and optionally for the left-hand model, according to Proposition 5). In this regard, AIAs are a more direct and natural representation of input-failure traces, since the input-failure closure is not needed.

Proposition 13. *For* $s \in \mathcal{AIA}$, $\mathrm{Ftraces}(s)$ *is input-failure closed.*

Another motivation to represent input-failure traces with AIAs is the connection between the distributive lattice $\mathcal{D}(Q)$ and the lattice of sets of input-failure traces: $\wedge$ and $\vee$ are connected to intersection and union of input-failure traces, respectively, and $\top$ and $\bot$ represent the largest and smallest possible input-failure trace sets.

Proposition 14. *Let* $s \in \mathcal{AIA}$, *and* $e, e' \in \mathcal{D}(Q_s)$. *Then*

1. $\text{Ftraces}(e \wedge e') = \text{Ftraces}(e) \cap \text{Ftraces}(e')$
2. $\text{Ftraces}(e \vee e') = \text{Ftraces}(e) \cup \text{Ftraces}(e')$
3. $\text{Ftraces}(\bot) = \emptyset$
4. $\text{Ftraces}(\top) = \mathcal{FT}_{I,O}$
5. $\text{Ftraces}(e) = \{\epsilon\} \cup \{\overline{a} \in \overline{I_s} \mid e \text{ after } a = \top\}$
   $\qquad \cup \left(\bigcup_{\ell \in L_s} \ell \cdot \text{Ftraces}(e \text{ after } \ell) \right) \qquad \textit{if } e \neq \bot$

Propositions 14.3 and 14.5 show why Definition 7 does not allow transitions to $T(q, a) = \bot$ for an input a: in that case, $\text{Ftraces}(q)$ would contain trace ϵ, but it would not contain extension a nor $\overline{a}$ of ϵ, meaning that after trace ϵ it is not allowed to accept nor to refuse a.

We can lift configurations $\top$ and $\bot$, as well as $\wedge$ and $\vee$, to the level of AIAs. This provides the building blocks to compose specifications. Specifications $s_\top$ and $s_\bot$ can be used to specify that any or no behaviour is considered correct, respectively. The operators $\wedge$ and $\vee$ on specifications fulfill the same role as existing operators in substitutivity refinement [7], and have similar properties, described in Proposition 14.

Definition 15. *Let* $s_1, s_2 \in \mathcal{AIA}$. *Without loss of generality*[1], *assume that* Q_1 *and* Q_2 *are disjoint. We define*

$$s_\top = (\emptyset, I, O, \emptyset, \top) \qquad s_1 \wedge s_2 = (Q_1 \cup Q_2, I, O, T_1 \cup T_2, e_1^0 \wedge e_2^0)$$
$$s_\bot = (\emptyset, I, O, \emptyset, \bot) \qquad s_1 \vee s_2 = (Q_1 \cup Q_2, I, O, T_1 \cup T_2, e_1^0 \vee e_2^0)$$

Proposition 16. *Let* $i, i', s, s' \in \mathcal{AIA}$. *Then*

$$i \leq_{if} s \text{ and } i \leq_{if} s' \iff i \leq_{if} (s \wedge s')$$
$$i \leq_{if} s \text{ or } i \leq_{if} s' \implies i \leq_{if} (s \vee s')$$
$$i \leq_{if} s \text{ and } i' \leq_{if} s \iff (i \vee i') \leq_{if} s$$
$$i \leq_{if} s \text{ or } i' \leq_{if} s \implies (i \wedge i') \leq_{if} s$$
$$i \leq_{if} s_\top$$
$$i \not\leq_{if} s_\bot \qquad \textit{if } e_i^0 \neq \bot$$

The converse of statement (2) does not hold. As a counter-example, choose $\text{Ftraces}(i) = \{\epsilon, x, y\}$, $\text{Ftraces}(s_1) = \{\epsilon, x\}$ and $\text{Ftraces}(s_2) = \{\epsilon, y\}$. In that case, $i \leq_{if} s_1 \vee s_2$ holds, but $i \not\leq_{if} s_1$ and $i \not\leq_{if} s_2$. The converse of statement (4) can be disproven similarly.

---

[1] If Q_1 and Q_2 are not disjoint, the disjoint union $Q_1 \uplus Q_2$ can be used instead of $Q_1 \cup Q_2$. The transition functions of $s_1 \wedge s_2$ and $s_1 \vee s_2$ should be adjusted accordingly.

3.3   AIA Determinization

In case of nestings of $\land$ and $\lor$, the after-set s after σ may not be clear immediately, so a transition function producing configurations without $\land$ and $\lor$ is easier to interpret. For this reason, we lift the notions of determinism and determinization from IAs [11] to the alternating setting.

Definition 17. Let $s \in \mathcal{AIA}$ and $e \in \mathcal{D}(Q_s)$. Then e is deterministic if $e = \top$ or $e = \bot$ or $e = \langle q \rangle$ for some $q \in Q_s$. Furthermore, s is deterministic if for all $\sigma \in L^*$, configuration s after σ is deterministic.

Compare the notions of determinism for IAs and AIAs. For every trace σ, a deterministic IA s is in a singleton state $(s \text{ after } \sigma) = \{q\}$, unless $(s \text{ after } \sigma) = \emptyset$ (that is, σ is not a trace of s). For AIAs, this singleton set $\{q\}$ is replaced by the embedding $\langle q \rangle$, and $\emptyset$ is replaced by $\top$ or $\bot$, depending on whether this set was reached by an undespecified action or a forbidden action.

We now define determinization, where we require the distinction between $\langle q \rangle$ and q to avoid ambiguity.

Definition 18. Let $s \in \mathcal{AIA}$. We define $\det : \mathcal{D}(Q_s) \to \mathcal{D}(\mathcal{D}(Q_s) \setminus \{\top, \bot\})$ as

$$\det(e) = \begin{cases} \top & \text{if } e = \top \\ \bot & \text{if } e = \bot \\ \langle e \rangle & \text{otherwise} \end{cases}$$

The determinization of s, or $\det(s) \in \mathcal{AIA}$, is defined as

$$\det(s) = (\mathcal{D}(Q_s) \setminus \{\top, \bot\}, I, O, T_{\det(s)}, \det(e_s^0)), \text{ with}$$
$$T_{\det(s)}(e, \ell) = \det(e \text{ after}_s \ell) \qquad \text{for } \ell \in L$$

Proposition 19. For $s \in \mathcal{AIA}$, $\det(s)$ is deterministic.

Example 20. Figure 4 shows (the reachable part of) the determinizations of s_A and s_B from Figure 3. In $\det(s_A)$, state $q_A^0 \land q_A^2$ has no outgoing !x-transition. This expresses $T_{\det(s_A)}(q_A^0 \land q_A^2, !\text{x}) = \bot$, which is because q_A^2 has no x-transition, so $T_A(q_A^2, !\text{x}) = \bot$. In contrast, state $q_A^0 \land q_A^2$ has an outgoing ?a-transition, $T_{\det(s_A)}(q_A^0 \land q_A^2, ?\text{a}) \neq \top$, because q_A^0 has an ?a-transition, $T_A(q_A^0, ?\text{a}) \neq \top$.

Example 20 shows that an input is specified by a conjunction of states in the determinization if *any* of the individual state specify this input, whereas an output is allowed by a conjunction of states only if *all* of the individual state allow this output. In the setting of IA, [11] already established that this works in a reversed way for non-determinism, following their definition of determinization: *all* individual states of a disjunction should specify an input to specify it in the determinization, and *any* individual state should allow an output to allow it in the determinization. Their so-called *input-universal determinization* is an instance of the determinization from Definition 18, using only disjunctions.

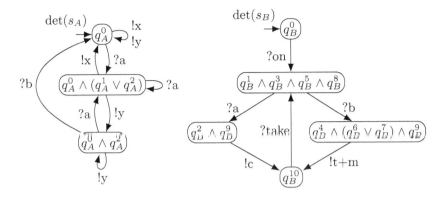

Fig. 4. Examples of determinization.

This duality arises from Definition 10 of after, since the determinization directly represents the after-function: the determinizations in Example 20 correspond to the after-sets such as those derived in Example 11. This correspondence is formalized in Proposition 21.

Proposition 21. *Let $s \in \mathcal{AIA}$ and $\sigma \in L^*$. Then*

$$(\det(s) \text{ after } \sigma) = \det(s \text{ after } \sigma).$$

Proposition 22. *Let $s \in \mathcal{AIA}$. Then* Ftraces(s) = Ftraces$(\det(s))$.

Corollary 23. *Let $s \in \mathcal{AIA}$. Then $s \equiv_{if} \det(s)$.*

A known result [6] is that alternating automata are exponentially more succinct than non-deterministic automata, and double exponentially more succinct than deterministic automata. Although alternating automata are not a special case of AIAs (as AIAs lack the accepting and non-accepting states of alternating automata), we expect AIAs to be exponentially more succinct than IAs, as well.

3.4   Connections between IAs and AIAs

IAs and AIAs are used to represent sets of input-failure traces, and are in that sense interchangeable. First, we show that any IA can be translated to an AIA.

Definition 24. *For $s \in \mathcal{IA}$, the AIA induced by s is defined as* AIA$(s) = (Q_s, I_s, O_s, T, \bigvee Q_s^0) \in \mathcal{AIA}$, *where for all $q \in Q_s$ and $\ell \in L$:*

$$T(q, \ell) = \begin{cases} \top & \text{if } \ell \in I \text{ and } q \not\xrightarrow{\ell} \\ \bigvee T_s(q, \ell) & \text{otherwise} \end{cases}$$

Proposition 25. *Let $s \in \mathcal{IA}$. Then* Ftraces(AIA(s)) = fcl(Ftraces(s)).

Corollary 26. *Let $s_1, s_2 \in \mathcal{IA}$. Then $s_1 \leq_{if} s_2 \iff$ AIA$(s_1) \leq_{if}$ AIA(s_2)*

Definition 29 formalizes how disjunction in an AIA corresponds to non-determinism in IA. Specifically, if no transitions are present for some output in an IA, then the transition function of the corresponding AIA gives $\bigvee \emptyset = \bot$ for this output, analogous to the explicit case $\top$ for inputs. Note that the graphical representation of an IA and that of its induced AIA are the same.

The translation from AIAs to IAs is more involved. For disjunctions of states $(q \text{ after } \ell) = q_1 \vee q_2$, the translation of Definition 24 can simply be inverted, but this is not possible for conjunctions. As such, we represent any configuration by its unique disjunctive normal form.

Definition 27. *Let $e \in \mathcal{D}(Q)$. Then $\mathrm{DNF}(e)$ is the smallest set in $\mathcal{P}(\mathcal{P}(Q))$ such that $e = \bigvee\{\bigwedge Q' \mid Q' \in \mathrm{DNF}(e)\}$.*

The set $\mathrm{DNF}(e)$ can be constructed by using the axioms from Definition 6.

Example 28. To find $\mathrm{DNF}(q^1 \vee (q^2 \wedge (q^1 \vee q^3)))$, we first rewrite the expression by using distributivity, associativity, commutativity and absorbtion, as follows:

$$q^1 \vee (q^2 \wedge (q^1 \vee q^3)) = q^1 \vee (q^2 \wedge q^1) \vee (q^2 \wedge q^3) = q^1 \vee (q^2 \wedge q^3)$$

So we find $\mathrm{DNF}(q^1 \vee (q^2 \wedge (q^1 \vee q^3))) = \{\{q^1\}, \{q^2, q^3\}\}$. Two other examples are $\mathrm{DNF}(\bot) = \mathrm{DNF}(\bigvee \emptyset) = \emptyset$ and $\mathrm{DNF}(\top) = \mathrm{DNF}(\bigvee\{\bigwedge \emptyset\}) = \{\emptyset\}$.

Definition 29. *Let $s \in \mathcal{AIA}$. Then the* induced IA *of s is defined as*

$$\mathrm{IA}(s) = (\mathcal{P}(Q_s), I, O, T, \mathrm{DNF}(e_s^0)) \in \mathcal{IA}, \text{ with for } Q \subseteq Q_s \text{ and } \ell \in L:$$

$$T(Q, \ell) = \begin{cases} \mathrm{DNF}((\bigwedge Q)[T_s \ell]) \setminus \{\emptyset\} & \text{if } \ell \in I \\ \mathrm{DNF}((\bigwedge Q)[T_s \ell]) & \text{if } \ell \in O \end{cases}$$

A state of $\mathrm{IA}(s)$ acts as the conjunction of the corresponding states in s. In particular, a singleton state $\{q\}$ in $\mathrm{IA}(s)$ acts as the contained state q in s, and state $\emptyset$ in $\mathrm{IA}(s)$ acts as a chaotic state, having $\mathrm{Ftraces}_{\mathrm{IA}(s)}(\emptyset) = \mathcal{FT}_{I,O}$.

Proposition 30. *Let $s \in \mathcal{AIA}$. Then $\mathrm{Ftraces}(s) = \mathrm{fcl}(\mathrm{Ftraces}(\mathrm{IA}(s)))$.*

Corollary 31. *Let $s_1, s_2 \in \mathcal{AIA}$. Then $s_1 \leq_{if} s_2 \iff \mathrm{IA}(s_1) \leq_{if} \mathrm{IA}(s_2)$*

4   Testing Input-Failure Refinement

So far, we have introduced refinement as a way of specifying correctness of one model with respect to another. Often, a specification is indeed a model, but we use it to ensure correctness of a real-world software implementation. To this end, we assume that this implementation behaves like a IA. We cannot see the actual states and transitions of this IA, but we can provide inputs to it and observe its outputs. We assume that this IA must have an initial state, i.e. it is *non-empty*.

Definition 32. *[1] An IA i is* empty *if $Q_i^0 = \emptyset$.*

In this section, we introduce a basis for *model-based testing* with AIAs, analogously to ioco test case generation [15]. Given a specification AIA, we derive a testing experiment on non-empty implementation IAs, in order to observe whether input-failure refinement holds with respect to the specification. This requires an extension of input-failure refinement to these domains.

Definition 33. *Let $i \in \mathcal{IA}$ and $s \in \mathcal{AIA}$. Then*

$$i \leq_{if} s \iff \text{Ftraces}(i) \subseteq \text{Ftraces}(s).$$

4.1 Testers for AIA Specifications

From a given specification AIA, we derive a tester. We model this tester as an IA as well, which can communicate with an implementation IA through a form of parallel composition. The tester eventually concludes a verdict, indicating whether the observed behaviour is allowed. To communicate, the inputs of the implementation must be outputs for the tester, and vice versa (note that I and O denote the inputs and outputs for the *implementation*, respectively). The tester should not block or ignore outputs from the implementation, meaning that the tester should be input-enabled. If the tester intends to supply an input to the implementation, it should also be prepared for a refusal of that input. A verdict is given by means of special states **pass** or **fail**. Lastly, to give consistent verdicts, a tester should be deterministic. This leads to the following definition of testers.

Definition 34. *A tester for (an IA or AIA with) inputs I and outputs O is a deterministic, input-enabled IA $t = (Q_t, O, I \cup \overline{I}, T, q_t^0)$ with $\textbf{pass}, \textbf{fail} \in Q_t$, such that $\textbf{pass}$ and $\textbf{fail}$ are sink-states with $\text{out}(\textbf{pass}) = \text{out}(\textbf{fail}) = \emptyset$, and $a \in \text{out}(q) \iff \overline{a} \in \text{out}(q)$ for all $q \in Q_t$ and $a \in I$.*

Testing is performed by a special form of parallel composition of a tester and an implementation. If the tester chooses to perform an input while the implementation also chooses to produce an output, this results in a race condition. In such a case, both the input or the output can occur during test execution. We assume a synchronous setting, in which the implementation and specification agree on the order in which observed actions are performed (in contrast to e.g. a queue-based setting [13], in which all possible orders are accounted for). These assumptions are in line with the assumptions in e.g. ioco-theory [15], and lead to the following definition of test execution.

Definition 35. *Let $i \subset \mathcal{IA}$ be non-empty, and let t be a tester for i. We write $q_t \,]|\, q_i$ for $(q_t, q_i) \in Q_t \times Q_i$. Then test execution of i against t, denoted $t \,]|\, i$, is defined as $(Q_t \times Q_i, \emptyset, I \cup \overline{I} \cup O, T, q_t^0 \,]|\, q_i^0) \in \mathcal{IA}$, with*

$$T(q_t \,]|\, q_i, \ell) = \{q_t' \,]|\, q_i' \mid q_t \xrightarrow{\ell} q_t', \, q_i \xrightarrow{\ell} q_i'\} \qquad \text{for } \ell \in L$$

$$T(q_t \,]|\, q_i, \overline{a}) = \{q_t' \,]|\, q_i \mid q_t \xrightarrow{\overline{a}} q_t', \, q_i \xrightarrow{a}\hspace{-0.9em}/\;\} \qquad \text{for } a \in I$$

*We say that i **fails** t if $q_t^0 \,]|\, q_i^0 \xrightarrow{\sigma} \textbf{fail} \,]|\, q_i$ for some σ and q_i, and i **passes** t otherwise.*

We reuse the notions of *soundness* and *exhaustiveness* from [15], to express whether a tester properly tests for a given specification.

Definition 36. *Let $s \in \mathcal{AIA}$ and let t be a tester for s. Then t is* sound *for s if for all $i \in \mathcal{IA}$ with inputs I and outputs O, i* **fails** *t implies $i \not\leq_{if} s$. Moreover, t is* exhaustive *for s if for all $i \in \mathcal{IA}$, i* **passes** *t implies $i \leq_{if} s$.*

A simple attempt to translate specification AIA s to a sound and exhaustive tester would be similar to the determinization of s, but replacing every occurence of $\perp$ and $\top$ by **fail** and **pass**, respectively.

$$f_t(e) = \begin{cases} \textbf{fail} & \text{if } e = \perp \\ \textbf{pass} & \text{if } e = \top \\ e & \text{otherwise} \end{cases}$$

Taking special care of input failures, the function f_t then induces a tester $(\mathcal{D}(Q_s) \cup \{\textbf{pass}, \textbf{fail}\}, O, I \cup \overline{I}, T, f_t(e_s^0))$, with

$$T(e, \ell) = \{f_t(e \text{ after}_s \ell)\} \qquad\qquad \text{for } e \in \mathcal{D}(Q_s), \ell \in L$$

$$T(v, \ell) = \begin{cases} \{v\} & \text{if } \ell \in O \\ \emptyset & \text{if } \ell \in I \end{cases} \qquad\qquad \text{for } v \in \{\textbf{pass}, \textbf{fail}\}$$

$$T(e, \overline{a}) = \begin{cases} \{\textbf{pass}\} & \text{if } (e \text{ after}_s a) = \top \\ \{\textbf{fail}\} & \text{otherwise} \end{cases} \qquad \text{for } e \in \mathcal{D}(Q_s), a \in I$$

This tester is sound and complete for s: each possible input-failure trace is in Ftraces(s) if and only if it does not lead to **fail**, by construction. Here, we make use of the fact that Ftraces($\perp$) = $\emptyset$, meaning that $\perp$ cannot be implemented correctly by a non-empty IA and can thus be replaced by **fail**. Likewise, Ftraces($\top$) = $\mathcal{FT}_{I,O}$ means that $\top$ is always implemented correctly, and can be replaced by **pass**.

However, this tester is quite inefficient. If a tester reaches **pass** after both σa and $\sigma \overline{a}$, then this input a does not need to be tested after σ. Specifically, this is the case if and only if trace σa leads to specification configuration $\top$. We thus improve the tester for a given specifications as follows.

Definition 37. *Let $s \in \mathcal{AIA}$. Then* tester(s) $\in \mathcal{IA}$ *is defined as*

$$\text{tester}(s) = (\mathcal{D}(Q_s) \cup \{\textbf{pass}, \textbf{fail}\}, O, I \cup \overline{I}, T, f_t(e_s^0)), \text{ with } f_t \text{ as before, and}$$

$$T(e, \ell) = \begin{cases} \{f_t(e \text{ after}_s \ell)\} & \text{if } \ell \in O, \text{ or } \ell \in I \text{ and } (e \text{ after}_s \ell) \neq \top \\ \emptyset & \text{if } \ell \in I \text{ and } (e \text{ after}_s \ell) = \top \end{cases} \quad \text{for } \ell \in L$$

$$T(e, \overline{a}) = \begin{cases} \emptyset & \text{if } (e \text{ after}_s a) = \top \\ \{\textbf{fail}\} & \text{otherwise} \end{cases} \qquad\qquad \text{for } e \in \mathcal{D}(Q_s), a \in I$$

$$T(v, \ell) = \begin{cases} \{v\} & \text{if } \ell \in O \\ \emptyset & \text{if } \ell \in I \end{cases} \qquad\qquad \text{for } v \in \{\textbf{pass}, \textbf{fail}\}, \ell \in L$$

Example 38. The tester for s_B in Figure 3 is shown in Figure 5.

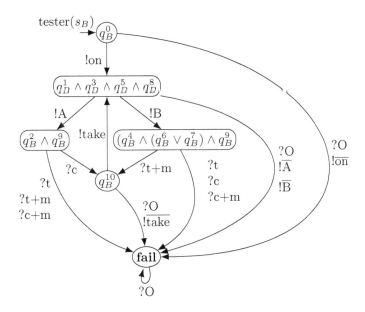

Fig. 5. The tester for the vending machine. The label ?O denotes a transition for every label in O. Remark that inputs for s_B are outputs for tester(s_B), and vice versa.

Theorem 39 shows that soundness and exhaustiveness of a tester corresponds to refinement of the corresponding AIA.

Theorem 39. *Let $s_1, s_2 \in \mathcal{AIA}$. Then*

    1 tester(s_1) *is sound and exhaustive for* IA(s_1)

    2   tester(s_1) *is sound for s_2* $\iff$ $s_2 \leq_{if} s_1$

    3 tester(s_1) *is exhaustive for s_2* $\iff$ $s_1 \leq_{if} s_2$

4.2 Test Cases for AIA Specifications

In [15], an algorithm was introduced to generate *test cases*. These are testers as in Definition 34 with additional restrictions, so that they can be used as unambiguous instructions to test a system. In particular, states of a test case should have at most one outgoing input transition. This ensures that no choice between different inputs has to be resolved during test execution. Additionally, all paths of a test case lead to **pass** or **fail** in a finite number of steps, to ensure that test execution terminates with a verdict.

Definition 40. *A tester t for I and O is a* test case *if*

– *for all* $q_t \in Q_t$, $|\operatorname{out}(q_t)| \leq 1$, *and*
– *there are no infinite sequences* $q_t^0, q_t^1, \ldots$ *for* $q_t^0, q_t^1, \ldots \in Q_t \setminus \{\textbf{pass}, \textbf{fail}\}$
  such that $q_t^0 \xrightarrow{\ell^0} q_t^1 \xrightarrow{\ell^1} \ldots$

The test case generation algorithm of [15] is non-deterministic, since it must choose at most one inputs in every state, and it must choose when to stop testing. We avoid defining a separate test case generation algorithm, and instead use Theorem 39 to obtain sound test cases. If specification s_1 is weakened to s_2, such that tester(s_2) is a test case, then soundness of tester(s_2) for s_1 is guaranteed by the theorem. Such a weakened *singular specification* s_2 describes a finite, tree-shaped part of the original specification s_1.

Definition 41. *Let* $s_1, s_2 \in \mathcal{AIA}$. *Then* s_2 *is a* singular specification *for* s_1 *if* Q_2 *is a finite subset of* L^*, *with* $e_2^0 \in \{\epsilon, \top, \bot\}$, $e_1^0 = \top \implies e_2^0 = \top$ *and* $e_2^0 = \bot \implies e_1^0 = \bot$, *and having that for every* $\sigma \in Q_2$, *the following holds:*

1. $T_2(\sigma, \ell) = \bot \implies (s_1 \text{ after } \sigma\ell) = \bot \text{ for } \ell \in L$,
2. $(s_1 \text{ after } \sigma\ell) = \top \implies T_2(\sigma, \ell) = \top \text{ for } \ell \in L$
3. $T_2(\sigma, \ell)$ *is either* $\bot$ *or* $\top$ *or* $\sigma\ell$ *for* $\ell \in L$, *and*
4. *there is at most one* $a \in I$ *with* $T(\sigma, a) \neq \top$.

It can be created from s_1 similarly to test case generation in [15]. In every state σ of the tree s_1, we either decide to pick one input specified in s_1 and also specify that in s_2; or we do not specify any input, but only outputs; or we leave any successive behaviour unspecified ($\top$).

Test cases based on singular specifications are inherently sound, and for any incorrect implementation, it is possible to find a singular specification which induces a test case to detects this incorrectness.

Theorem 42. *If* s_2 *is a singular specification for* s_1, *then* tester(s_2) *is a sound test case for* s_1.

Theorem 43. *Let* $i \in \mathcal{IA}$ *and* $s_1 \in \mathcal{AIA}$. *If* $i \not\leq_{if} s_1$, *then there is a singular specification* s_2 *for* s_1 *such that* i **fails** tester(s_2).

Example 44. Specification s_B in Figure 3 can be weakened to singular specification s_C shown in Figure 6. Indeed, $s_B \leq_{if} s_C$ holds, which can be established by comparing s_C with det(s_B) in Figure 4. Therefore tester(s_C) is a sound test case for s_B.

5   Conclusion and Future Work

Alternating interface automata serve as a natural and direct representation for sets of input-failure traces, and therefore also for refinement of systems with inputs, outputs, non-determinism and conjunction. We have used the observational nature of input-failure traces to define testers, describing an experiment to observationally establish refinement of a black-box system.

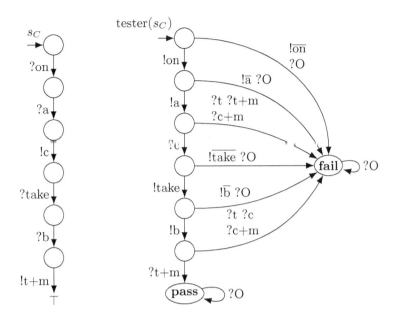

Fig. 6. A weakened version s_C of the vending machine, and the test case tester(s_C). Question and exclamation marks are interchanged in tester(s_C) to indicate that the input and output alphabets have been interchanged with respect to s_C.

The disjunction and conjunction of alternation brings interface automata specifications closer to the realm of logic and lattice theory. On the theoretical side, a possible direction is to extend configurations from distributive lattices to a full logic. On the practical side, classical testing techniques acting on logical expressions, such as combinatorial testing, could be translated to our black-box configurations of states.

Possible criticism on our running example of a vending machine s_B in Figure 3 may be that its representation as an AIA is not concise, since the determinization $det(s_B)$ is much smaller and more understandable than s_B itself. This is because the individual specifications offer a choice between outputs, such as tea with or without milk, whereas the intersection of all choices is singleton. A more natural encoding for this example is to express the types of drink with data data parameters, and the restrictions on them by logical constraints. This requires an automaton model in style of symbolic transition systems [9], which could be enriched with the concepts of alternation of AIAs.

Interface automata typically contain internal transitions, and the interaction between internal behaviour and alternation is not immediately clear. A possible approach to extend AIAs with internal behaviour is to lift the ϵ-closure of [1], the set of states reachable via internal transitions, to the level of configurations.

Acknowledgement.

We thank Jan Tretmans and Frits Vaandrager for their valuable feedback.

References

1. Alfaro, L.d., Henzinger, T.: Interface Automata. In: Gruhn, V. (ed.) Joint 8th Eur. Softw. Eng. Conf. and 9th ACM SIGSOFT Symp. on the Foundation of Softw. Eng. – ESEC/FSE-01. SIGSOFT Softw. Eng. Notes, vol. 26, pp. 109–120. ACM Press (2001). https://doi.org/10.1145/503271.503226

2. Alur, R., Henzinger, T., Kupferman, O., Vardi, M.: Alternating Refinement Relations. In: Sangiorgi, D., Simone, R, d. (eds.) 9th Int. Conf. on Concurrency Theory – CONCUR'98. LNCS, vol. 1466, pp. 163–178. Springer (1998). https://doi.org/10.1007/BFb0055622

3. Beneš, N., Daca, P., Henzinger, T., Křetínský, J., Ničković, D.: Complete composition operators for ioco-testing theory. In: Kruchten, P., Becker, S., Schneider, J.G. (eds.) Proc. 18th Int'l ACM SIGSOFT Symp. on Comp.-Based Softw. Eng. pp. 101–110. ACM (2015). https://doi.org/10.1145/2737166.2737175

4. Bijl, M.v.d., Rensink, A., Tretmans, J.: Compositional Testing with ioco. In: Petrenko, A., Ulrich, A. (eds.) Formal Approaches to Software Testing. LNCS, vol. 2931, pp. 86–100. Springer (2004). https://doi.org/10.1007/978-3-540-24617-6_7

5. Brinksma, E.: Constraint-Oriented Specification in a Constructive Formal Description technique. In: de Bakker, J., Roever, W.P.d., Rozenberg, G. (eds.) Stepwise Refinement of Distributed Systems Models, Formalisms, Correctness: REX Workshop, Mook, The Netherlands. pp. 130–152. Springer Berlin Heidelberg (1990). https://doi.org/10.1007/3-540-52559-9_63

6. Chandra, A.K., Kozen, D.C., Stockmeyer, L.J.: Alternation. J. ACM **28**(1), 114–133 (Jan 1981). https://doi.org/10.1145/322234.322243

7. Chilton, C., Jonsson, B., Kwiatkowska, M.: An algebraic theory of interface automata. Theoretical Computer Science **549**, 146–174 (2014). https://doi.org/10.1016/j.tcs.2014.07.018

8. Doyen, L., Henzinger, T.A., Jobstmann, B., Petrov, T.: Interface theories with component reuse. In: Proceedings of the 8th ACM International Conference on Embedded Software. pp. 79–88. EMSOFT '08, ACM, New York, NY, USA (2008). https://doi.org/10.1145/1450058.1450070

9. Frantzen, L., Tretmans, J.: Model-based testing of environmental conformance of components. In: de Boer, F.S., Bonsangue, M.M., Graf, S., de Roever, W. (eds.) Formal Methods for Components and Objects. pp. 1–25. Springer (2007). https://doi.org/10.1007/978-3-540-74792-5_1

10. Janssen, R.: Combining partial specifications using alternating interface automata. Report, Radboud University, Nijmegen (2020), https://arxiv.org/abs/2002.08754

11. Janssen, R., Vaandrager, F., Tretmans, J.: Relating alternating relations for conformance and refinement. In: Ahrendt, W., Tapia Tarifa, S. (eds.) Integrated Formal Methods. pp. 246–264. LNCS, Springer (2019). https://doi.org/10.1007/978-3-030-34968-4_14

12. McNaughton, R., Yamada, H.: Regular expressions and state graphs for automata. IRE Transactions on Electronic Computers **EC-9**(1), 39–47 (1960). https://doi.org/10.1109/TEC.1960.5221603

13. Petrenko, A., Yevtushenko, N., Huo, J.L.: Testing transition systems with input and output testers. In: Hogrefe, D., Wiles, A. (eds.) Testing of Communicating Systems. pp. 129–145. Springer Berlin Heidelberg, Berlin, Heidelberg (2003). https://doi.org/10.1007/3-540-44830-6_11

14. Priestly, H., Davey, B.: Introduction to lattices and order. Cambridge University Press, England (1990)
15. Tretmans, J.: Model Based Testing with Labelled Transition Systems. In: Hierons, R., Bowen, J., Harman, M. (eds.) Formal Methods and Testing. LNCS, vol. 4949, pp. 1–38. Springer (2008). https://doi.org/10.1007/978-3-540-78917-8_1

Permissions

All chapters in this book were first published by Springer; hereby published with permission under the Creative Commons Attribution License or equivalent. Every chapter published in this book has been scrutinized by our experts. Their significance has been extensively debated. The topics covered herein carry significant findings which will fuel the growth of the discipline. They may even be implemented as practical applications or may be referred to as a beginning point for another development.

The contributors of this book come from diverse backgrounds, making this book a truly international effort. This book will bring forth new frontiers with its revolutionizing research information and detailed analysis of the nascent developments around the world.

We would like to thank all the contributing authors for lending their expertise to make the book truly unique. They have played a crucial role in the development of this book. Without their invaluable contributions this book wouldn't have been possible. They have made vital efforts to compile up to date information on the varied aspects of this subject to make this book a valuable addition to the collection of many professionals and students.

This book was conceptualized with the vision of imparting up-to-date information and advanced data in this field. To ensure the same, a matchless editorial board was set up. Every individual on the board went through rigorous rounds of assessment to prove their worth. After which they invested a large part of their time researching and compiling the most relevant data for our readers.

The editorial board has been involved in producing this book since its inception. They have spent rigorous hours researching and exploring the diverse topics which have resulted in the successful publishing of this book. They have passed on their knowledge of decades through this book. To expedite this challenging task, the publisher supported the team at every step. A small team of assistant editors was also appointed to further simplify the editing procedure and attain best results for the readers.

Apart from the editorial board, the designing team has also invested a significant amount of their time in understanding the subject and creating the most relevant covers. They scrutinized every image to scout for the most suitable representation of the subject and create an appropriate cover for the book.

The publishing team has been an ardent support to the editorial, designing and production team. Their endless efforts to recruit the best for this project, has resulted in the accomplishment of this book. They are a veteran in the field of academics and their pool of knowledge is as vast as their experience in printing. Their expertise and guidance has proved useful at every step. Their uncompromising quality standards have made this book an exceptional effort. Their encouragement from time to time has been an inspiration for everyone.

The publisher and the editorial board hope that this book will prove to be a valuable piece of knowledge for researchers, students, practitioners and scholars across the globe.

List of Contributors

Jiao Jiao and Shang-Wei Lin
Nanyang Technological University, Singapore

Jun Sun
Singapore Management University, Singapore

Lars Tveito, Einar Broch Johnsen and Rudolf Schlatte
Department of Informatics, University of Oslo, Oslo, Norway

Joxan Jaffar , Rasool Maghareh , Sangharatna Godboley and Xuan-Linh Ha
National University of Singapore, Singapore

Claudio Menghi
University of Luxembourg, Luxembourg

Alessandro Maria Rizzi and Anna Bernasconi
Politecnico di Milano, Milano, Italy

Aleksandar S. Dimovski
Mother Teresa University, 12 Udarna Brigada 2a, 1000 Skopje, N. Macedonia

Axel Legay
Université catholique de Louvain, 1348 Ottignies-Louvain-la-Neuve, Belgium

Raffi Khatchadourian
CUNY Hunter College, New York, NY USA
CUNY Graduate Center, New York, NY USA

Yiming Tang
CUNY Graduate Center, New York, NY USA

Mehdi Bagherzadeh
Oakland University, Rochester, MI USA

Baishakhi Ray
Columbia University, New York, NY USA

Donato Clun and Antonio Filieri
Imperial College London

Phillip van Heerden and Willem Visser
Stellenbosch University

Hoang M. Le
Insitute of Computer Science University of Bremen, Germany

Themistoklis Diamantopoulos, Nikolaos Oikonomou and Andreas Symeonidis
Electrical and Computer Engineering Dept., Aristotle University of Thessaloniki, Thessaloniki, Greece

Maurice H. ter Beek
ISTI–CNR, Pisa, Italy

Sjef van Loo, Erik P. de Vink and Tim A. C. Willemse
TU Eindhoven, Eindhoven, The Netherlands

Alexander Knüppel, Inga Jatzkowski, Marcus Nolte, Tobias Runge and Ina Schaefer
TU Braunschweig, Braunschweig, Germany

Thomas Thüm
TU Braunschweig, Braunschweig, Germany
University of Ulm, Ulm, Germany

Ramon Janssen
Radboud University, Nijmegen, The Netherlands

Index

A

Abstract Analyses, 72, 76, 85, 88
Abstract Domains, 71-72, 88, 90
Abstract Semantics, 76
Abstraction Learning, 44-45
Active Object Language, 23-26, 28, 30-34, 40
Active Object Systems, 23-24, 26, 32, 40
Asynchronous Calls, 24-25, 38
Asynchronous Message, 24, 35, 40, 109

B

Bamboo Smart Contract, 6-7
Benchexec Tool-info, 46-47
Black-box Testing, 44
Blockchain, 1-2, 4-5, 10, 19-21

C

Cloud-deployed Software, 24
Code Coverage, 44, 137-140
Code Semantic Analysis, 142
Computing Program Reliability, 71, 87-88
Configuration, 7, 10, 17, 26-28, 30-32, 46-47, 140, 163, 169-171, 173-176, 179-180, 210-212, 214, 216
Content-based Replay, 23, 39
Cooperative Scheduling, 24, 34-35

D

Dynamic Symbolic Execution, 44, 137, 139

E

Empirical Studies, 91, 108
Equivalence Classes, 31, 40, 209
Ethereum Virtual Machine, 2, 20
Evm Bytecode, 1-2, 4, 18
Executable Formal Semantics, 1-4, 18-19

F

Formal Methods, 41-42, 49, 67-70, 90, 163, 181, 184-185, 201-202, 222-223
Formal Semantic, 1, 3, 18
Forward Analysis, 72, 85

G

General Semantic Model, 1, 3-4, 10, 18
Generalized Semantics, 1
Global Reproducibility, 23, 26, 32, 34, 40
Global Trace Set, 31-32, 34, 36
Global-activate, 31
Global-async-call, 31
Global-load, 30-32

H

Hybrid Fuzzing, 137-138, 141

I

Interval Domain, 72
Iterative Design, 49, 69

J

Java, 1, 7, 19, 26, 91-95, 97-98, 101, 107-112, 114, 129-130, 143, 146-147, 149-150, 153, 157, 196

K

K-framework, 2, 4, 7, 10, 12

L

Linear Constraints, 71-72, 87

M

Memory Operations, 10, 12
Model Checking, 43, 49-51, 55-56, 58, 65-70, 87, 89, 163-164, 167-172, 178, 180-183, 201, 204
Model Counting, 71-73, 79-80, 87, 89, 134
Multi-paradigm Programming, 91
Multicore Systems, 24

N

Natural Language, 51-52, 69, 101, 143-146, 151, 159-160, 162
Non-determinism, 23-24, 26, 34-35, 38-40, 73, 81, 91-92, 100, 204-207, 209, 211, 214, 220
Numeric Abstract, 71, 79, 83, 90

Function Calls, 10, 12, 17-18
Functional Programming, 91-92, 94, 98, 112

O

Object Languages, 23-24, 34, 40-41
Operational Semantics, 20, 25-26, 32, 40

P

Path Explosion, 44, 139
Place Holder Statement, 17
Polyhedra Domain, 72, 79, 83
Program Paths, 44, 87
Program Verification, 1, 71, 89
Programming Languages, 1-4, 6-7, 18-20, 43, 70, 89-90, 110, 152
Prototype Implementation, 71, 129

Q

Question-answering Systems, 142

R

Real-time Abs Models, 35, 39
Real-world Software, 72, 108, 204, 216
Recursive Memory Operations, 12
Reflecting Local Transitions, 23-24
Resource-aware Behavior, 23-24, 34, 38, 40
Runtime Syntax, 26-27

S

Semantic Framework, 1-3, 18, 20-21
Semantic Model, 1-4, 10, 18
Smart Contracts, 1-7, 12, 18-22

Snippet Mining, 142-144, 159
Software Architecture, 44-45, 138
Software Engineering, 20-22, 41-42, 48-49, 67-70, 90, 101, 109-113, 135-136, 160-163, 181, 191, 201-203
Solidity Contracts, 1, 19
Stable Configurations, 27-28, 31-33
Static Analysis, 20-21, 71-73, 85-86, 88-91, 93, 95, 183, 186
Symbolic Execution, 2, 21, 44-46, 48, 86-87, 90, 116, 123, 133, 137, 139, 141
Syntactic Check, 49, 51, 62, 66
Syntax, 3, 6-7, 10, 22, 26-27, 74, 81, 84, 98, 102, 133, 188
System Development, 49, 51

T

Test Programs, 17, 46
Theorem Proving, 49-50, 184, 201, 203
Topological Proofs, 49, 51, 57, 59
Tracerx, 44-47

U

Uniformly Distributed, 72-73, 75, 79-81
Unsatisfiable Core, 49, 60-61, 65, 67-69

V

Vacuum-cleaner Robot, 51-52

Printed in the USA
CPSIA information can be obtained
at www.ICGtesting.com
JSHW051352221024
72173JS00006B/1306